# HISTORY
# ALIVE

## NEW Junior Cycle History

**Gráinne Henry • Bairbre Kennedy • Tim Nyhan • Stephen Tonge**

D1407223

The Educational Company of Ireland

Edco

First published 2018
The Educational Company of Ireland
Ballymount Road
Walkinstown
Dublin 12
www.edco.ie

A member of the Smurfit Kappa Group plc

ISBN: 978-1-84536-780-0

**Cover:** emc design; images: Alamy Stock Photos: David Lyons, Stephen Barnes;
Bridgeman Images: Vatican Museums and Galleries, Vatican City
**Design:** emc design
**Editors:** Jennifer Armstrong, Jane Rogers
**Layout:** emc design
**Proofreader:** Neil Burkey
**Artists:** Keith Barret, Mike Lacey, Wes Lowe, Andrew Pagram, Dusan Pavlic

# Acknowledgments

**The authors and publisher would like to thank the following for permission to reproduce images:**

**Alamy Stock Photos:** Page 1, repeated on page 2, Amanda Fiedler; Page 4, Dreamworks; Page 7, World History Archive; Page 7, Heritage Image Partnership Ltd; Page 7, Sabena Jane Blackbird; Page 13, Martin Shields; Page 20, Photo 12; Page 22, Rob Whitworth; Page 23, www.BibleLandPictures.com; Page 23, Keith Heron; Page 29, Photo Art Collection (PAC); Page 32, JHPhoto; Page 37, Vibrant Pictures; Page 38, St. Patrick preaching at Tara, from 'The Trias Thuamaturga, or Three Wonder-Working Saints of Ireland', by Mary Cusack (1829-99) published c.1890s (litho) (b/w photo), Irish School, (19th century) / Private Collection / The Stapleton Collection / Bridgeman Images; Page 42, Photo 12; Page 44, INTERFOTO; Page 47, TadhgD; Page 53, Lebrecht Music and Arts Photo Library; Page 53, Lebrecht Music and Arts Photo Library; Page 53, PAINTING; Page 56, Timewatch Images; Page 58, London Aerial Photo Library; Page 61, ART Collection; Page 62, Granger Historical Picture Archive; Page 64, INTERFOTO; Page 68, PRISMA ARCHIVO; Page 49 and page 70, North Wind Picture Archives; Page 71, Design Pics Inc; Page 71, sante castignani; Page 74, Neamt Monastery, Neamt county, Romania; Page 75, Granger Historical Picture Archive; Page 75, North Wind Picture Archives; Page 80, PRISMA ARCHIVO; Page 80, kevers; Page 81, MARKA; Page 78 and page 83, Art Collection 2; Page 83, Heritage Image Partnership Ltd; Page 83, age fotostock; Page 84, World History Archive; Page 85, PAINTING; Page 85, Dennis Hallinan; Page 86, Heritage Image Partnership Ltd; Page 86, Paul Fearn; Page 86, imageBROKER; Page 87, FineArt; Page 87, Tomas Abad; Page 87, Heritage Image Partnership Ltd; Page 87, INTERFOTO; Page 87, FineArt; Page 88, Granger Historical Picture Archive; Page 88, INTERFOTO; Page 88, Artokoloro Quint Lox Limited; Page 89, Peter Barritt; Page 90, age fotostock; Page 90, WorldPhotos; Page 90, John Baran; Page 91, Sergey Borisov; Page 91, Classic Image; Page 92, Stefano Politi Markovina; Page 78 and page 94, World History Archive; Page 96, IanDagnall Computing; Page 97, Heritage Image Partnership Ltd; Page 99, Science History Images; Page 99, Science History Images; Page 100, The Granger Collection; Page 100, Everett Collection Inc; Page 102, Hirarchivum Press; Page 102, Peter Horree; Page 105, Heritage Image Partnership Ltd; Page 106, B Christopher; Page 109, The Artchives; Page 104 and page 110, imageBROKER; Page 110, Granger Historical Picture Archive; Page 111, Ian G Dagnall; Page 114, The Granger Collection; Page 119, The Granger Collection; Page 124, Commission Air; Page 125, North Wind Picture Archives; Page 125, Pictorial Press Ltd; Page 126, Georgios Kollidas; Page 127, Ian Dagnall; Page 129, Falkenstein Heinz-Dieter; Page 130, Lanmas; Page 132, Peter Horree; Page 133, North Wind Picture Archives; Page 134, Pictorial Press Ltd; Page 135, Peter Barritt; Page 136, Paul Fearn; Page 123 and page 138, Lanmas; Page 138, Heritage Image Partnership Ltd; Page 140, Reflex Picture Library; Page 140, PRISMA ARCHIVO; Page 141, FL Historical 1A; Page 142, ART Collection; Page 147, Arco Images GmbH; Page 148, Universal Images Group North America LLC / DeAgostini; Page 153, GL Archive; Page 154, Historical Images Archive; Page 155, GL Archive; Page 164, Radharc Images; Page 164, Stephen Barnes; Page 166, Mike Kipling Photography; Page 167, SOTK2011; Page 167, North Wind Picture Archives; Page 168, Pictorial Press Ltd; Page 168, PRISMA ARCHIVO; Page 168, AA World Travel Library; Page 168, World History Archive; Page 169, GL Archive; Page 169, North Wind Picture Archives; Page 170, Granger Historical Picture Archive; Page 171, KGPA Ltd; Page 172, Pictorial Press Ltd; Page 173, mooziic; Page 173, Rolf Richardson; Page 173, Lebrecht Music and Arts Photo Library; Page 174, World History Archive; Page 175, Granger Historical Picture Archive; Page 175, The Print Collector; Page 175, GL Archive; Page 176, Lebrecht Music and Arts Photo Library; Page 165 and page 177, Chronicle; Page 177, GL Archive; Page 177, Lebrecht Music and Arts Photo Library; Page 178, World History Archive; Page 178, PRISMA ARCHIVO; Page 165 and page 183, Orcea David; Page 187, culliganphoto; Page 189, Zivica Kerkez; Page 191 and page 192, imageBROKER; Page 192, PAINTING; Page 193, Lebrecht Music and Arts Photo Library; Page 194, Archive Images; Page 195, The Granger Collection; Page 196, The Granger Collection; Page 197, Masterpics; Page 198, Niday Picture Library; Page 199, Granger Historical Picture Archive; Page 202, 19th era; Page 203, INTERFOTO; Page 203, Photo 12; Page 204, AM Stock 3; Page 205, Pictorial Press Ltd; Page 206, David Lyons; Page 207, Pictorial Press Ltd; Page 209, Pictorial Press Ltd; Page 210 and page 211, Werner Dieterich; Page 213, Thomas Weightman; Page 213, Historical Images Archive; Page 214, The Granger Collection; Page 216, 19th era; Page 217, Classic Image; Page 220, Granger Historical Picture Archive; Page 220, Pictorial Press Ltd; Page 221, North Wind Picture Archives; Page 223, World History Archive; Page 223, Ed Rooney; Page 223, Scott B. Rosen; Page 224, Granger Historical Picture Archive; Page 210 and page 225, Radharc Images; Page 227, AF archive; Page 228, lev radin; Page 228, Steve Bukley; Page 229, Pictorial Press Ltd; Page 229, Adam Stoltman; Page 229, Granger Historical Picture Archive; Page 229, Granger Historical Picture Archive; Page 230, NASA Archive; Page 230, Christoph Furlong; Page 230, Granger Historical Picture Archive; Page 231, mark reinstein; Page 232 and page 233, Loop Images Ltd; Page 233, McPhoto/Scholz; Page 233, Tom Corban; Page 234, Andrew Aitchison; Page 235, Pictorial Press Ltd; Page 235, Pictorial Press Ltd; Page 236, Classic Image; Page 236, World History Archive; Page 237, Barry Mason; Page 238, Pictorial Press Ltd; Page 238, Paul Fearn; Page 238, Paul Fearn; Page 238, Pictorial Press Ltd; Page 239, Frymire Archive; Page 240, Chris Hellier; Page 241, World History Archive; Page 246, Hilary Morgan; Page 249, Pictorial Press Ltd; Page 249, Paul Fearn; Page 150, Pictorial Press Ltd; Page 250, Paul Fearn; Page 251, Pictorial Press Ltd; Page 253, Pictorial Press Ltd; Page 255, IanDagnall Computing; Page 256, Pictorial Press Ltd; Page 259, Pictorial Press Ltd; Page 270 and page 271, Trinity Mirror / Mirrorpix; Page 272, Marshall Ikonography; Page 273, Atomic; Page 274, Granger Historical Picture Archive; Page 277, Neil McAllister; Page 270 and page 278, Trinity Mirror / Mirrorpix; Page 280, Trinity Mirror / Mirrorpix; Page 281, Pictorial Press Ltd; Page 286, Heritage Image Partnership Ltd; Page 288, Heritage Image Partnership Ltd; Page 290, Shawshots; Page 290, Chronicle; Page 292, Peter Horree; Page 293, David Cole; Page 298, OsmanPhotos.com; Page 300, World History Archive; Page 301, Pictorial Press Ltd; Page 303, Eddie Gerald; Page 307, dpa picture alliance; Page 308, Pictorial Press Ltd; Page 308, AF archive; Page 308, INTERFOTO; Page 308, Pictorial Press Ltd; Page 308, SPUTNIK; Page 311, Prisma by Dukas Presseagentur GmbH; Page 311, War Archive; Page 311, Lordprice Collection; Page 311, Pictorial Press Ltd; Page 312, dpa picture alliance; Page 312, WS Collection; Page 317, World History Archive; Page 318, ITAR-TASS News Agency; Page

## Digital Resources

The *History Alive* digital resources will enhance classroom learning by encouraging student participation and engagement. They support the New Junior Cycle Specification's emphasis on the use of modern technology in the classroom and are designed to cater for different learning styles.

To provide guidance for the integration of digital resources in the classroom and to aid lesson planning, they are **referenced throughout the textbook** using the following icons:

 **PowerPoint** presentations provide a summary of every section of the student textbook, highlighting main themes and topics.

 **Section summary** documents that highlight the learning intentions of each section.

 Useful **Weblinks** documents provide links to additional material.

Teachers can access the *History Alive* digital resources via the *History Alive* interactive e-book, which is available online at **www.edcolearning.ie.**

 Students work in pairs or groups to complete the activity.

 Every activity involves at least one of the eight key skills of Junior Cycle; direct links have been highlighted.

 **Learning Outcomes:** Each section specifically addresses one or more of the Learning Outcomes. Some of the more general Learning Outcomes (1.1, 1.2, 1.3, 1.4, 1.7, 1.8, 1.9, 1.10, 1.11, 2.11, 2.13) are covered throughout the text.

# CONTENTS

# INTRODUCTION

Welcome, history students, to the textbook *History Alive*! History is about how humans lived in the past and how their experience has shaped the world that we live in today. Our aim is to bring history alive for you. You are going to become a detective! Through clues called **sources** you will learn how to find out about the past and how to judge what happened at a particular time.

At the start of each section there is a list of **learning intentions**. These tell you what you will learn about in this part of the history course. You will be asked to think about what you already know about a topic and then examine relevant sources before being introduced to the main story. At the start of each section in the student activity book you will be asked to think about what you already know about the topics covered in that section.

Throughout the book there are **visual and written primary and secondary sources** which will help you to find out what happened at that time and why it happened. A lot of the activities can be done in pairs or groups. Detective work is more successful when you work as a team!

As you work with different types of sources you will develop new **historical skills**. You will learn how to collect information and put clues together. You will learn how to look at an event or person in the past from the point of view of people living at that time. You will learn to look at the past from different points of view. As you discover the stories of people who lived in the past you will understand more about how people live today. You will even find that learning about history helps you solve today's problems!

In the new Junior Cycle there are eight key skills, which you will also be learning throughout your history course. They are:

> Being numerate
> Being literate
> Being able to reflect on your own learning
> Managing information
> Being creative
> Being able to communicate ideas
> Working with others
> Staying well.

At the end of each section there is a list of **key terms** that you need to know to be able to talk or write about the topic. You can use the questions at the end of each section to check what you have learned about a topic and the skills you have acquired. These activities can be done on your own or you can work in pairs or with groups of other students. A good idea is to check each other's work. There are a wide variety of activities in the *History Alive Student Activity Book* (anticipation and reflection exercises; pair and group activities; key terms revisited and revised) and the *History Alive Graphic Organiser* (graphic organisers to help you summarise and revised information). These books will help you to remember what you have learned about a topic.

Good luck and happy investigating!

*Gráinne Henry, Bairbre Kennedy, Tim Nyhan, Stephen Tonge*

# 1 WORKING WITH EVIDENCE

The job of the historian — 2

The importance of archaeology — 9

# THE JOB OF THE HISTORIAN

## 🎯 LEARNING INTENTIONS

**At the end of this section, you should be able to:**

◎ Define the word 'history'

◎ Outline the types of evidence historians use

◎ Distinguish between primary and secondary sources

◎ Explain how historians examine and evaluate sources

◎ Describe how historians record events in order.

## What is history?

**History** involves the study of the past. It is the story of human activity. Events that happened before you came into class are now part of history.

History is not just about battles and the lives of kings and queens. **Historians** are also interested in answering questions about the lives of ordinary people. What were their homes like? What food did they eat? What jobs did they do? What did they wear? What games did they play?

Historians make a distinction between history and prehistory.

> The **historic period** is when people used writing. For example, we know a lot about the lives of ancient Romans because they wrote books.

> The **prehistoric period** is the time before writing was used. We rely on archaeology for our evidence from this period (see The Importance of Archaeology, page 9).

## What evidence do historians use?

Historians are similar to police detectives. Both try to piece together the story of what happened from the clues or evidence available. For historians, a clue about what life was like in the past is called a **source**. Sometimes the evidence is very good and so the story is accurate. Sometimes there are few sources and so our knowledge of an event remains poor.

A source could be a written document, a photograph or an object from the past. Archaeologists discover and examine objects from the past (see The Importance of Archaeology, page 9).

**Historian**
A person who studies the past.

### Activity 1

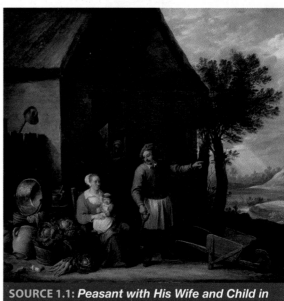

**SOURCE 1.1:** *Peasant with His Wife and Child in Front of the Farmhouse* (1640–1670) by David Teniers

1  In pairs, examine the picture and give four pieces of evidence about life at the time.

**Archaeology**
The study of the remains left by people in the past.

**Source**
Evidence used by historians to find out what happened in the past, e.g. a document, a picture.

## Activity 2

Examine this source and then answer the question below.

**SOURCE 1.2:** *The Irish Times* examines the European Commission (EU) action ordering Apple Inc. to pay Ireland unpaid taxes, 31 August 2016

1 How useful, do you think, are newspaper headlines and articles to historians?

Historians divide sources into two main types: primary sources and secondary sources.

> **Primary sources** come directly from the time of the event being studied. For example, a newspaper from 1900 could tell us a lot about the sports played at that time.

> **Secondary sources** come from a later date. For example, a 2018 book about leisure activities in 1900 could tell us a lot about the sports played at that time. This book is a secondary source as it was written long after most of the events that it describes. The tables below list a selection of primary sources and secondary sources that historians use.

| Primary sources | Description |
|---|---|
| Interviews | These are also called **oral sources**. An example would be an interview with an older person describing how their life has changed over the last fifty years. |
| Diaries | A record a person keeps of day-to-day events. Diaries give us evidence of personal events in the writer's life and important public events that were happening at the time. |
| Letters, emails | Written communications between people are very useful sources of evidence for historians. They include letters and emails. |
| Speeches | Formal and recorded talks can contain views on important events or government policies. |
| Government records | These include laws passed by parliament and reports carried out for the government. Probably the most important is the calculation of the population (number of people who live in a place) held every five years – the **census**. It gives us valuable information on the lives of ordinary people. |
| Autobiographies | An account of a person's life written by the actual person. These can be a very useful source for historians. |
| Photographs, posters, paintings | Visual records of the past. These sources reveal what people looked like, what they wore, where they lived, etc. |
| Newspapers, magazines | These are very useful sources. They contain reports on important political, social and sporting events, and reveal the interests of readers at the time. |
| Artefacts | Human-made objects found by archaeologists. |

| Secondary sources | Description |
|---|---|
| Biographies | The story of a person's life written by another person. Biographies have been written about most important people in history. |
| Movies | Some films tell the story of real people and historical events. They can give us some understanding about a subject; but teaching us about history is not their primary purpose. |
| TV or radio documentaries | An investigation into a particular event, person or period of history. |
| The Internet | Searching online is a popular way to research events. This is a very useful source, but historians must check the accuracy of the information they find. |
| History books | Most authors of history books lived many years after the events that they write about. |

## DID YOU KNOW?

Before the invention of the printing press, all books and documents were written by hand. These books were called **manuscripts**.

**SOURCE 1.3: Monk writing a manuscript**

SOURCE 1.4: Re-enacting history in *Saving Private Ryan*

## How do historians examine sources?

Historians want to examine why an event happened (the **cause**), what happened (the **course**) and the effects of the event (the **consequences**). They are not just interested in the event itself; they also want to investigate how the event affected the people of the time and the people of later generations.

First, historians have to find sources of information about the event they want to study. They could visit a place where written sources are stored, such as archives, libraries and museums. They could interview participants or witnesses to the event. They could read books written by other historians. They could research the topic using the Internet. This is becoming an increasingly valuable resource as more and more documents in archives and libraries become available online.

When researching a source to gather evidence about the past, historians follow a number of steps. Here is an example for a written source:

**Activity 3**

**Archives** are collections of documents and records that contain historical information. They are used by anyone doing historical research. The **National Archives of Ireland** contains many important documents about Irish history. However, many records are missing because they were destroyed during an attack on the Four Courts in Dublin in 1922, which marked the start of the Irish Civil War.

SOURCE 1.5: National Archives of Ireland

1   Why would historians visit the National Archives?

2   Why were so many records lost in 1922?

**1** Read or look at the source carefully.

**2** Find out *who* wrote the source, *what* kind of information it has, *when* it was written, *where* the content came from and *why* it was written. These are called the **5 Ws**.

**3** Establish whether the author of the source was present at the event being described and how soon afterwards the account was written. Historians call this the **time and place rule**. An eyewitness account written days after the event is more useful than an account of the same event written decades later by someone who was not there.

**4** Interpret what evidence from the source is valuable and whether the source can be trusted. No piece of evidence is taken at face value!

**5** Look at many different sources and compare the findings to make sure that the story of the past is as accurate as possible. This is called **cross-checking**.

## How do historians evaluate a source?

All sources have some use to historians, but they may also have limitations or weaknesses. To determine how useful a source is, historians have to judge its **reliability**. This involves considering factors such as:

> **Bias:** Is the source one-sided? Does it favour one side's version of events over another's? Sometimes authors or interviewees deliberately leave out facts or details that would not support their view of the event.

> **Viewpoint:** Does the source contain the personal opinions of the author? If the source gives no views about the event it is said to be **objective**. Historians have to be able to separate fact from opinion, especially when reading diaries, letters, speeches and newspapers.

> **Accuracy:** Some sources supply incorrect information. That is why historians use more than one source. For example, many history sites on the Internet contain errors and falsehoods.

> **Exaggeration:** This can be a major problem, especially with eyewitness accounts. Is the person being interviewed overstating his or her role in an event? The number of people claimed to have been involved in an event also has to be checked carefully as these figures are often inflated.

> **Propaganda:** Does the source make one side look good and another look bad? Propaganda is widely used during wars.

### Remember!

Primary sources are not necessarily more (or less) reliable than secondary sources. It depends on the source itself. In some cases, secondary sources can be more reliable as they are based on many primary sources.

### Activity 4

Read the following brief description of the American leader George Washington.

> George Washington was born in 1732. He was the commander of the American army that defeated the French who ruled America. He was a great leader … Afterwards he became the first president of the United States. He served as president for years. He was the best American president and the American people were very happy while he was president. He died in 1799.

1 Pick out two facts and two opinions.
2 Do you think this account is biased?
3 Research a biography of George Washington online to check the accuracy of this account.
4 From your research, write down four more facts about the life of George Washington.

## How do historians record events in order?

When historians find out information about the past, they must place the events in the right order. They usually use dates to do this. **Date order** makes it easier for people to follow the story of what happened.

There are a number of ways to put events in date order. For example:

⟩ If the event happened over a short period of time, historians might use years, months, days or even hours.

⟩ For events that happened over a longer period, they can use centuries. A **century** lasts 100 years. The twenty-first century started in 2001 and will end in 2100.

⟩ If the event happened over a very long period or a very long time ago, historians may use a **millennium** – this is a period of 1,000 years.

⟩ Events may be dated as taking place before or after the birth of Christ. The letters BC (Before Christ) or AD (Anno Domini – the year of our Lord) placed next to a date tell us this. For example, the first Roman emperor, Augustus Caesar, was born in 63 BC and died in AD 14. In recent years BC and AD have often been replaced by BCE and CE, which mean Before the Common Era and Common Era.

**Activity 5**

Examine this source and then answer the questions below.

SOURCE 1.6: Cork, 1900

1 Write down five pieces of information that you can infer from this photograph.
2 Consider how the picture would be different if taken today. Suggest three changes.

## Timelines

Historians can use **timelines** to show the order in which events happened. For example, when studying the lives of famous people it is useful to know the year they were born and the year they died. The important events in their lives can be placed in between these two dates. On the right is a short timeline of the life of the Irish politician Seán Lemass.

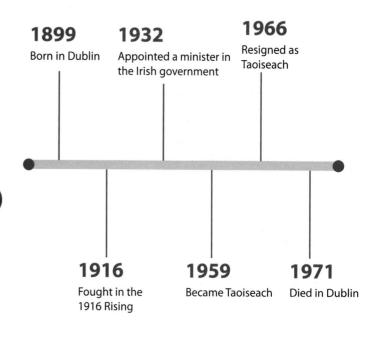

**1899**
Born in Dublin

**1932**
Appointed a minister in the Irish government

**1966**
Resigned as Taoiseach

**1916**
Fought in the 1916 Rising

**1959**
Became Taoiseach

**1971**
Died in Dublin

SOURCE 1.7: **Timeline for Seán Lemass**

---

### Activity 6

1   Draw up timelines for **two** of the four countries below, showing five important events that happened in their history:
- United States of America
- United Kingdom
- Germany
- Russia.

---

## Eras

Historians also organise events into historical eras. This is often done when there are few or no written sources. The table below shows early Irish historical eras, which are based on the main materials used to make tools and weapons.

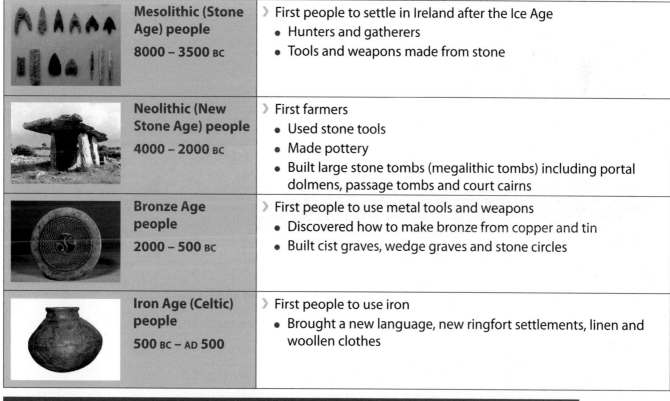

| | **Mesolithic (Stone Age) people** 8000 – 3500 BC | › First people to settle in Ireland after the Ice Age <br> • Hunters and gatherers <br> • Tools and weapons made from stone |
|---|---|---|
| | **Neolithic (New Stone Age) people** 4000 – 2000 BC | › First farmers <br> • Used stone tools <br> • Made pottery <br> • Built large stone tombs (megalithic tombs) including portal dolmens, passage tombs and court cairns |
| | **Bronze Age people** 2000 – 500 BC | › First people to use metal tools and weapons <br> • Discovered how to make bronze from copper and tin <br> • Built cist graves, wedge graves and stone circles |
| | **Iron Age (Celtic) people** 500 BC – AD 500 | › First people to use iron <br> • Brought a new language, new ringfort settlements, linen and woollen clothes |

SOURCE 1.8: **Eras of early Irish history**

The more recent historical eras are:

› **The Middle Ages:** This refers to events that happened between AD 500 and 1500.

› **Early Modern Period:** This covers events from 1500 until 1800.

› **Late Modern Period:** This refers to events after 1800.

## CENSUS OF IRELAND, 1901.

*(Two Examples of the mode of filling up this Table are given on the other side.)*

### FORM A.

No. on Form B. ___4___

RETURN of the MEMBERS of this FAMILY and their VISITORS, BOARDERS, SERVANTS, &c., who slept or abode in this House on the night of SUNDAY, the 31st of MARCH, 1901.

| No. | NAME and SURNAME — Christian Name | Surname | RELATION to Head of Family. | RELIGIOUS PROFESSION. | EDUCATION. | AGE — Years on last Birthday. | Months for Infants under one Year. | SEX. | RANK, PROFESSION, OR OCCUPATION. | MARRIAGE. | WHERE BORN. | IRISH LANGUAGE. | If Deaf and Dumb; Dumb only; Blind; Imbecile or Idiot; or Lunatic. |
|---|---|---|---|---|---|---|---|---|---|---|---|---|---|
| 1 | Patrick | Quinn | Hd of Family | Roman Catholic | cannot read | 52 | - | M. | Farmer | married | Co Donegal | | |
| 2 | Bridget | Quinn | Wife | - Do - | cannot read | 40 | | F. | | married | Do | | |
| 3 | Daniel | Quinn | Son | Do | read & write | 18 | | M. | Farmers Son | Not married | Do | | |
| 4 | Bridget | Quinn | Daughter | Do | read & write | 16 | . | F. | Farmers Daughter | Not married | Do | | |
| 5 | Patrick | Quinn | Son | Do | read & write | 13 | | M. | Scholar | Not married | Do | | |
| 6 | Edward | Quinn | Son | Do | read & write | 11 | | M. | Scholar | Not married | Do | | |
| 7 | Maggie Jane | Quinn | Daughter | Do | read | 7 | . | F. | Scholar | Not married | Do | | |
| 8 | Rose | Quinn | Daughter | - Do | cannot read | 4 | | F. | | Not married | Do | | |
| 9 | John | Quinn | Son | Do | cannot read | 7 | | M. | | Not married | Do | | |
| 10 | Cassie | Quinn | Daughter | Do | cannot read | | 9 | F. | | | | | |
| 11 | Jane | Quinn | Mother | Do | cannot read | 86 | | F. | | | | | |
| 12 | | | | | | | | | | | | | |
| 13 | | | | | | | | | | | | | |
| 14 | | | | | | | | | | | | | |
| 15 | | | | | | | | | | | | | |

I hereby certify, as required by the Act 63 Vic., cap. 6, s. 6 (1), that the foregoing Return is correct, according to the best of my knowledge and belief.

I believe

*Frances A W Lunel* (Signature of Enumerator.)

**SOURCE 1.9: Census form from 1901**

### Activity 7

Working in groups:
1. Identify five pieces of information from the census form.
2. Name two other types of source that would help you learn more about this family.

## DO YOU UNDERSTAND THESE KEY TERMS?

| | | | |
|---|---|---|---|
| archaeology | history | propaganda | timeline |
| autobiography | manuscript | reliability | viewpoint |
| bias | millennium | secondary source | |
| century | prehistory | source | |
| cross-checking | primary source | time and place rule | |

 PowerPoint summary

## SELF-ASSESSMENT – CAN YOU?

1. Explain the difference between prehistory and history.
2. Identify four things that interest historians besides famous people and battles.
3. Explain the difference between a primary source and a secondary source, and list three types of each.
4. List four places where historians go to find written sources.
5. Identify the 5 Ws and explain why they are important when studying a source.
6. Demonstrate why it is good practice for historians to cross-check sources.
7. Outline four reasons for agreeing or disagreeing with this statement: 'All sources are very reliable.'
8. Pick a historical figure you are familiar with and draw up a timeline containing five important events in his or her life.

# THE IMPORTANCE OF ARCHAEOLOGY

## ◎ LEARNING INTENTIONS

**At the end of this section, you should be able to:**

- ◎ Define the word 'archaeology'
- ◎ Describe how archaeologists choose sites to investigate
- ◎ List the steps archaeologists take to investigate a site
- ◎ Outline the methods archaeologists use to date objects
- ◎ Recognise why the discovery of a skeleton is important
- ◎ Explain the role of DNA analysis in modern archaeology.

## What is archaeology?

**Archaeology** is the study of what has been left behind by people from the past. **Archaeologists** work closely with historians to build up a better picture of what life was like for people long ago. For example, thousands of years ago there was no writing, so historians need the evidence provided by archaeologists to find out what life was like then.

Archaeologists look to find clues left by our ancestors. These may be human or animal bones, buildings or objects that people have made. The man-made objects they find are called **artefacts**. These include jewellery, pottery, tools and weapons.

Archaeology is not about hunting for treasure. An old rubbish tip can often tell an archaeologist more about what life was like for our ancestors than a find of gold or silver.

## Why do objects end up in the ground?

There are many reasons why evidence of human activity ends up in the ground. Here are some of the common ones:

- ❯ Some objects are lost. How many times have you lost something?
- ❯ Valuable objects were buried for safekeeping. There were no banks to store valuables.
- ❯ Food items were buried for preservation. There were no fridges to preserve food.
- ❯ In pre-Christian times bodies were buried with objects that it was believed the person would need in the afterlife. These are called **grave goods** and can provide a wealth of information.
- ❯ Old buildings are knocked down and new buildings may be built over them, especially in cities.
- ❯ Abandoned buildings are covered by soil over time.

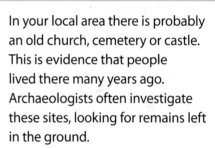

**Artefacts**
Objects made by humans (e.g. coins, axes and bowls).

### Activity 1

In your local area there is probably an old church, cemetery or castle. This is evidence that people lived there many years ago. Archaeologists often investigate these sites, looking for remains left in the ground.

1 In groups of four, make a list of old buildings in your area that archaeologists might be interested in investigating for remains from the past.

### Activity 2

1 In pairs, list ten items that you would bury today in a time capsule to be opened in 100 years. Explain how each object that you choose would tell somebody in the future about life today.

In most cases living things decay when buried in soil. That is why archaeologists usually find bones rather than bodies. However, this is not always the case. Bodies found in very wet soil conditions or in very cold climates are sometimes well preserved. In Ireland, well-preserved bodies have been found in bogs where the soil is waterlogged. They are called **bog bodies**.

## How do archaeologists choose sites to investigate?

An area of ground where archaeologists decide to dig is called a **site**. There are three main reasons that a site may be chosen:

> There is evidence that objects might be found at the site. There might be a ruined building there, or there might be an old document showing that a building once existed at the location. This is called **research archaeology**.

> Archaeologists often dig at a site before construction work on roads or buildings starts, especially if there is strong evidence that there may be remains of human activity. They want to make sure that no objects from the past are lost or damaged. This is called **rescue archaeology**.

> Many finds are discovered by accident by a member of the public. Archaeologists are then called in to investigate. This is called **salvage archaeology**.

## What steps do archaeologists take to investigate a site?

When archaeologists decide to investigate a site they are very careful to make sure that all evidence from the past is collected.

### Preparing to dig

A **survey** of the site is carried out to help the archaeologists decide where to start digging. The survey may include:

> A **geophysical survey**, which involves using a machine like an X-ray to look at the soil underneath the surface. It shows how much the earth has been disturbed by human activity.

> Digging **test trenches** to get an idea of the amount of remains they can expect to find.

> Taking **aerial photographs** to determine the size of the site. These often reveal features that may be missed on the ground. Kites, balloons, model planes and, in recent years, drones have been used to take the images.

The archaeologists will then draw up a detailed plan of where they will dig. The site is divided into numbered squares measuring one metre by one metre. The archaeologists will follow this plan when investigating the site.

### DID YOU KNOW?

- Large numbers of gold and silver objects are often found together. They were buried for safekeeping but their owners did not come back for them. Archaeologists call this type of find a **hoard**.

- In 2013, 50 kg of butter was discovered buried in a bog near Tullamore, Co. Offaly. Called bog butter, it was found to be 5,000 years old!

- Two of the most famous archaeological finds in Irish history were discovered by accident. The **Broighter Hoard** was found by two farmers ploughing a field near Limavady in Co. Derry in 1896; it was about 35 cm below the surface. The **Ardagh Chalice** (see page 43) was discovered by two boys digging for potatoes near Ardagh in Co. Limerick in 1868. Both of these finds are on view at the National Museum of Ireland in Kildare Street, Dublin.

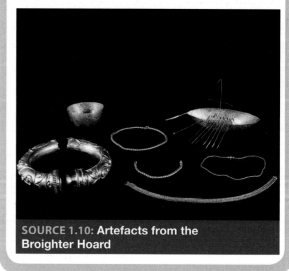

**SOURCE 1.10: Artefacts from the Broighter Hoard**

## During the dig

The excavation or **dig** starts by removing the topsoil, often with a digger. Spades and pickaxes are also used. With this cleared, the archaeologist can begin to look for remains from the past.

Archaeologists use a large number of tools to look for objects. For example:

> Layers of earth are scraped away using a **trowel**.
> A **hand-pick** is used to loosen soil.
> Archaeologists have to be careful not to damage any objects they discover, as they can be very fragile. They use **brushes** and even toothbrushes to help unearth them.
> As some objects are very small, the soil is often put through a **sieve** to make sure that nothing is missed.

Once an object has been uncovered, a **photograph** will be taken of it.

Even if no objects are found, the soil itself can tell an archaeologist a lot about the past. For example:

> Wooden poles that were used for building houses will have decayed but they will have left dark round patches called **post-holes**.
> A fireplace will leave a square-shaped dark patch in the soil.
> Evidence that the site may have been destroyed by fire will be seen by a dark layer of soil between two lighter ones.

Careful records are made of all objects found. The objects are cleaned and put into labelled bags to record where they were found on the site. Computers are used to help to record this information.

The objects discovered are then sent to a university or a museum. Some will go on display to the public.

### Activity 3

Examine this source and then answer the questions below.

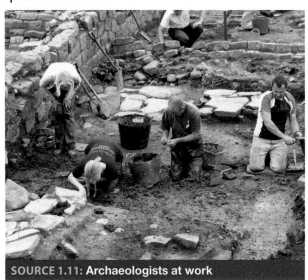

SOURCE 1.11: Archaeologists at work

1. Outline the activities being carried out in the picture.
2. Identify the main tools being used.

### Activity 4

Examine this source and then answer the questions below.

SOURCE 1.12: Excavation of Viking Dublin, 1996

1. Who carries out an excavation?
2. List two reasons why these kinds of excavation are so useful to historians.

## What methods do archaeologists use to date objects?

One of the biggest challenges archaeologists face is working out the age of the artefacts they have found.

If artefacts do not have a written source to help with dating, archaeologists can use some of the following indicators:

› **Coins:** Finding a coin with artefacts is a great help. Coins usually have dates on them and this can help the archaeologist to determine how old an object is.

› **Depth:** As a rule, the deeper an object is found, the older it is. This is called **stratigraphy**.

› **Design:** An object's design or the decoration on it (e.g. on a piece of pottery) can indicate its age.

› **Carbon 14: Carbon** or **radiocarbon dating** is a scientific method used to find the age of an object that was once alive. All living objects (humans, plants and animals) contain carbon 14. After death the amount of carbon 14 begins to decline – the older an object, the less carbon 14 will be present.

› **Tree rings:** Each year a tree grows a new ring. The number of rings inside the trunk tells you the age of the tree. By studying the pattern of these rings, known as **dendrochronology**, archaeologists can estimate the age of wooden objects such as parts of buildings or ships.

## Why is the discovery of a skeleton important?

Archaeologists can learn a lot from human bones when they are discovered. Analysis of the bones enables them to piece together a picture of the person's life. For example, damage to a bone could prove that the person died from a wound. The bones can be examined scientifically and this can tell us about the person's diet.

**1** The pelvic bone and the skull reveal whether it was a man or a woman.

**2** The femur (thigh bone) indicates the person's height.

**3** The teeth can help tell the person's age at death.

**4** A well-preserved skull can help archaeologists to reconstruct the face, showing us what the person looked like.

---

🔍 **DID YOU KNOW?**

Artefacts found at Mount Sandel near Coleraine in Co. Derry were clearly very old, but how old? Archaeologists used carbon dating on burnt hazelnut shells and discovered that the site was 9,000 years old. Radiocarbon dating of butchered bear bones found in Co. Clare showed that people lived in Ireland 12,500 years ago. Previously it had been thought that Mount Sandel was the oldest site in Ireland.

🔍 **DID YOU KNOW?**

A painting of Mary Queen of Scots (1542–1587) in the National Gallery in London was thought to be an eighteenth-century copy. Dendrochronological analysis of the wooden panel around the painting proved it was actually from the sixteenth century when Mary lived.

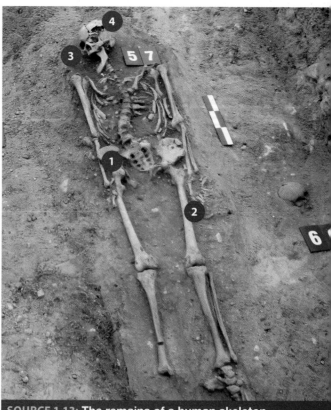

SOURCE 1.13: **The remains of a human skeleton**

# Ötzi

In 1991 two hikers stumbled on a body sticking out of a melting glacier high in the Ötztal Alps on the Italian–Austrian border. The body had been well preserved by the ice and it became a very important discovery for archaeologists.

Nicknamed Ötzi, or the Iceman, carbon dating showed the body to be 5,300 years old. Examination of the body provided a lot of evidence about life at that time. For example:

> It could be the oldest murder case in history. An X-ray revealed that he had been killed by an arrow to the shoulder. It is likely that he was being pursued by his killers high into the mountains.

> He was about 1.7 metres tall and between forty and forty-five years old.

> Analysis of pollen found on the body established that he died in the early summer.

> Examination of his stomach found that his last meal consisted of deer and a type of bread.

> His clothes were made from a variety of animal hides – sheep, goat and bear.

> A backpack discovered beside his body contained items he needed for his journey, including a first-aid kit to help treat the stomach problems he suffered from.

> He also had a mixture of copper and stone tools and weapons – a copper-headed axe, a flint dagger and a bow made of wood. Copper tools were rare at the time and this find suggests he was an important person in his village.

> He had sixty-one different tattoos on his body.

> He had no wisdom teeth and was missing two ribs.

> DNA testing found that nineteen men living in the Alps today could be descended from Ötzi.

A reconstruction was made (pictured here) to show what Ötzi looked like.

SOURCE 1.14: Ötzi reconstruction

---

**Activity 5**

Use the Internet to research more details about Ötzi and to answer the following questions:

1 How was the body discovered and removed from the ice?

2 What was discovered by examining his body?

3 What was learned from Ötzi's clothing and equipment?

# What is the role of DNA analysis in archaeology?

Archaeologists make use of modern scientific methods to investigate artefacts. One of these is **DNA analysis**, which they use to discover more evidence from skeletons. DNA is present in the cells of our bodies. It is passed from generation to generation. DNA samples taken from bones can be matched with the DNA of living relatives to identify a body.

## Activity 6

In 2013 a skeleton found in England helped solve a historical mystery. It was identified as King **Richard III**. He had been killed in a battle in 1485, but it was not known where he had been buried. He was identified through DNA testing of living descendants. Archaeologists were also able to use his skull to reconstruct what he looked like.

SOURCE 1.15: Richard III's skeleton, discovered in 2013

SOURCE 1.16: Reconstruction of Richard III's face

1 What historical mystery was solved in 2013?
2 How was the skeleton identified?

## DO YOU UNDERSTAND THESE KEY TERMS?

| | | | |
|---|---|---|---|
| artefact | a dig | post-hole | stratigraphy |
| bog body | DNA analysis | research archaeology | survey |
| carbon dating | excavation | rescue archaeology | test trench |
| dendrochronology | hoard | salvage archaeology | |

 Chapter summary      Weblinks      PowerPoint summary

# SELF-ASSESSMENT – CAN YOU?

1 Explain why archaeology is important.

2 Explain how objects such as bodies can be well preserved in certain conditions.

3 Demonstrate two ways in which sites are chosen to be excavated.

4 Explain why archaeologists survey a site before they dig.

5 Identify three tools that archaeologists use during excavations.

6 Explain why archaeologists have to be careful with objects that they find.

7 Identify and explain two methods archaeologists use to date objects they discover.

8 Describe what information an archaeologist can discover from a skeleton.

9 Identify and explain two examples from this section where archaeology has improved our knowledge of the past.

10 List four examples to support this statement: 'Archaeologists use a lot of modern technology to help them.'

# 2 HOW AN ANCIENT CIVILISATION INFLUENCED OUR WORLD

Who were the Romans?

16

What was life like in Rome in AD 100?

22

How has the Roman Empire influenced us?

32

# WHO WERE THE ROMANS?

## 🎯 LEARNING INTENTIONS

**At the end of this section, you should be able to:**

◎ Define and describe the Roman Empire

◎ Outline how we can find out about the Romans

◎ Explain how Roman society was organised.

## What was the Roman Empire?

Rome started out as a group of small villages around 750 BC. Gradually, the villages came together to form the city of Rome.

By AD 200 Rome was the largest city in the world. About one million people lived there. It controlled all the land around the Mediterranean Sea, including much of Western Europe and parts of the Middle East and North Africa. We call this area the **Roman Empire**.

The areas conquered by Rome were called **provinces**. Each province was run by a governor. Each province paid huge taxes and sent grain to Rome. Many of these provinces later became countries.

> **Empire**
> Where a number of different countries are controlled by one ruler.

> **KS** 👥 **Activity 1**
>
> In pairs, examine this source and then answer the questions.
> 1. What names of countries do you recognise? Make a list.
> 2. Where, do you think, did Rome's wealth come from?

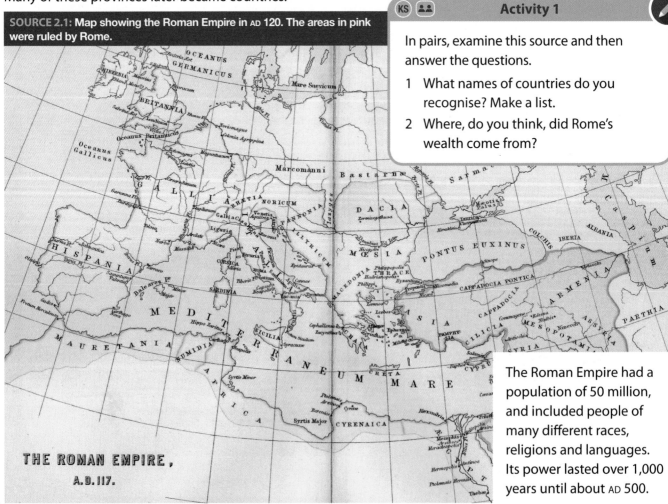

**SOURCE 2.1:** Map showing the Roman Empire in AD 120. The areas in pink were ruled by Rome.

> The Roman Empire had a population of 50 million, and included people of many different races, religions and languages. Its power lasted over 1,000 years until about AD 500.

# How can we find out about the Romans?

One of the most important ways of learning about the Romans is to look at what they left behind. For example:

› **Buildings:** Archaeologists have **excavated** (dug up) many places where the Romans lived and they have found Roman artefacts including coins, statues and paintings. There are also many ruins of Roman buildings.

› **Texts:** The Romans wrote many stories, histories, plays and other books, making it easy for us to find out how they thought and felt. They wrote in **Latin** and for centuries people all over Europe learned Latin. It is still taught in some schools today.

**Forum**
The main public space in the centre of Rome. It was originally a marketplace.

---

**KS** **Activity 2**

Examine these four sources and then answer the questions below.

**A**

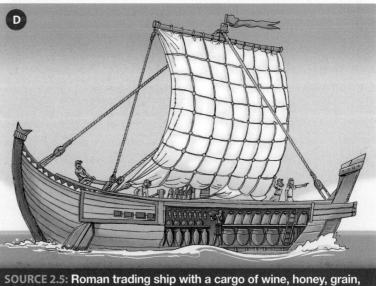

SOURCE 2.2: Ruins of the Forum

**B** Here is the unlovely tomb of a lovely woman. Her parents gave her the name of Claudia. She loved her husband with all her heart. She had two sons, one of whom she buried. She was charming to talk to and gentle to be with. She looked after the house and spun wool.

SOURCE 2.3: Translation of words on a tombstone near Rome

**C**

SOURCE 2.4: Replica Roman coin

**D**

SOURCE 2.5: Roman trading ship with a cargo of wine, honey, grain, fish and olive oil

1 What is a primary source? Which of these sources is a primary source?
2 List five things these sources tell us about the Roman Empire.
3 Which source do you find most interesting? Explain why.

**Learning Outcome** 3.1

## Rome

**Activity 3**

Examine this source and then answer the questions below.

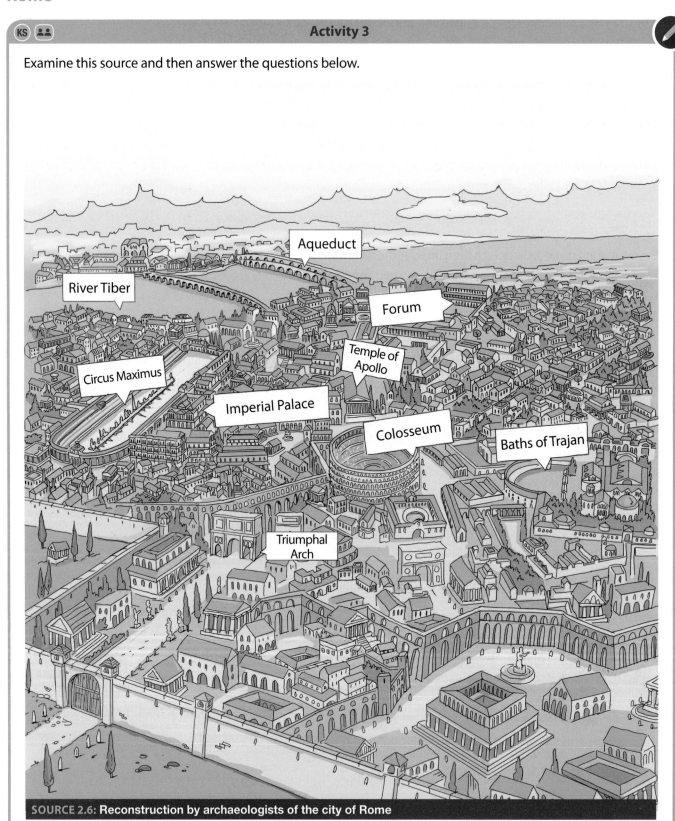

SOURCE 2.6: Reconstruction by archaeologists of the city of Rome

1   What buildings can you identify from this source?
2   Describe the streets.
3   What building materials were used, do you think?
4   Why is a source like this useful for historians?

## Pompeii

In the late 1700s archaeologists discovered two Roman cities, almost exactly as they had been 1,500 years earlier. They were called **Pompeii** and **Herculaneum**. They were wealthy cities, located south of Rome on the side of a volcano called **Mount Vesuvius**.

Vesuvius had been quiet for 800 years until it erupted on a sunny August day in AD 79. Red-hot rock, gas and ash began to pour from the volcano. Travelling at 100 km per hour, the rocks and ashes quickly covered Pompeii and Herculaneum.

Thousands of people died horribly. Archaeologists excavating the ruins found people lying where they fell when the ashes covered them. Houses with their furniture and beautiful wall paintings were just as they had been when their owners died. Meals lay uneaten on tables.

 **Activity 4**

Examine this source and then answer the question below.

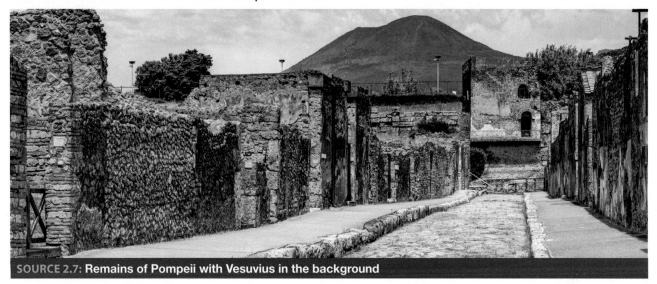

SOURCE 2.7: Remains of Pompeii with Vesuvius in the background

1   Identify three pieces of information this source tells you about Pompeii.

## How was Roman society run?

Rome was ruled at first by kings, but soon the Romans set up a new type of government called a **republic**. This meant that Roman citizens could choose their own government. They elected people to the **Senate**.

There were three main groups of people in Roman society: patricians, plebeians and slaves. The **patricians** were rich landowners and the **plebeians** were ordinary workers and farmers. You had to be a member of one of these two groups to be a Roman **citizen**. In reality the patricians had all the power. Women and slaves were not allowed to be citizens.

About one-third of the people living in Rome were **slaves**. Some slaves were criminals, but most were foreigners whom Roman soldiers had taken prisoner when they conquered their land.

Slaves belonged to their masters and had no rights. They were not paid but they did most of the hard work. They worked in houses, on farms and building sites and down mines. They fought as gladiators and raced chariots. Some slaves were educated and worked as teachers and doctors.

Sometimes a master freed a slave who had served him well. Freed slaves lived like ordinary Romans, but they could never become Roman citizens.

**Citizens**
People who live freely in a state and who have certain rights and responsibilities.

**Activity 5**

Examine this source and then answer the questions below.

SOURCE 2.8: After every victory the Roman army would return to Rome and parade through the city. Triumphal arches were built for each parade. Still from the film *The Fall of the Roman Empire*.

1   Give two reasons why the Roman army might be described as impressive in this image.
2   The real rulers of the Roman Empire were the soldiers. Suggest why this was the case.
3   This source is taken from a film. Identify one advantage and one disadvantage of this type of source for historians.
4   Is this a secondary or a primary source? Give reasons for your answer.

## The army

The Roman army held the empire together and remained unbeaten for centuries. Soldiers had excellent discipline and training. They marched more than 30 km a day. They were well paid and were also allowed to sell any prisoners they captured as slaves.

The army was divided into thirty **legions**. Each legion had about 5,000 soldiers. Most soldiers were volunteers. Many were the sons of soldiers. They were very proud of their legion and they fought very hard in battle.

Additional army units were made up of conquered soldiers and friendly tribes. These soldiers served for twenty-five years and at the end of their service they became citizens of Rome.

## Rome becomes an empire

The Romans loved their army generals and sometimes they became very powerful. One of these generals was **Julius Caesar**, who lived around 50 BC. He became so popular that he was able to rule Rome without the Senate.

His adopted son became the first emperor of Rome, **Emperor Augustus**, in 27 BC. He did away with the Senate and ruled alone. After that the Roman Empire was always ruled by an emperor.

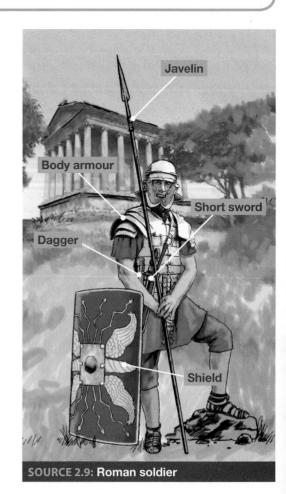

SOURCE 2.9: Roman soldier

## Activity 6

Examine this source and then answer the questions below.

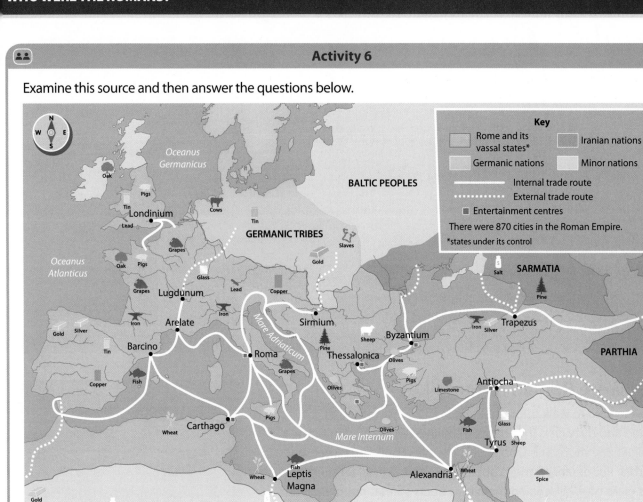

**SOURCE 2.10: Map showing trade in the Roman Empire in the second century AD**

1 Name three important cities in the Roman Empire other than Rome.

2 Can you guess the two biggest expenses that Rome had in running this empire?

3 How, do you think, did the Romans manage to run their empire so efficiently? Give two examples in your answer.

4 List ten items that the Romans traded.

PowerPoint summary

## DO YOU UNDERSTAND THESE KEY TERMS?

| citizen | empire | Forum | legion | plebeian | republic | slave |
|---------|--------|-------|--------|----------|----------|-------|
| emperor | excavated | Latin | patrician | province | Senate | |

# SELF-ASSESSMENT – CAN YOU?

1 Give the size of the Roman Empire's population.

2 Explain the geographic areas the Roman Empire covered.

3 Give five examples of primary sources from which we can find out about the Romans.

4 Explain why Pompeii and Herculaneum are so important for historians and give two examples of what they can tell us about Ancient Rome.

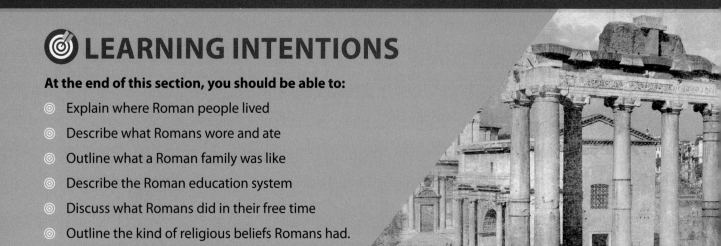

## 🎯 LEARNING INTENTIONS

**At the end of this section, you should be able to:**

◎ Explain where Roman people lived

◎ Describe what Romans wore and ate

◎ Outline what a Roman family was like

◎ Describe the Roman education system

◎ Discuss what Romans did in their free time

◎ Outline the kind of religious beliefs Romans had.

## What were Roman homes like?

If we were able to walk through Rome in AD 100 we would find a crowded and dirty city. The streets were lined with wooden houses, blocks of flats, shops and workshops. The main buildings were made of marble. People threw their rubbish onto the streets. Stepping stones were often placed on the filthy streets so that people could avoid getting their feet dirty.

**SOURCE 2.11: Stepping stones on a Roman street**

### Patricians

A rich (patrician) Roman family would live in a big country house called a **villa**. In the town their house was called a **domus**. Archaeologists think a domus looked like this.

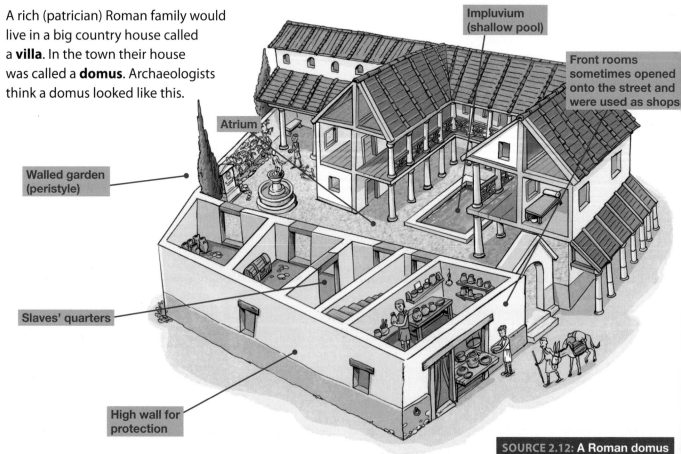

Impluvium (shallow pool)

Front rooms sometimes opened onto the street and were used as shops

Atrium

Walled garden (peristyle)

Slaves' quarters

High wall for protection

**SOURCE 2.12: A Roman domus**

## Activity 1

Examine this source and then answer the question below.

> The fear of fires, the constant collapse of houses, ... however fast we hurry, there's a huge crowd ahead and a mob behind pushing and shoving. You get dug in the ribs by somebody's elbow. Then someone hits you with a long pole, another with a beam from a building or a wind-barrel. The streets are filthy – your legs are plastered with mud.

**SOURCE 2.13: Extract from the writings of Juvenal, describing Rome in the second century** AD

1  List five hazards walkers faced on the streets of Rome.

**SOURCE 2.14: Roman mosaic from Israel**

Inside the front door of the domus was a hall, open to the sky, called an **atrium**. The atrium had marble columns and bronze statues of gods or of the owner. There were pools, fountains and flowers. Other rooms opened off the atrium. These were bedrooms, a dining room, reception rooms, kitchens, storerooms and places for the slaves to live.

There was very little furniture – just chairs, couches and beds. The floors had colourful **mosaics** and there were bright paintings (**murals**) on the walls. At night, light came from oil lamps, which burned olive oil.

**Mosaic**
Pictures and designs made from tiny pieces of glass, stone, pottery or tile.

**Mural**
Picture painted on a wall.

## Activity 2

Examine this source and then answer the questions below.

**SOURCE 2.15: Roman mural**

1  What is a mural?
2  Do you think this mural is in a rich person's house? Give reasons for your answer.

KS

Activity 3

Examine this source and then answer the questions below.

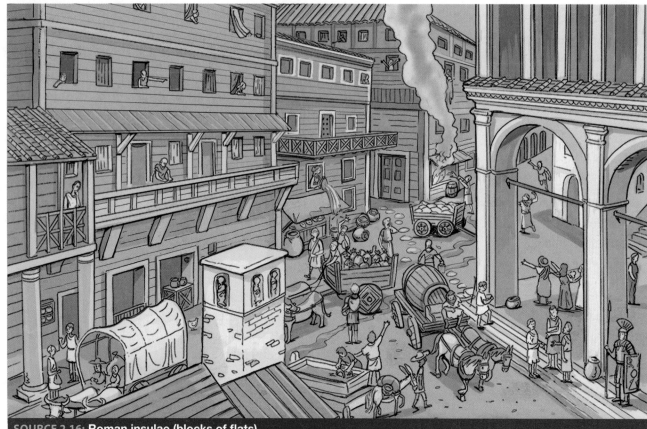

SOURCE 2.16: Roman insulae (blocks of flats)

1   How many storeys are there in most of the buildings?
2   What material is the insula made of? Why could this be dangerous?
3   Suggest what kinds of items would be sold in the shops below.
4   Which rooms, do you think, were the cheaper ones to rent? Give a reason.
5   There were no indoor toilets. Suggest where people went to the toilet.
6   From the information given in this section, do you think that this image is an accurate portrayal of Ancient Rome? Verify your answer by referring to the sources above.

## Plebeians

Plebeian families lived in blocks of flats called **insulae**.

The flats were small. The whole family – parents, grandparents and children – lived in one or two rooms. We think that people used insulae for sleeping only. It was dangerous to have fires for cooking indoors, so the plebeians probably ate at the food shops called **thermopolia**, which lined the streets.

The higher up you lived in an insula, the cheaper the rent. Piped water was supplied to the ground floor only, so people had to carry buckets of water and everything else they wanted up many flights of stairs.

There were no indoor toilets. People went to the public toilets or used pots. They threw the contents of these pots, along with other rubbish, out of the window onto the street!

**DID YOU KNOW?**

There were on average two house fires a day in Ancient Rome.

# What did Romans eat?

The Romans did not eat much during the day. For breakfast, they had bread dipped in wine, with olives, cheese or raisins. For lunch, they had cold food such as bread, salad, fruit and nuts. The usual drink was wine, often mixed with water. The main meal, known as the **cena**, was in the evening. For rich people, it often lasted several hours and included entertainment such as dancers or gladiator fights.

A patrician dinner would have three courses:

- **Starter** of savoury dishes such as oysters, mussels and raw or cooked vegetables
- **Main course** of roast or boiled meat, covered in rich, spicy sauces that disguised the taste of food that was not very fresh
- **Dessert** of pastries, nuts and fruit such as figs and grapes. Honey was used to sweeten the food.

 **DID YOU KNOW?**

The Romans had spoons and knives, but no forks.

Poor Romans ate bread, porridge, beans, lentils and maybe a little meat. Most Romans depended on handouts of bread from the government to survive. This was called **dole**.

 **DID YOU KNOW?**

In his eleventh year of power Emperor Augustus (63 BC–AD 14) gave free grain to at least 250,000 people.

## Activity 4

Examine this source and then answer the questions below.

**SOURCE 2.17:** Patricians eating their evening meal. Note how they are propped up on couches.

1 What was the evening meal called in Rome?
2 Who is serving the wine?
3 How are the people eating their food?
4 What kind of furniture do you see in this picture?

## How did Romans dress?

The official dress of a Roman citizen was the **toga**. However, togas were uncomfortable and most of the time men wore a **knee-length tunic**. It was like a long T-shirt with a belt tied at the waist. The tunic was made of cool linen in summer and warm wool in winter.

After a girl married, which could be as young as twelve, she wore a long woollen tunic called a **stola**. Rich women used plenty of make-up and often dyed their hair red. They wore a lot of jewellery – rings, earrings, bracelets and necklaces.

Both men and women wore leather sandals in the house and shoes outside.

## How was the Roman family organised?

The **father** was the head of the Roman family. He had power over everyone in the household, from his wife to the slaves. Men often beat their wives and children, or sold them into slavery. When a baby was born, the father decided whether it lived or died. The father arranged the marriages of his children. Girls married young, usually in their early teens. Children were expected to obey their parents in all things.

Roman **women** could not become citizens or vote in elections. But they could inherit property and we know that some were successful in business. Among the plebeians, women ran shops and worked in trades and crafts. They were especially good at weaving, silverwork and making perfumes. Women could also become priestesses, hairdressers, midwives and even gladiators. There were some female doctors but most were men.

## Did Roman children go to school?

Education was important to the Romans. Most children from poor families did not go to school, but many still learned to read and write.

Some rich girls had tutors at home who taught them about Greek literature and how to play a musical instrument. Mothers taught daughters how to manage a household and how to spin, weave and sew.

Boys from rich families might be taught by an educated slave; others went to school. The school day started at dawn. The boys sat on backless benches. They studied reading, writing and arithmetic. Older boys learned about Greek and Latin writers, and discussed their ideas. They practised **oratory**, the art of public speaking, which would help them later if they were elected to the Senate.

SOURCE 2.18: **Roman dress**

### 🔍 DID YOU KNOW?

- Most Romans preferred to have sons. The Senate had to pass a law forbidding people from leaving newborn baby girls out in the rubbish to die.

- Romans made ink from a mixture of soot, vinegar and a sticky gum from tree bark. Roman writings have survived for over 2,000 years!

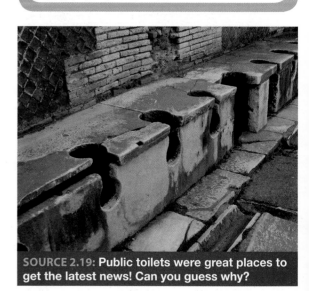

SOURCE 2.19: **Public toilets were great places to get the latest news! Can you guess why?**

# Did Romans have religious beliefs?

**Shrine**
Place of worship.

The Romans worshipped **gods**, each of which had his or her own temples. Romans often wrote prayers on clay **tablets** and left them at the temple. Thousands of these tablets survive and they tell us a lot about the worries of ordinary Romans.

Every family had a shrine at home to its household gods. These gods or guardian spirits were called the **lares**. Romans thought they were the spirits of their ancestors who watched over them. The family prayed to them each day.

## Activity 5

Read the inscriptions and then answer the question below.

> Crush, kill Fistus the senator. May Fistus dilute, languish, sink and may all his limbs dissolve.
>
> _____
>
> Most holy goddess Sulis curse whomever stole my hooded cloak whether man or woman slave or free that the Goddess Sulis inflict death on him. Do not let him sleep or have children now or in the future until he brings my cloak to the temple of her divinity

**SOURCE 2.20:** Two inscriptions on clay tablets; some people's 'prayers' were curses!

1 Find out who Sulis was.

## Activity 6

Examine these four sources and then answer the questions below.

**A** The Romans believed in many gods and saw them as a kind of family. Here are some of them:

- The father of the gods was **Jupiter** and all the other gods feared him. His wife was **Juno**.
- **Venus** was the goddess of love.
- **Mars** was the god of war.

Romans prayed to different gods, depending on what they wanted. For example, a soldier going into battle might pray to Mars for his own safety and to Venus if he wanted success in love.

**SOURCE 2.21:** from *Living History 1* by M.E. Collins, Stephen Tonge, Gráinne Henry

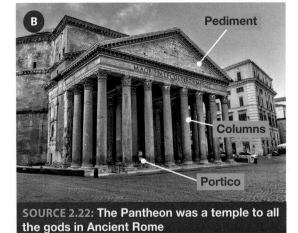

**SOURCE 2.22:** The Pantheon was a temple to all the gods in Ancient Rome

**SOURCE 2.23:** Household gods: the lares

**SOURCE 2.24:** Tablet left at a temple

1 The Pantheon is a typical example of Roman architecture. Describe it.
2 What were the lares?
3 Why are Roman tablets that were left in temples so useful to historians now?
4 Why is the tablet in Source D hard for us to read?
5 Would you say that religion was important to the Romans? Give two reasons for your answer.
6 Identify two details about Ancient Rome from these sources.

## A new religion

Romans were tolerant of foreign gods. As long as people obeyed the emperor and did not cause trouble, the Romans did not mind which gods they followed. However, everyone was expected to worship Roman gods alongside their own. The emperors saw this as the best way to keep the empire united.

**Christianity** was started after AD 30 by the followers of Jesus. Christians were taught that there was only one god and therefore they refused to give offerings to the Roman gods. The Romans saw this as treason. Christians were tortured and hundreds were executed. But the new religion became more and more popular. Then, in the fourth century, the **Emperor Constantine** became a Christian and Christianity was made the official religion of the empire.

## Death

When people died, their family put coins on their eyes to pay their fare to the next world. People believed the dead person's spirit was rowed across a mystical river called the **Styx** to the afterlife.

It was forbidden to cremate or bury a person in the city, so the remains were placed outside the city walls. Bodies were cremated and the ashes were placed in **urns** (jars). With the coming of Christianity, many Romans were buried in the underground cemeteries, the **catacombs**, which lined the roads into Rome.

# What did Romans do in their free time?

The city of Rome became very rich from its control of the Roman Empire. This meant that entertainment was cheap, and even plebeians could afford many luxuries.

## Roman baths

The Romans loved bathing, so there were public baths in every Roman city. Pompeii had three and there were said to be 900 in Rome. They were cheap, and children were allowed in free.

Men and women bathed separately. The baths had either separate male and female areas, or men and women went at different times.

**Treason**
Betraying your country.

**Activity 7**

Examine this source and then answer the questions below.

SOURCE 2.25: **Emperor Constantine** (AD 272–337)

1 Why are sculptures useful to historians?
2 Find out three facts about Emperor Constantine.

SOURCE 2.26: **The catacombs. Christians were often buried here.**

**DID YOU KNOW?**

Some Roman baths had room for up to 3,000 people.

Most Romans went to the baths every day, not just to bathe but also to exercise, meet friends and perhaps shop or read in the library.

A visit to the baths typically involved four stages:

1 First, a slave would massage the bather with olive oil.

2 The bather then had the option to go to the exercise yards and do weightlifting or wrestling.

3 Next, the bather would either relax and chat with friends in the warm room, or sit in a tub of very hot water in the **caldarium**.

4 Finally, the bather visited the cold room, called a **frigidarium**, which had a refreshingly cool pool.

**SOURCE 2.27: Visiting the public baths**

**Activity 8**

Examine this source and then answer the question below.

> I live over the public baths. It's sickening. First, there are the 'strongmen' doing their exercises and swinging their heavy lead weights about with grunts and groans. Next the lazy ones having a cheap massage. I can hear someone being slapped on the shoulders ... then there is the man who likes the sound of his own voice in the bath.

**SOURCE 2.28: Translation of the words of Roman poet Seneca (4 BC–AD 65)**

1 What information does this source give us about Roman baths?

## Chariot racing

Chariot races were held at the **Circus Maximus** (see Source 2.29), a great racetrack on the edge of Rome. It had room for 250,000 people.

Usually four teams competed in the race. They were called after colours: the Reds, the Greens, the Whites and the Blues. The fans wore the colours of their team and there was heavy betting on each race.

Four horses, running abreast, pulled the chariot. At breakneck speed, they raced seven times around the track (about 8 km). Crashes were common and drivers and horses were often killed.

**Chariot**
Two-wheeled vehicle pulled by horses.

**SOURCE 2.29: Artist's impression of a chariot race in the Circus Maximus**

## Gladiator contests

Romans also loved to watch fights between gladiators. The fights were held in the **Colosseum**, which was near the Forum.

The Colosseum held nearly 50,000 people and shows could go on for weeks. Sometimes a great awning or shade would be drawn across to protect the audience from the hot sun. There were special seats for the patricians and for important people such as the emperor.

Gladiators were usually slaves. They belonged to the men who managed the fights. Each man had a team of fighters.

**Gladiators**
Slaves who fought each other or animals for the entertainment of the crowd.

The gladiators wore armour and had to fight each other. Sometimes both men had swords. Usually one man had a sword, while the other had a net and a forked spear called a **trident**. The latter, known as a **retiarius**, would try to entangle his opponent in the net and kill him with the trident.

To make the contests more interesting, gladiators might be made to fight blindfolded or against wild animals. The games organisers sometimes flooded the centre of the Colosseum with water and staged mock naval battles.

**DID YOU KNOW?**

The Emperor Trajan held games that went on for 123 days – 10,000 men took part and 11,000 animals were killed.

**SOURCE 2.30: Ruins of the Colosseum in Rome**

## Activity 9

1 Using the information and sources in this section:
  - Identify five similarities between Roman lives and our lives
  - Identify five differences between Roman lives and our lives.

2 Take part in a class discussion to see how many similarities and how many differences the class can identify.

3 Imagine you are putting up a post on social media from a time-travelling spacecraft. You are describing a visit to Ancient Rome.
  - Say what you liked most about Rome
  - Mention three things about the Romans' lives that you didn't like.

### DID YOU KNOW?

Successful gladiators were often adored by their fans, a little like football players today. If they lived, they could win their freedom and retire wealthy. The writer Juvenal wrote about a senator's wife who went off to Egypt with her favourite fighter: 'What did she see in him to make her put up with being called "Gladiator's Moll" [woman]? He wasn't exactly young, and he had a dud arm. Besides his face looked a proper mess … But he was a gladiator. This made her prefer him to her children, her country, her sister and her husband.'

### DO YOU UNDERSTAND THESE KEY TERMS?

| | | | | | |
|---|---|---|---|---|---|
| atrium | dole | impluvium | mural | tablet | trident |
| caldarium | domus | insula | oratory | thermopolia | tunic |
| catacombs | frigidarium | lares | Pantheon | toga | urn |
| cena | gladiator | mosaic | stola | treason | villa |

 PowerPoint summary

## SELF-ASSESSMENT – CAN YOU?

1 Explain, giving reasons for your answer, whether you agree or disagree with this statement: 'Rome was a filthy city.'

2 Describe a patrician's home and draw a diagram of it.

3 Describe an insula and give two advantages and two disadvantages of living in an insula.

4 Explain, giving two reasons, whether you agree or disagree with this statement: 'The father was the head of the Roman family.'

5 Describe the role of women in Ancient Rome. Name two trades that women specialised in.

6 Name three Roman gods and say what each of them was believed to look after.

7 Explain how we know today what ordinary Roman people prayed for.

8 Say what new religion started around AD 30 in the Roman Empire and explain why the Romans did not like it.

9 Describe a typical visit to a Roman bath.

10 Name two favourite sports of the Romans.

11 Describe a chariot race.

12 Explain how we know that gladiators were popular.

13 Explain what writers like those in sources 2.20 and 2.28 tell us about Ancient Rome.

14 Describe the Roman entertainment that you would have liked best and say why.

15 Say which of these statements are true and which are false. Correct any false ones:

  - The Romans worshipped one god
  - Mars was the father of the gods
  - Chariot racing took place in the Circus Maximus
  - It was expensive to go to the baths in Rome.

**Learning Outcome 3.1** 31

# HOW HAS THE ROMAN EMPIRE INFLUENCED US?

## 🎯 LEARNING INTENTIONS

**At the end of this section, you should be able to:**

◎ Outline ways in which the Romans have influenced our lives today.

## Have Romans influenced how we build?

The Romans have had a great influence on our engineering and styles of building. They were able to build solid roads, tunnels and bridges. They were the first people in Europe to make **concrete** by mixing lime water and ash from volcanic soil. They learned how to build **arches**, which meant they could construct very large buildings.

### 🔍 DID YOU KNOW?

The Romans built 120,000 km of roads – that's more than twice the circumference of the world!

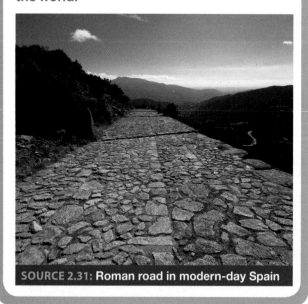

**SOURCE 2.31: Roman road in modern-day Spain**

The Romans built the first apartment blocks and shopping centres. They used a system of underfloor heating in their homes, where warm air rose from furnaces in the cellar.

---

### KS 👥 Activity 1

Examine these five sources and then answer the question below.

**A** circus   exodus   fridge   villa   century

**SOURCE 2.32:** Some English words that come from Latin

**B**  'I see wars, horrid wars, the Tiber foaming with much blood.' *The Aeneid*, Book 6, lines 122–3

**SOURCE 2.33:** Long poem by Roman poet **Virgil** about a hero who lived in the city of Troy; many books and films have been based on its stories

**C**

**SOURCE 2.34:** Christian crucifix

**D**

**SOURCE 2.35:** Roman temple

**E**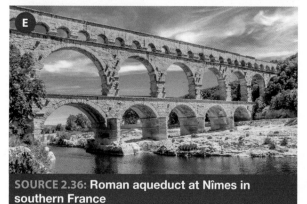

**SOURCE 2.36: Roman aqueduct at Nîmes in southern France**

1  In pairs, write down five ways in which the Romans still influence us today.

**Aqueducts** were able to bring in 130 million gallons of water to Rome every day (almost the equivalent amount of water as 300 Olympic-sized swimming pools). There are many surviving today (see Source 2.36).

> **Aqueduct**
> Bridge that carries water over a valley.

## Have Romans influenced how we speak and write?

**Latin** became the language used throughout the Roman Empire. Italian, French, Romanian, Spanish and Portuguese are modern versions of Latin. Over 30 per cent of the words we use in English come from Latin. You have read some of them already in this book. Three examples are: villa (a house), circus (a round area) and senate (an elected body). In science, all plants, animals and insects are known officially by their Latin names.

Many **names** of modern-day countries and cities are in fact Roman names, for example, Syria and London. Look back at the maps of the Roman Empire (Sources 2.1 and 2.10) to find other examples. Roman names or names based on Latin words are still given to children in some parts of the world. Examples include Diana (after the moon goddess), Patricia or Patrick (meaning noble), Marcus (after the god of war) and Laura (meaning laurel tree).

We also still use the **Roman alphabet** and form our letters in mostly the same way as the Romans did.

---

### Activity 2

Examine this source and then complete the tasks below.

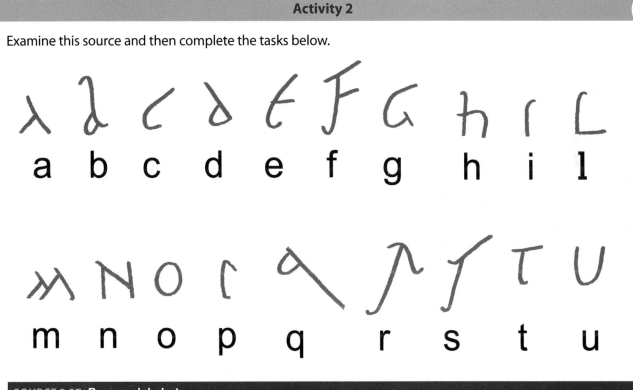

**SOURCE 2.37: Roman alphabet**

1   Compare this alphabet with the one we use today. Which letters have changed?
2   What modern letters are missing from the Roman alphabet?
3   Try writing your name or a short message using the Roman alphabet.

## Numerals

Sometimes we use the Roman system of numbers, known as **Roman numerals**. They are often used on clocks and watches or when we are referring to the name of monarchs such as Henry VIII and Elizabeth II.

> **Numeral**
> Written symbol used to represent a number.

## Calendar

We use a version of the **Roman calendar**, with all months having thirty or thirty-one days, except February which has twenty-eight, or twenty-nine in a leap year. We have also kept the Roman names for the months.

## Have the Romans influenced how we run our country?

The Romans had a well-developed system of laws. Today, Roman law still forms the basis of the legal systems of many European countries. For example, who has the right to inherit property is influenced by Roman ideas. The way the courts are run in Ireland, the names of court officials (e.g. barrister) and the way cases are recorded all come from Roman law.

### DO YOU UNDERSTAND THESE KEY TERMS?

aqueduct    numeral

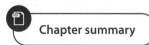
Chapter summary

Weblinks

PowerPoint summary

---

### Activity 3

Examine this source and then answer the questions below.

| | | | |
|---|---|---|---|
| I = 1 | VII = 7 | XX = 20 | CC = 200 |
| II = 2 | VIII = 8 | XL = 40 | D = 500 |
| III = 3 | IX = 9 | L = 50 | DC = 600 |
| IV = 4 | X = 10 | XC = 90 | CM = 900 |
| V = 5 | XI = 11 | C = 100 | M = 1,000 |
| VI = 6 | XV = 15 | CXL = 140 | MM = 2,000 |

*Example:* 2019 = MM (2,000) + X (10) + IX (9) = MMXIX

**SOURCE 2.38: Roman numerals**

1  Write out the year of your birth in Roman numerals.

2  Write out the following numbers in Roman numerals: 82, 349, 1,914, 1,592.

3  Imagine you run a business. What problems might arise when using these numbers?

4  In pairs, write out three Roman numbers each and see if your partner can read them correctly.

### Activity 4

1  Which emperors, do you think, are the months of July and August named after?

2  Suggest two months that were called after Roman gods.

---

## SELF-ASSESSMENT – CAN YOU?

1  Describe how the Romans have influenced our lives, giving at least ten examples.

2  Explain and describe what you think is the best Roman invention, giving a reason for your choice.

3  Give two reasons why you would like to have lived in Ancient Rome and two reasons why you would not.

# 3 HOW CHRISTIANITY INFLUENCED IRISH CULTURE AND SOCIETY

## How did Christianity come to Ireland?

36

## How did Christianity develop in Ireland?

39

## How has Christianity influenced modern Ireland?

46

# HOW DID CHRISTIANITY COME TO IRELAND?

## ⊚ LEARNING INTENTIONS

**At the end of this section, you should be able to:**

⊚ Explain how Ireland became a Christian country

⊚ Discuss the role of St Patrick in converting Ireland to Christianity.

## How did Ireland become Christian?

Fifth-century Ireland was divided into about 150 kingdoms called **tuatha**. Each tuath was ruled by a chieftain or clan leader called a **rí**. Their chief advisers were **pagan** priests called **druids**. There were very few towns.

At the time when Jesus lived, the Romans ruled most of Europe. In AD 43 they conquered Britain. In the fourth century **Christianity** began to spread rapidly throughout the lands ruled by Rome, including Britain. It is said that **St Patrick** brought Christianity from Britain to Ireland in the fifth century, but is this true?

**Christianity**
Religion based on Jesus Christ and the belief that he is the son of God.

**Pagan**
Worshipper of many gods and of nature.

| Activity 1 | ✏ |
|---|---|

Examine this source and then answer the questions below.

> Blessed by Pope Celestine, Palladius was sent as the first bishop to the Irish who believe in Christ.

**SOURCE 3.1: Words of a French priest named Prosper in AD 431**

1 Who did the pope send as the first bishop to Ireland?
2 How do we know from this document that there were Christians in Ireland already?

We do not know whether **Palladius** ever arrived in Ireland, but we do know from the above document that there were already Irish Christians in 431. As the Romans never ruled Ireland, these early Christians were probably traders from Roman Britain who had settled on the east coast of Leinster.

In pairs, examine these two sources and then answer the questions below.

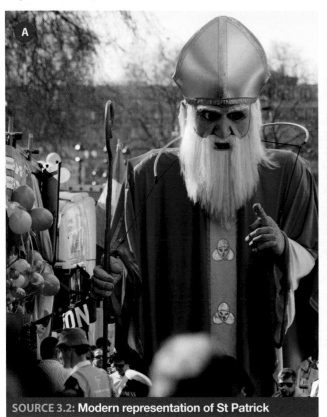

SOURCE 3.2: Modern representation of St Patrick

SOURCE 3.3: Earliest surviving picture of St Patrick *(right)*

1  Describe the similarities and differences between the two St Patricks.
2  Do you think Patrick really looked like either of these representations? How would we know?
3  Which source is more accurate, in your opinion? Give reasons for your answer.

## Who was St Patrick?

As a young boy, Patrick lived in Roman Britain and his family were Christians. Historians think he came to Ireland sometime between the 430s and 490. His story is unique because he was the only Roman citizen we know about at this time who was captured by raiders and sold into slavery.

He was captured 'along with many thousands of others' by Irish raiders and sold as a slave to a farmer in Co. Antrim. After six years he escaped from Ireland. Later he became a priest and returned as a missionary to convert the Irish people to Christianity.

Patrick's story is famous because he wrote two books about his time in Ireland:

> *The Confession:* an account of his life in Ireland and his reasons for coming to preach Christianity to the Irish.

> *A Letter to the Soldiers of King Coroticus:* Coroticus was a king in Britain. His soldiers raided Ireland and kidnapped people to sell as slaves. Patrick wrote this book asking them to stop the raids.

Examine this source and then answer the questions below.

> I went to outlying regions beyond which no man dwelt and where never had anyone come to baptise or ordain clergy [priests] or confirm the people.

SOURCE 3.4: St Patrick, *The Confession*

1  Where does this quote come from?
2  Is this a reliable source? Give a reason for your answer.
3  What is the main point Patrick is making here?

**Learning Outcome** 2.6    37

## How did Patrick convert people?

In *The Confession* Patrick tells us he 'baptised thousands' and 'ordained clerics everywhere'. We know that the druids and some of the ríthe (kings) did not accept the new religion, because Patrick wrote that he 'lived in daily expectation of murder, treachery or captivity'.

Usually when a chieftain converted to Christianity, the whole clan followed. People in early Christian Ireland still lived much as they had done for hundreds of years, but after Patrick the power of the druids ended. Christian priests and bishops gradually replaced them.

Patrick became a hero after his death. Many legends were told about him; for example, it is said that he banished all the snakes from Ireland (we know now that there were never any here in the first place!); and that he won great battles with the druid priests on the Hill of Tara and elsewhere. People transferred some of the stories the Celts had told about their gods to St Patrick and other early Christian leaders like St Brigid.

---

### Activity 4

In pairs, examine this source and then answer the questions below.

Laeghaire the king and his Druids had returned from their journey to Slane and had sat hungry to a lunch in their great hall, when who should walk in but Patrick himself, along with his companions. The king had previously set traps, snares and ambushes for Patrick, who had escaped them all, and so the king was much surprised to see him enter …

The Druids brought him his wine but craftily dropped a dose of poison from an ebony ring into his cup just before passing it to him. Patrick didn't notice this but made the sign of the cross over the wine, turning the poison into a lump and spilling from the cup as he raised it to his lips, so he drank unharmed.

**SOURCE 3.5: Extract from a story about St Patrick at the royal court of Tara. After a contest of spells between Patrick and the chief druid, the druid burned to death. We do not know if this story is true because it was written down by monks long after Patrick had died.**

1  Who wrote down this story?
2  What, do you think, was the purpose of a story like this?

PowerPoint summary

---

### Activity 5

Examine this source and then answer the question below.

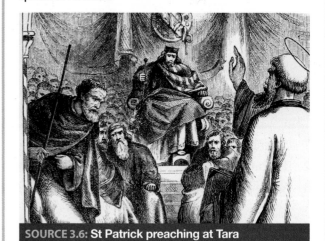

**SOURCE 3.6: St Patrick preaching at Tara**

1  Is this picture realistic, do you think? Explain your answer.

---

**DO YOU UNDERSTAND THESE KEY TERMS?**

| Christianity | pagan | tuath |
|---|---|---|
| druids | rí | |

---

## SELF-ASSESSMENT – CAN YOU?

1  Explain how we know that there were Christians in Ireland before St Patrick.

2  Name the first bishop appointed to Ireland.

3  List the sources we have about St Patrick.

4  Say who ruled Ireland in the fifth century.

5  List five pieces of information that we *know* about St Patrick.

6  Describe how the arrival of St Patrick changed the lives of people in Ireland, giving two examples.

7  Was Christianity welcomed by everyone in Ireland? Explain your answer.

# HOW DID CHRISTIANITY DEVELOP IN IRELAND?

## LEARNING INTENTIONS

**At the end of this section, you should be able to:**

◎ Describe life in an early Christian monastery in Ireland

◎ Discuss the importance of Christian monasteries

◎ Outline why the Golden Age ended.

## What were the early Christian centres in Ireland?

The first groups of Christians in Ireland often came together to dedicate their lives to God. Some believed they could get closer to God by devoting their lives to prayer in remote places. They were called **hermits**.

However, most lived in **monasteries**. They became known as **monks** (men) and **nuns** (women). Male and female monasteries were built side by side for protection. Married people lived in monasteries also as there was no strict rule about remaining celibate (single).

It was through a network of these monasteries that Christianity spread throughout Ireland.

### What were the monasteries like?

The buildings in the earliest monasteries were made from timber and have not survived. However, using sources written by the monks, and archaeological evidence, we know what they looked like.

Early Christian or Celtic monasteries were surrounded by an outer stone wall (or banks of piled-up earth) for protection. Inside the wall, the monks grew their own food, wrote books and made beautiful works of art.

**Celtic Ireland**
The Celts arrived in Ireland from Europe around 500 BC, marking the start of the Iron Age in Ireland.

**Monastery**
A place where people devote their lives to God.

### Activity 1

**KS**

Examine this source and then answer the questions below.

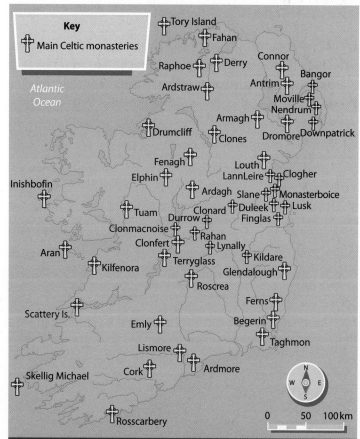

**SOURCE 3.7: Map showing monasteries in early Christian Ireland. The first recorded monastery was established by St Brigid in Kildare in 500.**

1 Where are most of the monasteries located? Why? (*Hint:* think about the life of St Patrick.)

2 There were only about ten monasteries for women. Suggest why that was.

An early Christian monastery had several buildings:

1. The **church** was where the monks went to pray.
2. A **round tower** was used as a bell tower to call the monks to religious services, and as a look-out post and hiding place for the monks and their valuables when any raiders attacked the monasteries. Remains of sixty-three round towers can be found across Ireland.
3. The **scriptorium** was where manuscripts were copied.
4. The **refectory** was where the monks had their meals.
5. The **cells** were where the monks lived, in single huts (**beehive huts**).
6. Monks who died were buried in a **graveyard** beside the church, inside the walls of the monastery.

**SOURCE 3.8:** Artist's impression of an early Christian monastery

Some monasteries remained small, while others developed into bigger complexes. Some were built near rivers, which made them easy to get to. **Clonmacnoise**, set up by St Ciarán in AD 545, is on the River Shannon. It grew to be the largest monastery in Ireland. People came from all over Europe to study there. Many kings are buried at this site. Monasteries became the centre of communities in Ireland because there were so few towns.

**SOURCE 3.9: Monastery at Glendalough (founded by St Kevin) with round tower**

Examine this source and then answer the questions below.

SOURCE 3.10: **Monastic ruins at Clonmacnoise, Co. Offaly**

1  Can you identify three buildings? (Use Source 3.8 to help you.)
2  Why, do you think, was a wall built around the monastery?
3  How would you know from this photo that a lot of monks lived at this monastery?

## DID YOU KNOW?

One of the more remarkable monastery locations was **Sceilig Mhichíl**, a rock in the Atlantic Ocean, off the coast of Co. Kerry. You can still see the remains of six small stone huts where the monks once lived. Monks brought soil from the mainland so that they could make a garden to grow vegetables on the rock.

SOURCE 3.11: **Beehive huts on Skellig Michael (Sceilig Mhichíl)**

It is hard to find out what early Christian preachers were really like, but we have some clues. Surviving stories and writings give us a sense of how they lived and the ideas they had (see Source 3.12).

## Why were monasteries so important?

The monks have left us with rich sources of art in the form of manuscripts, metalwork and stonework.

### Manuscripts

Art and learning were very important to the early Christians. The monks introduced reading and writing to Ireland. Since printing had not yet been invented, books had to be copied by hand. These books are called **manuscripts**. The monks copied down the Bible, and many of the old Celtic laws and legends.

They wrote in **Irish** as well as in Latin. Their books in Irish are the first examples of writing in a modern European language (educated people elsewhere in Europe wrote in either Latin or Greek). Our modern version of written Irish comes from these monks.

The Irish monks were among the first to use capital letters at the start of sentences and spaces between words, making their writing much easier to read.

The manuscripts were made by **scribes**, who worked in a **scriptorium**. The scribes wrote on **vellum** (calf skin) or on **parchment** (sheep skin). For pens they used **quills** (goose or swan feathers) dipped in ink made from plants and powdered rocks. Many of the manuscripts were beautifully illustrated (decorated). Some illustrations were made from gold leaf.

Many manuscripts still survive today. These are the most famous:

> The **Cathach of St Columba** is the oldest Irish manuscript. It dates from the sixth century. It got its name from the old Irish word for battle. The O'Donnell clan took it into battle with them as a good luck charm.

> The **Book of Kells** is a copy of the four gospels. It dates from around AD 800. Historians think it was written by Irish monks in Iona, Scotland. You can see it on display at Trinity College in Dublin. Many people regard it as the most beautiful manuscript in the world.

---

**KS**          **Activity 3**

Examine this source and then answer the questions below.

> Two monks, Finnian and Columcille, fell out over who owned a copy of a book of psalms, the writer or the publisher. This ended up in the Battle of Cul Dremhe in AD 561. The battle was a massacre for both sides and soon after Columcille left Ireland for Scotland.

> Some monks were returning up river with wood for their monastery on rafts. When a storm suddenly swept them out to sea they were jeered by onlookers. The onlookers said they had no pity for the monks because they had 'robbed men of their old ways of worship'.

**SOURCE 3.12: Extracts from *Life of Cuthbert* (AD 700)**

1  How long after St Patrick did the above events take place?

2  Is there anything that surprises you about how monks lived at that time?

3  What, do you think, did the people mean when they said that the monks had 'robbed men of their old ways of worship'?

4  Would you say that life was difficult for early Christians in Ireland? Give two reasons for your answer based on the evidence in these two extracts.

**SOURCE 3.13: A page from the *Book of Kells***

## Metalwork

The monks made beautiful objects in gold and silver, and decorated them with precious stones. The designs are Celtic with curving 'swirly' decorations.

The monks used a style of raised-metal decoration known as **filigree**. It is made by intertwining thin strips of gold and silver. The **Ardagh Chalice**, a vessel used for giving out Communion wine, is an excellent example and it is on display at the National Museum in Dublin. These elements and designs were copied by craft workers from all over Europe.

SOURCE 3.14: Typical Celtic design

Silver bowl decorated with gold, glass, amber and enamel

Band of gold filigree and studs

Silver foot

SOURCE 3.15: Ardagh Chalice

## Stonework

Between the eighth and eleventh centuries the monks made stone **high crosses**. As few people could read or write, the monks carved scenes from the Bible on these huge crosses to teach them about Christianity. Examples can be seen at Clonmacnoise and Moone.

### KS          Activity 4

Examine this source and then answer the questions below.

SOURCE 3.16: **High Cross of Moone, Co. Kildare**

1   What is the main purpose of the carvings on this type of cross?
2   Suggest why this cross has been moved inside from outside the monastery.
3   Can you work out who these twelve men from the Bible are?

## How did Irish ideas spread abroad?

Irish monks went abroad to set up monasteries and spread Christianity. **St Columcille** set up a monastery in Iona, Scotland. Monks from Iona preached to the Scots and English. **St Gall** set up a monastery in Switzerland (see Source 3.17). The town of St Gallen is named after him. The Irish monks are still remembered today in parts of France, Italy and Germany.

Irish monks brought a lot of their new ideas in writing and artwork to other parts of Europe. By AD 800 the Irish monasteries had become famous all over Europe. Many students came to study at them. The period is known as the **Golden Age** in Irish learning.

# How did the Golden Age end?

Stories about the rich treasures kept in monasteries spread and they became targets for attack. Raiders from Scandinavia, called **Vikings**, began arriving in search of treasures. In AD 795 they attacked a monastery on Lambay Island near Dublin. Over the next few centuries many other monasteries were attacked. Treasures from Irish monasteries have been discovered by archaeologists in Denmark and Sweden. The arrival of the Vikings ended the Golden Age of Irish monasteries.

PowerPoint summary

## Activity 5

Examine this source and then answer the question below.

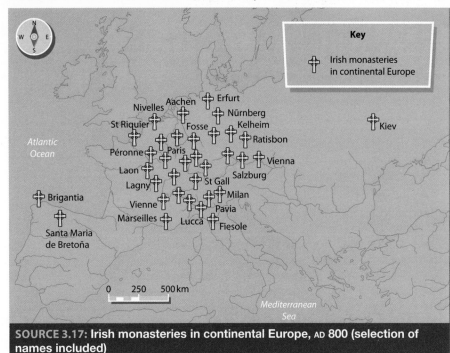

**SOURCE 3.17: Irish monasteries in continental Europe, AD 800 (selection of names included)**

1 What parts of Europe were the Irish monasteries located in?
2 Suggest why they are not found in other parts of Europe.

## DO YOU UNDERSTAND THESE KEY TERMS?

| | | | | |
|---|---|---|---|---|
| beehive hut | filigree | monastery | parchment | scriptorium |
| cell | Golden Age | monk | quill | vellum |
| Celtic Ireland | hermit | nun | round tower | Vikings |
| Dark Ages | manuscript | refectory | scribe | |

## SELF-ASSESSMENT – CAN YOU?

1 Explain what a monastery is.

2 Give two reasons why monasteries had round towers.

3 Name two other buildings found in early monasteries and describe the activities that took place in them.

4 Name two monasteries that were set up in early Christian Ireland.

5 Explain where the monks got the materials they used to produce a manuscript.

6 Name the oldest manuscript in Ireland.

7 Name another famous manuscript and say where it was written.

8 Name two important ways in which monks have influenced our writing today.

9 Describe the other works of art that were produced in monasteries.

10 Name two places in Dublin where you could find some of these works of art.

11 Explain why Irish monks became so important in Europe.

12 Explain what is meant by the Golden Age in Irish history and describe how it ended.

# HOW HAS CHRISTIANITY INFLUENCED MODERN IRELAND?

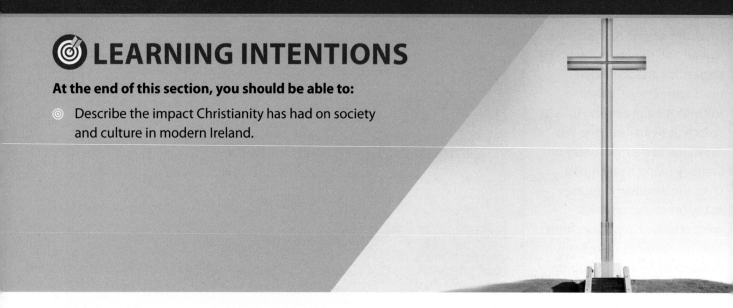

## ⊚ LEARNING INTENTIONS

**At the end of this section, you should be able to:**

◎ Describe the impact Christianity has had on society and culture in modern Ireland.

## How did Christianity evolve?

Christianity remains the major religion in Ireland. Most people belong to the Roman Catholic Church, but there are also members of other Christian churches and denominations, as well as people of different faiths. In the Middle Ages all Christians in Western Europe were called Roman Catholics. In the 1500s the Christian Church in Western Europe split into two main groups: Roman Catholics and Protestants (see Section 7).

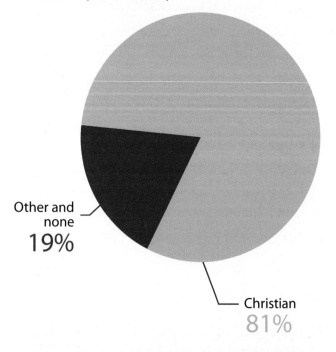

Other and none
**19%**

Christian
**81%**

**SOURCE 3.18: Religion in the Republic of Ireland, Census 2016**

## How has Christianity shaped modern Ireland?

Christianity has had a huge influence on people's lives in Ireland. Almost 93 per cent of people living in the **Irish Free State** in 1922 were Catholic. They went to Mass every Sunday. Most hospitals, schools and orphanages were run by the Catholic Church. Others were run by Protestant churches.

Church leaders had a big influence on politics and society. In the 1930s **divorce** and **contraception** were made illegal because they were against Catholic teachings. Sex before marriage was seen as a sin. If a woman got pregnant before she married, the whole family could be shunned. These women and girls were often sent away to homes (including **Magdalene laundries**) and their babies were given up for adoption.

The **Ne Temere** decree issued by the Catholic Church in 1908 meant that the children of mixed Catholic and Protestant marriages had to be reared as Catholics. This is one of the reasons why there was a huge drop in the number of Protestants living in the Republic of Ireland by the 1960s.

The **Second Vatican Council** in the 1960s began to modernise the Catholic Church. Irish society changed too. Television helped to spread new ideas and attitudes. Church teachings began to have less influence on how people lived their lives. In the 1990s details about child abuse and sex scandals further undermined the Catholic Church.

Nevertheless, the visit of **Pope John Paul II** to Ireland in 1979 attracted huge crowds and showed how important the Catholic Church still was in Ireland. It continues to have a strong influence on Irish society, especially in schools and hospitals.

**Activity 1**

In pairs, examine the images in this section. What do they tell us about Christianity in Ireland?

KS

**Activity 2**

Examine these sources and then answer the questions below.

1. For each source, write down how Christianity has influenced modern Ireland.
2. Look at Source 3.25 on page 48. How did each of these places get their name?
3. Are any place names in your area linked to churches or monasteries?
4. Is there a grotto in your area? Would you say they are common in Ireland?

**A** As many as 2.7 million people were estimated to have turned out to greet and worship with the pope [in 1979] at one or another of the major venues of his visit … This estimated total of 2.7 million represented more than half the people then living on the island of Ireland.

SOURCE 3.19: from 'A Church in Crisis: The Irish Catholic Church Today' by James S. Donnelly Jr, *History Ireland*, Vol. 8, No. 3, Autumn 2000, pp. 12–17

**B** In the 2016 Census, 78.3% of the population in the Irish Republic identified as Roman Catholic, and 2.65% as Protestant (Church of Ireland).

| Religion | 2011 (000s) | 2016 (000s) | % change |
|---|---|---|---|
| **Roman Catholic** | 3,861.3 | 3,729.1 | -3.4 |
| **Church of Ireland** | 129.0 | 126.4 | -2.0 |
| **Muslim (Islamic)** | 49.2 | 63.4 | 28.9 |
| **Orthodox** | 45.2 | 62.2 | 37.5 |
| **Christian** | 41.2 | 37.4 | -9.1 |
| **Presbyterian** | 24.6 | 24.2 | -1.6 |
| **Hindu** | 10.7 | 14.3 | 34.1 |
| **Apostolic or Pentecostal** | 14.0 | 13.4 | -4.9 |
| **Other** | 70.2 | 97.7 | 39.1 |
| **No religion** | 269.8 | 468.4 | 73.6 |
| **Not stated** | 72.9 | 125.3 | 71.8 |
| **Total** | 4,588.3 | 4,761.9 | 3.8 |

SOURCE 3.20: Population of Ireland by religion, 2011 and 2016

**C** In the 2011 Census in Northern Ireland, 45% of the population identified or had been brought up as Catholic and 48% as Protestant.

SOURCE 3.21: UK 2011 Census

**D** State-funded primary schools under Church control in the Republic of Ireland, 2013: 90% Catholic and 6% Protestant.

SOURCE 3.22: Department of Education and Skills

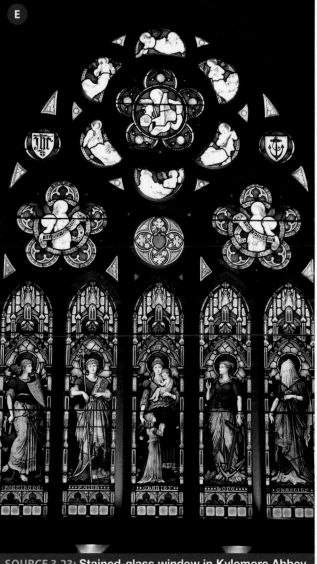

SOURCE 3.23: Stained-glass window in Kylemore Abbey, Co. Mayo

SOURCE 3.24: St Vincent's Private Hospital, Dublin

G Thousands of Irish places are named after religious settlements. Here are just a few examples: Monasterevin, Abbeyfeale, Kildare, Abbeyleix, Churchtown, Glendalough, Kill, Kilkenny, Monkstown. Note: Cill means church in Irish.

SOURCE 3.25

SOURCE 3.26: Grotto in the Claddagh, Galway

I In 1900 there were 368 convents in Ireland.

SOURCE 3.27: Historian Catriona Clear

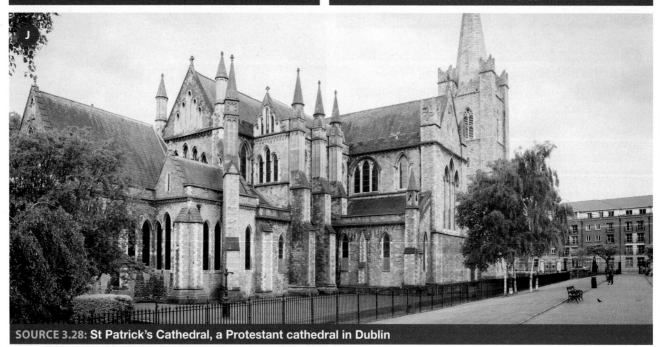

SOURCE 3.28: St Patrick's Cathedral, a Protestant cathedral in Dublin

Chapter summary    Weblinks    PowerPoint summary

## SELF-ASSESSMENT – CAN YOU?

1 Name five different types of built remains that are evidence of Ireland's Christian heritage.

2 Discuss five ways in which Christianity influences your life.

3 Identify three places you know of that get their names from early Christian settlements.

# 4 LIFE AND DEATH IN MEDIEVAL TIMES

## What was life like in a medieval village?

50

## What was life like in a medieval castle?

58

## What was life like in a medieval town?

65

## Why was religion so important in medieval times?

70

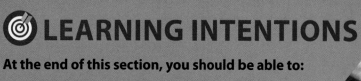

# WHAT WAS LIFE LIKE IN A MEDIEVAL VILLAGE?

## ◎ LEARNING INTENTIONS

**At the end of this section, you should be able to:**

◎ Outline what the feudal system was

◎ Describe a medieval manor

◎ Discuss life in a medieval village

◎ Explain how law and order operated in the Middle Ages.

## What were the Middle Ages?

The time from about AD 500 to 1500 is called the **Middle Ages** or the **medieval period**. It covers the period between the end of the Roman Empire and what we call modern times.

Europe in the Middle Ages was very different from today's Europe. Most of the land had not been changed by humans. Huge areas of forest and grassland were home to wild pigs (boar), wild cats and wolves. Nine out of ten people lived in the countryside and worked on the land.

### Population size

The population of Europe in the early Middle Ages was probably between 25 and 30 million. It grew significantly after AD 1000, reaching perhaps 100 million by the end of the medieval period. Now there are over 740 million people living in Europe.

## What was the feudal system?

When the Roman Empire broke up in the fifth century there was no central government and no single currency in Europe. Roads and towns fell into ruins. Bandits and outlaws attacked people, making travel and trade very difficult. People looked to local lords to protect them and the lords became very powerful. Gradually they set up the **feudal system**.

> **Feudal system**
> The way land was owned and society was organised in the Middle Ages.

---

**KS**  **Activity 1**

Examine this source and then answer the questions below.

| Year | Population |
|------|------------|
| 1000 | 56.4 million |
| 1100 | 62.1 million |
| 1200 | 68 million |
| 1250 | 72.9 million |
| 1300 | 78.7 million |
| 1350 | 70.7 million |
| 1400 | 78.1 million |
| 1450 | 83 million |
| 1500 | 90.7 million |

**SOURCE 4.1: Population of Europe 1000–1500**

1  Between which years is there a decrease in the population of Europe?

2  What was the overall increase or decrease in population between 1000 and 1500?

3  How do we measure the size of a population?

4  Why, do you think, are historians not sure of the size of the population of medieval Europe?

5  Research 'population change in Europe between 1000 and 1500' online. Identify two countries where the population more than doubled and two countries where the population remained more or less stable during this period.

6  Suggest why the population would grow at a quicker rate in some countries than it did in others.

---

**Activity 2**

Examine this table showing how the feudal system worked and then answer the questions below.

| | |
|---|---|
|  SOURCE 4.2: The king | ⟩ The **king** owned all the land <br> • He could not control or farm it all himself, so he gave some to his followers <br> • He kept about a quarter of the land for his own use |
|  SOURCE 4.3: The king's vassals | ⟩ The king's followers were called his **vassals** <br> • Some vassals were **lords** with titles such as earl or count <br> • Others were **bishops** or **abbots** |
|  SOURCE 4.4: A knight | ⟩ The lords gave some of their land to their **knights** in return for their loyalty <br> • Knights were soldiers who rode into battle on horseback and fought for their lords |
|  SOURCE 4.5: Peasants | ⟩ **Peasants** farmed the land <br> • They had to pay heavy taxes and rents <br> • There were two types of peasant: **serfs** and **freemen** |

1  Who had the most power in the Middle Ages?
2  Who, do you think, did the most work?
3  What problems might a king have had?
4  Which person would you prefer to have been? Say why.

 **DID YOU KNOW?**

The land a king rules is called a **kingdom.** The word **county** used to mean the land that a count got from the king.

## What was a medieval manor?

Most people lived in small villages and farms owned by the local lord or knight. These were called **manors**. There were usually twenty to thirty houses in a village. The **peasants** farmed the land around the village, which was divided into three big fields and a **commons**.

Most peasants were **serfs**. They belonged to the lord and farmed his land. They got their own small piece of land to farm, and in return they had to work for free on the lord's private land (his **demesne**). They could not leave the manor or get married without the lord's permission. They also paid taxes to him and to the priest.

Some peasants were **freemen**. They did not have to give free labour to the lord but they did have to pay him rent for their land. They could travel and marry as they pleased. They still had to pay their taxes to the lord and to the priest.

The priest lived beside the church in the centre of the village. He said Mass for the peasants on Sundays, and baptised, married and buried them. They paid him by giving him one-tenth of their crops. This payment was called a **tithe**.

 **Manor**
The land, and everything on it, owned by the lord.

 **Peasant**
A person who worked on the land.

 **Serf**
A person who belonged to the lord and farmed his land. Sometimes called a **villein**.

 **Freeman**
A peasant who paid rent and tax to the lord but could travel as he pleased.

## Activity 3

Examine Source 4.6 and then answer the questions below.

1 **Manor house**, where the lord lived; usually at the edge of the village

2 **Demesne**, the lord's private land

3 **Commons**, where all the peasants' animals grazed together

4 **Forge**, where the blacksmith made nails, knives, axes, horseshoes and other iron goods

5 **Water mill**, where the miller ground wheat into flour

6 **River**, where peasants washed themselves and their clothes

7 A **serf's house**

8 **Serf's one-acre strip of land** (every serf had a strip of land in each of the big fields)

9 **Forest**, where peasants got wood for their fires and to build their houses

10 **Church** and **priest's house**

11 **Alehouse**, where peasants drank beer (only taverns could sell wine and this was more expensive)

12 **Bailiff's house**

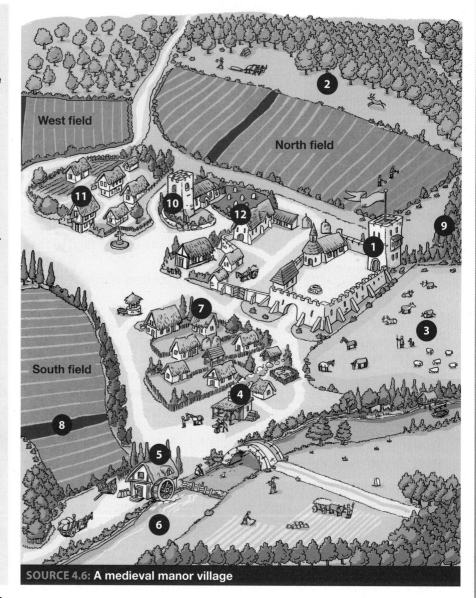

SOURCE 4.6: **A medieval manor village**

1 What is the lord's demesne?

2 Apart from the church and the lord's manor house, the buildings were made of wood. Suggest why.

3 Was it a good idea to have all the animals together in the commons?

4 Why did the peasants pay taxes to a priest?

5 Why, do you think, was it a crime to fish in the river without permission?

## Farming

The peasants farmed the land of the manor using a method called the **open-field system**. There were two types of land.

> A big meadow called the **commons**, where all the animals belonging to the peasants grazed.

> **Three huge open fields**, where crops were grown. Each field was divided into long strips and every peasant family had one or more strips in each of the three fields. The peasants rented these strips from the lord of the manor.

**Bailiff**
Person who looked after the lord's accounts and kept law and order on the lord's manor.

**Learning Outcome 3.6**

This is how the open-field system worked. Each year one of the three open fields was left **fallow** (i.e. with nothing growing). This meant that the soil was rested and would be fertile again the next year. This system is called rotating the crops or **crop rotation** (see Source 4.7).

| | North field | West field | South field |
|---|---|---|---|
| **Year 1** | Oats, rye or barley | Wheat | Fallow |
| **Year 2** | Fallow | Oats, rye or barley | Wheat |
| **Year 3** | Wheat | Fallow | Oats, rye or barley |

SOURCE 4.7: Crop rotation

## Activity 4

Examine these images of peasants at work on a medieval farm and then answer the questions below.

**A**

SOURCE 4.8: **Ploughing with four oxen**

**B**

SOURCE 4.9: **Breaking up the ploughed earth**

**C**

SOURCE 4.10: **Sowing seeds**

**D**

SOURCE 4.11: **Women carrying pails on their heads**

**E**

SOURCE 4.12: **Separating grains from their husks using a flail (two sticks tied together)**

**F**

SOURCE 4.13: **Cutting hay; women reaping with sickles**

1  Write down three pieces of information these images give us about peasants in the Middle Ages.
2  Describe the tools and methods used for sowing and harvesting on a medieval manor farm.
3  How was the land ploughed?
4  'Women did the same work on a medieval farm as the men.' Is this statement true or false? Referring to the images above, give a reason for your answer.
5  Most of these pictures come from a medieval church calendar. Are they a primary or a secondary source?
6  Examine Source D. How are the women carrying their loads? Where might you see that today?
7  Imagine you are a medieval peasant. Write an account of how you sow and harvest your crops.

**Oxen**
A type of cattle used for heavy work.

## Housing

A peasant's house usually had just one room. Families cooked and slept in the same room. Children slept in a loft if the house was big enough.

---

**KS** | **Activity 5**

Examine this source and then answer the questions below.

**SOURCE 4.14:** Artist's impression of a medieval peasant's home

1 What materials were used to build this house?
2 Where do the family cook?
3 Where does the smoke from the fire go?
4 Would there be glass in the window?
5 Describe the furnishings.
6 What smells would there have been inside this house?

---

Peasants built their own houses using a method called **wattle and daub**. They wove branches of trees together to make the walls of the house and dabbed or 'daubed' them with mud. The roof was thatched with straw. There was no chimney. In winter, they brought their animals into the house for safety and warmth.

## Clothing

Peasants made their own clothes from linen or wool. They dyed them with berries or mosses. The women wore long dresses and a bonnet or headscarf. It was not thought proper for a married woman to go out with her head uncovered. The men wore a tunic and a belt.

## Food and drink

Peasants rarely ate meat. Their usual diet was bread and cheese. Ale (weak beer) was safer to drink than water, which was usually dirty.

**SOURCE 4.15: Typical peasant dress**

## Activity 6

In pairs, examine this source and then answer the questions below.

### Breakfast at dawn
Lump of dark bread, ale

### Lunch at 11 a.m.
Dark bread, cheese, ale or cider

### Main meal at 5 p.m.
Pottage (vegetable soup with oatmeal), bread, cheese, ale or cider

**SOURCE 4.16: Typical peasant diet**

1 List two things missing from this menu that most of us would have every day.
2 Suggest why they are not there.
3 Why, do you think, did peasants have to get up at dawn?

## Pastimes

Music, dancing and singing were popular activities. Some medieval pastimes remain popular today, such as noughts and crosses, draughts, wrestling and carol singing. One popular game was called 'hoodsman blind'. Children still play this game today: can you think what we call it? Peasants were free on church holidays. These could add up to 90 days a year!

## Law and order

See also **Section 20: Crime and punishment over time**

The lord appointed a **bailiff** to oversee the village for him. The bailiff made sure the peasants paid rents and taxes. He also looked after law and order. Sometimes peasants stole from the lord's orchards or poached deer in his forest. Some got drunk or started fights. Serfs were often caught running away. If a serf could remain free for a year and a day he could become a **freeman**. The bailiff brought those accused of a crime to the manor house, where the lord decided their punishment.

### DID YOU KNOW?

- Even the dung on a manor farm belonged to the lord.
- Peasants occasionally bathed in rivers and lakes. Most of the time they were dirty. Lice crawled in their hair, and their bodies were covered with fleas and bugs they picked up from sleeping on straw.

## Activity 7

Examine this source and then answer the question below.

**SOURCE 4.17: Medieval musicians**

1 Identify as many of these instruments as you can.

### DID YOU KNOW?

People were not put in prison. The local castle had **dungeons**, but these were used only for soldiers captured in a war.

## Activity 8

Examine this source and then answer the questions on crime below.

> John Shepherd fined because the clay he took to place on the outside of the walls of his house was taken from the common roadway
>
> Alice Kaa fined because she broke down the door and windows and took away lamps and oil from a house
>
> John Smith was fined 12d for not producing what he said he would
>
> Agnes who is poor gave birth to a child when she was not married
>
> Hugh Trees' beasts were caught in the lord's garden. Fined 6d
>
> Isabella Winters, widow, fined because her son John trespassed in the lord's woods 18d
>
> The whole township of Little Ogbourne, except seven, for not coming to wash the lord's sheep, 6s. 8d.

**SOURCE 4.18: Records from medieval manor courts in England (Note: d = penny, s = shilling)**

1  What is the most common type of crime?
2  What is the most common form of punishment?
3  Who was fined the most?
4  Do you think these crimes were very serious? Give a reason for your answer.
5  Who, do you think, got most of the money when people were fined?
6  What do we find out about everyday life on a manor farm from these court records? Give two examples.

The most common punishment for small crimes was a **fine**. Another punishment was to put people in the **stocks**. Their legs and sometimes hands were locked between planks of wood. Passers-by spat at them or threw things at them.

A **pillory** was like the stocks, but it held both the head and hands. A **ducking stool** was used to punish women who were thought to be troublesome – they were tied to a chair and lowered into the water, again and again.

## Activity 9

Examine these sources and then answer the questions below.

**SOURCE 4.19: Pillory**

**SOURCE 4.20: Stocks**

1  What is the difference between a stocks and a pillory?

A thief could have his hand cut off. Really serious criminals like murderers or traitors were **hanged**. Another crime that was harshly punished was witchcraft – witches could be hanged, and sometimes they were **burned alive at the stake**.

**DID YOU KNOW?**

Sometimes a person hunted by the bailiff ran into a church or monastery. The bailiff could not arrest anyone there. This was called **sanctuary**.

## Activity 10

In pairs, examine these sources and then answer the questions below.

**A** The Miller was a chap of sixteen stone, A great stout fellow big in brawn and bone. He did well out of them, for he could go And win the ram at any wrestling show … He could heave any door off hinge and post, Or take a run and break it with his head.

**SOURCE 4.21: Extract from *The Canterbury Tales* by Geoffrey Chaucer (a fourteenth-century poet)**

**B** Poor folk in hovels Charged with children and overcharged by landlords, What they may save by spinning they spend on rent On milk or on meal to make porridge

**SOURCE 4.22: Extract from *Piers Plowman* by William Langland (a fourteenth-century priest)**

1 What does document A tell you about how people in the Middle Ages spent their free time?

2 Many surnames come from the Middle Ages. What common surname do you see in A? Where does the name come from?

3 Does Langland present a positive or negative view of the life of a serf? Give a reason for your answer by referring to the source.

4 Look back over this section. Would you agree that the daily life of the serf was hard? Give three pieces of evidence to support your answer.

## Activity 11

Imagine you are a serf living in a medieval village in 1300. You are being interviewed by a time traveller, who asks you to answer these questions:

1 How do you farm your land?

2 What sort of house do you live in?

3 What do you eat and drink in a typical day?

4 What kind of clothes do you wear?

5 How would you be punished if you committed a crime?

6 What do you do in your free time?

7 What do you enjoy about being a serf? List three advantages.

8 What do you not like about being a serf? Give three examples.

### DO YOU UNDERSTAND THESE KEY TERMS?

| | | |
|---|---|---|
| bailiff | manor | serf |
| commons | medieval | stocks |
| county | Middle Ages | sanctuary |
| demesne | open-field system | tithe |
| ducking stool | | vassal |
| feudal system | peasant | wattle and daub |
| freeman | pillory | |
| knight | pottage | |

 PowerPoint summary

## SELF-ASSESSMENT – CAN YOU?

1 Define 'the medieval period'.

2 Give two differences between Europe now and Europe in the Middle Ages.

3 Name the most important person in a medieval kingdom.

4 Name two kinds of people who could be vassals of the king.

5 Describe the knights and explain what they did.

6 Identify the largest class or category of people in the Middle Ages.

7 Define the difference between serfs and freemen.

8 Name three buildings you would find in a medieval village.

9 Explain what a tithe was.

10 Identify the person who worked in the forge and describe what he made there.

11 Explain, with the aid of a drawing, how the open-field system worked and give two reasons why this was not a very efficient method of farming.

**Learning Outcome 3.6**

# WHAT WAS LIFE LIKE IN A MEDIEVAL CASTLE?

## ⊚ LEARNING INTENTIONS

**At the end of this section, you should be able to:**

- ◎ Explain how medieval castles were built
- ◎ Describe a siege
- ◎ Discuss what life was like for medieval lords and ladies
- ◎ Distinguish between the different types of medieval soldier
- ◎ Explain how a boy became a knight.

## How were medieval castles built?

As soon as a lord got land from his king, he built a castle on it. He needed it to defend himself and his people from enemies.

### Motte and bailey castles

The first castles were made of wood and were easy to build. Historians call them motte and bailey castles.

> 1 The lord got his peasants to construct a small hill. This was a **motte**.
> 2 On top of the motte they built a wooden **fort**. From this lookout post the lord's soldiers could see an enemy approaching.
> 3 Below the motte was a big enclosure called the **bailey**. Most of the time, the lord and his soldiers lived in the bailey, but if an enemy attacked, they went up to the fort.

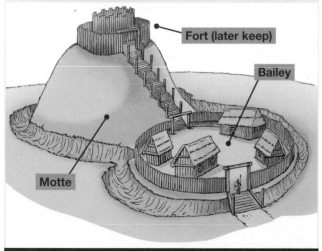

**SOURCE 4.23:** Motte and bailey castle

---

### Activity 1

Examine this source and then answer the questions below.

**SOURCE 4.24:** Remains of a motte and bailey castle

1 Identify where the motte and the bailey were located in this aerial photo.
2 Suggest why the ruins of the castle are gone.
3 Give one advantage of aerial photographs as a source for historians.

## Stone castles

Once the lord had control of the local countryside he replaced the motte and bailey castle with a stone castle.

1. **Keep:** The main building in the castle. It was where the lord and lady, their family and some soldiers lived.
2. **Battlements:** A walled platform at the top of the keep.
3. **Curtain walls:** The outer walls of the castle.
4. **Turrets:** Strong towers along the walls.
5. **Drawbridge:** A bridge that could be raised at night or if an enemy approached.
6. **Portcullis:** An iron grille that could be lowered in front of the castle gate.
7. **Ramparts:** Platforms along the top of all the walls that were wide enough for soldiers to walk along.
8. **Moat:** A ditch at the foot of the castle walls, filled with water. Often it was part of a nearby river or stream.
9. **Courtyard:** An open space in front of the keep. Also called a **bailey** or a **bawn**. Much of the life of the castle went on in the courtyard. It usually contained stables, pigeon houses, kitchens, a forge, and a well for fresh water.
10. **Latrines:** The toilets of the castle, usually in the corner of one of the towers in the keep.

**SOURCE 4.25: Stone castle**

# What was a siege?

When an enemy approached a castle, local people rushed inside the walls for safety. They often brought their animals with them. The castles were strong and at that time there was no gunpowder to blast the walls. The enemy surrounded the castle to stop anyone going in or out. This was called **laying a siege**. A castle could hold out for several months under siege.

Gradually weapons were invented that could help attackers to take over a castle.

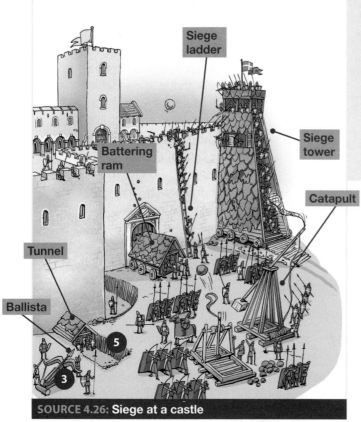

SOURCE 4.26: Siege at a castle

1 **Battering rams** were used to pound the gate.
2 Giant **catapults** hurled huge boulders or fireballs over the walls.
3 A **ballista** was like a giant crossbow and was used to fire large arrows.
4 **Siege towers** were like enclosed ladders and were used to scale the walls.
5 **Tunnels** were dug with the aim of collapsing the walls.
6 **Siege ladders** were used to climb the walls.

After gunpowder and the cannon were invented in the 1400s, it was much easier to capture castles.

## What was it like to be the lord of a medieval castle?

The most important person in a castle was the lord, who lived there with his family. The castle and its land belonged to him. But if he betrayed the king, he would lose it all.

### The keep

The lord and his family lived in the **keep**. It had a **narrow spiral staircase** that circled to the right. Since most people held their sword or spear in their right hand, that made it easier to fight coming down the stairs than going up.

### Activity 2

Examine this source and answer the question below.

SOURCE 4.27: Artist's reconstruction of Trim Castle, Co. Meath

1 Identify the labelled parts of the castle.

On the **top floor** were the lord's private apartments, the **solar** and the chapel. The great hall took up the entire **middle floor**. This is where everyone ate. The lord also used the hall to give orders to his soldiers and to collect rents and taxes from the peasants. Suspected criminals were brought there to be tried. On the **lower floor** there were storerooms for food and drink. There were also **dungeons** to hold enemy soldiers captured in war.

## Education

Up to the 1300s most lords could barely read or write. They had no need to because they kept a priest to do that for them. The priest also acted as schoolmaster to the lord's sons until they were seven years old. Good manners and fighting skills were considered more important than reading or writing.

## Food

In the castle there were usually two meals a day: dinner at noon and supper at about 4 p.m. The amount of food could be enormous. One meal might include duck, rabbit, hare, pork, boar, lamb and birds. Rich people ate a lot of meat!

At a feast, important people sat at the top tables in the dining hall. The food was served on wooden plates or on big slices of bread called **trenchers**. They cut meat with their knives and ate with their fingers. They drank wine or ale.

**Keep**
A large square tower where the lord's family lived.

**Minstrel**
Travelling musician who entertained wealthy families.

**Solar**
The room which the lady of the castle used for work such as embroidery.

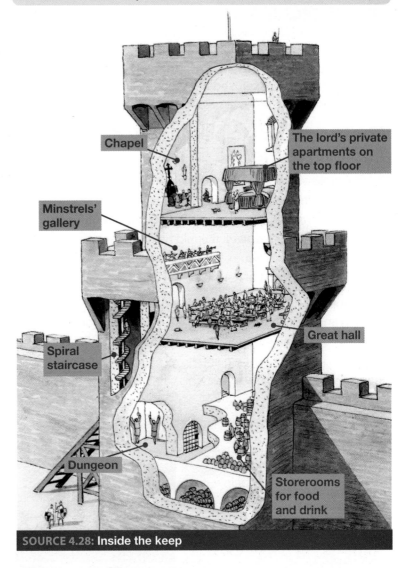

Chapel

The lord's private apartments on the top floor

Minstrels' gallery

Great hall

Spiral staircase

Dungeon

Storerooms for food and drink

**SOURCE 4.28: Inside the keep**

### DID YOU KNOW?

In 1465 an English bishop invited 2,500 people to be his guests for a few days. Between them they ate 1,000 sheep, 4,000 pigeons and 2,000 pigs.

## Entertainment

A favourite pastime for rich people was **hawking**. The hawk was trained to sit on a person's hand and to hunt for songbirds, ducks and small animals.

**Hawking**
Hunting with trained birds of prey (hawks).

**SOURCE 4.29: Hawking was popular with men and women**

**Tournaments** were also popular. Knights acted out mock battles. They could fight in teams (**melées**) or one knight could fight against another (**jousting**). Blunt swords and lances were used, but there were still many deaths.

> 🔍 **DID YOU KNOW?**
>
> So many knights were killed in tournaments that the Church banned them. Until 1300 knights who died in them were refused a Christian burial.

## What was it like to be the lady of a medieval castle?

The main role of a woman in medieval times was to marry and have children. A noblewoman did not marry for love. Her parents arranged her marriage like a business contract. They would give her a **dowry**. It could be money, cattle or household utensils. In return, her husband would agree to support her for the rest of her life.

Most noblewomen could not read or write, but they learned spinning and weaving, needlework, music and embroidery so that they could make beautiful **tapestries**. They also learned how to run a large household and how to use herbs to cure illnesses. When the lord was away, his wife had to look after and defend the castle.

**Tournament**
An event where knights fought mock battles against each other.

### Activity 3

Examine this source and then answer the questions below.

SOURCE 4.30: **Jousting at a modern re-enactment show**

1 Have you ever been to a re-enactment show of any historical event? Describe it.
2 Are they a good idea, do you think? Give a reason for your answer.

**Dowry**
Money or goods that a woman's family gave to her husband when she got married.

###  Activity 4

Examine this source and then answer the questions below.

1 What is a tapestry?
2 Is this a primary or a secondary source? Explain your answer.
3 List three pieces of information this tapestry tells us about life in the Middle Ages.
4 Would you agree that tapestries are very useful sources for historians trying to find out about the Middle Ages? Give reasons for your answer.
5 Is this source completely accurate, do you think? Explain your answer.

SOURCE 4.31: **French medieval tapestry about making wine**

## Clothes

Women wore long dresses. It was fashionable for them to trail on the floor. They were usually made of wool, but sometimes merchants or knights brought back silk from Asia. The headdress was called a **wimple**. Rich men wore long tunics. Shoes were made of leather and were pointed. The long toes were stuffed with horsehair.

## Who were the lord's soldiers?

There were three kinds of soldier in the castle.

> **Foot soldiers** carried swords, daggers and shields.
> **Archers** used bows and arrows. Some had longbows and some crossbows, which were more powerful.
> **Knights** were the most important soldiers in a medieval army.

## How did a boy become a knight?

It took thirteen years of training for a boy to become a knight. There were three stages.

> When a lord's son was seven years old, he was sent to another castle to be a **page**. He was taught to ride a horse and use a sword. He also learned singing, dancing and good manners.
> When the boy was fourteen, he became a **squire**. He learned to fight on horseback.
> When the squire was twenty-one, he became a **knight** in a ceremony called **dubbing**. The squire would first spend a night praying in the church. The next morning, he knelt before his lord, who put on his armour, piece by piece. The squire then swore to uphold the **code of chivalry** – a promise to be loyal to God, to protect women and children, and never to run away in a battle. Then his lord touched him on the shoulder with his sword and said, 'Arise, Sir Knight.'

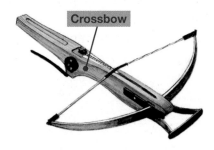

Crossbow

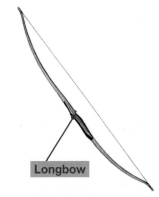

Longbow

**SOURCE 4.32: Weapons used by archers. Why, do you think, was the crossbow a better weapon?**

**Chivalry**
A code of honour that said a knight should be brave, love God and protect women and children.

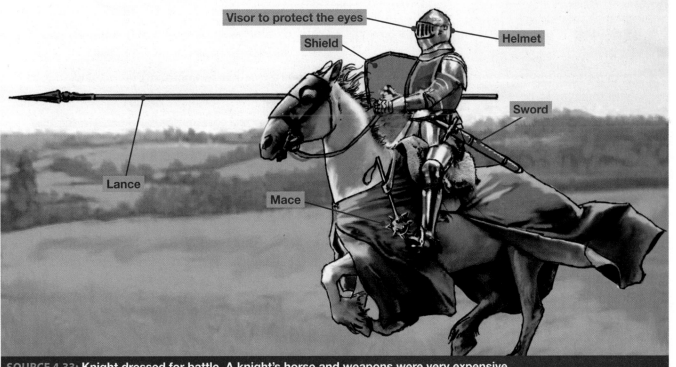

**SOURCE 4.33: Knight dressed for battle. A knight's horse and weapons were very expensive.**

Visor to protect the eyes

Shield

Helmet

Sword

Lance

Mace

## Activity 5

Examine this source and then answer the questions below.

Norman soldiers                                                                     English soldiers

**SOURCE 4.34:** Part of the Bayeaux Tapestry, which is kept in the Bayeux Museum in France and depicts how William, Duke of Normandy, became King of England in 1066

1   What weapons can you identify in this image? List three.
2   Why, do you think, did the Normans win this battle?
3   Which side do you think made the tapestry: the Normans or the English? Give a reason for your answer.
4   What can a source like this tell historians?

### DO YOU UNDERSTAND THESE KEY TERMS?

| | | | | | | |
|---|---|---|---|---|---|---|
| archer | battlements | drawbridge | jousting | motte | siege tower | tournament |
| bailey | catapult | dubbing | keep | page | solar | wimple |
| ballista | chivalry | dungeon | latrine | portcullis | squire | |
| battering ram | curtain walls | fort | melée | ramparts | tapestry | |
| | dowry | hawking | moat | siege | trencher | |

 PowerPoint summary

## SELF-ASSESSMENT – CAN YOU?

1   Name the first kind of castle and describe how it was built.

2   List three activities that took place in the castle courtyard.

3   Explain why a well was vital for a castle.

4   Describe three ways in which an enemy might try to capture a castle and say which you think was most effective.

5   Suggest why castles were usually built near rivers or the sea, or on high ground.

6   Explain why castles were no longer used after the 1400s.

7   Describe where the lord and his family lived.

8   Describe what you would find in (a) a solar and (b) a dungeon.

9   Describe how the lord of a castle was educated.

10   Outline what kind of food rich people ate, and list three examples.

11   List three entertainments enjoyed by the people of the castle.

12   Describe a tournament and explain the two types of mock battle fought by knights.

13   Explain how marriages were arranged.

14   Outline the main duty of a medieval noblewoman.

15   List four things the lady of a castle had to see to.

16   Name the three kinds of soldier found in a medieval castle and the weapons each carried.

17   Describe the Bayeux Tapestry and name where it is kept.

18   Explain the three stages a boy went through to become a knight.

19   Describe a dubbing.

# WHAT WAS LIFE LIKE IN A MEDIEVAL TOWN?

## 🎯 LEARNING INTENTIONS

**At the end of this section, you should be able to:**

◎ Discuss what it was it like to live in a medieval town

◎ Outline the types of people who lived in medieval towns

◎ Explain what a guild is

◎ Describe how a boy became a master craftsman.

## What did a medieval town look like?

Medieval towns grew up next to big castles or monasteries or beside rivers. Most towns in Europe had fewer than 1,000 people.

**Toll**
A tax that traders had to pay at the town's gates.

---

### KS 👥 | Activity 1 | ✏️

Examine Source 4.35, which shows some of the important buildings and places in a medieval town, and then answer the questions below.

1 Which building looks the most important?
2 What are the buildings around the square made of?
3 What material are most of the houses built from?
4 Why, do you think, was the square important to the people of the town?
5 Why is there a wall around the town?
6 Why, do you think, was a town built at this location?

1 High outer wall
2 Gates
3 High Street
4 Parish church
5 Rich merchant's house
6 Market square
7 Fair green

**SOURCE 4.35:** Artist's reconstruction of a medieval town

Anyone who wanted to sell goods in the town had to pay a **toll**. The gates were closed between sunset and dawn.

**Activity 2**

Examine this source and then answer the questions below.

SOURCE 4.36: Medieval gate at Drogheda, Co. Louth

1 Suggest what happened at the gate in a medieval town.
2 What can you infer about Drogheda from this photograph?
3 Find Drogheda on a map of Ireland. Suggest why a town developed at that location.

**DID YOU KNOW?**

The names of some gates still survive in modern place names. In Dublin, for example, St James's Gate (where Guinness is made) was the site of a medieval gate.

Only the main street of a town was paved with stones or wooden planks. It was often called **High Street**. Other streets were narrow lanes. They were not paved so they usually became very muddy in wet weather.

## Buildings

Every medieval town had a **parish church** and a **town hall**, which were made of stone. Most other buildings were made of wood.

Rich merchants had their **houses** on the High Street. These had three storeys, each storey leaning out over the one below, which made the street dark. Craftspeople lived over their **shops**. Some houses had a long back garden, where the family grew vegetables and kept pigs, hens or even a cow. As you moved away from the town centre, the houses became smaller and the people poorer.

**Activity 3**

Examine this source and then answer the questions below.

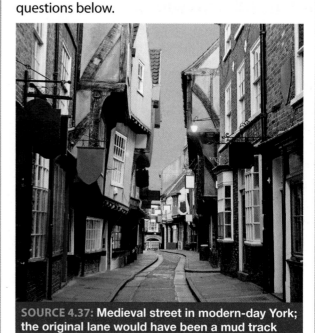

SOURCE 4.37: Medieval street in modern-day York; the original lane would have been a mud track

1 What does this street tell us about medieval towns?
2 How does the modern street pictured differ from the way it would have been in the Middle Ages? State two changes.

**DID YOU KNOW?**

People of the same trade liked to live in the same area, so you often have streets named after trades, such as Fishamble Street, Dublin. Some streets were so narrow that two people could shake hands with each other out of their top-floor windows!

Because the houses were made of wood, there were strict rules about fire safety. At sunset, church bells rang out to mark the arrival of the **curfew**. That meant that all fires and candles in the town had to be put out. The word curfew means 'cover the fire'.

## Dirt and disease

Towns were very dirty. There were no sewers. An open drain ran down the middle of the street. People threw everything into it, including the contents of their chamber pots.

People seldom washed and they all had fleas. Many suffered from skin diseases. A common one was **leprosy**, where sores broke out all over the person's body. Lepers were not allowed to mix with others and had to live in a special place, usually outside the town walls. This is how Leopardstown in south Dublin got its name (see Black Death, pages 75–76).

## Fairs

The highlight of the year was the annual fair. It could last up to three weeks and took place on the **fair green** outside the town walls. Merchants came from all over the world. They sold silk and spices from Asia, brightly dyed woollen cloth from Italy and furs from Russia. Craftspeople bought things they needed for their work. Acrobats, musicians and jugglers entertained the crowds.

# What was a guild?

## Craftspeople

The **craftspeople** made the things that people needed. Even the smallest town had over thirty different craftspeople. Many surnames come from the names of crafts that people did. For example, Robert the (black)smith became known as Robert Smith.

## Guilds

Every craftsperson who worked in a town had to belong to a **guild**. There was a bakers' guild, a carpenters' guild and so on. Each guild regulated its trade. For example, the guild set examinations to make sure the craftspeople were good at their trade. It set standards of work and decent wages. It looked after old or sick members, paid for their funerals and looked after their orphans.

**Guild**
An organisation that controlled its own craft or trade.

---

**Curfew**
The time when all fires had to be out in a medieval town.

**DID YOU KNOW?**

In medieval Dublin, almost one-third of children died before the age of ten. Average life expectancy of men and women was just thirty years.

**Chamber pot**
Container shaped like a giant cup that was used as a toilet.

### Activity 4

Examine this list of crafts and trades and then answer the questions below.

| | |
|---|---|
| Shoemakers | Fishmongers |
| Weavers (made cloth) | Masons (builders who used stone) |
| Tailors (made clothes) | |
| Carpenters | Tanners (made leather) |
| Blacksmiths | |
| Coopers (made barrels) | Chandlers (made candles) |
| Bakers | Apothecaries (pharmacists) |
| Butchers | |
| Millers (made flour) | Merchants (traders) |

1. How many familiar surnames can you find? Make a list.
2. What trades do you think were once carried out in (a) Smith's Lane, Cork (b) Winetavern Street and Cook Street, Dublin?

**Craftsperson**
Someone who has learned a skilled manual craft or trade (e.g. a carpenter).

**DID YOU KNOW?**

There were also merchant guilds who looked after trade in the towns. Merchants bought and sold goods made by craftspeople.

### Activity 5

Examine this source and then answer the questions below.

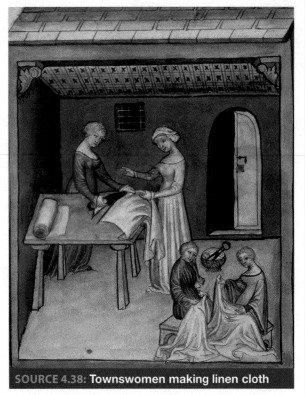

SOURCE 4.38: Townswomen making linen cloth

1  What kind of craft work are these people doing?
2  Was it possible for a woman to be a member of a guild, do you think?

There were many **craftswomen**, but as time went on guilds began to exclude female members. In most towns women were allowed to become members of a guild only if their husband had died and they wanted to carry on his trade.

## How did a boy become a master craftsman?

A boy who wanted to practise a craft went through three stages.

> At twelve years of age, he became an **apprentice** and went to live in the house of a master craftsman to learn the trade. He stayed there for seven years, working without pay.

> At nineteen, the apprentice became a **journeyman**. He could leave his old master and look elsewhere for the best-paid work.

> To become a **master craftsman**, a journeyman had to produce a **masterpiece**. For example, a carpenter might make a table or a tailor a coat. Then he could have his own workshop and sell his goods in the town. Along with the masterpiece, the man had to make a large payment to the guild. Most journeymen could not afford this, so they never got to be masters.

### Activity 6

Examine this source and then answer the question below.

In 1492 the masters of medicine in London complained about female members of the barber-surgeons' (doctors') guild. They wanted to ban female members because: 'They have neither natural ability nor professional knowledge, make the gravest possible mistakes (thanks to their stupidity) and very often kill their patients.'

SOURCE 4.39: Fifteenth-century records of the Masters of Medicine Guild, London

1  Explain in your own words why the masters of medicine wanted to ban women from their guild.

### Activity 7

In pairs, examine this source and then answer the questions below.

- All craftsmen must be members of a guild.
- The guild sets the price for all your goods.
- All members of the guild pay workers the same wage.
- Shoddy workmanship is not allowed.
- You are not allowed to advertise.
- No other guild member will have anything to do with a member who lives in **adultery** [living with someone outside marriage].

SOURCE 4.40: Guild rules

1  Suggest why guild members were not permitted to advertise their goods or services.
2  List two benefits of being a guild member.
3  List two disadvantages of being a guild member.

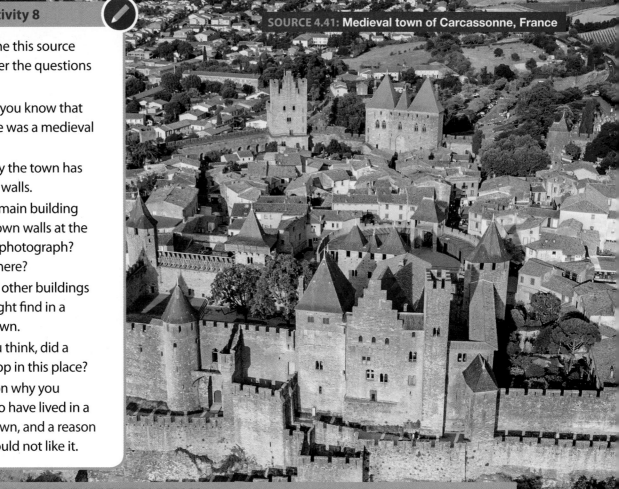

SOURCE 4.41: Medieval town of Carcassonne, France

## Activity 8

KS 👥

In pairs, examine this source and then answer the questions below.

1   How would you know that Carcassonne was a medieval town?

2   Suggest why the town has two rows of walls.

3   What is the main building inside the town walls at the front of the photograph? Who lived there?

4   Identify any other buildings that you might find in a medieval town.

5   Why, do you think, did a town develop in this place?

6   Give a reason why you would like to have lived in a medieval town, and a reason why you would not like it.

## DO YOU UNDERSTAND THESE KEY TERMS?

| | | | | |
|---|---|---|---|---|
| adultery | charter | curfew | journeyman | masterpiece |
| apprentice | corporation | fair green | leprosy | merchant |
| chamber pot | craftsperson | guild | master | toll |

🖥 PowerPoint summary

## SELF-ASSESSMENT – CAN YOU?

1   Explain where towns developed in the Middle Ages.

2   Describe what a toll was.

3   Explain where in a medieval town you would find the homes of rich merchants.

4   Define a curfew and explain why it was imposed on medieval towns.

5   Outline why diseases were common in medieval towns.

6   Explain which buildings in a medieval town were made of stone.

7   Explain why fairs were so popular, giving two reasons.

8   Name the group of people who ran a medieval town.

9   Name at least five different crafts and trades that were carried out in even small towns.

10   Explain what a guild was.

11   List three kinds of service provided by guilds to their members.

12   List two guild rules.

13   Explain the process a person had to follow to become a master in a guild.

# WHY WAS RELIGION SO IMPORTANT IN MEDIEVAL TIMES?

##  LEARNING INTENTIONS

**At the end of this section, you should be able to:**

◎ Discuss how the Christian Church influenced medieval people's lives

◎ Outline how the Church was organised in medieval Europe

◎ Explain what the Black Death was and how it affected people

◎ Distinguish between Romanesque churches and Gothic churches

◎ Discuss what it was like to be a medieval monk or friar.

## Were medieval people religious?

In the Middle Ages religion was very important to people. Most Europeans could not imagine a world without God. Even rulers believed they would go to hell if they did not obey the Christian Church's teachings.

---

**KS**             **Activity 1**

Examine these sources and then answer the questions below.

There was once a worthy woman who had hated a poor woman for more than seven years. When the worthy woman went to confession the priest told her to forgive her enemy. She said she had forgiven her. But the woman added, 'Do you think I forgave her with my heart as I did my mouth? No!' Then the devil came down and strangled her there in front of everyone. So make sure that when you make a promise you make it with your heart without any deceit.

**SOURCE 4.42: Medieval priests told this story to teach people how they should live**

**SOURCE 4.43: Medieval image of hell**

1 Why did priests tell stories like the one above, do you think?

2 Who are the creatures with pitchforks meant to represent in the image of hell?

3 If you had lived in medieval times, how would you have felt seeing such images and listening to such stories? Worried? Bored? Afraid? Amused? Give a reason for your answer.

---

## How was the Christian Church organised?

The leader of the Christian Church in Western Europe was the **pope**. At local level the Church was divided into **parishes** and **dioceses**. The parish priest ran the parish and the bishop ran the diocese. Usually the manor farm was also a parish and the local priest baptised, married and buried everyone in the parish.

Bishops were rich and owned a lot of land. In each diocese, the bishop built a big church called a **cathedral**. Many churches were very impressive in the Middle Ages. They were meant to help people think of heaven and to show their devotion to God.

**DID YOU KNOW?**

The priest was sometimes the only person in a parish who could read or write. He helped people with legal documents and advised them on all kinds of problems.

## How powerful was the Christian Church?

We have evidence that the Christian Church had a huge influence on Europe. One of the ways we can see this is in the thousands of churches built during the Middle Ages.

### Romanesque churches

Around AD 1000 Christians began to build big stone churches. The first stone churches were built in a style called **Romanesque**. The external features of a Romanesque church include round arches and square towers. The interior is dark and gloomy. The roof is held up with heavy round columns and thick walls, which means that all windows are small and little light gets in.

### Activity 2

Examine these sources and then answer the question below.

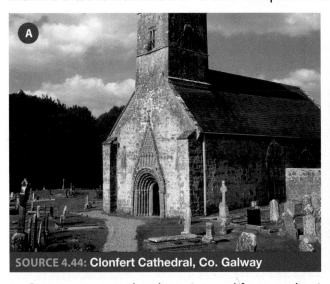

SOURCE 4.44: Clonfert Cathedral, Co. Galway

SOURCE 4.45: Church in Umbria, Italy

1   State two external and two internal features that indicate these are Romanesque churches.

### Gothic churches

Later, a new style of architecture called the **Gothic** style became popular. Gothic cathedrals usually have spires. The arches over the windows and doors are pointed and there are often stone statues carved into the doorways.

Arches on the outside of the church support the weight of the roof. These are called **flying buttresses**. Therefore slim columns could hold up the church walls on the inside, leaving more space for windows. These churches often have beautiful **stained glass**. When the sun shines through the glass, the whole church glows with light and colour. Other dramatic features include rose windows and gargoyles.

**DID YOU KNOW?**

**Gargoyles** are common on the sides and doorways of Gothic churches. They help to drain off the water from the roof. They are also meant to ward off evil.

SOURCE 4.46: Flying buttresses

SOURCE 4.47: A stained-glass rose window

SOURCE 4.48: Gargoyle

## Summary

| Romanesque style | Gothic style |
| --- | --- |
| Square towers | Tall spires |
| Rounded arches | Pointed arches |
| Thick, round columns | Slim columns |
| Thick walls to support roof | Flying buttresses |
| Small windows | Bigger windows, rose windows |
| Dark interiors | Brighter interiors, glow from stained glass |
| Plain exterior | Stone statues over doors and windows |

## Were monasteries important in the Middle Ages?

Monasteries were very important in medieval Europe. They were communities of men (**monks**) or women (**nuns**) who wanted to devote their lives to God. They followed strict rules. They had to pray seven times every day, fast regularly and always obey the **abbot** or the **abbess**, the head of the monastery. A monastery was sometimes called an abbey. There were different orders of monks and nuns, such as Benedictines, Cistercians and Poor Clares.

The monks slept in the **dormitory**, ate meals in the **refectory**, prayed in the **church**, walked and prayed in the **cloisters** and studied in the **library**. The **chapter house** was where the monks met to discuss the business of the monastery and to elect the abbot. The **guest house** was where they gave food to poor people and travellers, and monks nursed the sick in the **infirmary**.

> **Cloister**
> A square in the centre of the monastery with a covered walkway where monks would walk and pray.

### Activity 3

Examine this source and then answer the questions below.

SOURCE 4.49: Cologne Cathedral, Germany

1   Identify three features of Gothic architecture on this cathedral.

2   Can you name a church you have visited (in Ireland or abroad) that has similar features?

## Activity 4

Examine this source and then answer the question below.

Church · Chapter house · Dormitory · Refectory · Library and scriptorium

**SOURCE 4.50: Reconstruction of a medieval monastery**

1 A cloister is a covered walkway around a courtyard in the centre of a monastery. What did the monks do there?

2 Monasteries were not just places where people prayed. Which services provided by a medieval monastery can you identify from this reconstruction?

Boys and sometimes girls were educated in monasteries. The monks also wrote books and recorded events.

Monks and nuns did everything for themselves, such as making their furniture and clothes and growing their food. They even brewed their own beer! They trained many boys and girls in their skills. Some of the larger monasteries were like small towns.

## What was it like to be a monk in a medieval monastery?

The Rule of St Benedict, which most monasteries followed, laid down a strict timetable for the monks.

> **DID YOU KNOW?**
>
> Part of a monk's job was to read and copy books by hand in a special room called the **scriptorium**. If it weren't for these books, we would know very little about what happened during the Middle Ages.

> **KS** | **Activity 5** |
>
> Examine this source and then answer the questions below.
>
> | 3 a.m. | Matins (morning prayers) |
> | --- | --- |
> | 6 a.m. | After a sleep, silent prayers |
> | 7 a.m. | Breakfast in silence |
> | 8 to 9.30 a.m. | Work in the fields |
> | 10 a.m. | Mass |
> | 11 a.m. to 2 p.m. | Work again |
> | 2 p.m. | Dinner |
> | 2.30 p.m. | Reading |
> | 3 to 5 p.m. | Work |
> | 5 p.m. | Vespers (evening prayers) |
> | 6 p.m. | Supper |
> | 8 p.m. | Compline (night prayers) and retire to bed |
>
> SOURCE 4.51: Daily routine in a medieval monastery
>
> 1 Explain the terms 'matins' and 'vespers'.
> 2 Calculate how many hours each day were spent at prayer, and how many at work.
> 3 What would you have liked most and least about this life?
> 4 Look back over this section and name two advantages of being a monk.

> **Activity 6**
>
> Examine this source and then answer the questions below.
>
>
>
> SOURCE 4.52: **Large medieval monastery in Romania**
>
> 1 Why, do you think, is the monastery in the photograph in such an isolated area?
> 2 Do you think that it was a wealthy monastery? How would you know?

Each monk or nun had a special job. The abbot (or abbess) was head of the monastery, elected by the monks (or nuns). In his absence, the **prior** (or prioress) was in charge. The **almoner** looked after visitors and the poor. The **infirmarian** looked after the sick and kept a record of the herbs used in the monastery. The **librarian** looked after the library.

> **DID YOU KNOW?**
>
> Poorer women rarely became nuns. Their labour was needed too much in the lord's fields.

# How did a boy become a monk?

SOURCE 4.53: **Can you see these monks' tonsures?**

When a boy joined a monastery he was called a **novice**. If the abbot thought the novice would make a good monk, he let him take **solemn vows**. These were promises of **poverty** (he must not own anything), **chastity** (he must not marry) and **obedience** (he must do what the abbot told him). Then his hair was cut in a **tonsure**, a shaved patch on the crown of his head, to show that he was a monk.

# What were friars?

If people needed the help of monks or nuns, they had to go to them at the monastery. But around 1200, a different kind of monk appeared. They were called **friars**. Friars travelled from place to place, working with the poor. One group of friars was called the Franciscans after its founder, St Francis of Assisi. Other groups included the Dominicans and the Augustinians.

# What was the Black Death?

Between 1347 and 1350 a terrible **plague** raged in Europe. It wiped out nearly one-third of the population. Historians later gave this plague the name the **Black Death**. Given the power and influence of the Christian Church, people looked to their religious leaders for help.

Various remedies to stop the plague were tried. Church bells were rung. There were all-night prayers. In some places, Jews were blamed and thrown out of towns. But the Church was unable to stop the plague, and some people saw it as God's punishment for their sins.

The plague probably started in Asia and travelled westward along the **Silk Road** trade route (see Section 6). The disease was carried by fleas that lived on rats.

SOURCE 4.54: **Medieval nuns in France**

## Activity 7

Examine this source and then answer the questions below.

SOURCE 4.55: **A medieval friar**

1　How do we know that this is a friar and not a monk?
2　Suggest what he is doing.

**Plague**
Infectious disease that spreads quickly.

Historians think that black rats living on European merchant ships caught the disease, and brought it to Europe. Many victims had swellings in their neck, armpit or groin.

The following quotes give an idea of the effect of the plague:

# EFFECTS OF THE PLAGUE

## CONTEMPORARY SOURCES

### SOURCE 4.56

'On the same day twenty, forty, sixty and very often more corpses were committed to the same grave' – Registrar of London, 1349

### SOURCE 4.57

'Men and women bore their own dead children on their shoulders to the church and cast them in to a common pit' – English eyewitness account

### SOURCE 4.58

'Plague stripped villages, towns and castles and swallowed them up … This pestilence was so contagious that those who touched the sick or the dead were immediately infected themselves and died … I see the whole world placed within the grasp of Satan.' – John Clyn, Irish friar, Kilkenny Chronicle (Clyn later died from the plague while trying to help others)

## MODERN SOURCES

### SOURCE 4.59

'The period between 1348 and 1420 saw the heaviest loss. In parts of Germany, about 40% of the named inhabitants disappeared… and in some parts of Tuscany, 70% were lost during this period.' – 'The Economic Consequences of the Black Death' by Economic Historian Paolo Malanima

### SOURCE 4.60

'It is estimated that somewhere between 75 million and 200 million people died of the plague' – 'The Economic Consequences of the Black Death' by Economic Historian Paolo Malanima

### SOURCE 4.61

'Jews were burned in Strasbourg in 1349. It was believed that the Jews had caused the plague by poisoning drinking water' – *A History of the Jews* by Paul Johnson, 1988, p. 217

## Activity 8

Examine these sources and then answer the questions below.

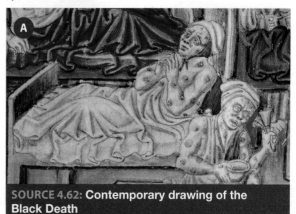

SOURCE 4.62: **Contemporary drawing of the Black Death**

BRING OUT YOUR DEAD!

MORE LAND!

FAIRER PAY FOR LABOUR!

SOURCE 4.63: **Modern cartoon strip of the Black Death**

1 How many people in Europe are thought to have died from the Black Death?

2 According to A, how would you know if someone had the Black Death?

3 According to B, explain two effects of the Black Death.

4 Which of these two sources is primary and which is secondary? Give a reason for your answer in each case.

5 Give an example of where one of these visual sources agrees with one or more of the written sources on the left about the Black Death.

**Contemporary**
Belonging to the same period of time.

Many more townspeople than peasants died from plague. This was because the towns were crowded and very dirty. The rate of death among priests was particularly high because they were in close contact with the sick. As monasteries also operated as inns and hospitals, they were often a breeding ground for the plague.

## Effects of the Black Death

The Black Death led to massive changes for people in Europe.

> Law and order broke down in towns and the countryside. Peasants revolted against their landlords. They no longer wanted to provide landlords with free labour.

> Exports fell and trade almost stopped.

> Jews were often blamed for the plague. Many were attacked, forced to become Christians and even expelled from some countries.

It took Europe fifty years to recover from the Black Death, and many other plagues followed that were nearly as bad. Peasants' revolts were brutally put down, but their conditions did begin to improve. There were fewer of them so they had more bargaining power.

### Activity 9

Examine these sources and then answer the questions below.

**A** The Black Death 1348–1350 killed so many villeins that the lord of the manor could not get enough people to live and work on his estates. Some villages were deserted.

SOURCE 4.64: *Durham Priory Manorial Accounts 1277–1310*

**B** On the estates of Durham Priory things were changing before the Black Death. The lord was already renting out his lands to people who would pay him rent instead of doing services ... The lord decided he could make more money from rents.

SOURCE 4.65: *Durham Priory Manorial Accounts 1277–1310*

1 According to A, what change came about because of the Black Death?

2 How does the text in Source B contradict that in Source A?

### DO YOU UNDERSTAND THESE KEY TERMS?

| | | | | |
|---|---|---|---|---|
| abbot | diocese | Gothic | parish | solemn vows |
| almoner | dormitory | hosteller | plague | stained glass |
| cathedral | flying buttress | infirmarian | prior | tonsure |
| chapter house | friar | infirmary | Romanesque | |
| cloisters | gargoyle | novice | rose window | |

 Chapter summary    Weblinks    PowerPoint summary

## SELF-ASSESSMENT – CAN YOU?

1 Identify one reason why the Christian Church had so much power over people in the Middle Ages.

2 Name the head of the Christian Church in Western Europe.

3 Outline what a parish priest did in the Middle Ages.

4 Name the style of church building that developed in Europe around AD 1000, and list three of its main features.

5 Name the other style of medieval church building and list four of its features.

6 Give three reasons why monasteries were so important to people in medieval times.

7 Name an order of monks and an order of nuns.

8 Explain what each of the following places in a medieval monastery was for: cloister, library, dormitory and chapter house.

9 Describe how a boy became a monk.

10 Explain what (a) the abbot, (b) the prior and (c) the almoner did.

11 Explain who friars were and outline how they were different from monks.

12 Name two groups of friars.

13 Explain what the Black Death was.

14 Decide whether this statement is true or false: 'About one-third of the population of Europe was wiped out.'

15 Explain two other effects of the Black Death in Europe.

# 5 THE IMPACT OF THE RENAISSANCE ON ARTS AND SCIENCE

## What was the Renaissance?

79

## How did visual arts change in the Renaissance?

83

## How did writing change in the Renaissance?

94

## How did science change in the Renaissance?

98

# WHAT WAS THE RENAISSANCE?

## ◎ LEARNING INTENTIONS

**At the end of this section, you should be able to:**

◎ Explain what the Renaissance was and why it started

◎ Recognise the role of patrons

◎ Comment on the role of women in the Renaissance.

## What was the Renaissance?

About AD 1400 people began to question the ideas of the Middle Ages and took a new interest in the world of Ancient Greece and Rome. This was the start of the **Renaissance**.

The Renaissance lasted over 200 years and saw an explosion of new ideas in the arts (e.g. painting, literature and architecture). There were also new discoveries in science. Many historians believe that it marks the beginning of the modern world.

> **Renaissance**
> A time when people began to see their world in a different way. This change was inspired by a new interest in Ancient Greece and Rome.

## Humanism

The renewed interest in the ancient world was called **humanism**. It put human beings at the centre of everything. People in the Renaissance were interested in all aspects of earthly life, unlike medieval people, who focused more on the afterlife in heaven. They studied and painted the natural world, especially human beings.

### DID YOU KNOW?

The word Renaissance means '**rebirth**'. Historians call this age the Renaissance because it was almost as if the Greeks and Romans had come back to life.

---

### Activity 1

Examine this source and then answer the questions below.

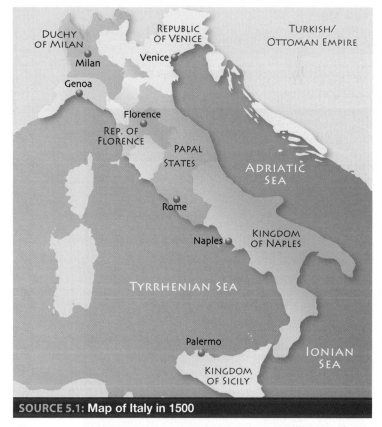

SOURCE 5.1: **Map of Italy in 1500**

1 Looking at the map, can you guess why the Renaissance began in Italy?

2 Find the following important cities on the map:

- **Rome**, home to the pope, who ruled over the city and the Papal States
- **Florence**, which was ruled by the Medicis, a wealthy banking family
- **Milan**, which was ruled by the Sforza, a military family
- **Venice**, where the richest families elected a council to run the city.

## Where did the Renaissance start?

**1** The Renaissance began in Italy. Italy had been the centre of the old Roman Empire and every town had ruins of old Roman buildings.

**2** **Rich Italian merchants:** brought silks and spices from Asia and sold them to the rest of Europe. This trade made them very wealthy. They spent money on grand buildings and beautiful pictures and statues.

**3** **Contact with other cultures:** Italian merchants brought home many ideas from their travels and became more critical of the old ways of doing things in Europe.

**4** **Independent city-states:** Italy was divided into **city-states** and each city had its own ruler. The citizens were very independent and were open to new ideas.

### Activity 2

Examine this source and then answer the question below.

SOURCE 5.2: *Holy Family with St John* (1517) by Raphael

**1** In pairs, discuss how the painter, Raphael, shows the holy family as a real human family.

### Activity 3

Examine this source and then answer the question below.

SOURCE 5.3: **Basilica (large church) of San Lorenzo in Florence, designed by Brunelleschi**

**1** In what ways does the architecture copy the ideas of the Romans?

## Why were patrons important?

A **patron** is a person who commissions (i.e. sponsors) an artist to produce a work of art. In Italy at the time of the Renaissance, many people and cities had enough money to become patrons. They also funded science research and buildings. Two important patrons were **Cosimo de' Medici** and his grandson **Lorenzo de' Medici**. They were members of the richest family of bankers in Florence in the fifteenth century. Many popes were also patrons.

**Patron**
Person who commissions an artist to produce a work of art.

### DID YOU KNOW?

In 1550 a famous book called *The Lives of the most Excellent Painters, Architects and Sculptors* was published. Written by the artist Giorgio Vasari, it contains details of 150 Renaissance artists. It is one of the most important sources we have on the Renaissance.

Examine these sources and then answer the questions below.

**A**   Florence is more beautiful than your Venice. We have 30,000 homes owned by noblemen, merchants, craftsmen and citizens. Our city has 270 shops belonging to the wool merchants' guild and 83 splendid warehouses of the silk merchants' guild. We also have ... 44 goldsmiths and jewellers and 33 banks.

**SOURCE 5.4: Words of a merchant from Florence in 1472**

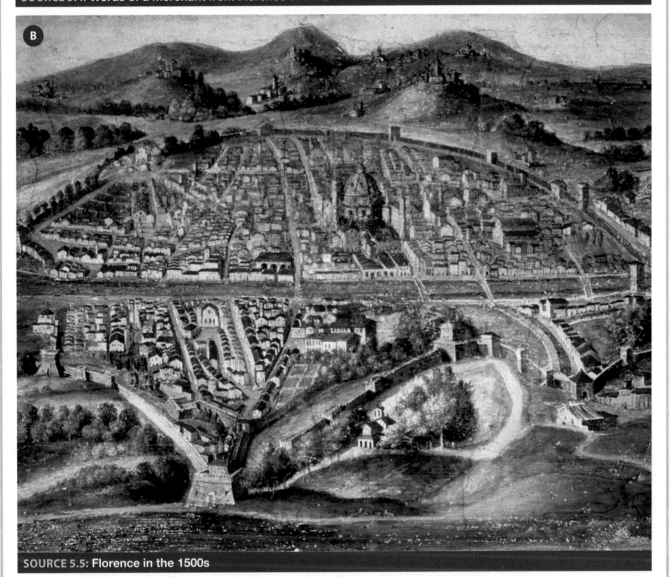

**SOURCE 5.5: Florence in the 1500s**

1.   Write down two pieces of evidence from A that show that Florence was a wealthy city.
2.   What is a guild?
3.   How can you tell from B that Florence was a wealthy city? Give two reasons for your answer.
4.   What was the main industry of the city, do you think? Give a reason for your answer.
5.   Where would the merchants have sourced their silk?

## Why were there so few famous women in the Renaissance?

As you read about famous artists and writers of the Renaissance you will notice that they were mainly men.

### Activity 5
KS

Examine these sources from the 1500s and then answer the questions below.

> Our parents have the laudable [well-meaning] custom
> In order to deprive us of our wits
> Of keeping us locked up at home
> And of handing us the spindle [part of a spinning wheel] instead of a pen.

**SOURCE 5.6: Madeleine des Roches, a French writer in the 1500s, from *Women and Gender in Early Modern Europe* by Merry E. Wiesner, 2000**

> … this we know, that she was not damned along with her sex to dullness and stupidity.

**SOURCE 5.7: Words of male scholar Angelo Politian about fellow Renaissance Italian scholar Cassandra Fedele, from *Women and Gender in Early Modern Europe* by Merry E. Wiesner, 2000**

1 Summarise in your own words what each writer is saying about the general view of women in the 1500s.

2 What do these comments tell you about attitudes to women at this time?

### DO YOU UNDERSTAND THESE KEY TERMS?

| | |
|---|---|
| city-state | patron |
| humanism | Renaissance |

PowerPoint summary

During the Renaissance most people believed that a woman's role was to be a good housekeeper and a good mother. Learning was for men, not for women. When sons went to school, most daughters stayed at home and learned household skills. Women were not allowed to attend universities and most never learned to read and write. They were not welcomed into the male-dominated areas of painting, sculpting, writing, architecture and science.

### Activity 6
KS

Examine this source and then answer the questions below.

> Up to the Middle Ages most healers were women. But during the Renaissance women were not allowed to attend lectures and demonstrations in anatomy and new medical learning. They were banned from the surgeon guilds. By the late 1600s, even midwives who helped women during childbirth were mainly men!

**SOURCE 5.8: from *Women and Gender in Early Modern Europe* by Merry E. Wiesner, 2000**

1 What point is the writer making in this extract?

2 In the 1500s women were thought to be intellectually inferior to men. Does the evidence in this modern source and in the two sources from the 1500s in Activity 5 support that viewpoint? Justify your answer.

## SELF-ASSESSMENT – CAN YOU?

1 Explain what the Renaissance was, giving at least two examples.

2 Outline two differences between the way medieval and Renaissance people thought.

3 Explain what 'humanism' means in relation to the Renaissance.

4 Give four reasons why the Renaissance began in Italy, choose the one you think is most important and justify your choice.

5 Explain patronage and name one Renaissance patron

6 Decide whether the Renaissance would have been possible without patrons and decide why or why not.

7 List two sources of information from this section that you can use to find out about what happened during the Renaissance.

8 Outline why people in Renaissance times thought there was no need to educate women.

9 Give two reasons why there were so few women artists in the Renaissance.

# HOW DID VISUAL ARTS CHANGE IN THE RENAISSANCE?

## LEARNING INTENTIONS

**At the end of this section, you should be able to:**

◎ Outline how painting changed in the Renaissance

◎ Discuss some of the great Renaissance artists and their work

◎ Identify some female Renaissance artists

◎ Outline how sculpture changed in the Renaissance

◎ Discuss Michelangelo Buonarroti and his work

◎ Outline how architecture changed in the Renaissance

◎ Discuss some of the great Renaissance architects and their work.

## How did painting change in the Renaissance?

### Activity 1

Examine these sources and then answer the questions below.

**SOURCE 5.9:** Medieval painting of the Virgin Mary and Jesus

**SOURCE 5.10:** Renaissance painting of the Virgin Mary and Jesus

1  Based on the above sources, list four differences between medieval and Renaissance paintings. Look at the colours, the details in the pictures and the depiction of the Virgin Mary.

2  Which is more realistic, A or B? Explain your answer.

**Visual arts**
The arts that we appreciate through sight, for example painting, drawing, sculpture, architecture.

Renaissance artists developed new techniques to make their paintings more lifelike.

❭ **Anatomy:** Some artists cut up dead bodies to find out where the bones were and how the muscles worked. Their knowledge of anatomy made their paintings of bodies more accurate.

❭ **Perspective:** Artists began to paint people and objects at the back of the picture smaller than those at the front. This gives the illusion of depth and space (perspective) in a painting.

❭ **Sfumato:** Artists used tiny brush strokes to blend areas into each other and avoid hard outlines. This technique is called **sfumato**, from the Latin word meaning 'smoke'. It produces a hazy effect. They used it to paint very realistic shadows and skin tones.

**Anatomy**
The study of the human body.

**Perspective**
Adding depth to a picture.

> **Oil paint:** Medieval painters mixed their colours with egg white. It dried quickly so they had little time to get the effects they wanted. Renaissance artists began to mix their paints using **linseed oil**. Oil paints dried more slowly and gave artists time to work in more detail.

> **Canvas:** Medieval artists painted on wooden boards, whereas Renaissance artists started to use canvas to paint on. The paint dries more slowly on canvas, making it less likely to crack.

Two popular forms of Renaissance painting were **portraits** and **frescos**. A fresco is a painting done directly onto wet plaster. Frescos were used to decorate the walls and ceilings of churches and houses.

These changes started in Italy, but soon artists came from all over Europe to see the new art and apply it to their own work.

**Canvas**
Cloth from which sails are made. It makes a good surface for painting when stretched tight.

**Portrait**
A picture of a real person.

**Fresco**
A picture painted straight onto a wall or ceiling. The paint is applied to wet plaster.

SOURCE 5.11: *Mona Lisa* (1503–06) by Leonardo da Vinci

SOURCE 5.12: Portrait of Leonardo da Vinci

## Special Study: Leonardo da Vinci (1452–1519)

**Leonardo da Vinci** was one of the greatest geniuses of the Renaissance. He was a marvellous **painter and inventor**.

Leonardo was born in 1452 near Florence, in Vinci, which is where he got his name. At fifteen he was apprenticed to **Verrocchio**, a leading Florentine artist, and learned to paint.

After Florence became involved in war, Leonardo moved to Milan. There he painted *The Last Supper* (see Source 5.13) on the wall of a convent church. It was a fresco, but Leonardo tried out a new recipe for making the paint. It did not work. Soon after the picture was done, the paint began to peel away.

## Activity 2

Examine this source and answer the questions below.

SOURCE 5.13: *The Last Supper* (1495–6), a fresco by Leonardo da Vinci

1 Describe the use of perspective in this painting.
2 Symmetry was very important in Renaissance painting. Identify three different mathematical shapes in the painting.
3 Describe the emotions you see on the faces of the apostles.
4 How is Jesus feeling, do you think?

**Symmetry**
Where two sides or parts are even or balanced.

SOURCE 5.14: *The Virgin of the Rocks* (1483–6)

Leonardo was the first artist to use sfumato. You can see it in his most famous picture, the **Mona Lisa** (see Source 5.11). The scenery in the background is typical of a Renaissance painting. People have argued for a long time about the expression on her face. Is it one of sadness or happiness? What do you think?

Another well-known painting, **The Virgin of the Rocks** (see Source 5.14), depicts the Virgin Mary with baby Jesus, John the Baptist and an angel. The angel is meant to show Leonardo's ideal of female beauty.

Leonardo had a strong **interest in nature, plants and animals**. He made great discoveries. He worked out how rocks were formed and how to tell the age of a tree by counting the rings.

Leonardo always carried **notebooks** with him so he could jot down any ideas he had. When he wrote in his notebooks he used mirror writing (from right to left). For that reason no one read his notes until many years after his death. Today, we have over 5,000 pages of his notebooks. They contain diagrams of machines as well as notes on botany, geology and engineering.

SOURCE 5.15: Leonardo's notebook sketch of rushes

Leonardo **invented several weapons of war** for Sforza, the Duke of Milan, such as a tank and a cannon. His notebooks were full of new ideas including designs for a helicopter, a submarine and a parachute. But Sforza would not give any funding for them.

## DID YOU KNOW?

Leonardo said, 'A bird is an instrument working according to mechanical law.' His notebooks contain designs for a 'flying machine'. Modern archaeologists constructed the helicopter-type design shown here from his notebooks. It stayed in the air for 30 seconds.

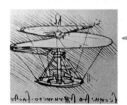 

SOURCE 5.16: Leonardo's design and a modern reconstruction of it

When a French army captured Milan, Leonardo had to leave. The King of France invited Leonardo to France to work for him. He died there three years later.

## Some other famous Renaissance artists

### Raphael (1483–1520)

Another Italian painter was **Raphael Sanzio**. Raphael became famous for his paintings of the **Madonna** (Mary, the mother of Jesus – see Source 5.2. The paintings were modelled on real women.

**Activity 3**

Examine this source and then answer the questions below.

SOURCE 5.17: *The School of Athens* (1509–11) by Raphael (featuring people from Ancient Greece and Rome)

1  What Renaissance artistic techniques does this picture show? Give two examples.
2  How else would you know that it is a Renaissance painting?

### Pieter Bruegel the Elder (c.1525–1569)

Belgian artist **Pieter Bruegel the Elder** is famous for his paintings of **scenery and nature**. He was the first European painter to paint landscapes for their own sake rather than as a backdrop to something else. Most of his paintings of the countryside tell a story or have a moral message. Bruegel also painted **ordinary people**. This was rare at that time because most artists painted portraits of rich people who could pay them. Both his sons became artists, with Pieter Bruegel the Younger copying his father's style.

## Activity 4

Examine this source and then answer the questions below.

1. Identify three features of Renaissance art in this painting.
2. List three things we can learn about everyday life in Belgium in the 1500s from this painting.
3. Describe the expressions on the people's faces.
4. Some art historians believe that Bruegel was sorry for the peasants because they were so poor and uneducated. He wanted to show in his paintings that they didn't have much chance in life. Does *Peasant Wedding* support this view? Give reasons for your answer.

SOURCE 5.18: *Peasant Wedding* (1567) by Pieter Bruegel the Elder

## Activity 5

Examine these sources and then answer the questions below.

SOURCE 5.19: *The Harvesters* (1565) by Pieter Bruegel the Elder

SOURCE 5.20: *Winter Landscape with a Bird Trap* (1601) by Pieter Bruegel the Younger

1. Name the four artists and their nationalities.
2. How long did it take El Greco to complete his painting of St Martin?
3. Identify any differences between this artwork and the paintings of the Italian artists you have seen already.
4. Identify two features in these paintings that are similar to Italian Renaissance art.
5. Why is Dürer's painting *Young Hare* so unusual for the time?

SOURCE 5.21: *Young Hare* (1502) by German artist Albrecht Dürer

SOURCE 5.22: *St Martin and the Beggar* (1597–9) by Spanish artist El Greco

## Were there female artists?

Although they were few in number, there were some female Renaissance painters. For example:

> **Artemisia Gentileschi** (1593–c.1653), who was Italian and drew women in most of her works. It was difficult for female artists to draw men as they were forbidden to study the male nude.

> **Judith Leyster** (1609–1660), who was Dutch and painted domestic scenes and still lifes.

> **Rachel Ruysch** (1664–1750), another Dutch artist who specialised in still lifes.

---

**KS**          **Activity 6**

Examine this source and then answer the questions below.

SOURCE 5.23: *Self-Portrait* (1630) by Leyster

1. What do you learn about Judith Leyster from this self-portrait? Suggest at least two ideas.
2. Identify two features of Renaissance painting in this portrait.
3. Is there any difference between the paintings you have seen by male artists and those by female artists in this section? (*Hint:* Look at the themes of the paintings.)

---

SOURCE 5.24: *Self-Portrait* (1638–9) by Gentileschi

SOURCE 5.25: *Flower Still Life* (c. 1726) by Ruysch

**Still life**
Painting of an object (e.g. a vase of flowers or a bowl of fruit).

## How did sculpture change in the Renaissance?

### Activity 7

Examine this source and then answer the questions below.

SOURCE 5.26: Statues carved on a Gothic church

1  What is a Gothic church?
2  Do these statues look realistic? Why/why not?
3  What is a sculpture? What is the name of the person who makes a sculpture?

Medieval sculptors carved statues that were part of buildings, usually churches. These statues were not lifelike. Older Greek and Roman statues stood alone and were skilfully carved to show the human body as it really was. Renaissance sculptors copied them and made realistic figures. **Renaissance sculpture is lifelike and not part of a building.** Many Renaissance statues are nudes.

## Special Study: Michelangelo Buonarroti (1475–1564)

The greatest sculptor of the Renaissance was **Michelangelo Buonarroti**. He was born near Florence. His father apprenticed him to a sculptor when he was thirteen. **Lorenzo de' Medici** saw his work and invited Michelangelo to join the school for sculptors in his palace.

SOURCE 5.28: Portrait of Michelangelo

**Sculptor**
An artist who makes statues or other sculptures, using stone, metal or wood.

**Nude**
An artwork of a person who is not wearing any clothes.

After Lorenzo's death, Michelangelo went to Rome. There he made a marble statue called the **Pietà**, which means 'sorrow'. It shows Mary holding Jesus after his death on the cross. Notice how realistic the folds in the material look.

**Pietà**
Any artwork showing Mary holding the dead Jesus in her arms.

SOURCE 5.27: *David* (c. 1430) by Donatello

SOURCE 5.29: Michelangelo's *Pietà* (1498–99)

To celebrate Florence's victory in a war with France, the town council held a competition and Michelangelo won the contract. Florence's victory reminded Michelangelo of the biblical story of the boy David defeating the giant Goliath. He found a block of white marble and carved a huge statue, *David*. It is five metres high. Notice how you can see every vein and muscle.

SOURCE 5.30:
**Michelangelo's** *David*
(1501–4)

### Activity 8

1 Today a copy of Michelangelo's *David* stands in the central square of Florence. The original is kept in a museum. Suggest two possible reasons for this.

2 How, do you think, was Michelangelo able to sculpt David's muscles so accurately?

3 What material is this statue made of?

4 Which is the better sculpture: Donatello's *David* or Michelangelo's *David*? Give a reason for your choice.

5 How could you tell that these statues were made in the Renaissance period? Give two reasons.

**Pope Julius II** hired Michelangelo to paint frescos on the ceiling of the **Sistine Chapel** in the Vatican. For four years he worked on the frescos. They depict the Bible story of the creation of the world, from God creating Adam to Noah and the flood. When he finished, the whole ceiling was covered with over 300 figures. The figures are life-size and done in beautiful colours. It is one of the greatest masterpieces of all time. Would you agree?

SOURCE 5.31: Part of the ceiling of the Sistine Chapel called *The Creation of Adam* (1512)

Michelangelo was also a great **architect**. Before his death he designed the great dome of **St Peter's Basilica** in Rome.

# How did architecture change in the Renaissance?

Renaissance architects turned away from the medieval Gothic style and brought in their own ways of building that were based on the ideas of the Greeks and the Romans. The table below summarises the differences between the two architectural styles.

**Pediment**
Structure in architecture, usually triangular, that is supported by columns.

| Gothic style | Renaissance style |
| --- | --- |
| Spires | Domes |
| Less symmetry | More symmetry |
| Pointed arches | Rounded arches |
| Flying buttresses | Pediments and columns |

## The dome

The first famous architect of the Renaissance was **Filippo Brunelleschi** (1377–1446). He built the dome on the cathedral in Florence. It took sixteen years to complete and became part of the typical architecture of the Renaissance.

## Symmetry

All Renaissance buildings followed an exact **symmetrical plan**. Houses had the same number of windows on each side of the door. Churches had the same number of arches on each side of the aisle.

**KS** — Activity 9

Examine this source and then answer the questions below.

SOURCE 5.33: St Peter's Basilica, Rome

1  What is a basilica?
2  What Roman influences can you see in this architecture? Give two examples.

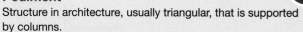
SOURCE 5.32: Cathedral in Florence with Brunelleschi's dome

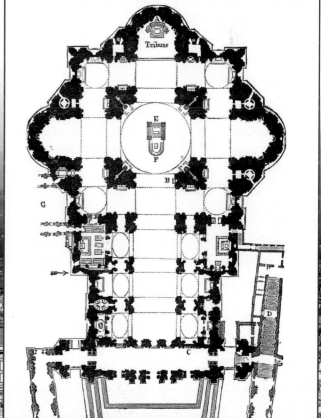
SOURCE 5.34: Raphael's unused plan for St Peter's Basilica. Notice how symmetrical it is.

## Other features

**Rounded arches** became hugely popular and architects used them to support and decorate buildings. **Pediments** and **columns** in the Roman style became fashionable again. Look at the house in Source 5.35 designed by the architect **Andrea Palladio** (1508–1580). He designed 150 houses for wealthy Italians. His style became known as **Palladian**, and can be seen in houses and important buildings all over the world.

---

KS    **Activity 10**

Examine this source and then answer the questions below.

SOURCE 5.35: Villa 'La Rotonda', designed by Palladio

1    How many columns can you see in this photo of the Rotonda villa?
2    Can you find any rounded arches?
3    Can you guess how many columns there would be in the whole building?
4    Can you identify three features of Roman architecture in this building?
5    Give an example of symmetry in this building.

---

## Activity 11

KS 👥

Imagine that you are working in an art gallery. You have been asked to explain to a group of young people how art changed during the Renaissance. You need to:

- Mention five things to look out for in Renaissance art
- Explain how these ideas or techniques were different from medieval art
- Briefly describe three paintings by Italian artists that illustrate your ideas
- Refer to a non-Italian artist and explain how their art might differ from Italian art
- Tell your group which is your favourite painting and explain why.

## Activity 12

KS

1. Describe three main changes in (a) sculpture and (b) architecture in the Renaissance. Use diagrams to illustrate your answer.
2. Which is your favourite development in either architecture or sculpture? Explain why you chose this feature.
3. Many newer buildings have been built in the Palladian style. Find out the names and locations of two of these buildings in Ireland and write a short account of each.

## DO YOU UNDERSTAND THESE KEY TERMS?

| | | | | | |
|---|---|---|---|---|---|
| anatomy | fresco | nude | perspective | sculptor | symmetry |
| canvas | Madonna | oil paint | pietà | sfumato | visual arts |
| dome | mirror writing | pediment | portrait | still life | |

 PowerPoint summary

# SELF-ASSESSMENT – CAN YOU?

1. List two ways in which a Renaissance painting differs from a medieval painting.
2. Describe how Renaissance artists began to mix their paints. Say why this was better than the method used by medieval artists.
3. What was a painting on a wall called? Where else did Renaissance artists use this technique?
4. Describe one of Leonardo da Vinci's paintings, and name two of the techniques he used in the picture.
5. Explain what was strange about Leonardo's notebooks.
6. List two of Leonardo's discoveries.
7. Name one other Italian Renaissance painter and one of his/her pictures.
8. Describe the features that identify a painting as being from the Renaissance, using Leonardo's *Virgin of the Rocks* (Source 5.14) or any other painting in this section as an example.
9. Name two famous Renaissance artists from outside Italy and one work by each of them.
10. Give two reasons why Bruegel's paintings are so famous.
11. Name two features of medieval sculpture and three features of Renaissance sculpture.
12. Name the most famous Renaissance sculptor and two of his patrons.
13. List three features of Renaissance architecture and explain where the ideas for them came from.
13. Name two Italian architects and say why they are famous.

Learning Outcome 3.7

## ⊚ LEARNING INTENTIONS

**At the end of this section, you should be able to:**

◎ Discuss the invention of printing and how it changed the world

◎ Explain how literature changed in the Renaissance

◎ Identify some female Renaissance writers.

## How did books change in the Renaissance?

Ever since writing was invented, books (known as **manuscripts**) had been written by hand. It was a very slow process, which meant that books were rare and expensive. Only rich people like the Medicis or the popes could afford to own more than one or two books. Most people were **illiterate**. But all that changed when **printing** was introduced to Europe during the Renaissance.

**Illiterate**
Unable to read or write.

The Chinese invented printing. They carved pictures in wood or metal and pressed them onto paper. Around 1439 **Johannes Gutenberg** in Europe invented a **printing press** that used **moveable type**. Gutenberg was a goldsmith from Mainz in Germany. His system made it much quicker and cheaper to produce a book.

**Moveable type**
Small metal letters used to make words; they can be reused over and over again.

**SOURCE 5.36: Printing a book**

This is how a printing press worked:
1  The men put the letters of the alphabet into separate compartments.
2  A printer lays out the letters on a frame to make a page.
3  The apprentice covers each page with ink.
4  The hand screw press brings the page down on to the paper.
5  The newly printed sheets of paper are hung up to dry.
6  A boy stacks up the printed sheets. Later they will be bound together to make a book.
7  The master printer oversees the work.

## 🔍 DID YOU KNOW?

Gutenberg produced the first printed book in Europe. It was a copy of the Bible and had 1,300 pages. Only forty-seven copies of it still exist. The estimated value of one copy is about $30 million!

Printing spread quickly. By 1500 there were over a thousand printers working in Europe and over one million printed books had appeared.

## Activity 1

Examine this source and then answer the questions below.

SOURCE 5.37: Gutenberg's printed Bible on display

1  What language is this book written in, do you think?
2  How does this book look different from a modern book?
3  Suggest three ways in which access to printed books would have changed people's lives.

## How did printing change the world?

The invention of printing is one of the most important events in human history. It changed the world in many ways. For example:

> Books became much cheaper, so more people could afford to own them.
> Books were easily available, so more people learned to read and write.
> New ideas spread more easily because people could write and read books about them.
> It became harder for kings or popes to stop a new idea that they disliked, because people could make many copies of a book about it. We will see in Section 7 how this helped the Reformation to develop.

## Activity 2

A Spanish writer, Miguel de Cervantes, wrote a novel called *Don Quixote* in 1605. It is a funny story about the travels of an idealistic knight and his world-weary servant. It was one of the first books to tell the story of ordinary people such as shepherds and innkeepers.

Examine this source and then answer the question below.

'Hunger is the best sauce in the world.'

'… he who's down one day can be up the next, unless he really wants to stay in bed, that is …'

'Thou hast seen nothing yet.'

SOURCE 5.38: Quotes from *Don Quixote* by Cervantes

1  Do you find it easy to understand what Cervantes is saying? Change these excerpts into your own words.

## How did literature change in the Renaissance?

Most medieval manuscripts were written in Latin. During the Renaissance people wanted to read books written in their own language, so writers began to write in the everyday language of the people. This is called **vernacular literature**.

Writers also began to write more about everyday human problems and less about religious themes. New styles of literature such as **plays** and, later, **novels** became popular.

**Vernacular literature**
Literature written in the everyday language of the people (e.g. Spanish, Irish, English) and not in classical Greek or Latin.

**DID YOU KNOW?**

In the ninth century the biggest library in Europe had only 36 books!

# Special Study: William Shakespeare (1564–1616)

A famous Renaissance writer who wrote in English was **William Shakespeare**. Shakespeare was born in Stratford-upon-Avon in England. He lived in the time of Queen Elizabeth I (1533–1603).

Shakespeare was one of the owners of a theatre company who performed at the royal court and at their own open-air theatre, the **Globe**, on the banks of the River Thames in London.

The Globe could hold 3,000 people. Poor people stood in the pit below the stage and wealthier people had seats in the balconies or galleries. Plays were put on during the day, when it was bright.

Shakespeare's plays included **histories** such as *Henry V* and *Richard III*, **comedies** such as *Twelfth Night* and *As You Like It*, and **tragedies** such as *Hamlet* and *Romeo and Juliet*. Like many Renaissance writers, he based some of his plots on stories from Ancient Greece or Rome (e.g. *Antony and Cleopatra* and *Julius Caesar*).

His characters are often kings and queens and nobles, but there are always ordinary people in his plays as well. He wrote about **everyday problems** and the common mistakes people make in their relationships with others. His plays are still popular today because they deal with our shared **human emotions** such as love and jealousy.

SOURCE 5.41: William Shakespeare

SOURCE 5.42: Artist's impression of the Globe, where Shakespeare's theatre company performed plays. Both male and female roles were acted by men.

## Activity 3

Examine the sources and answer the questions below.

> My drops of tears I'll turn to sparks of fire.

SOURCE 5.39: Shakespeare, *Henry VIII*, Act II, Scene iv

> This above all: to thine own self be true,
> And it must follow, as the night the day,
> Thou canst not then be false to any man.

SOURCE 5.40: Shakespeare, *Hamlet*, Act I, Scene iii

1. What is Shakespeare saying in these extracts? Explain in your own words.
2. How do you know that these quotations are from a Renaissance and not a medieval writer? Give two reasons.

## Were there female writers?

There were some famous female scholars and writers during the Renaissance. For example:

> An Italian, **Isabelle d'Este** (1474–1539), collected manuscripts and made her own translations of Greek and Roman authors.

> A German-Dutch woman, **Anna Maria van Schurman** (1607–1678), was so brilliant at school that she got special permission to attend lectures at the University of Utrecht in Holland. Even then she had to stand behind a curtain! She knew fourteen languages, including Hebrew, Arabic, Latin and Greek, and she wrote an Ethiopian grammar book.

Most female scholars came from very wealthy families and they were often related to male scholars. While it became accepted practice for noble and very rich women to have private tutors, the Renaissance did not bring great learning opportunities for the majority of women.

**SOURCE 5.43: Anna Maria van Schurman**

### DO YOU UNDERSTAND THESE KEY TERMS?

| | |
|---|---|
| comedy | play |
| illiterate | tragedy |
| moveable type | vernacular literature |
| novel | |

PowerPoint summary

## SELF-ASSESSMENT – CAN YOU?

1. Explain why books were so expensive before the Renaissance.
2. Name the person who first used moveable type in Europe.
3. Explain how books were printed in the Renaissance.
4. Name the first printed book in Europe and explain why it is so valuable now.
5. List two ways in which Renaissance writing differed from medieval literature.
6. Define 'vernacular literature', name two famous writers who wrote in the vernacular and say where they came from.
7. Explain why plays were so popular in sixteenth-century England.
8. List three ways in which printing changed the world.
9. Decide what you think was the most important change brought about by the invention of printing and give a reason for your choice.
10. Name one female writer of the Renaissance.

# HOW DID SCIENCE CHANGE IN THE RENAISSANCE?

## LEARNING INTENTIONS

**At the end of this section, you should be able to:**

◎ Discuss the new ideas in medicine during the Renaissance

◎ Discuss the new ideas in astronomy during the Renaissance

◎ Explain who Galileo was and describe his work.

◎ Assess the importance of the Renaissance.

## How did medicine change in the Renaissance?

During the Middle Ages people knew a lot about **herbal medicine**, but doctors did not understand how the human body worked. They based their ideas on the writings of an Ancient Greek doctor called **Galen**. But Galen had never dissected the human body and many of his ideas were wrong.

The Church banned the dissection of bodies in 1300. It believed that the human body should be left intact for the next world. This made it difficult for doctors to find out about the organs of the human body and how they work.

The most common killer diseases were plague, typhoid, smallpox and measles. Nobody knew what caused them. They did not know about germs or bacteria.

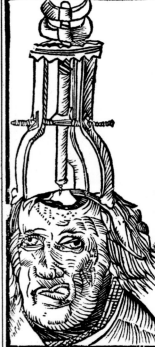

**SOURCE 5.44: Engravings from 1525. Medieval doctors believed that drilling holes in the skull could cure mental disorders.**

**SOURCE 5.45: A blood-letting**

🔍 **DID YOU KNOW?**

The most common cure for any illness at this time was **blood-letting**. Doctors cut a person's arm to make it bleed. They believed the 'bad' blood was being let out.

## Breakthroughs

In 1543 **Andreas Vesalius** published the first accurate drawings of the human body. He held public dissections at Padua University and huge crowds of students came to see them. He even stole bodies from graveyards in order to dissect them. His book *On the Fabric of the Human Body* has 270 drawings of every part of the human body and is still used today. He is called the **'Father of Anatomy'**.

In 1575 a French army surgeon called **Ambroise Paré** developed a new way of treating wounds. Up to this time gunshot wounds had been treated by pouring boiling elderberry oil on the wound and sealing it with red hot irons. Paré began using an ointment made of egg yolk and turpentine on the wound. He then bandaged it to keep it clean. He also found ways of stopping soldiers bleeding to death and new ways of binding arms. He is often regarded today as the **'Father of Modern Surgery'**. However, he was not allowed to become a member of a surgeons' guild because he did not know Latin.

**DID YOU KNOW?**

Paré wrote: 'I would rather do the right thing on my own than follow the guidance of experts and do the wrong thing.'

### Activity 1

Examine these sources and then answer the questions below.

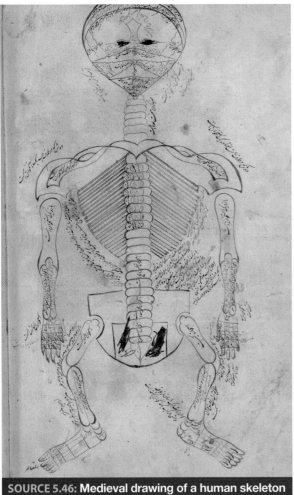

**SOURCE 5.46: Medieval drawing of a human skeleton**

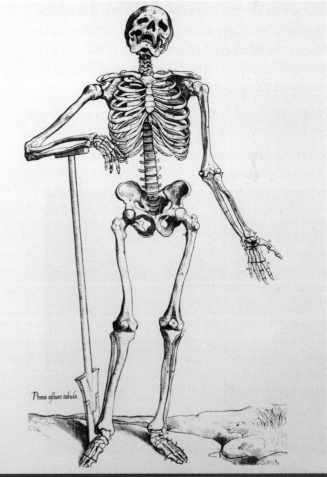

**SOURCE 5.47: Vesalius's drawing of a human skeleton**

1. What faults can you see in the medieval drawing?
2. List three differences between the medieval drawing and Vesalius's drawing.

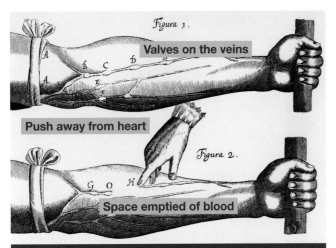

Figura 1.

**Valves on the veins**

**Push away from heart**

Figura 2.

**Space emptied of blood**

SOURCE 5.48: **Harvey's experiment on blood circulation**

In 1628 an English doctor called **William Harvey** discovered how blood circulated round the body. Galen had written that blood was burned up in the body and remade in the liver. But Harvey showed that the heart pumped blood round the body.

He observed that if you tightly bandage your upper arm, you can see the valves in your veins. Then if you push with your finger away from the heart the space between the two valves (O and H on the sketch) will empty of blood. This proved that the blood is going only one way round the body.

## How did astronomy change in the Renaissance?

In the Middle Ages people believed that the Earth was at the centre of the universe. Every day they saw the sun rise in the east, move across the sky and set in the west; the moon and planets also moved across the sky. So people believed they moved around the Earth, which stood still. The Bible and the Church supported this theory. Two Renaissance astronomers – **Copernicus** and **Galileo** – had different ideas.

### Nicholas Copernicus (1473–1543)

**Nicholas Copernicus** was a Polish priest. Every day he watched the movements of the sun, moon and stars. Using mathematics, he worked out that **the Earth revolves round the sun**, and not the other way around. However, there were no telescopes then, so he could not prove his idea.

SOURCE 5.50: Nicholas Copernicus

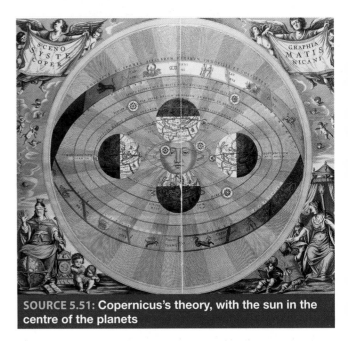

SOURCE 5.51: Copernicus's theory, with the sun in the centre of the planets

### Activity 2

KS

Examine this source and then answer the questions below.

SOURCE 5.49: **Harvey demonstrating his theory of blood circulation to Charles I of England**

1　Why would Harvey demonstrate this to the king?

2　This is a painting. How can a painting help historians find out about the past? Explain your answer.

**Astronomy**
The study of the universe, including the sun, moon, stars and planets.

## Galileo Galilei (1564–1642)

**Galileo Galilei** was born in Pisa in Italy. He believed that all the laws of nature could be proved by calculation and experiment.

### Activity 3

Examine the source and answer the question below.

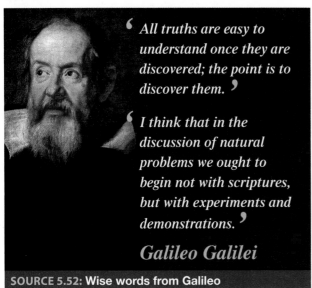

' All truths are easy to understand once they are discovered; the point is to discover them. '

' I think that in the discussion of natural problems we ought to begin not with scriptures, but with experiments and demonstrations. '

*Galileo Galilei*

SOURCE 5.52: **Wise words from Galileo**

1   What was Galileo saying about science?

Dutchman **Hans Lippershey** invented the telescope in 1608, but Galileo designed and built a more powerful version. Galileo's telescope could magnify something thirty-two times. He built over one hundred telescopes and was the first person to use the telescope to study the skies.

Galileo was able to see things no human being had ever seen before. He realised that **Copernicus was right**. The Earth could not be the centre of the universe. The sun was the centre of the solar system and the Earth moved round it.

When the Catholic Church heard about Galileo's theories, it banned his books. The Church believed that the Earth had to be the centre of the universe because the Earth was created by God. It is where Christ was born.

Galileo published his findings in a book known as the *Dialogue*. The pope summoned him to Rome, where he was put on trial. The trial was held in secret. Galileo was very ill when he attended. Afraid that he was going to be burned at the stake, Galileo finally agreed to say he was wrong. He was not allowed to write about astronomy after this, but his ideas still lived on.

**Magnify**
Make things look bigger.

### DID YOU KNOW?

Galileo was the first to come up with the idea of a pendulum clock. This is a mechanical clock powered by a pendulum. Christiaan Huygens made the first clock in 1656.

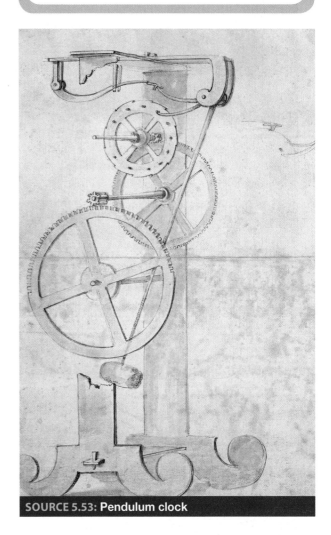

SOURCE 5.53: **Pendulum clock**

SOURCE 5.54: **Galileo's telescope 1610, replica**

## Activity 4

Examine this source and then answer the questions below.

SOURCE 5.55: Trial of Galileo, Rome, 1633

1   The men on the left with red hats are called cardinals. Who are cardinals?
2   Was this painted during the trial or after, do you think? Give a reason for your answer.
3   From what you have read about the trial, identify two historical inaccuracies in the painting.

## What was the importance of the Renaissance?

The Renaissance changed the way people in Europe did things and the way they thought about the world. These changes have influenced the modern world. Here are just a few of the changes the Renaissance brought.

### New skills and discoveries

> Art: perspective, sfumato, humanism.
> Medicine: anatomy, blood circulation.
> Science: experiments, the Earth moves round the sun, telescope, pendulum clock.

### Invention of printing

> Made books more available and cheaper.
> Encouraged more people to read and write.
> Helped ideas to spread more quickly.

## Activity 5

Examine this source and then answer the questions below.

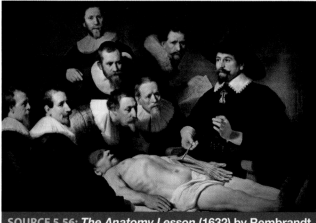

SOURCE 5.56: *The Anatomy Lesson* (1632) by Rembrandt

1   Why were examinations of dead bodies such as that shown here not very common before the Renaissance?
2   Why did Renaissance artists study anatomy?
3   What information does this painting give us about medical practice in the 1600s?

## Confidence grew

> People began to think for themselves.
> People challenged old ideas about geography and the human body.

## People questioned the Church

> People challenged the power of the Church, which led to the Reformation.

---

### Activity 6

Examine this source and then answer the questions below.

| Printing | Invention of moveable type (Gutenberg); books no longer copied by hand |
|---|---|
| Literature | Writers using vernacular languages, not Latin; Shakespeare (English) and Cervantes (Spanish) writing plays and novels about human interests such as love and revenge |
| Medicine | Better knowledge of the human skeleton (Vesalius); improved ways of treating wounds (Paré); recognition of circulation of the blood (Harvey) |
| Science | Importance of experimenting; telescope invented; pendulum clock invented (Galileo); proving that the Earth goes round the sun (Copernicus, Galileo) |

**SOURCE 5.57:** Advances made in learning during the Renaissance

1  Make a timeline of the scientific discoveries that had been made by 1650.
2  Which discovery, do you think, was the most important? Justify your answer.
3  Which discovery would have the greatest impact on ordinary people's lives?
4  Look back at what people believed in the Middle Ages about medicine. What had **not** changed in the Renaissance?
5  Look at the quotes from Paré (page 99) and Galileo (page 101). What did these two scientists believe about how new discoveries are made?

---

### DO YOU UNDERSTAND THESE KEY TERMS?

| | | | |
|---|---|---|---|
| anatomy | blood-letting | magnify | telescope |
| astronomy | circulation of the blood | pendulum clock | |

Chapter summary    Weblinks    PowerPoint summary

## SELF-ASSESSMENT – CAN YOU?

1  Outline two incorrect medical ideas held by medieval doctors.
2  Explain why it was almost impossible for medical experts to dissect bodies in the Middle Ages.
3  Outline why Vesalius is called the 'Father of Anatomy'.
4  Describe the new type of treatment that Paré came up with for soldiers' wounds.
5  Describe what William Harvey discovered.
6  Outline Copernicus's theory about the sun and the Earth.
7  Name the invention that Galileo developed and explain what it helped to prove.
8  Say who opposed Galileo's theories and explain why.

# HISTORY ALIVE

# 6 THE IMPACT OF PORTUGUESE AND SPANISH EXPLORATION

**What factors led to the Age of Exploration?**

 105

**Who were the main explorers?**

110

**What was the impact of the Age of Exploration?**

118

# WHAT FACTORS LED TO THE AGE OF EXPLORATION?

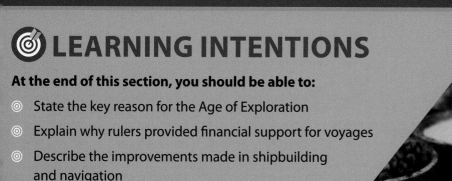

## LEARNING INTENTIONS

**At the end of this section, you should be able to:**

◎ State the key reason for the Age of Exploration

◎ Explain why rulers provided financial support for voyages

◎ Describe the improvements made in shipbuilding and navigation

◎ Discuss life on board a ship and the main dangers crews faced.

## What was the key reason for the Age of Exploration?

Sea voyages from Europe made many important discoveries about the world during the fifteenth and sixteenth centuries. This period has been called the **Age of Exploration** by historians.

The key reason for the Age of Exploration was the need to find a new sea route to Asia in order to gain control of the **spice trade**. Spices from Asia were worth a lot of money and control of this trade would make a country very wealthy.

Spices were used to flavour and preserve food. They were also used as medicines. The main spices used in Europe were:

> Cinnamon, which came from China

> Nutmeg and cloves from the Spice Islands (the Moluccas)

> Pepper, which was grown only in India.

Getting spices to Europe was difficult and dangerous in 1400. They were transported overland on a long and slow route known as the **Silk Road**. When the traders reached the Mediterranean, merchants from Genoa and Venice shipped the spices around Europe, where they were sold for a great profit.

### Activity 1

Examine these two maps and then answer the questions below.

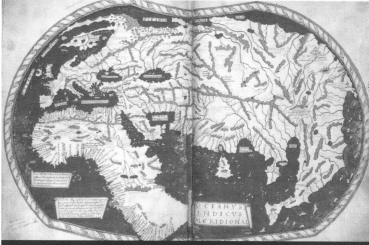

**SOURCE 6.1: The world as known by Europeans c. AD 1400**

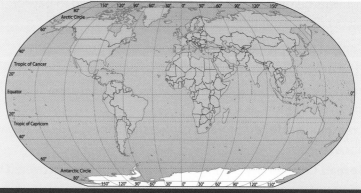

**SOURCE 6.2: The world as we know it today**

1 List three differences between the maps. (*Hint:* What is missing in the first map?)

2 How, do you think, did sea voyages from Europe change our knowledge of the world?

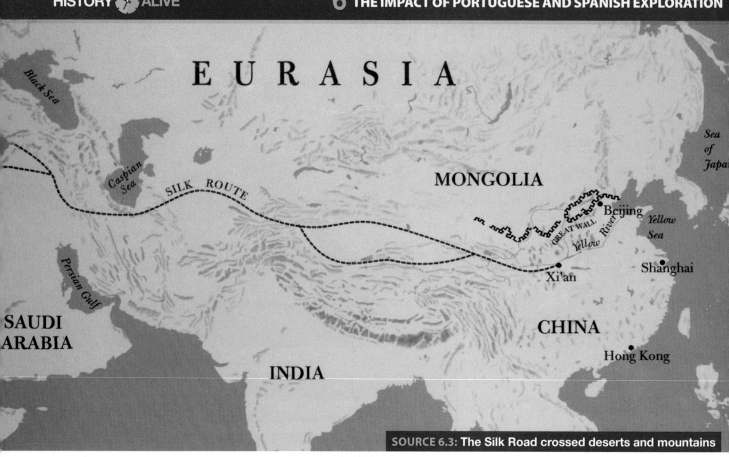

SOURCE 6.3: **The Silk Road crossed deserts and mountains**

> The Silk Road was controlled by Muslim rulers, who charged high taxes.
> Muslims and Christians were often at **war**, which frequently cut off trade.
> The capture of the Christian city of Constantinople (modern-day Istanbul in Turkey) in 1453 was an important factor in pushing the Europeans to find a new sea route to bring goods from Asia.

The Portuguese set off on voyages of discovery down the coast of Africa, the Spanish headed west and the English sought a northwest or northeast passage to Asia.

## Why did rulers provide money for voyages?

European explorers needed the permission and financial support of kings and queens before they set sail. Rulers were prepared to pay for the voyages of discovery because they wanted to:

> **Control the spice trade**, which would bring great wealth
> **Find other sources of wealth**, such as gold and precious jewels, in undiscovered lands (there were stories that great wealth could be discovered in Africa)
> **Create powerful empires** by conquering other lands as they were discovered
> **Spread Christianity** among the peoples of newly discovered lands.

The explorers themselves hoped to gain fame and wealth by making important discoveries. As with other areas of learning, the Renaissance brought a great curiosity and desire to find out about the world. One area where there was a particular interest was **mapmaking**. The invention of the printing press also meant that the accounts of voyages were widely read.

**Mapmaking**
The making of maps is also called cartography.

# How was shipbuilding changing?

Traditionally, ships on ocean-going voyages remained in sight of land. They relied on square sails, using the wind to power them. The square sail could catch the wind in only one direction. As a result the ships were slow and difficult to steer, especially into the wind. They were not suited to exploring close to the coast, where the water was shallow.

The Age of Exploration would not have been possible without improvements in ships and navigational instruments. These allowed ships to make longer and more dangerous voyages and have a good chance of returning home safely.

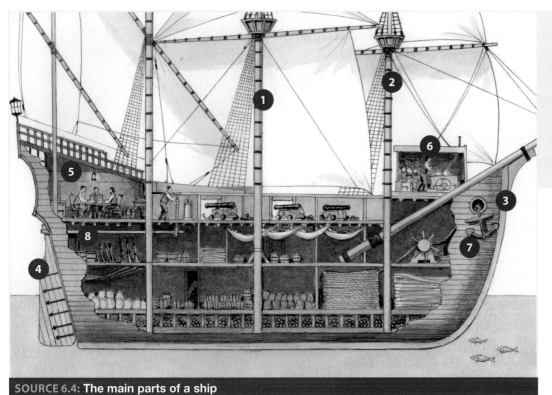

1  Main mast
2  Foremast
3  Bow of ship
4  Rudder for steering
5  Captain's cabin
6  Cook
7  Anchor
8  Guns

**SOURCE 6.4: The main parts of a ship**

Around 1450 the Portuguese invented a new type of ship called a **caravel**. The famous explorers of the time (e.g. **Bartolomeu Dias**, **Vasco da Gama** and **Christopher Columbus**) all used caravels on their voyages. Caravels had several advantages:

> They were **small, fast and easy to steer**.
> At first they had only triangular lateen sails but soon they used a combination of a square sail and triangular lateen sails. The lateen **sails could catch the wind in both directions** and allowed the ship to sail into the wind. These sails were copied from Arab ships in the Mediterranean.
> They had strong **clinker-built hulls** to protect the ships in storms.
> **Watertight decks** stopped water getting into the ship during bad weather.
> They were ideal for exploring as they could **sail close to the coast and up rivers**.

The main drawback of a caravel was that it could not carry much cargo. Later, bigger ships were built to overcome this problem.

**Hull**
Main body of a boat.

**Clinker-built**
Made with overlapping planks of wood.

**SOURCE 6.5: Drawing of a Portuguese caravel**

## How was navigation changing?

When going on a voyage it is vital to have some idea about where you are going – this is called **navigation**. To navigate properly, sailors need to know the ship's current position, the direction the ship is going in and the speed at which the ship is travelling. Traditionally, sailors relied on observing the sun or stars, wind speed and sea current. At this time a number of instruments were developed to help sailors navigate their ships.

### To calculate position

The ship's position north or south of the equator is called **latitude**. An instrument called an **astrolabe** was first used to measure latitude at sea by the Portuguese in the fifteenth century.

> It measured the angle of the sun or the North Star.
> It was difficult to use if the sea was rough, so sailors often went ashore to get a better reading.
> A similar instrument called a **quadrant** was also used.
> **Cross-staffs** were developed around 1500. They were not affected by stormy seas.

However, using all these instruments involved looking directly at the sun, which could damage sailors' eyesight.

### To calculate direction

Most ships were equipped with a **compass**.

> Originally invented by the Chinese, the compass was much improved by the start of the fifteenth century.
> A magnetic needle pointed to magnetic north.
> In order to use the compass in stormy seas, it was kept in a secure case on deck.
> At night it was read with the aid of a lamp.

### To calculate speed

Speed was measured using a newly developed technique called the **log and line**.

> A piece of wood (log) was thrown into the sea from the back of the boat. It was attached to a reel of knotted rope (line).
> The amount of rope that was pulled by the wood in one minute was then measured.
> Time was measured using a sand **hourglass**. Sailors would then be able to calculate the ship's speed by multiplying distance by time.

**DID YOU KNOW?**

North of the equator sailors usually relied on the North Star for navigation. South of the equator they used the sun.

**(KS)** **Activity 2**

SOURCE 6.6: An astrolabe measures latitude

Search online using the phrase 'How to use an astrolabe'. Write a brief explanation of how an astrolabe worked, using evidence from your research.

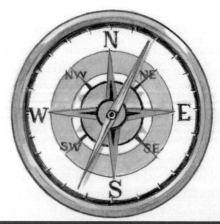

SOURCE 6.7: A compass measures direction

**Activity 3**

1 Find out the main navigational instruments that are used on ships today. Make two lists: one showing the instruments used around 1500, the other showing the instruments used today.

**DID YOU KNOW?**

Today the speed of a ship is still measured in knots based on the knotted rope used in the log and line. A knot is equal to 1.85 km per hour.

## Activity 4

Look at the picture and answer the question below.

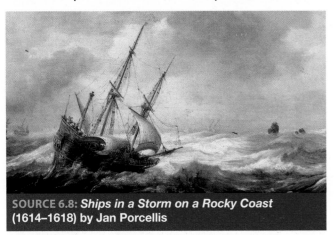

**SOURCE 6.8:** *Ships in a Storm on a Rocky Coast (1614–1618) by Jan Porcellis*

1  From evidence in the picture, describe two dangers ships faced.

## What was life like on board a ship?

Life at sea was tough.

> The ships were little bigger than modern yachts, they had no radio and if they got into trouble there was little chance of help.

> The **captain** was in charge of the ship and at times he could be very harsh on his crew. He was helped by the **first mate**.

> At mealtimes sailors ate with their fingers. Biscuits called **hardtack** were commonly eaten. Other foods included cheese, onions, dried beans, and fresh or salted fish.

> The lack of fresh fruit and vegetables could lead to a deadly disease called **scurvy**. This disease was the biggest killer on voyages during the Age of Exploration.

> A lack of fresh water was another major problem. Water was stored in barrels and it often went bad when the ship was at sea for a long time.

> Drinking infected water spread a horrible disease called **dysentery**. This was another big killer on voyages at the time.

Voyages during the Age of Exploration were very risky. Many sailors were afraid of sea monsters or of falling off the edge of the world. These fears were imaginary, but others were very real. The **main dangers** were: disease; storms, which could wreck wooden ships and drown those on board; attack by hostile natives; and hunger and thirst if food and water supplies ran out. Captains often set sail with twice the number of men they needed because they knew so many would die.

### DID YOU KNOW?

Scurvy was caused by a lack of vitamin C, which is normally consumed in fresh fruit and vegetables. The disease causes gums to bleed and teeth to fall out. When left untreated, it led to death. The simple cure – eat fresh fruit – was not discovered until the late 1700s.

### DO YOU UNDERSTAND THESE KEY TERMS?

| | | | | |
|---|---|---|---|---|
| astrolabe | cross-staffs | lateen sails | mapmaking | scurvy |
| caravel | dysentery | latitude | navigation | Silk Road |
| compass | hardtack | log and line | quadrant | spice trade |

PowerPoint summary

## SELF-ASSESSMENT – CAN YOU?

1  Explain why countries in Western Europe began to look for new routes to Asia.

2  Identify three spices that were popular in Europe and say what they were used for.

3  Outline two reasons why rulers were prepared to sponsor voyages of exploration.

4  Explain how the Renaissance influenced the Age of Exploration.

5  Examine the benefits of the caravel in voyages of exploration.

6  Describe how two instruments of navigation were used.

7  Explain why life on board a ship in the fifteenth century was very tough.

##  LEARNING INTENTIONS

**At the end of this section, you should be able to:**

◎ Outline the main achievements of the Portuguese explorers

◎ Discuss the impact of the Portuguese voyages

◎ Describe the voyages of Christopher Columbus and their impact

◎ Explain the contribution of Ferdinand Magellan to the Age of Exploration.

## What were the main achievements of the Portuguese explorers?

It was **Portugal** that began the Age of Exploration. In looking for a sea route to Asia and the Spice Islands, the Portuguese explorers mapped the coast of Africa and discovered Brazil.

### Prince Henry the Navigator (1394–1460)

**Prince Henry** was the man who started Portuguese exploration. He set up a **school for exploration at Sagres** on the southern tip of Portugal. Look at Activity 1 to see what happened there. Although he did not actually sail himself, Henry paid for ships to explore the coast of Africa. His role was similar to that of a Renaissance patron.

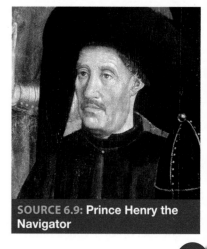

**SOURCE 6.9: Prince Henry the Navigator**

His sailors mapped the coastline of Africa on **portolan charts**. They discovered the islands of **Madeira** and the **Azores**. They also opened up trade links with African rulers, and gold and slaves began arriving in Portugal. By the time of Henry's death in 1460, over 2,400 kilometres of the African coastline had been mapped.

**Portolan charts**
Maps made of the coastline on voyages of discovery. Later voyages used these maps.

---

**KS** **Activity 1**

Read this description of the school at Sagres and answer the questions that follow.

> Henry gathered people from all nations to help him understand ... their navigation technology. The research center ... became famous throughout Europe. Henry invited the finest minds of navigation, the cleverest ship carpenters, the most accomplished navigators, the most knowledgeable cartographers (map makers), and the most experienced sea captains. This wise counsel helped Henry overcome the technological obstacles that prevented his captains from traversing the southern seas.

**SOURCE 6.10: from *Crossing The Ocean Sea* website by Mary Ames Mitchell**

1 What does this source tell us about the purpose of the school?
2 Identify the types of people Henry invited to Sagres.
3 What was the school's main benefit to Henry?

## Bartolomeu Dias (1450–1500)

The Portuguese continued to send ships down the African coast. One such voyage set off in 1487, led by an experienced sailor called **Bartolomeu Dias**.

> In January 1488 his ship was caught in a violent storm and lost sight of land for thirteen days.

> When the storm ended, he realised he had rounded the southern tip of Africa. His was the first European ship to enter the Indian Ocean.

Due to the stormy weather, Dias called the tip of Africa the **Cape of Storms**. However, the King of Portugal, **John II**, who wanted sailors to round the Cape again, renamed it the **Cape of Good Hope**.

## Vasco da Gama (1460–1524)

Vasco da Gama left Lisbon in 1497 with three ships to try to sail to Asia. He used the maps drawn by Dias and five months later had rounded the Cape of Good Hope. In May 1498 he reached the rich city of **Calicut** in India. This was a major trading port where spices from the East could be bought. Da Gama returned to Portugal in 1499.

SOURCE 6.11: Vasco da Gama

Da Gama had made one of the greatest discoveries in history, the sea route to Asia.

> It gave Portugal an opportunity to exploit the wealth of the **Spice Islands**.

> Despite the length of the voyage, the Portuguese were determined to keep control of this new route.

> Later Portuguese expeditions were not ones of discovery but of **conquest**.

> The Portuguese seized Goa in India and captured the main port in the Spice Islands. Da Gama died in India in 1524.

---

## Activity 2

Look at the map in pairs and answer the questions below.

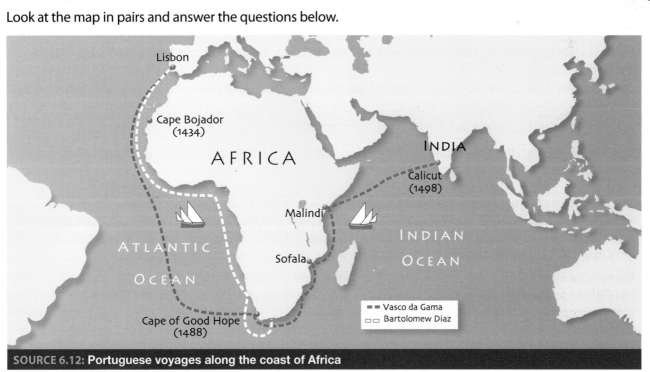

SOURCE 6.12: Portuguese voyages along the coast of Africa

1   Draw up a timeline of five important Portuguese discoveries – you can use your textbook to help you.

2   What was the major difference between da Gama's voyage and Dias's voyage in the Atlantic Ocean? Find out the reason for the difference by researching online.

## Activity 3

Pedro Cabral discovered Brazil in 1500.

1 Find out four facts about his voyage.

2 Name one long-term impact of his discovery that is still relevant today.

## What was the importance of the Portuguese voyages?

Portugal began the Age of Exploration and its expeditions of discovery had a number of important effects:

> Discovery of the sea route to the East

> Greatly improved knowledge of the coast of Africa

> Trade links were established with African rulers; gold and slaves were brought to Europe

> End of Muslim control of the spice trade

> Increased supply of spices made them more affordable for ordinary Europeans

> Portugal built a large empire in Asia and in Brazil.

## Activity 4

In groups of four, look at the picture below and answer the questions that follow.

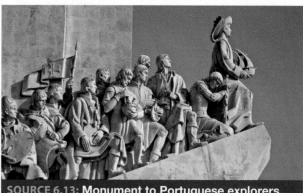

SOURCE 6.13: **Monument to Portuguese explorers, Belem, Lisbon**

1 Identify the figure leading the explorers. Why, do you think, was he put at the front of the monument?

2 What is the name of the type of ship he is holding in his hand?

3 How, do you think, are the explorers regarded in Portugal today? Explain your answer.

## DID YOU KNOW?

It was very important for countries to protect their discoveries. They would build a fort and send more voyages with soldiers and settlers. This was in order to show other countries that they had got there first and had made it their own.

## Activity 5

Examine this source, which describes the inhabitants of the coastal region of present-day South Africa, and then answer the questions below.

The inhabitants of this country are tawny-coloured [light brown]. Their food is confined to the flesh of seals, whales and gazelles, and the roots of herbs. They are dressed in skins ... Their numerous dogs resemble those of Portugal, and bark like them. The birds of the country, likewise, are the same as in Portugal ... The climate is healthy and temperate [mild], and produces good vegetation.

On the day after we had cast anchor, Thursday (November 9), we landed with the captain-major [da Gama], and made captive one of the natives, who was small of stature ... This man had been gathering honey in the sandy waste ... He was taken on board the captain-major's ship, and being placed at table he ate of all we ate. On the following day the captain-major had him well dressed and sent ashore.

SOURCE 6.14: **Extract from an account of da Gama's voyage to Calicut**

1 What did you learn about the inhabitants discovered by da Gama?

2 What similarities were there between the land described and Portugal?

3 Do you think the author admired da Gama? Give reasons for your answer.

## What role did Spain play in the Age of Exploration?

The other country that led the Age of Exploration was Spain.

> The Spanish tried to reach Asia by sailing westwards but instead stumbled on an unkown continent, America.

> It was discovered by the most famous explorer in history, **Christopher Columbus**, an Italian who sailed for Spain.

Columbus needed a ruler to agree to and support a proposed voyage west of Europe. The Portuguese were more interested in searching for a route to Asia by going down the coast of Africa. So Columbus put his proposal to **King Ferdinand** and **Queen Isabella** of Spain, who agreed to finance his voyage. They hoped to beat Portugal in the race to find a sea route to the East. They also wanted to spread Christianity.

### Christopher Columbus (1451–1506)

Columbus was born in the large port of **Genoa** in 1451. An experienced sailor, he studied old maps and thought that he could reach Asia and the Spice Islands (an area also known as the **East Indies**) by sailing west from Europe. He called his proposal the **Enterprise of the Indies**.

**SOURCE 6.15:
Christopher Columbus**

Columbus set sail on 3 August 1492 with ninety crew in total on three ships: the *Nina*, the *Pinta* and the *Santa Maria*. Columbus travelled on the *Santa Maria*. Most of the crew were worried. Ships rarely went out of sight of land unless they knew where they were going, but they were now sailing out into the open ocean. To calm his crew, Columbus lied to them about the distances they had travelled each day.

Land was sighted on the morning of 12 October 1492 and Columbus soon set foot on an island he named **San Salvador**. Thinking he had reached Asia, he named the native people **Indians**. As he searched for a passage to the East, he discovered **Cuba**, which he thought was Japan.

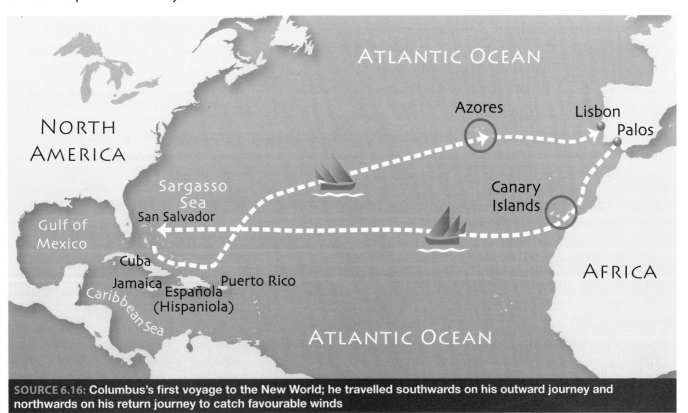

**SOURCE 6.16: Columbus's first voyage to the New World; he travelled southwards on his outward journey and northwards on his return journey to catch favourable winds**

### Activity 6

Historians are not sure on which island Columbus first landed. Find out the modern name of the island that most historians think it was.

**Learning Outcome 3.2** 113

## Activity 7

In pairs, examine this source and then answer the questions below.

SOURCE 6.17: *Landing of Columbus* (1846) by John Vanderlyn

1　What is Columbus doing in the picture?
2　The picture was painted long after Columbus reached San Salvador. Do you think the artist approved of this moment in history? Give reasons for your answer.

Columbus discovered the island of **Hispaniola**, where, on Christmas day, the *Santa Maria* hit a rock and had to be abandoned. Leaving thirty-nine men behind, Columbus decided to return home on the *Nina*. He survived terrible storms and reached Portugal in March 1493.

Columbus received a hero's welcome in Spain and news of his discovery spread throughout Europe. Ferdinand and Isabella wanted to conquer this land for Spain and agreed to a second voyage.

Columbus urged them to protect the new discoveries. So in 1494, at the **Treaty of Tordesillas**, Portugal and Spain agreed to divide the unknown world between them. Any land discovered to the west of a line drawn in the Atlantic Ocean went to Spain and land to the east went to Portugal.

Columbus sailed on three more voyages. He explored Central and South America, discovering Puerto Rico, Trinidad, Jamaica, Panama and the mouth of the Orinoco River. He did not reach North America or Asia. He returned to Spain for a final time in 1504 and died there in 1506.

### DID YOU KNOW?

Columbus brought back items from the New World that had not been seen in Europe before. These included pineapples, turkeys, tobacco and a hammock for sleeping.

SPAIN　PORTUGAL

SOURCE 6.18: The Treaty of Tordesillas divided the undiscovered world between Spain and Portugal

## Activity 8

In pairs, examine this source, which describes the discovery of the New World in 1492, and then answer the questions below.

> [The crew] of the caravel *Pinta* saw a cane and a pole, and they took up another small pole which appeared to have been worked with iron; also another bit of cane, a land-plant, and a small board. The crew of the caravel *Nina* also saw signs of land, and a small branch covered with berries. Everyone … rejoiced at these signs … As the caravel *Pinta* was a better sailer, and went ahead of the Admiral [Columbus], she found the land, and made the signals ordered by the Admiral. The land was first seen by a sailor named Rodrigo de Triana. But the Admiral, at ten in the previous night, being on the castle of the poop, saw a light, though it was so uncertain that he could not affirm it was land … the Admiral asked and admonished the men to keep a good look-out on the forecastle, and to watch well for land; and to him who should first cry out that he saw land, he would give a silk doublet, besides the other rewards promised by the Sovereigns, which were 10,000 maravedis [Spanish coins] to him who should first see it. At two hours after midnight the land was sighted at a distance of two leagues [approximately 10 km].

**SOURCE 6.19:** Extract from *The Journal of Christopher Columbus (During his First Voyage, 1492–93)* (it was common in this period for a person to write an account in the third person, i.e. using 'the Admiral' rather than 'I')

1  Who was the author of the account? Why, do you think, was it written?
2  What evidence of land had the crew of the *Pinta* found on 11 October?
3  What time was land spotted? Who spotted it first?
4  Is there evidence that Columbus was claiming that he sighted land first?
5  What was promised to the first sailor to spot land?
6  Is this a primary or a secondary source? Give a reason to support your answer.

Although Columbus believed that he had found a new route to Asia, other people soon realised that he had in fact discovered a **New World**. This inspired many later explorers to sail westwards.

## What was the importance of the voyage of Ferdinand Magellan?

The **Treaty of Tordesillas** had divided the newly discovered world between Portugal and Spain. The main issue for both countries was the location of the Spice Islands – were they in the Spanish or the Portuguese half? A Portuguese sailor, **Ferdinand Magellan (1480–1521)**, persuaded the young Spanish king, **Charles I**, that he could reach the Spice Islands by sailing west down the coast of America. He would then cross the ocean and claim the islands for Spain.

Magellan set sail from Seville with a crew of 270 in August 1519. There were five ships: the *Trinidad*, the *Concepcion*, the *San Antonio*, the *Santiago* and the *Victoria* (Magellan's ship). They sailed down the coast of South America looking for the passage that would lead to the Spice Islands. The *Santiago* was wrecked in a storm.

**SOURCE 6.20: Ferdinand Magellan**

## Activity 9

America was not named after Columbus but after another explorer. Prepare a class presentation answering the following questions:

1  After whom was America named?
2  Why was it named after this explorer?
3  Identify two places in North or South America that are named after Columbus.

Eventually Magellan found a passage through the straits that are named after him today, **Strait of Magellan**. The *San Antonio* deserted the voyage and returned to Spain. The straits had very rough seas and Magellan was relieved to reach a calm ocean. He called it the **Pacific** (peaceful).

The Pacific Ocean was much bigger than Magellan expected. Magellan's crew suffered from scurvy and over one hundred men died. Eventually the three remaining ships reached the **Philippines**. Magellan got involved in a tribal war there and was killed in battle on 26 April 1521.

> **Strait**
> A narrow passage of sea between two land masses.

**DID YOU KNOW?**

As Magellan did not survive his voyage we rely on two sources for information about his journey.

1 The account of Italian sailor **Antonio Pigafetta**, who was a member of the crew (see Activity 10).

2 The interviews conducted by the king's secretary, **Maximilianus Transylvanus**, with the survivors of the voyage.

---

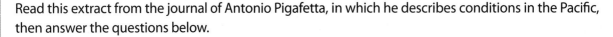

**Activity 10**

Read this extract from the journal of Antonio Pigafetta, in which he describes conditions in the Pacific, then answer the questions below.

> We … entered into the Pacific sea, where we remained three months and twenty days without taking in provisions or other refreshments, and we only ate old biscuit reduced to powder, and full of grubs [insects], and stinking from the dirt which the rats had made on it when eating the good biscuit, and we drank water that was yellow and stinking.
>
> Besides the above-named evils, this misfortune which I will mention was the worst, it was that the upper and lower gums of most of our men grew so much that they could not eat, and in this way so many suffered, that nineteen died. Besides those who died, twenty-five or thirty fell ill … However, thanks be to the Lord, I had no sickness.

**SOURCE 6.21: from *The First Voyage Round the World, by Magellan*, Antonio Pigafetta**

1 How long did Magellan's ships travel in the Pacific without taking in 'provisions or other refreshments'?

2 What food were they forced to eat?

3 Describe their worst misfortune, according to Pigafetta.

4 What, do you think, is the disease he describes in the account? Explain your answer.

---

In September 1522 the *Victoria*, captained by **Sebastian del Cano**, with eighteen survivors on board, reached Spain. They were the only survivors of the 270 men who had left three years earlier. Nonetheless their achievement was very important. They were the first people to **circumnavigate** (sail round) the world. In doing so, they had proved beyond any doubt that the world was round.

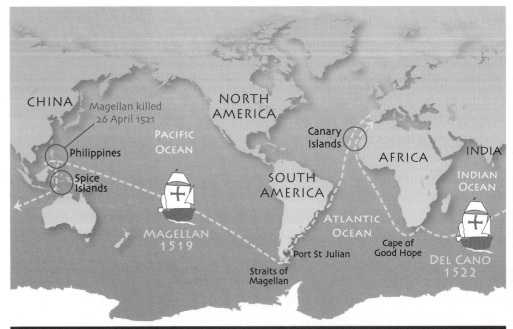

**SOURCE 6.22: Magellan's voyage, as completed by del Cano**

# Summary: Importance of the Age of Exploration

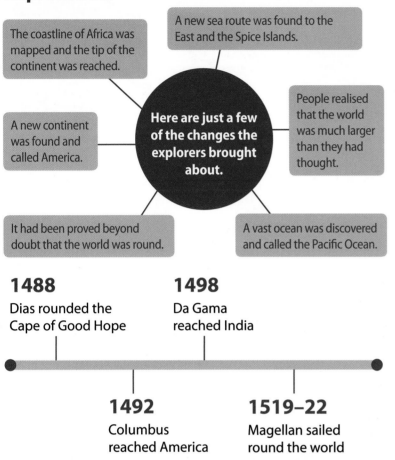

The coastline of Africa was mapped and the tip of the continent was reached.

A new sea route was found to the East and the Spice Islands.

**Here are just a few of the changes the explorers brought about.**

A new continent was found and called America.

People realised that the world was much larger than they had thought.

It had been proved beyond doubt that the world was round.

A vast ocean was discovered and called the Pacific Ocean.

**1488**
Dias rounded the Cape of Good Hope

**1498**
Da Gama reached India

**1492**
Columbus reached America

**1519–22**
Magellan sailed round the world

**6.23: Timeline of exploration**

## DO YOU UNDERSTAND THESE KEY TERMS?

| | | |
|---|---|---|
| circumnavigate | log | strait |
| Enterprise of the Indies | New World | |

## Activity 11

1. Work in groups of four to prepare and deliver a PowerPoint presentation to the class on one of the following explorers: Jean Cabot, Marco Polo, Vasco Núñez de Balboa, Vasco da Gama, Bartolomeu Dias, Amerigo Vespucci, Francis Drake, James Cook.

   The presentation could take the following structure: Early life → Main voyages → Land discovered → Why they are famous today.

   Each group will need to allocate roles such as: researching information, sourcing visual images, typing up the PowerPoint, giving the presentation, taking questions from the class.

2. Following the presentations, discuss which of these explorers you find most interesting and give reasons for your choice.

PowerPoint summary

# SELF-ASSESSMENT – CAN YOU?

1. Explain the purpose of the school set up at Sagres by Prince Henry.

2. Outline the importance of the voyage of Bartolomeu Dias.

3. Identify the main achievement of Vasco da Gama's voyage.

4. Demonstrate how Portugal established control of the route to the East.

5. Outline three important results of the Portuguese voyages of exploration.

6. Explain what the 'Enterprise of the Indies' was.

7. Explain why Ferdinand and Isabella of Spain agreed to support Columbus.

8. Explain why Columbus called the American natives 'Indians'.

9. Identify what was agreed in the Treaty of Tordesillas.

10. Outline the reason for Magellan's voyage.

11. Describe the difficulties Magellan faced in the Pacific.

12. Demonstrate the significance of Magellan's voyage.

# WHAT WAS THE IMPACT OF THE AGE OF EXPLORATION?

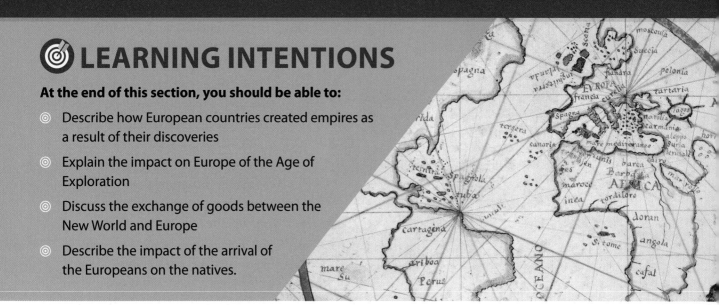

## LEARNING INTENTIONS

**At the end of this section, you should be able to:**

◎ Describe how European countries created empires as a result of their discoveries

◎ Explain the impact on Europe of the Age of Exploration

◎ Discuss the exchange of goods between the New World and Europe

◎ Describe the impact of the arrival of the Europeans on the natives.

## How did European countries create empires?

As a rule, a voyage of discovery was followed by a voyage of conquest. For example, Columbus's first voyage of discovery was followed by his second, much larger, voyage of conquest.

Countries were keen to exploit the new lands that had been discovered, which meant they had to conquer them first. This process is called **colonisation**. It enabled the European occupiers to exploit the wealth (especially gold) of the **colony**, establish new trading routes, send settlers and convert the natives to Christianity.

Portugal soon gained a large empire in Asia as a result of the discoveries of Portuguese explorers. But it was in South America that some of the most dramatic conquests were made. There, ruthless soldiers called **conquistadors** or conquerors built a large empire for Spain.

**Conquistadors**
Sixteenth-century Spanish soldiers who conquered Central and South America.

### DID YOU KNOW?

Throughout history, the country conquering a weaker country usually has technological advantages in battle. The conquistadors had steel armour and swords, while the native populations, the **Aztecs** and the **Incas**, used stone weapons. The Spanish also used muskets, cannon, horses and even dogs in battle. This enabled them to defeat armies that were much bigger in size than theirs. When Europeans colonised Africa in the late nineteenth century they had artillery, accurate repeating rifles and machine guns, while the natives had older single-shot muskets or spears. In one battle in Sudan in 1898 the British killed or wounded 25,000 Sudanese for the loss of 50 men killed and 400 wounded.

**Colonisation**
The process of one country establishing control over another country.

**Colony**
A country that is controlled by another more powerful country.

### Activity 1

Examine this source and then answer the question below.

SOURCE 6.24: An armed conquistador

1 What advantages did the conquistadors have over natives who relied on stone weapons in battle?

## Hernando Cortes (1485–1547)

**Hernando Cortes** set out from Cuba in 1519 with a force of 600 men. When he landed in Mexico, he learned from the native people about the **Aztec Empire**. He travelled to the Aztec capital, **Tenochtitlan**, where **Montezuma**, the Aztec ruler, at first welcomed the Spanish. Soon the Aztecs rose up against the Spanish. Montezuma was killed and Cortes was forced to flee.

The next year Cortes returned with a much larger force made up of Spaniards and native Indian allies. After a three-month siege the Spaniards captured Tenochtitlan. It was then destroyed and Cortes built Mexico City on its ruins. The rest of the Aztec Empire was quickly captured.

SOURCE 6.25: Hernando Cortes

### DID YOU KNOW?

The Aztecs controlled a large empire and were very cruel rulers. They practised human sacrifice on a scale that shocked the Spanish. The tribes ruled by the Aztecs had to supply young men and women for sacrifice. As a result many of these tribes supported the Spanish.

### DID YOU KNOW?

The Incas ruled a large empire covering much of present-day South America. They worshipped their ruler as a living god. Like the Aztecs, the Incas practised human sacrifice.

## Francisco Pizarro (1471–1541)

After the victory of Cortes over the Aztecs, **Francisco Pizarro** was given permission to conquer the **Inca Empire** in South America. In 1531 he set sail with only 180 men to conquer an empire of 12 million people. Although vastly outnumbered, his small force captured the Inca emperor, **Atahualpa**, at Cajamarca in 1532.

Atahualpa offered to fill a room full of gold and silver if he was released. Pizarro agreed and the Incas brought the precious metals. The gold and silver was melted down and sent back to Spain. Pizarro had Atahualpa killed anyway. It was too dangerous to keep him alive in case he led a rebellion against Spanish rule.

Pizarro soon captured the Inca capital, **Cuzco**. He founded the city of Lima, which became the capital of a new Spanish colony, Peru.

### DID YOU KNOW?

Gold and silver mines were discovered in the Inca empire. The most famous was at Potosí. By 1560 the gold shipped back from the New World had doubled the amount of the metal in Europe.

### Activity 2

Examine this source and then answer the questions below.

SOURCE 6.26: The capture of Atahualpa

1  Describe what is happening in this scene.
2  This engraving was made 200 years after the capture of Atahualpa. What, do you think, is the artist's attitude to this historical event? Give a reason for your answer.

**Learning Outcome 3.2**  119

## Spanish Main

The Spanish set up the **Council of the Indies** to run the new lands that had been conquered. Spain's colonies in the New World became known as the **Spanish Main**. Every year a treasure fleet sailed for Spain loaded with gold, silver and spices. This wealth made Spain Europe's most powerful country.

## Other empires

Other European powers also built up large empires as a result of discoveries and conquest. The English settled on the east coast of North America. The French Empire in the Americas consisted of Canada and the valley of the Mississippi River.

# What was the impact on Europe of the Age of Exploration?

As a result of the new trade routes from Asia and the Americas, the ports of the Mediterranean, particularly Venice and Genoa, went into decline. They were replaced by the **Atlantic ports** of Seville, Antwerp, Amsterdam and Rotterdam.

With the great wealth and land available as a result of exploration, **rivalry** and **wars** soon developed between European countries. For example:

> The English attacked Spanish colonies. The ships bringing gold and silver back to Spain were particular targets.

> The Dutch conquered many Portuguese colonies, including some of the Spice Islands.

> Wars later broke out between the Dutch and the English over colonies.

> The French and the English were rivals in America, the Caribbean and India.

**DID YOU KNOW?**

As a result of one war, the Dutch swapped New Amsterdam (New York) with the English for a tiny spice island called Run.

# What goods were exchanged between the New World and Europe?

The exchange of goods between Europe and the New World had a very important impact on people's diets and lifestyles. For example:

> The Europeans introduced **crops** such as wheat, cotton, sugar cane and coffee. They grew very well in the Americas. Cotton, coffee and sugar were usually grown on large farms called **plantations**. These farms were created on land stolen from the native people.

**Plantation**
Large farm growing crops such as sugar and tobacco. They were usually farmed by native forced labour or slaves.

> **Animals** such as horses, cattle, pigs, goats and sheep were also taken to America for the first time. Columbus introduced them on his second voyage (1493–96).

> New goods were introduced to Europe from the New World, including chocolate (cocoa beans), turkeys, tobacco, pineapples, corn, vanilla, chilli peppers and potatoes.

> Spices and crops grown in the New World became more widely available to Europeans.

> Sugar grown in the New World was added to coffee, and coffee houses sprang up throughout Europe in the seventeenth and eighteenth centuries.

> Smoking tobacco became a popular pastime in Europe.

> The potato soon became the main part of the diet of the Irish people.

**DID YOU KNOW?**

Chocolate was originally taken as a drink by the Indians. When sugar was added it became a very popular drink in Europe. Chocolate bars date from the 1840s.

# What was the impact of the arrival of the Europeans on the natives?

The colonisation of the New World affected the natives in three main ways: forced labour, disease and slavery.

## Forced labour

The native populations lost their land and were forced to work for their new European masters.

› When a settler was granted land in the New World by the Spanish, the native people living on the land were granted to him as well.

› The Spanish copied the Inca **mita system**, forcing native villagers to provide labour to work in mines, building roads or on plantations.

› The Spanish government did pass laws to improve the treatment of natives but they were difficult to implement given the distance from Spain.

› Conversion of the natives to Catholicism was important for the Spanish. Some priests and monks tried to defend the natives against poor treatment.

## Disease

The most dramatic impact on the natives was the arrival of new diseases. The Europeans brought smallpox, influenza, measles, typhoid and the bubonic plague.

› The natives had not experienced these before and so had no immunity to them; millions died.

› The native population of the Caribbean was wiped out by European diseases.

› **Smallpox** was a particular killer. The native population in Mexico fell from about 30 million in 1519 to 3 million in 1568 as a result of smallpox.

### Activity 3

Examine this source and then answer the questions below.

> As the Indians did not know the remedy of the disease ... they died in heaps … In many places … everyone in a house died and, as it was impossible to bury the great number of dead, they pulled down the houses over them so that their homes became their tombs.

**SOURCE 6.28: A description of the impact of smallpox by a Spanish Franciscan**

1 Give two pieces of evidence that large numbers of Indians died from smallpox.

2 How were many victims of the disease buried?

### Activity 4

Examine the picture and answer the question below.

**SOURCE 6.27: Workers on a South American plantation**

1 Describe the main activities in this picture.

## Slave trade

Another terrible consequence of the European discoveries was the growth of the **slave trade**. The Portuguese began the slave trade with Africa in 1441. In the New World there was a great demand for workers to mine gold and silver and to work on the plantations. As millions of natives died of disease, a new source of labour was needed.

The Spanish and the Portuguese were the first to ship enslaved **Africans** to their colonies in America and the Caribbean. The English, French and Dutch soon followed.

### Activity 5

Examine this source and then answer the question below.

> The closeness of the place, and the heat of the climate, added to the number in the ship … almost suffocated us. This produced copious perspirations [great sweating], so that the air soon became unfit for respiration [breathing] … and brought on a sickness among the slaves, of which many died … This … was again aggravated by the galling [annoyance] of the chains … and the filth of the necessary tubs [buckets used as toilets] …

**SOURCE 6.29: Olaudah Equiano's account of his journey as an eleven-year-old captive on a slave ship from Africa to Barbados in 1756**

1 List five hardships that Equiano endured on the journey.

This horrible trade in human beings lasted for hundreds of years. It made great fortunes for European merchants. The slave trade was also called the **Middle Passage**.

> Goods grown on plantations worked by slaves (e.g. cotton, tobacco and sugar) were shipped to Europe.

> Merchants traded goods manufactured from these products (e.g. rum and clothes) to African rulers in exchange for more slaves.

**SOURCE 6.30:** Conditions on board a slave ship

> These slaves were then transported across the Atlantic – hence the name Middle Passage.

> The slaves were sold in the New World and more goods (sugar, tobacco, etc.) were bought.

The slave trade brought terrible misery. Historians are unsure of the exact figures but estimate that 12 million Africans were shipped to the New World, with up to half dying during the voyage. The United States (after independence in 1783) was also involved in the slave trade.

The slave trade was abolished in the British Empire in 1807. Most countries in South America ended it in the 1820s. In the USA, it was not abolished until 1865.

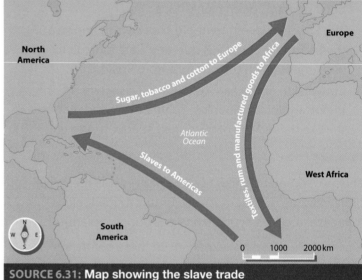

**SOURCE 6.31:** Map showing the slave trade

## DO YOU UNDERSTAND THESE KEY TERMS?

| | | | | |
|---|---|---|---|---|
| Aztec | colony | Inca | plantation | smallpox |
| colonisation | conquistador | Middle Passage | slave trade | |

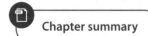 Chapter summary      Weblinks     PowerPoint summary

# SELF-ASSESSMENT – CAN YOU?

**1** Describe the role of the conquistadors.

**2** Explain why other Indians were prepared to help the Spaniards against the Aztecs.

**3** Describe how Pizarro overcame the Inca ruler Atahualpa.

**4** Identify one major consequence for Spain of the conquest of the Inca Empire.

**5** Name two other countries that developed empires as a result of the Age of Exploration.

**6** Draw up a list of four goods introduced from Europe into America and four goods introduced into Europe from America.

**7** Describe the treatment of the native populations by the Europeans and give evidence to support your choice.

**8** Outline the impact smallpox had on the native populations.

**9** Explain why the Spanish and the Portuguese introduced slavery into the New World.

# 7 THE IMPORTANCE OF RELIGION IN HISTORY: THE REFORMATION

## What factors led to the Reformation?

124

## Who were the main reformers?

128

## What was the impact of the Reformation?

138

# WHAT FACTORS LED TO THE REFORMATION?

## 🎯 LEARNING INTENTIONS

**At the end of this section, you should be able to:**

◎ Describe the situation of the Catholic Church in 1500

◎ Explain why many people were unhappy with the Church

◎ Appreciate how the Renaissance contributed to the Reformation.

## What was the Reformation?

Major changes occurred in religious ideas in sixteenth-century Europe that led to reform in the Christian Church. Historians call this movement the **Reformation**. The changes led to a division among Christians and gave us a new word – **Protestant**.

## What was the Catholic Church like in 1500?

Nearly all people in Western Europe were members of the Catholic Church at the start of the sixteenth century. There were also small Jewish communities in some countries. If you were Christian, you were Catholic.

The Catholic Church was far more powerful than it is today and it had great control over the lives of the people.

> The head of the Church was the **pope** in Rome. He was also the ruler of central Italy – the Papal States – which meant that he had a political role.

> The next most important officials were **cardinals**. They elected the pope and helped him run the Church.

> Every country in Europe was divided into **dioceses**. Each diocese was controlled by a **bishop**.

> Each diocese was divided into **parishes**. Each parish had at least one **priest**.

> The people of the parish paid a **tithe** or tax to the Church. This money was used to pay the priest to perform Masses, weddings and funerals.

**Reformation**
Period of religious change that led to a division among Christians.

**Protestants**
Christians who disagreed with the teachings of the Catholic Church.

**Catholic**
The word 'catholic' means universal.

---

### Activity 1 ✏️

Examine this source and then answer the questions below.

**SOURCE 7.1: Lincoln Cathedral, England**

1 Describe the cathedral in relation to its surroundings.

2 In 1500 Lincoln Cathedral was the tallest building in Europe. What does this suggest about the role of the Catholic Church in society?

> There were also **monasteries** and **convents**, where **monks** and **nuns** lived. They helped to look after the sick and the poor.

> Monks called **friars** (such as the Franciscans and Augustinians) lived and worked in towns. They helped the poor and preached the word of God.

> The church was usually the largest building in every European town. Townspeople showed their devotion to God by building beautiful churches.

Religion played a very important role in most people's lives. They wanted to go to heaven when they died, which is called **salvation**. The Catholic Church taught people that they could earn salvation through a mixture of **faith** in God and **good works** such as charitable acts and going on pilgrimages.

---

**KS** | **Activity 2**

Pilgrimages were very important in the Middle Ages. A pilgrimage is when someone makes a journey to a holy place associated with a saint or the life of Jesus.

SOURCE 7.2: **A medieval pilgrimage**

1  Research online to identify four important pilgrimage sites in Ireland and Europe.

2  Explain why people went on pilgrimages in the Middle Ages.

3  Are these people rich or poor? How can you tell?

---

## Why were many people unhappy with the Church?

Problems with the Church caused many people to lose confidence in its teachings.

### Abuses of power

The problems started at the top of the Church. At that time many popes were not very holy men. Called the **Renaissance popes** by historians, they were more interested in art or politics than in religion. Here are some examples:

> **Pope Sixtus IV** (1471–1484) was a patron of art and science. He was also involved in a plot to assassinate Lorenzo de' Medici, the ruler of Florence, during Mass.

> **Pope Julius II** (1503–1513) and his successor **Pope Leo X** (1513–1521) were patrons of artists such as Leonardo da Vinci and Michelangelo. They were also involved in wars in Italy.

> **Pope Alexander VI** (1492–1503) lived a very unholy life. He had mistresses and made his son a cardinal.

 **DID YOU KNOW?**

Pope Leo X was the son of Lorenzo de' Medici. He was made a cardinal at the age of thirteen.

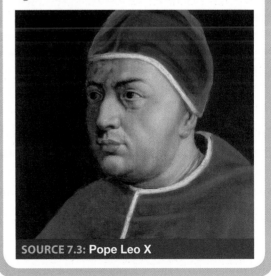

SOURCE 7.3: **Pope Leo X**

The absence of leadership from the popes meant that, over time, a number of serious abuses spread throughout the Church. Many of the popes were guilty of these abuses themselves. The four main abuses were:

> **Nepotism:** This was appointing a relative to an important position in the Church (such as bishop or cardinal) whether or not they were suitable. Pope Sixtus IV appointed six of his nephews as cardinals, including the future Pope Julius II.

> **Simony:** The practice of selling Church positions could earn a lot of money. It was widely believed that Alexander VI bribed some cardinals to elect him pope.

> **Pluralism:** Some people held more than one position in the Church at the same time. A bishop of two dioceses, for example, could accumulate a lot of wealth in tithes.

> **Absenteeism:** Bishops or priests often did not live in their dioceses or parishes. Most bishops were from wealthy, noble families. These families traditionally provided ministers and military commanders to kings and other rulers. It was quite common for bishops to act as advisers to kings. Some built great palaces for themselves to show their power and wealth.

## Indulgences

A further abuse was the **selling of indulgences**. It was believed that if you prayed for a person who died it would shorten the time they would spend in purgatory. An indulgence could be given to a living person who prayed or gave time or money to a good cause. The Church started selling these indulgences in the Middle Ages to make money.

## Excessive wealth

The Church was also an important landowner. Many rich people left large sums of money to monasteries to pray for their souls after they died. Some monasteries became very rich and owned huge amounts of land. The **abbots**, who ran the monasteries, did not always make sure that monks led holy lives.

## Poorly educated priests

While bishops and abbots were usually well educated, the same could not be said for ordinary priests. Some had very little knowledge of the Bible. They could not speak or understand Latin, which was the language used during Mass.

---

### Activity 3

Cardinal Wolsey was King Henry VIII's chief minister for fourteen years. Search online to find answers to the questions below.

SOURCE 7.4: **Cardinal Thomas Wolsey**

1 Identify four pieces of information about his life that interest you.

2 From your research, do you think he led a holy life?

---

**Purgatory**
According to Church teaching, this is the place where people are punished for their sins and purified before going to heaven. Those who led very sinful lives went to hell.

---

### Activity 4

1 'By 1500 reform was needed in the Catholic Church.' Do you agree with this statement? Give four reasons to support your answer. Present your findings to the class.

---

# How did the Renaissance contribute to the Reformation?

The Renaissance was a time when people questioned accepted ideas. As a result, many people also began to doubt both the power and the teachings of the Catholic Church. They argued for reform of the Church.

Writers known as **humanists** were very critical of the abuses and the lives of leading churchmen. In England, **Sir Thomas More** was a humanist writer and critic of the Church.

**Erasmus of Rotterdam** was the most famous critic. A priest himself, he wrote a book called *In Praise of Folly* ('folly' means foolishness), which poked fun at the lives of leading churchmen.

The newly invented printing press meant that many people read the work of Erasmus, and his advice was sought by important people. It was said at the time that 'Erasmus laid the egg and Luther hatched it' – **Martin Luther** was the German monk who criticised the sale of indulgences and started the Reformation (see page 128, Who were the Main Reformers?).

**SOURCE 7.5: Erasmus of Rotterdam**

## Summary: Causes of the Reformation

The main factors that led to the Reformation were:

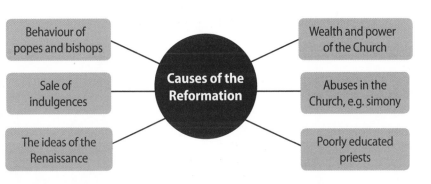

Behaviour of popes and bishops

Wealth and power of the Church

**Causes of the Reformation**

Sale of indulgences

Abuses in the Church, e.g. simony

The ideas of the Renaissance

Poorly educated priests

PowerPoint summary

### DO YOU UNDERSTAND THESE KEY TERMS?

| | | |
|---|---|---|
| absenteeism | indulgences | purgatory |
| faith | nepotism | Reformation |
| good works | pluralism | salvation |
| humanists | Protestant | simony |

## SELF-ASSESSMENT – CAN YOU?

1. Describe the role of a pope in the early sixteenth century.
2. Identify two examples to show that some popes did not live holy lives.
3. Analyse why the Catholic Church was very wealthy.
4. Outline how the Renaissance helped to cause the Reformation.
5. Explain why Erasmus was such an important writer at the time.

# WHO WERE THE MAIN REFORMERS?

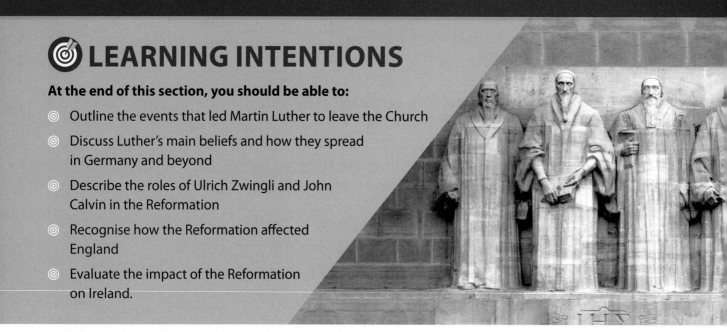

## Martin Luther (1483–1546)

**Martin Luther** was born at Eisleben in the German state of Saxony in 1483. He was from a large family and his father was a wealthy copper-miner. Following his father's wishes, he went to university to study law.

One day in 1505 he was caught in a thunderstorm. Frightened, he promised God that if he survived he would become a monk. He kept his promise and joined an order of monks called the Augustinians.

Luther studied **theology** at Erfurt University. He was a talented student and became Professor of Theology at the University of Wittenberg in 1512. This university had recently been founded by the ruler of Saxony, **Frederick the Wise**.

**Theology** 📖
The study of religion.

🔍 **DID YOU KNOW?**

We know that Luther came from a wealthy background because at the time very few people could afford to go to university.

SOURCE 7.6: **Martin Luther**

## How did Luther challenge the Church?

Although he led a very holy life, Luther was unhappy as a monk. He believed that he was a terrible sinner and that he would go to hell.

> He questioned whether Catholic Church teaching on how to get to heaven (win salvation) was right.

> The Church taught that a mixture of faith and good works was needed to get to heaven. But Luther had studied the Bible closely and was convinced that a person was saved by faith alone.

> He believed that good works such as going on pilgrimages and indulgences made no difference. His idea became known as **Justification by Faith Alone**.

The issue that saw Luther publicly express his views was the **sale of indulgences**. **Pope Leo X** had ordered their sale to pay for the rebuilding of St Peter's Basilica in Rome. In Luther's view, this encouraged people to think they could buy their way into heaven.

In 1517, as a protest against the sale of indulgences, Luther sent a letter to the bishop of his diocese, **Albrecht of Brandenburg**. His letter included a list called the **95 Theses** – these were his arguments against indulgences and their sale. He hoped the bishop would act against this practice. He is said to have nailed the *95 Theses* to the door of the castle church in Wittenberg on 31 October 1517.

Luther's ideas spread quickly across Germany. Pope Leo X ordered Luther to come to Rome to be questioned. This was a dangerous situation for Luther, but Frederick the Wise made sure he did not go. Frederick was proud that a professor at his new university had become so famous. Instead, Luther continued to write pamphlets explaining his beliefs. In these he was very critical of the Church and of the pope.

Pope Leo X wrote an official letter or **papal bull** condemning Luther in 1520. It was called *Exsurge Domine (Arise O Lord)*. It gave Luther sixty days to recant (withdraw) his beliefs. If he refused, he would be condemned as a **heretic** and **excommunicated**. Excommunication was a very serious punishment and meant that you were no longer a member of the Church.

---

### Activity 1

Examine this source and then answer the questions below.

**SOURCE 7.7:** Luther nailing the *95 Theses* to the church door

1 Describe the event shown in this picture in your own words.
2 What was the *95 Theses*?
3 Do you think the artist approved of Luther's actions? Give a reason for your answer.

---

**Pamphlet**
Small (thin) paper booklet giving information on something.

**Heretic**
A person who challenges the doctrines of an established religion.

In a daring act of defiance, Luther publicly burned the papal bull. In response, the pope asked the Holy Roman Emperor, **Charles V**, to deal with Luther. One of the emperor's roles was to defend the Catholic Church. Charles had to proceed very carefully, however. He had been elected emperor in 1519 and one of the seven electors was Frederick the Wise. To please Frederick, he agreed to allow Luther to attend a meeting of German princes known as a **Diet**. This meeting was to be held at Worms.

---

### Activity 2

Examine this source and then answer the questions below.

SOURCE 7.8: *Charles V* (1548) by Titian

1   What impression of Charles V is the painter trying to convey, do you think?
2   Research online and identify five other pictures by the artist Titian.

---

At the Diet, Luther refused to take back his teachings. He was condemned as an **outlaw** by the **Edict of Worms**. This meant that he could be killed and the person responsible would not be arrested. Promised safe conduct by Charles V, he was allowed to return to Saxony.

On the return journey Frederick the Wise had Luther kidnapped. He was hidden in a remote castle at **Wartburg**.

**Edict**
Law passed by an emperor.

---

🔍 **DID YOU KNOW?**

Charles V was not just the Holy Roman Emperor. He was the ruler of Spain and its new empire in the New World. In Spain his title was Charles I. Can you name the explorer he sponsored?

**Holy Roman Emperor**
Title given to the German king, who also ruled over a group of territories in central Europe.

**Diet**
Meeting of the princes of the Holy Roman Empire.

---

### Activity 3

Examine this source and then answer the questions below.

SOURCE 7.9: **Luther at the Diet of Worms**

1   What was the Diet of Worms?
2   The picture shows a confrontation. Who are the two sides?
3   What dangers was Luther facing in defending his beliefs?
4   This painting is from the nineteenth century. Is it reliable? Give a reason for your answer.
5   Suggest why Frederick the Wise had Luther kidnapped after the Diet.

---

**Outlaw**
Person outside the protection of the law.

**Safe conduct**
Permission to travel, with a guarantee that you will not be harmed.

## What were Luther's main beliefs?

While at Wartburg Luther translated the New Testament into German. He believed that it was very important for ordinary people to read the Bible in their own language. A few years later he translated the Old Testament as well.

By 1522 it was safe for Luther to return to Wittenberg. He took charge of the religious changes that were happening there and developed his main beliefs. The table below compares Luther's beliefs with those of the Catholic Church.

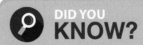

**DID YOU KNOW?**

The **Bible** is the best-selling book in history. It is divided into two parts. The Old Testament deals with events before the birth of Jesus. The New Testament is mainly about Jesus's life. Luther's translations became the basis of the modern German language.

| Teaching | Luther | Catholic Church |
|---|---|---|
| **What is the source of beliefs?** | Bible only | Bible and traditions |
| **How does a person get to heaven?** | Faith in God (Justification by Faith Alone) | Faith and good works are both needed |
| **Who is head of the Church?** | Ruler of each state | Pope |
| **What is the main weekly religious event?** | Communion (in German) | Mass (in Latin) |
| **How many sacraments are there?** | Two: Baptism and the Eucharist | Seven: Baptism, Eucharist, Confirmation, Reconciliation, Anointing (Last Rites), Marriage and Holy Orders |
| **Is Christ present at the Eucharist?** | Both the bread and wine and the body and blood of Christ are present | The bread and wine changes totally into the body and blood of Christ |
| **How important are priests?** | All Christians are equal and should read the Bible for themselves – the priesthood of all believers | Priests are a special group who have been trained to properly understand what the Bible means |
| **Are priests allowed to marry?** | Yes, allowed to marry | No, not allowed to marry |

Luther did not aim to set up a new church; rather, he sought to reform the existing one into the type of church he believed God had intended.

## How did Luther's ideas spread?

> Luther's ideas spread quickly in Germany, helped greatly by the newly invented printing press.

> The protection he received from Frederick the Wise was also crucial; without it he would have been handed over to the emperor and probably executed.

> Luther was a popular hero. More and more people became followers of Luther (**Lutherans**). Cities throughout Germany converted to Lutheran worship, with the Mass being replaced by a service in the German language.

> Church land was confiscated. Monasteries, convents and places of pilgrimage were closed.

> From 1525 onwards some of the rulers of the German states also started adopting Luther's ideas.

> Most of the states of northern Germany, including Saxony, left the Catholic Church. Soon **Denmark**, **Sweden** and **Norway** followed.

In 1529, when Charles V tried to ban Luther's ideas, a number of princes protested and Luther's followers became known as **Protestants**. This term was soon used to describe any group of Christians who broke away from the Catholic Church.

**Sacrament**
A very important Christian ritual where a person receives God's grace or favour.

**Lutheran**
Follower of the beliefs of Martin Luther.

**Learning Outcome** 3.8

Attempts to find a compromise solution failed and war broke out between the Protestant states and the Holy Roman Emperor. The war ended with the **Peace of Augsburg** in 1555. This agreement established the principle that the ruler of a state decided the religion of his people.

## What happened to Luther?

In 1525 Luther married a former nun, **Katharina von Bora**. Their marriage was happy and they had six children. He continued to write pamphlets and to preach. He also wrote a number of hymns, including the famous 'A Mighty Fortress is Our God'. He was not a rich man and rented rooms in his house to students to make some money.

He died in 1546 of a heart attack at his birthplace of Eisleben. The religious revolution he had started became known as the **Reformation**.

## Martin Luther timeline

| | |
|---|---|
| **1483** | Born at Eisleben in Saxony |
| **1505** | Became an Augustinian monk |
| **1512** | Appointed a professor at the University of Wittenberg |
| **1517** | Began his protest with his *95 Theses* against the sale of indulgences |
| **1518–20** | His ideas spread with the help of the printing press |
| **1520** | Pope Leo X condemned Luther Luther burned the papal letter |
| **1521** | Attended the Diet of Worms Condemned by the Edict of Worms |
| **1522** | Translated the New Testament into German Returned to Wittenberg |
| **1525** | German princes started converting to his ideas Married Katharina von Bora |
| **1534** | Published the complete Bible in German |
| **1546** | Died at his birthplace of Eisleben |

### DID YOU KNOW?

The ruler of Germany was called the **Holy Roman Emperor**. However, Germany was divided into many states and the rulers of these states jealously guarded their power. The most powerful states were ruled by **electors**, who chose the emperor.

One of those states was **Saxony**, and its elector, Frederick, was renamed **Frederick the Wise** by later generations because he protected Luther.

**SOURCE 7.10:** Map showing the Holy Roman Empire and the spread of Luther's ideas, 1550

**SOURCE 7.11:** Luther and his wife, Katharina von Bora, painted by Lucas Cranach in 1529. Cranach was Frederick the Wise's court painter. He was a follower of Luther and was best man at his wedding.

**Activity 4**

Examine this source and then answer the questions below.

October 31, 1517: Luther nailed his *95 Theses* to the door of the Castle Church in Wittenberg. It has become a symbol of the Reformation as nothing else has.

It was like a slap in the face when the Catholic Luther researcher Erwin Iserloh asserted in 1961 that the nailing of the theses to the door of the Castle Church belonged to the realm of legends. The facts are convincing. The first written account of the event comes from Philipp Melanchthon (one of Luther's followers), who could not have been an eye-witness to the event since he was not called to Wittenberg University as a professor until 1518. Also, this account appeared for the first time after Luther's death and he never commented on 'nailing anything up' in 1517. It is also worth noting that there was no open discussion of the theses in Wittenberg and that no original printing of the theses could be found.

One thing is sure: Luther wrote a letter to his superiors on October 31, 1517 in which he denounced the sale of indulgences and asked for repayment and removal of the misunderstandings. With the letter he included 95 theses, which were to be the basis for a discussion on the topic. Today, the majority of Luther researchers see it as fact that Luther did not nail his theses to the door of the Castle Church on that day.

**SOURCE 7.12:** Edited extract from 'Legends about Luther: Nailing the 95 Theses'

1 Outline three pieces of evidence presented in the article that suggest Luther did not nail up the *95 Theses* in 1517.

2 Why, do you think, is it important for historians to find out the truth about this event?

3 Search online for other articles about Luther's life. List two pieces of evidence from your research as to why historians believe that particular legend is a fact or a myth.

## What was the importance of Ulrich Zwingli?

Martin Luther began the Reformation, but soon other reformers were questioning the Catholic Church in countries throughout Europe. One of these countries was Switzerland.

**Ulrich Zwingli** (1484–1531) was a reformer in the Swiss town of Zurich.

> Like Luther, he believed that faith, not good works, earned a person salvation.

> He based his ideas solely on the Bible. Importantly, he believed that there was no presence of Christ at Communion.

> His ideas spread to other cantons in Switzerland. War broke out between the Protestant and Catholic cantons and Zwingli was killed during this war.

> His most important contribution to the Reformation was his belief about Communion. His view was adopted by later reformers such as **John Calvin**.

**SOURCE 7.13:** Ulrich Zwingli

**Canton**
Political region – Switzerland was divided into cantons that controlled their own affairs.

# What was the importance of John Calvin?

**John Calvin** (1509–1564) was born in France, but fled when the French king, Francis I, started persecuting followers of Luther. He settled in the Swiss town of Basel in 1535. There, he wrote a book called *The Institutes of the Christian Religion*. This book set out his main beliefs.

> He agreed with Luther that the Bible was the source of all faith, that faith alone was necessary for salvation and that a religious service should be in the language of the people.

> He agreed with Zwingli that there was no presence of Christ at Communion.

> He had developed his own ideas as well. He believed in **predestination**. In other words, God has chosen whether people will go to heaven (the Elect) before they are born. His followers had to lead good lives to show they were saved.

> He did not believe in bishops and rejected the authority of the pope.

Calvin moved to **Geneva**. He took total control of the city and put his religious ideas into practice. The city became known as the **City of God**. Gambling and dancing were banned. Churches were stripped of statues and decoration. The sermon became the main feature of a service. Calvin's church was called the **Reformed Church** or the **Presbyterian Church**.

Calvin's Geneva inspired many Protestants throughout Europe. They flocked to Geneva to learn more about Calvin's ideas, and then returned home to put those ideas into practice.

Many of his earliest followers were to be found in France, where they were known as **Huguenots**. His beliefs also became very popular in Holland and in Hungary. In England, his supporters were called **Puritans**. Many of the earliest European settlers in the United States were Puritans. **John Knox** very successfully introduced Calvin's ideas to Scotland, where the majority of people became Presbyterian.

SOURCE 7.14: **John Calvin**

## DID YOU KNOW?

- Followers of Calvin are known today as Presbyterians in Britain, Ireland and the United States. The word Presbyterian comes from the Latin word *presbyter*, meaning elder.

- One impact of the Protestant Reformation was the removal of statues of holy figures and images from churches. Most Protestant reformers regarded them as unbiblical and based on superstition. At times the process was accompanied with violence and there were riots. This destruction was named **iconoclasm** – 'icon' means image and 'clasm' means violence.

SOURCE 7.15: **Statues on Lyon cathedral in France today showing the damage done by Calvin's followers during the Reformation**

# How did England become Protestant?

## Henry VIII (1491–1547)

**Henry VIII** ruled England from 1509 until his death in 1547. At first, he strongly opposed the new religious ideas. This changed when he wanted to end his marriage to **Catherine of Aragon**.

The couple had one daughter, Mary, but Henry wanted a male heir to keep his family (the Tudors) on the throne of England. He asked **Pope Clement VII** for an annulment of his marriage to Catherine so he could marry **Anne Boleyn**. After a long delay the pope refused Henry's request.

Henry was angry and as a result passed the **Act of Supremacy**. This Act made Henry (and not the pope) head of the Church in England, which was now called the **Church of England**. He was then able to end his marriage.

Many people, especially monks, opposed Henry's changes. Henry responded by closing hundreds of monasteries in England, Wales and Ireland. This policy, called the **Dissolution of the Monasteries**, had an added benefit – Henry acquired the land and wealth of those monasteries. While Henry changed how the Church was run in England, he made few changes to religious teachings.

### Annulment

A ruling by the Church that a marriage did not exist as it was not legal in the eyes of the Church. It is different from divorce, which the Church opposes.

 **DID YOU KNOW?**

Catherine of Aragon was the daughter of Ferdinand and Isabella of Spain. She was also the aunt of the Holy Roman Emperor, Charles V.

**SOURCE 7.16: Henry VIII**

---

### Activity 5

Examine this source and then answer the questions below.

> Good Christian people, I am come hither to die, for according to the law, and by the law I am judged to die, and therefore I will speak nothing against it. I am come hither to accuse no man, nor to speak anything of that, whereof I am accused and condemned to die, but I pray God save the king and send him long to reign over you, for a gentler nor a more merciful prince was there never: and to me he was ever a good, a gentle and sovereign lord. And if any person will meddle of my cause, I require them to judge the best. And thus I take my leave of the world and of you all, and I heartily desire you all to pray for me. O Lord have mercy on me, to God I commend my soul.

**SOURCE 7.17: The last words of Anne Boleyn before her execution in 1536, as recorded at the time by Edward Hall**

1   What evidence is there to show in this source that Anne Boleyn called on people to support Henry VIII?

2   Would you agree that Anne was a religious person? Give reasons for your answer.

3   'Anne Boleyn showed great bravery at her execution.' Do you agree? Support your answer with evidence from the source.

---

### KS 👥 Activity 6

Henry VIII had six wives. In this section we have read about two of them: Catherine of Aragon and Anne Boleyn.

In groups of four, search online to find out five facts about one of Henry's other four wives.

When Henry died, his son, **Edward VI**, was aged nine. Because he was so young, a council of nobles ran England. They began to introduce Protestant teachings. A *Book of Common Prayer* was to be used in churches and religious services were to be held in English.

Edward died at the age of fifteen and was succeeded by his half-sister **Mary I**. Mary made England Catholic again. However, she made two decisions that turned the English people against her:

› Desperate for a child, she married her relative **Prince Philip of Spain**. This marriage was unpopular.

› She persecuted Protestants. Nearly 300 people were executed, which earned her the nickname 'Bloody Mary'.

When Mary died she was succeeded by her half-sister, **Elizabeth I**. Elizabeth, the daughter of Anne Boleyn, made England Protestant again. The *Book of Common Prayer* was reintroduced. The **Act of Uniformity** forced people to attend a Protestant service on Sundays. If they did not, they were fined. By the end of Elizabeth's long reign in 1603, the vast majority of English people were Protestant.

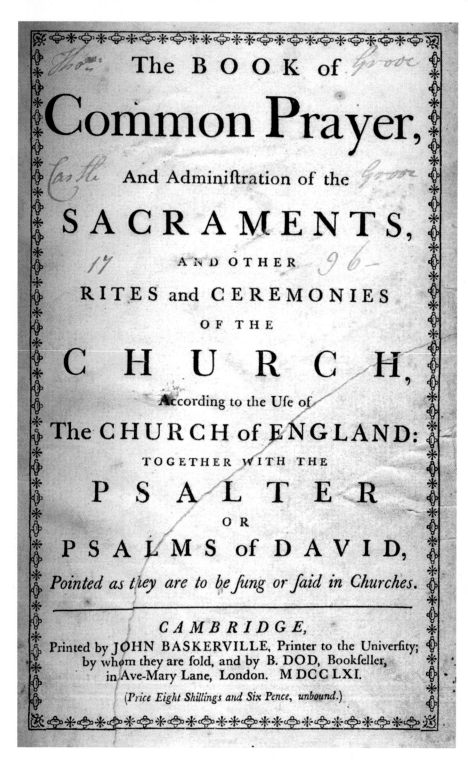

The BOOK of

# Common Prayer,

And Adminiftration of the

# SACRAMENTS,

AND OTHER

RITES and CEREMONIES

OF THE

# CHURCH,

According to the Ufe of

The CHURCH of ENGLAND:

TOGETHER WITH THE

# PSALTER

OR

# PSALMS of DAVID,

*Pointed as they are to be fung or faid in Churches.*

**CAMBRIDGE,**

Printed by JOHN BASKERVILLE, Printer to the Univerfity; by whom they are fold, and by B. DOD, Bookfeller, in Ave-Mary Lane, London. MDCCLXI.

*(Price Eight Shillings and Six Pence, unbound.)*

## Impact on Ireland

Henry VIII introduced his religious changes into the areas of Ireland that were under English control. Monasteries were closed and the **Church of Ireland** was set up, with Henry as its head. However, the reforms had little popular support.

› Most of the **Old English** (descendants of settlers who had come to Ireland with the Normans) refused to accept the new Church.

› The **Gaelic Irish** were very suspicious of anything English, and remained Catholic.

Elizabeth became worried that Ireland could be used as a base by England's Catholic enemy, Spain. To ensure English control it was decided to bring Protestant settlers to Ireland. Spreading Protestantism in Ireland became part of the English policy of conquering the country (see Section 8).

### Activity 7

KS

Henry VIII had three children who ruled England after he died:

- Edward VI (1547–1553)
- Mary I (1553–1558)
- Elizabeth I (1558–1603)

1  Find out four facts about the religious changes that were introduced during each of their reigns.

2  Prepare a PowerPoint presentation of your research and show it to the class.

### DO YOU UNDERSTAND THESE KEY TERMS?

| | | | |
|---|---|---|---|
| *95 Theses* | edict | Justification by Faith Alone | Puritan |
| Act of Supremacy | elector | Lutheran | Reformed Church |
| Act of Uniformity | excommunicate | papal bull | sacrament |
| annulment | heretic | predestination | theology |
| Diet | Holy Roman Emperor | Presbyterian | |
| Dissolution of the Monasteries | Huguenot | | |

PowerPoint summary

## SELF-ASSESSMENT – CAN YOU?

1  Explain Luther's idea of 'Justification by Faith Alone'.

2  Describe what caused Luther to publicly criticise the Church.

3  Comment on the reaction of the pope and Frederick the Wise to Luther's actions.

4  Identify why Charles V had to act carefully when dealing with Luther.

5  Explain what happened at the Diet of Worms.

6  Outline four beliefs Luther had that differed from Catholic teaching.

7  Explain the origin of the term 'Protestant'.

8  Describe what happened when a German town became Protestant.

9  Outline two reasons why Luther succeeded as a reformer.

10  Describe briefly Luther's life after 1525.

11  Explain Zwingli's major impact on the Reformation.

12  Describe the changes introduced by Calvin to Geneva.

13  Argue both sides of this view: 'Calvin and Luther agreed on some religious beliefs but disagreed on others.'

14  Name four countries to which Calvin's ideas spread.

15  Explain the religious changes introduced by Henry VIII to England.

16  Evaluate the impact of the Reformation on Ireland.

# WHAT WAS THE IMPACT OF THE REFORMATION?

## ◎ LEARNING INTENTIONS

**At the end of this section, you should be able to:**

◎ Describe the Catholic Church's reaction to the Reformation

◎ Discuss the religious persecution that occurred during the Reformation

◎ Outline the religious wars that broke out because of the Reformation.

## How did the Catholic Church react to the Reformation?

One of the most important consequences of the Reformation was the reaction of the Catholic Church to the growth of Protestantism. This became known as the **Counter-Reformation**.

As more and more people became Protestant, many people, including Charles V, demanded a Church council to look at reform. A Church council was a meeting of cardinals, bishops and other churchmen.

Traditionally, popes resisted such demands as they did not want to weaken their power. However, **Pope Paul III** (elected in 1534) was prepared to act and reform the Church.

> He agreed to a Church council, which became known as the **Council of Trent**.

> He approved the formation of the **Jesuits**.

**Counter-Reformation**
Response of the Catholic Church to the spread of Protestantism.

SOURCE 7.18: Pope Paul III

## The Council of Trent

The Church council met three times at Trent in the north of Italy between 1545 and 1563. It clearly stated the Church's beliefs (**Catholic doctrine**) and made important decisions on reform (**Church discipline**). For example:

> It ended the abuses of simony, nepotism, absenteeism and pluralism.

> It gave its view on what was wrong with Protestant teachings. For example, it declared that tradition and the Bible were the source of teachings, not just the Bible.

> The council also introduced the **Index** – a list of books that Catholics were forbidden to read.

The decisions reached at Trent improved standards within the Catholic Church and made it far stronger and better able to tackle the Protestant threat.

## The Society of Jesus (the Jesuits)

The Jesuits were the most influential of the new Catholic religious orders set up during the Counter-Reformation. They were founded by an ex-soldier from Spain called **Ignatius Loyola** (1491–1556), and approved by Pope Paul III in 1540. Modelled on an army, the order grew rapidly under Loyola's leadership.

The order was important in the struggle against Protestantism for a number of reasons:

> It carried out **missionary work** in Protestant lands to win people back to the Catholic Church. It was successful in parts of Poland, Austria and Hungary.

> It set up schools throughout Europe to offer a Catholic education to the children of the powerful and wealthy. Jesuit schools soon came to be regarded as the best in Europe.

SOURCE 7.19: *Council of Trent* (1633) by Elia Naurizio

**Doctrine**
List of beliefs of a religious group, e.g. the Catholic Church.

SOURCE 7.20: Ignatius Loyola

# What religious persecution was there during the Reformation?

The Reformation caused division in many countries. Most rulers did not want different religious views in society as they thought it would weaken their country.

Therefore, in most countries people were not allowed to practise the religion they wanted. This is called **persecution**.

Religious persecution was very common in Europe during the Reformation. It had a major impact on the lives of everyday people. Catholics in Protestant countries and Protestants in Catholic countries had to be careful. Many people were forced to leave their own country to practise their beliefs elsewhere.

Historians have to be careful when making a judgement about the scale of religious persecution in the sixteenth and seventeenth centuries as both Catholics and Protestants used propaganda to make the other side look bad.

## Inquisition

Probably the most famous example of religious persecution was the **Inquisition**. It played a very important role in the Counter-Reformation.

> It was a **Church court** set up to try heretics. These were people who held views that differed from the teachings of the Catholic Church.

> The court was active in Spain, Portugal and Italy. It targeted Protestants, Jews and Muslims.

> A person found guilty by the Inquisition could be fined, flogged, imprisoned or burned alive at the stake.

> The sentences were announced at a religious ceremony called an *auto-da-fé* (act of faith). During the ceremony those found guilty would wear a garment called a *sanbenito*.

**Auto-da-fé**
Religious ceremony at which those found guilty by the Inquisition received their sentences.

### Activity 1

Examine the source below and answer the questions that follow.

SOURCE 7.21: Gunpowder Plot

1   Can you name six of the people involved in the Gunpowder Plot?

2   Search online to find out the following facts about the Gunpowder Plot:
    - What the men in the picture were plotting to do
    - How their plans were discovered
    - What happened to the men involved in the plot
    - How the event is remembered in Britain today.

3   Imagine you are living in England in 1605. Write a letter to a friend describing your reaction to the discovery of the plot.

SOURCE 7.22: Burning heretics at the stake during an *auto-da-fé*

**Sanbenito**
Tunic worn by those who were condemned by the Inquisition.

The Inquisition in Italy was less harsh, but, famously, it tried the scientist **Galileo**. The Inquisition succeeded as Protestant ideas gained little support in Spain or Italy. To make the Catholic Church look bad, Protestant writers greatly exaggerated the numbers killed by the Inquisition.

## What wars broke out because of the Reformation?

**Religious wars** broke out. There were wars between countries and civil wars between Protestants and Catholics within countries.

> Most rulers persecuted religions they disagreed with and this led to war.

> The wars brought death and destruction.

The first religious war was in **Germany** between the princes who supported Luther and the emperor and his allies. The **Peace of Augsburg** of 1555 said that the prince of each state should decide the religion of his people.

In 1562 a civil war, known today as the **French Wars of Religion**, broke out in France.

> This war was between Catholics and followers of John Calvin, who were called **Huguenots**.

> During the war a terrible event occurred when Protestants were massacred in Paris in 1572. This event became known as the **St Bartholomew's Day Massacre**.

> In 1598 the **Edict of Nantes** ended the war. Protestants were allowed to practise their religion – one of the few examples of religious toleration in Europe.

### Activity 2

Examine this source and then answer the questions below.

Henry, by the grace of God king of France and of Navarre … do establish and proclaim:
I. First, that the recollection of everything done by one party or the other between March, 1585, and our accession to the crown, and during all the preceding period of troubles, remain obliterated and forgotten, as if no such things had ever happened. …
III. We ordain that the Catholic Apostolic and Roman religion [i.e. the Catholic Church] shall be restored and reestablished in all places and localities of this our kingdom … where the exercise of the same has been interrupted, in order that it may be peaceably and freely exercised, without any trouble or hindrance …
VI. And in order to leave no occasion for troubles or differences between our subjects, we have permitted, and herewith permit, those of the said religion called Reformed [i.e. followers of John Calvin] to live and abide in all the cities and places of this our kingdom … without being annoyed … or compelled to do anything in the matter of religion contrary to their consciences …

**SOURCE 7.23: Excerpts from the Edict of Nantes**

1 Who is the author of this edict? Provide one piece of evidence from the text to support your answer.

2 Would you agree that the aim of Article I of the edict is to promote peace in the future?

3 In your own words, what religious freedom is granted in Articles III and VI?

### Activity 3

In pairs, examine this source and then answer the questions below.

1 Describe what is happening in the picture.

2 Do you think this is a reliable source? Give evidence to support your answer.

SOURCE 7.24: St Bartholomew's Day Massacre

In the sixteenth century the **Netherlands** was ruled by Spain. Many Dutch people became followers of John Calvin and they revolted against their Spanish rulers. The war lasted for eighty years but in the end the Dutch won independence from Spain.

**Philip II of Spain** was annoyed that English ships were attacking Spanish ships that were bringing treasure back from the New World. Elizabeth I was also helping the Protestants in the Netherlands. Philip decided to invade England. His invasion fleet, called the **Spanish Armada**, was defeated by the English in 1588.

The most serious religious war was the **Thirty Years' War** from 1618 to 1648.

> It was fought in Germany and involved most of the countries of Europe.

> Historians think that about one-third of the population of Germany died as a result of the war.

> Most of the dead were ordinary people. Armies marching through the countryside would take food from farms, leaving farmers and their families to starve.

### Activity 4

Examine this source and then answer the questions below.

SOURCE 7.25: **Calvinist destruction of a Catholic church in the Netherlands, 1566**

1  Describe what is happening in the picture.
2  What is the name given to the destruction of churches?

### Activity 5

Find out more about either the Spanish Armada or the Thirty Years' War. Identify five facts that you found interesting.

### DO YOU UNDERSTAND THESE KEY TERMS?

| | | | |
|---|---|---|---|
| *auto-da-fé* | Counter-Reformation | Index | *sanbenito* |
| council | doctrine | persecution | |

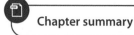 Chapter summary     Weblinks     PowerPoint summary

## SELF-ASSESSMENT – CAN YOU?

1 Outline two important decisions Pope Paul III made.

2 Explain why there were demands for a Church council in the 1500s.

3 Identify two important decisions reached by the Council of Trent.

4 Explain why the Jesuits were very important during the Counter-Reformation.

5 Outline the activities of the Inquisition in Spain.

6 Identify two reasons why religious wars broke out in Europe during the Reformation.

# 8 HOW SETTLEMENT AND PLANTATION AFFECTED IRISH IDENTITY

**How did the first towns develop in Ireland?** — 144

**What was the English policy of plantation?** — 150

**What was the impact of plantation?** — 159

# HOW DID THE FIRST TOWNS DEVELOP IN IRELAND?

## 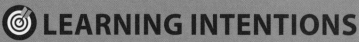 LEARNING INTENTIONS

**At the end of this section, you should be able to:**

◎ Discuss who built the first towns in Ireland

◎ Outline who the Vikings and the Normans were

◎ Explain how the Normans changed Ireland.

## Who built the first towns in Ireland?

The Irish population is made up of different groups of people. Most Irish people are descended from New Stone Age people but there have been waves of newcomers at different times in Irish history. They helped create the present Irish nation. For example, the arrival of the Vikings and later the Normans strongly influenced the development of towns in Gaelic Ireland.

### Vikings

The first people to build towns in Ireland were the **Vikings**. They were raiders from Scandinavia who were looking for treasures. A monk recorded their arrival near Dublin in AD 795. They did not come to Ireland in huge numbers, but they built and settled in the towns shown on the map.

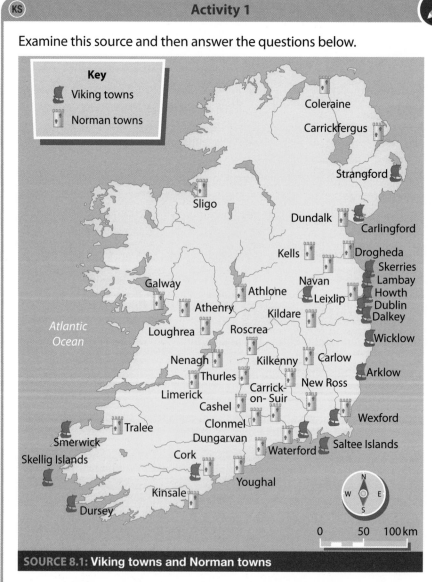

**Activity 1**

Examine this source and then answer the questions below.

**SOURCE 8.1: Viking towns and Norman towns**

1 List the three Viking towns and the three Norman towns closest to where you live.

2 Why are most of the towns on the coast?

3 In what part of Ireland are most of the Viking and Norman towns? Why?

4 Suggest two reasons why people build towns.

**KS**                       **Activity 2**

Examine these sources and then answer the questions below.

**A**   When the Vikings came to Dublin they introduced some words to the Irish language:

| Irish word | English translation |
|------------|---------------------|
| brea | fine, good |
| ancaire | anchor |
| bad | boat |
| margad | market |
| pingin | penny |

SOURCE 8.2: **Viking words still in use in Ireland today**

**B**

| Imports | Exports |
|---------|---------|
| ivory | wool |
| silver | fur |
| amber | hides (leather) |
| silk | slaves |
| ceramics | |

SOURCE 8.3: **Goods that Vikings traded in Dublin**

1   What did the new Irish words have in common?
2   Is there any item traded by the Vikings that surprised you? Say why.
3   Suggest where the Vikings got the goods they sold.
4   What did the Vikings use silver for, do you think? Write down two possibilities. (*Hint:* Table A might give you a clue.)
5   What does the information here tell you about the Vikings?

**Imports**
Goods sold into a country.

**Exports**
Goods sold out of a country.

## Normans

The **Normans** were the next settlers to arrive in Ireland.
They expanded the Viking towns and also established new towns.

**DID YOU KNOW?**

Until about AD 1000, people captured in Viking raids were bought and sold at slave fairs. At that time Dublin had the biggest slave market in northwest Europe.

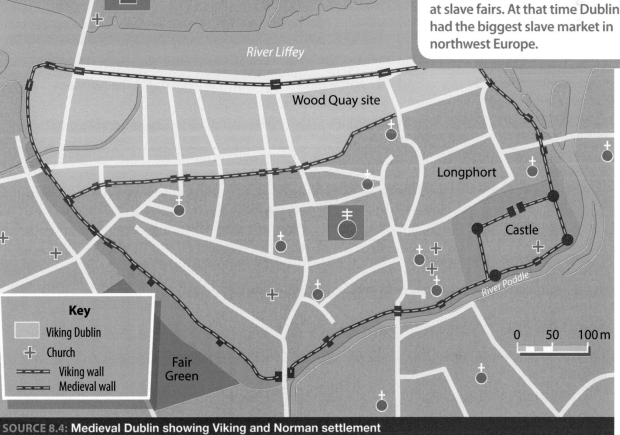

River Liffey

Wood Quay site

Longphort

Castle

River Poddle

**Key**
- Viking Dublin
- ✚ Church
- Viking wall
- Medieval wall

Fair Green

0   50   100 m

SOURCE 8.4: **Medieval Dublin showing Viking and Norman settlement**

## Who were the Normans?

The Normans were descended from Vikings who had settled in Normandy in northern France. They had conquered England in 1066.

They came to Ireland in 1169 when a band of Norman knights landed in **Wexford**. They had come at the request of the King of Leinster, **Dermot MacMurrough**. He wanted their help to defeat the other Gaelic kings and make himself High King of Ireland. Before long, the Norman lords had begun to plunder and capture lands in Ireland.

**Henry II** of England later followed these lords. He brought an army of 4,000 soldiers and 500 knights. The Gaelic lords swore loyalty to Henry, hoping he would protect them from the Norman lords. Henry declared himself the **Lord of Ireland**. However, when Henry left, the Norman lords went on taking over large parts of Ireland.

The Normans easily defeated the Irish because they were better equipped. They had knights on horses with heavy armour, lances and swords. They had archers who showered the Gaelic armies with thousands of arrows.

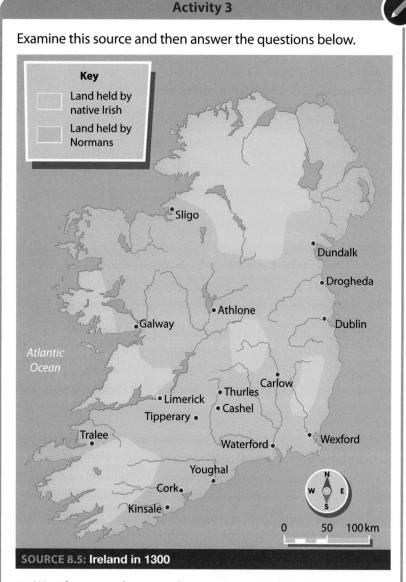

**Activity 3**

Examine this source and then answer the questions below.

**Key**
- Land held by native Irish
- Land held by Normans

SOURCE 8.5: Ireland in 1300

1  Was the area where you live conquered by the Normans?
2  Name three other places in Ireland that the Normans conquered.
3  Which areas of Ireland did the Normans *not* take over?

## What changes did the Normans bring?

The Normans brought the **feudal system** to Ireland (see Section 4), which greatly changed the landscape and culture of Ireland.

### Castles and manors

Once the Normans conquered an area, they built **motte and bailey castles** (see Section 4) so that they could immediately defend their territory.

Later, Norman lords built **stone castles** such as the one at Limerick on the next page. They usually built them on high places or near rivers. Four of the biggest Norman castles in Ireland are Dublin, Limerick, Trim and Carrickfergus.

## Activity 4

Examine this source and then answer the questions below.

SOURCE 8.6: **King John's Castle, Limerick**

1  Why, do you think, did the Normans replace motte and bailey castles with stone castles?
2  Suggest why a castle was built at the site shown in the photograph.
3  Look back at Source 8.5. Suggest why the Normans needed to build a strong castle here.

In the 1400s and 1500s the Normans and the Gaelic Irish built smaller castles. These are called **tower houses**. In all, the Normans built over 2,000 castles in Ireland.

The Normans set up **manor farms** near their castles. They encouraged peasants to come to Ireland from England and Wales and to farm the land like they did at home.

### New towns

The Normans established towns, mostly around their castles, so that people could trade in them (see Source 8.5).

## Changes in the Irish Church

The Normans built many monasteries and cathedrals. Most of them were in the Gothic style. They introduced the **parish system** we know today. Each manor farm would become a parish with a priest and a church.

---

### Activity 5

Examine this source and then answer the questions below.

SOURCE 8.7: **Jerpoint Abbey, Co. Kilkenny, one of the large monasteries built by the Normans**

1  What style of architecture can you see here? Give a reason for your answer.
2  List any towns in your area with the word 'abbey' in their name.

---

### Activity 6

Research Norman surnames in Ireland and answer the following questions.

1  Find five Norman surnames associated with the area where you live.
2  Are there any Norman surnames in your own family?
3  Name five famous Irish people with Norman surnames.
4  Identify five Norman surnames to do with a job or a place.

---

## Norman names

The Normans brought farmers, craftsmen and merchants from England, Wales and France. These people are the ancestors of many people in Ireland today. Many familiar surnames can be traced back to Norman settlers.

## English language

When the Normans arrived, everyone in Ireland spoke Gaelic. The Normans and the settlers who followed them were the first people living in Ireland to use a form of **English**.

### DID YOU KNOW?

Typical Norman surnames include Barry, Bermingham, Burke, Fitzgerald, Fleming, Jordan, Morris, Nugent, Power, Plunkett, Roche, Talbot, Walsh. *Fitz* was the Norman word for 'son of'. So, for example, the name Fitzmaurice meant 'son of Maurice'.

## Activity 7

Examine Source 8.8 and then answer the questions.

1 Write down two buildings that you would see in a medieval town.
2 Identify two other features that indicate Galway was a medieval town.
3 What can you see on an aerial map that you cannot see on the ground?
4 Outline two main reasons why the Vikings and Normans built towns.
5 How can archaeologists and historians find out where a town was, what its name was and what it looked like?

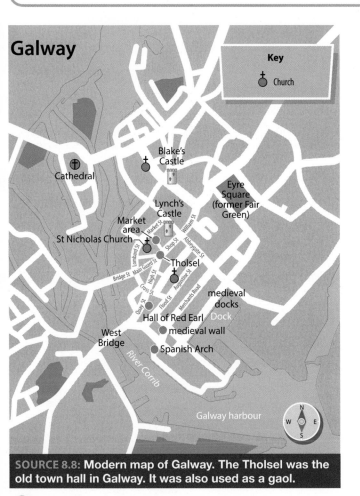

**SOURCE 8.8:** Modern map of Galway. The Tholsel was the old town hall in Galway. It was also used as a gaol.

PowerPoint summary

## Activity 8

**Investigation of a local town**

Working in a group, pick a town close to where you live and carry out some research into it.

1 Is it a Viking, medieval or plantation town?
2 Does it have elements of more than one of these different periods?
3 List some features of the town that would show a tourist that it is a Viking, medieval or plantation town.
4 From your study of this section, what impact do you think the development of the town had on your local area? In your answer consider population, local farms, cultural life and trade.

### DO YOU UNDERSTAND THESE KEY TERMS?

| | |
|---|---|
| Normans | tower house |
| parish system | Vikings |

## SELF-ASSESSMENT – CAN YOU?

1 Explain who set up the first towns in Ireland.

2 Name the trade that Dublin was at the centre of for northwest Europe and name four other items people traded in the towns.

3 List three words that the Vikings brought to the Irish language.

4 Say whether the Vikings used coins when they traded.

5 Give two reasons why the Normans were able to conquer Ireland.

6 Name the two types of castle the Normans built.

7 Name two surviving Norman castles in Ireland.

8 Outline the two changes the Normans made to the Irish Church.

9 Explain why the Normans considered towns important.

10 List four Irish surnames that came from the Normans.

# WHAT WAS THE ENGLISH POLICY OF PLANTATION?

## ⊚ LEARNING INTENTIONS

**At the end of this section, you should be able to:**

◎ Describe Ireland in 1500

◎ Outline the laws and customs under the three different types of ruler in Ireland

◎ Discuss the English policy of plantation and the reasons it was introduced to Ireland

◎ Discuss the Ulster plantation and describe how it worked.

## What was Ireland like in 1500?

Ireland in 1500 was very different from Ireland today. Thick forests and scrub covered a lot of the country. Travel was dangerous because of bandits and sometimes difficult because you needed the permission of the local lord.

There was no central government. The English rulers controlled only a small area around Dublin known as **the Pale**. Powerful noble lords ruled the rest of the country. Some areas were controlled by Gaelic lords and some by Old English lords. The Old English lords and the people of the Pale were descended from the Normans.

### Laws and customs

Laws and customs varied within Ireland depending on whether the area was ruled by Gaelic lords, by Old English lords or by the English monarch in the Pale.

> **The Pale**
> Dublin and a small area of land around it controlled by the English monarch.

### Activity 1

KS 👥

Examine this source and then answer the questions below.

1 Compare this map of Ireland in 1500 with the map of Ireland in 1300 (Source 8.5). List three differences.

2 Name two powerful Old English lords and two Gaelic lords in Ireland in 1500.

3 Was there a Gaelic or an Old English lord in your area? Do any of his descendants still live there?

4 How does this map of Ireland look different from a modern political map of Ireland? Explain two differences.

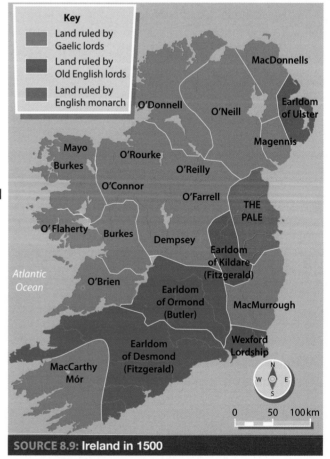

**SOURCE 8.9: Ireland in 1500**

Key
- Land ruled by Gaelic lords
- Land ruled by Old English lords
- Land ruled by English monarch

MacDonnells
O'Donnell
O'Neill
Earldom of Ulster
Magennis
Mayo Burkes
O'Rourke
O'Reilly
O'Connor
O'Farrell
THE PALE
O'Flaherty
Burkes
Dempsey
Earldom of Kildare (Fitzgerald)
Atlantic Ocean
O'Brien
Earldom of Ormond (Butler)
MacMurrough
Earldom of Desmond (Fitzgerald)
Wexford Lordship
MacCarthy Mór

0  50  100 km

|  | **Gaelic lords** | **Old English lords** | **The Pale** |
|---|---|---|---|
| **Who ruled?** | Gaelic lords ruled over a **clan** – a group of people with the same surname (e.g. O'Connor)<br><br>Most new lords were the brother or son of the previous lord | In theory, the English monarch was their overlord<br><br>In practice, they ruled their lands like countries (e.g. they had private armies and set their own taxes) | The English monarch ruled the people of this area, who were mostly descended from the Normans and followed English customs |
| **Language** | Irish | Mainly Irish – many had married into Gaelic families | English |
| **Law**<br>(See also Section 20) | **Brehon law**<br>The Brehon (judge) was in charge of carrying out the law<br><br>The only form of punishment was the **éiric** or fine, which the guilty person's family had to pay to the victim's family<br><br>No executions or use of prisons | Mostly Brehon law<br>Also used English law when it suited them | English **common law** (so called because it was common to all the English monarch's subjects)<br><br>The monarch appointed judges to go from place to place to try serious crimes<br><br>Courts were held in a courthouse in the town<br><br>People found guilty were beheaded or imprisoned |
| **Marriage laws** | A woman could keep her name and property when she married (and was still seen as part of her own clan)<br><br>Divorce was allowed<br><br>Children born outside marriage were entitled to a share in their father's property | Followed Brehon law | A wife took her husband's name and he took control of her property and money on marriage<br><br>Divorce was not allowed<br><br>Children born outside marriage could not inherit their father's property |

**SOURCE 8.10:** Types of ruler in Ireland, 1500

**Activity 2**

Examine this source and then answer the questions below.

1 How is this castle protected?

2 If you were an ordinary person living in sixteenth-century Ireland, would you prefer to live in a Gaelic area, in an area controlled by an Old English lord or in the Pale? Give two reasons for your choice.

3 Which area would you least like to have lived in? Give two reasons for your answer.

4 Would your answers be different if you were a man or a woman? Explain why.

5 Would your answers be different if you were a lord rather than an ordinary person? Explain why.

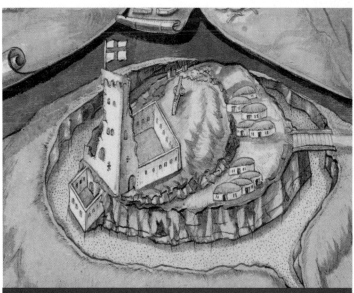

**SOURCE 8.11:** Gaelic lord's castle in the early 1600s. *This image is reproduced courtesy of the National Library of Ireland [Ms 2656/5 Richard Bartlett]. www.nli.ie*

## Activity 3

Examine this source and then answer the questions below.

1   Describe the clothes in the picture.
2   The woman is wearing a more English-style dress. Where in Ireland might she have lived?
3   Who, do you think, is richer, the man or the woman? Give a reason for your answer.
4   Why is a painting like this so useful to historians? Say two things we can learn about Irish society from this painting.

SOURCE 8.12: *Irish man and Irish woman* by Flemish artist Lucas d'Heere, c.1575

## What were plantations?

After the Vikings and Normans the next big group of newcomers to Ireland were English and Scottish settlers. They arrived during the 1500s and 1600s having received land in Ireland from the English monarch.

In the 1500s the English rulers introduced **plantation** as a new way of bringing Ireland under their control. It involved bringing English, and later Scottish, people to Ireland and giving them the land of the Gaelic Irish and the Old English.

Plantation had a lot of advantages for the English government:

›  It was cheaper than having an English army permanently based in Ireland.
›  Settlers replaced Irish laws and customs with English laws and customs.
›  Settlers built towns, increased trade and improved the economy.
›  Settlers spread the Protestant faith to Ireland.

A number of plantations were sponsored by different English rulers in the 1500s and 1600s. There were also some private plantations encouraged by the English government.

**Plantation**
People (known as **planters**) are sent from one country to another country where they have been given land to live and work on.

## Activity 4

Examine this source and then answer the question below.

We must change Irish government, clothing, customs, manner of holding land, language and habits of life to make them [the Gaelic Irish] obedient.

SOURCE 8.13: Sir George Carew, one of Queen Elizabeth's officials in Ireland

1   What reasons does Sir George Carew give for introducing the policy of plantation to Ireland?

## Activity 5

Examine this source and then answer the questions below.

1. The plantations of 1556 (Laois–Offaly) and 1586 (Munster) failed at first. Suggest two reasons why they might have failed.
2. What was the Pale?
3. In the 1650s the rest of Ireland outside of Connaught was planted. This plantation was organised by Oliver Cromwell and we call it the Cromwellian Plantation. Can you find out why Connaught was not included in this plantation?
4. Find out four facts about Oliver Cromwell.

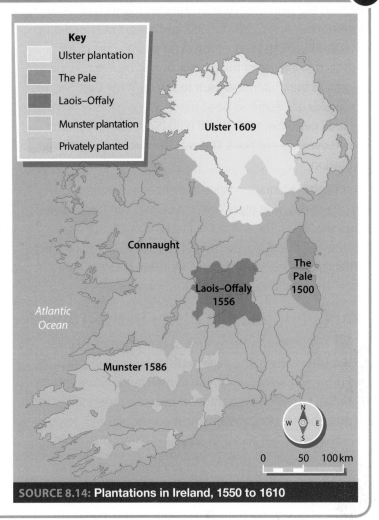

**Key**
- Ulster plantation
- The Pale
- Laois–Offaly
- Munster plantation
- Privately planted

Ulster 1609

Connaught

The Pale 1500

Laois–Offaly 1556

Atlantic Ocean

Munster 1586

0    50    100 km

**SOURCE 8.14:** Plantations in Ireland, 1550 to 1610

## The Laois–Offaly plantation

Queen **Mary I** planned the first plantation in Ireland in the 1550s. Two Gaelic clans – the O'Connors and the O'Mores – were raiding the Pale and stealing cattle. The lord deputy suggested to Mary that she give some of the clans' land to English soldiers. They would farm the land and at the same time guard the borders to the Pale. Mary agreed, but the plantation was not a success. Only eighty-eight planter families from the Pale settled there. None came from England.

**Lord deputy**
The English monarch's representative in Ireland.

**SOURCE 8.15: Queen Mary I**

**Learning Outcome 2.1** 153

### The Munster plantation

The next big plantation was in Munster. Mary's half-sister Elizabeth became queen in 1558 and ruled until her death in 1603. **Elizabeth I** was a Protestant and did not trust Catholics. She felt that the people should have the same religion as their ruler. She went to war with the Catholic Fitzgeralds of Desmond (see Source 8.9). When she won, she took over about 2,000 km² (200,000 hectares) of land spread over five counties. This was the start of the Munster plantation.

The Munster plantation failed at first because it was overrun in the Nine Years War (see below). But it did have some successes. The settlers built new towns such as Killarney, Glin and Mallow. By 1641 about 22,000 Protestant settlers had made their home in Munster. Many of their descendants still live there today.

SOURCE 8.16: Queen Elizabeth I

## What happened in Ulster in the 1590s?

By the 1590s the English controlled every part of Ireland except Ulster. The ruling lords in Ulster became worried about the spread of English law to their lands. Some of them had English titles because they had cooperated with English rulers in the past. The most powerful Gaelic lords were **Hugh O'Neill**, Earl of Tyrone, and **Hugh O'Donnell**, Earl of Tyrconnell.

### Nine Years War (1594–1603)

The remaining Gaelic lords were not impressed when English officials began telling them how to run their lands. Many Gaelic clans joined together and, led by Hugh O'Neill, went to war with the English. This was called the **Nine Years War**.

O'Neill, who was a very skilled soldier, won several battles against the English. But the Ulster lords knew they would need outside help to win the war. To get it, they claimed they were fighting for the Catholic faith against the Protestant Elizabeth. They asked the King of Spain, who was the most powerful Catholic monarch in Europe, to help them.

The Spanish king promised an army but it was a long time coming. When it arrived in 1601, it landed in Kinsale, Co. Cork, and not in Ulster. In the middle of winter, O'Neill and his army began to march south to join the Spaniards. An English army also rushed to Kinsale and it got there first. A fierce battle followed and the Irish and Spanish forces were defeated. O'Neill held out for two years, but he had to surrender in the end. The **Battle of Kinsale** (1601) is important because it was the last time Gaelic lords had a real chance to keep control in Ireland.

> **DID YOU KNOW?**
>
> Hugh O'Neill, Earl of Tyrone, was brought up in England and is usually referred to as 'Tyrone' in English sources from the time.

SOURCE 8.17: Hugh O'Neill

> **DID YOU KNOW?**
>
> The population of Ulster was estimated at between 25,000 and 40,000 people in 1600.

## Activity 6

Examine this source and then answer the questions below.

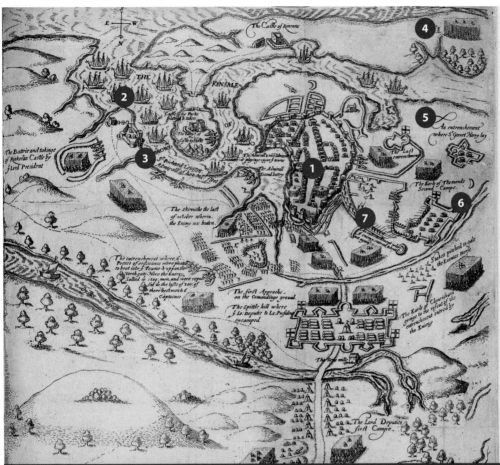

1. Town of Kinsale
2. Spanish ships
3. English fort
4. Gaelic Irish came from this direction
5. English camp
6. Earl of Thomond (O'Brien)
7. Forts and trenches built by the English

**SOURCE 8.18:** Map illustration of army besieging Kinsale in Ireland in 1601 © British Library Board

1. Where are the Spanish ships? Why would they find it difficult to contact their allies in the Irish camp?
2. Were there any Irish on the English side?
3. Why would some Irish clans support the English army, do you think?
4. Why is a map like this so useful to historians? Give a reason for your answer.

## Flight of the Earls

O'Neill was not harshly punished because the new monarch, **James I**, wanted peace in Ireland. However, most of the Gaelic Ulster lords found it impossible to accept English rule. They soon got into debt because they no longer had the power to collect rents and taxes. In 1607 the majority decided to leave Ireland and go to Europe, where they hoped to persuade the Spanish to send another army. This became known as the **Flight of the Earls**.

### DID YOU KNOW?

James VI of Scotland became **James I of England and Ireland** when Elizabeth I died in 1603.

**SOURCE 8.19: King James I**

# How did the Ulster plantation work?

With the Gaelic leaders gone, James decided to plant Ulster. He declared the Earls of Tyrone and Tyrconnell traitors and took over their land. As King of Scotland, England and Ireland, he wanted to bring people from all parts of his kingdom together. He saw Ulster as a land where he could do this. By 1609 his Ulster plantation plan was ready. It covered about 2,000 km$^2$ of farmland. It would be the most successful plantation in Ireland.

The land that had been taken was divided into **six counties**: Donegal, Derry, Tyrone, Armagh, Fermanagh and Cavan. He further divided the area into **estates** of 1,000 acres, 1,500 acres and 2,000 acres. These estates were given to the planters.

**Estate**
A large area of land.

**Acre**
Area of land measuring 4,047 m$^2$. One hectare is 2.47 acres.

There were three types of planter:

> **Undertakers:** Rich gentlemen from Britain who got grants of land and 'undertook' or promised to bring tenants to Ireland.
> **Servitors:** Mostly English or Scottish soldiers who were given land in the Ulster plantation.
> **'Loyal Irish':** Native Irish who had stayed loyal to the English during the Nine Years War.

They all had to promise to be loyal to the British monarch.

Land that had belonged to the Catholic Church was given to the Anglican (English Protestant) Church. Forests and bogs were not included in the plantation.

## Activity 7

Examine these sources and then answer the questions below.

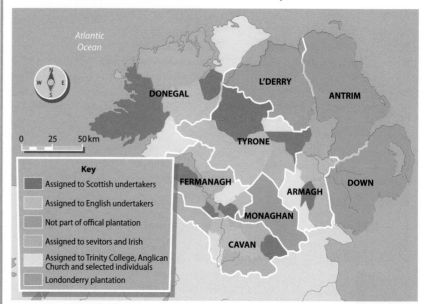

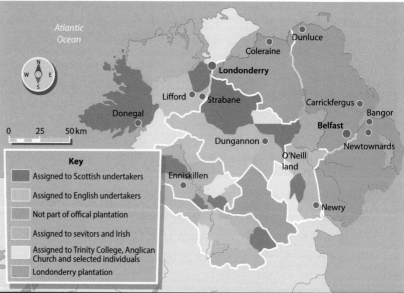

**SOURCE 8.20:** Maps of the Ulster plantation. In 1622 there were 3,100 adult Englishmen and 3,700 adult Scotsmen in a total of 19,000 settlers. By the 1630s that total had grown to an estimated 30,000.

1 Name the six Ulster counties that were planted by James I.
2 Which three Ulster counties were not part of the official Ulster plantation?
3 Suggest why the servitors and Irish were assigned land near each other.
4 Name four new plantation towns.

## Activity 8

Examine this source and then answer the questions below.

| | Undertakers | Servitors | Loyal Irish |
|---|---|---|---|
| **Who were they?** | English and Scottish landowners | English and Scots who worked for the government in Ireland; most were soldiers | Gaelic landowners who had been loyal to England during the Nine Years War |
| **What did they get?** | Mostly estates of 2,000 acres | Estates of 1,500 or 1,000 acres | Estates of 1,000 acres or less |
| **What rent did they pay to the king?** | £5 per 1,000 acres | £8 per 1,000 acres | £10 per 1,000 acres |
| **Who could they rent their land to?** | They had to bring in English or Scottish tenants<br><br>They could not rent land to Irish tenants | They could rent land to Irish tenants | They could rent land to Irish tenants |

**SOURCE 8.21:** Conditions planters had to agree to in order to get land

1 Who had to pay the most rent? Suggest why this was.
2 Why was some land given to Gaelic landowners?
3 What were undertakers not allowed to do?
4 Why were servitors allowed to have Gaelic tenants, do you think?

## Plantation in Derry

James made a special arrangement for Co. Derry. He persuaded twelve London companies (similar to medieval guilds) to invest money in planting it. They divided the land between them and renamed it Co. Londonderry.

The London businessmen built two large towns: Derry and Coleraine. In Derry, Gaelic people had to live outside the town walls. They settled on the boggy area nearby. The area is still called the Bogside.

## Activity 9

Examine this source and then answer the questions below.

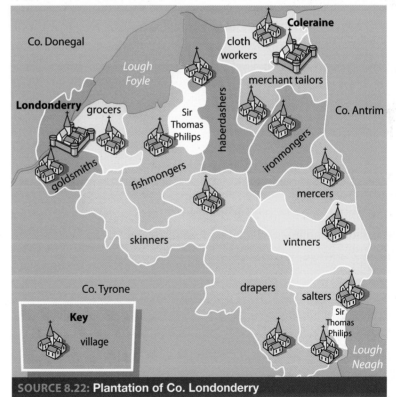

**SOURCE 8.22:** Plantation of Co. Londonderry

1 This map shows where each of the twelve London companies got land. Name the work of each company.
2 Why did the government want to bring these companies to Ireland, do you think?
3 One town in Co. Derry is called Draperstown. In your opinion, how did it get its name?

## Activity 10

Examine this source and then answer the questions below.

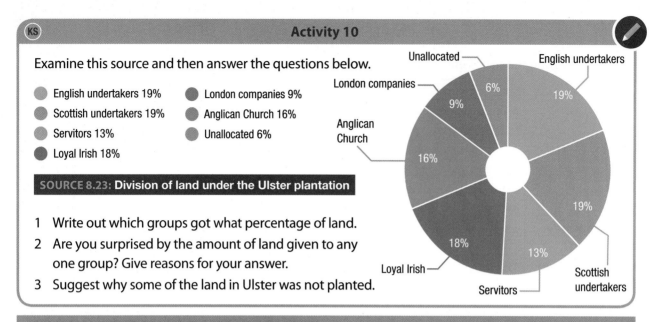

- English undertakers 19%
- Scottish undertakers 19%
- Servitors 13%
- Loyal Irish 18%
- London companies 9%
- Anglican Church 16%
- Unallocated 6%

**SOURCE 8.23: Division of land under the Ulster plantation**

1. Write out which groups got what percentage of land.
2. Are you surprised by the amount of land given to any one group? Give reasons for your answer.
3. Suggest why some of the land in Ulster was not planted.

## DO YOU UNDERSTAND THESE KEY TERMS?

| | | | |
|---|---|---|---|
| acre | estate | Nine Years War | servitor |
| Brehon law | Flight of the Earls | Old English | undertaker |
| common law | Gaelic lord | the Pale | |
| éiric | 'loyal Irish' | plantation | |

PowerPoint summary

# SELF-ASSESSMENT – CAN YOU?

1. Explain what Brehon law was.
2. Explain why land was very important to the Gaelic clans and say who owned it.
3. Explain how an Old English lord got his land.
4. Explain two ways in which Old English lords became more like Gaelic lords.
5. Define the Pale.
6. Explain how the people of the Pale were different from the people in the rest of Ireland.
7. Outline what was meant by common law.
8. Give three reasons why English rulers in the 1500s were attracted to the idea of plantation in Ireland.
9. Describe how the Laois–Offaly plantation came about.
10. Give one reason why Elizabeth I decided to have a plantation in Munster.
11. Say how much land was confiscated for the plantation in Munster.
12. Explain why the settlers had to build towns, giving two reasons.
13. Say how many new settlers had come to Munster by 1641.
14. Name the two strongest Gaelic lords in Ulster in the 1590s and explain why these lords had an English title.
15. Say which country the Gaelic lords asked for help to fight the English and outline the reason they gave for wanting help.
16. Name the battle that followed and say who won.
17. Explain the 'Flight of the Earls'.
18. Name the monarch who planted Ulster and explain what he hoped to achieve with this new plantation.
19. Distinguish between the three main types of planter.
20. Explain how 'Londonderry' got its name.

# WHAT WAS THE IMPACT OF PLANTATION?

## ◎ LEARNING INTENTIONS

**At the end of this section, you should be able to:**

◎ Explain how plantation changed life in Ulster

◎ Describe relations between the native Irish and the planters

◎ Assess the long-term impact of the Ulster plantation.

## How did plantation change life in Ulster?

The Ulster plantation changed Ulster. For example:

1 **New settlers:** By 1640 there were about 40,000 English and Scottish adult male settlers in Ulster. The settler population could have been as high as 200,000.

 Between 1690 and 1698 alone, 80,000 Scottish people came to Ulster because of a famine in their own country. Gaelic Irish people remained farming the land, but very few of them owned any land.

2 **New religions:** Most of the planters were Protestant. The Scottish were **Presbyterian** (followers of Calvin) and the English were **Anglican** (members of the Church of Ireland).

3 **New ways of farming:** The Gaelic way of farming, with huge herds of cattle roaming freely around the countryside, was finished. Forests were cleared and the land was divided into farms and fields. Each field was enclosed by a hedge and a ditch. Instead of raising cattle, farmers grew crops such as wheat.

4 **New ways of trading:** Markets and fairs were organised in the towns where settlers and the native Irish could sell their produce. Roads were built to link the towns and help trade develop.

5 **New towns:** By 1640 there were over twenty new towns. Some became large and successful; others remained villages. The new towns were well planned. Houses were laid out in streets with a square, often called the Diamond, in the centre. A Protestant church was usually built nearby.

### Activity 1

Examine this source and then answer the question below.

SOURCE 8.24: Aerial photograph of Fermanagh countryside

1 Give two advantages of dividing your land with ditches and hedges.

**Activity 2**

Examine this source and then answer the questions below.

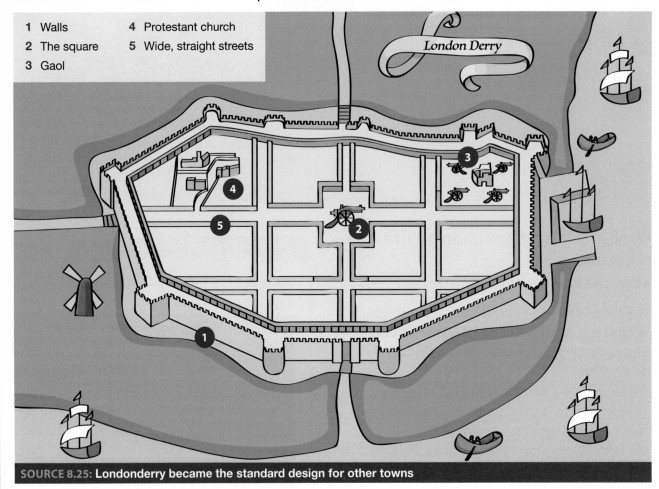

1 Walls          4 Protestant church
2 The square      5 Wide, straight streets
3 Gaol

London Derry

SOURCE 8.25: Londonderry became the standard design for other towns

1 What is the main feature in the centre of the town?

2 What was this area used for?

3 What information does this map give us about how people lived in Londonderry at this time? Identify three pieces of information it gives us and verify your answers.

4 Was this town easy to defend? Give reasons for your answer.

6 **New houses:** The settlers drew maps of their new estates. From these pictures we can see the kinds of houses and towns that they built.

7 **New laws:** English judges brought in common law. Brehon law was forbidden in the large towns. There were courthouses and a gaol to house prisoners. There was a sheriff in every county and a constable in each parish. The king's judges travelled around the country to judge serious crimes. (See Section 20)

8 **New customs:** The English banned Irish fashions such as the **glib**, a long fringe worn by Irish men, the Irish mantle, and harping. Settlers brought in English and Scottish styles of dress, food, music and dances such as the hornpipe.

9 **New language:** The Irish language was used less, and by 1700 most well-educated people in Ulster spoke only English.

Despite these changes, Irish culture remained strong. Irish scholars, especially in Europe, wrote down the history of Ireland and old Irish legends. Irish music and poetry remained popular.

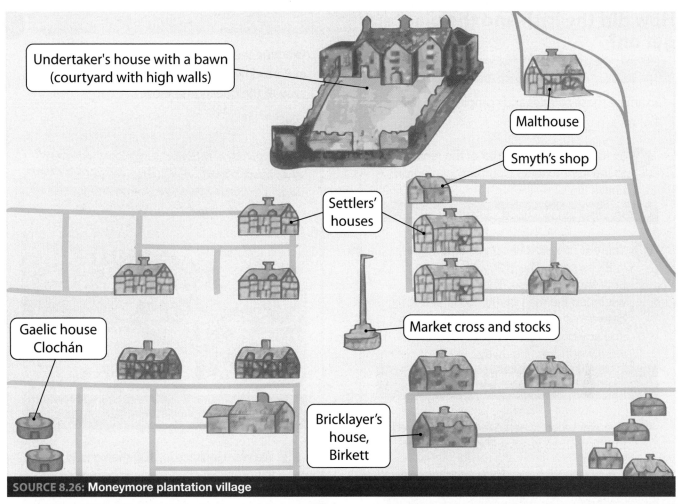

Undertaker's house with a bawn (courtyard with high walls)

Malthouse

Smyth's shop

Settlers' houses

Gaelic house Clochán

Market cross and stocks

Bricklayer's house, Birkett

**SOURCE 8.26: Moneymore plantation village**

## Activity 3

(KS) (👥)

Examine the village plan in Source 8.26 and then answer these questions.

1 Who, do you think, worked in Smyth's shop?

2 What, do you think, was made at the malthouse?

3 What building is *not* here that you might expect to find in a village?

4 What did undertakers promise to do in the Ulster plantation? List three promises they made.

5 From this map, how do we know that the undertaker broke his agreement with the government?

6 How does the map reveal that not as many settlers came here as was hoped?

## Activity 4

Examine this source and then answer the question below.

Sʳ Phillom O Neale
Cheife Traytor of all Ireland

**SOURCE 8.27: Phelim O'Neill in English dress, 1640s**

1 What does this picture tell us about Phelim O'Neill?

2 Describe two items of 'English' dress and fashion that you can see in the picture.

**Learning Outcome** 2.1   161

## How did the Irish and the planters get on?

Examine these sources and complete the task below.

**A** In 1616, over one quarter of the rents paid to the Ironmongers Company came from native Irish.

SOURCE 8.28: Ironmongers' plantation records

**B** There is nothing but constant struggle in these parts. The Irish went in to an Englishman's house. They severely wounded the man of the house and took between 7 and 8 pounds [a fortune now!] and any of the rest of his goods which were worth carrying away.

SOURCE 8.29: George Canning, agent for the ironmongers

**C** The plantation scheme in Ulster survived for thirty-three years without any major fighting.

SOURCE 8.30: from *The Plantation of Ulster* by Jonathan Bardon, Gill & Macmillan, 2011

**D** At the Hamilton Estate in Co. Tyrone in 1622 there were no settlers and 120 native Irish.

SOURCE 8.31: 1622 report on Ulster plantation

**E** Where have the Gaels gone? … We have in their stead an arrogant, impure crowd of foreigners' blood.

SOURCE 8.32: Seventeenth-century Gaelic Irish poet

1  Write a heading in your journal: 'How well did the settlers and native Irish get on?' and divide the page into two columns.
  • In the first column, write down which of the sources A–E support the idea that the native Irish and settlers mixed.
  • In the second, write down which sources suggest that the two groups did not get on.
  • Evaluate the evidence for and against the question. Write down your opinion and give two reasons for it.

Examine these sources about the Massacre at Portadown, Co. Armagh (1641), and then answer the questions below.

**A**

Driuinge Men Women & chi:dren by hund: reds vpon Briges & casting them into Riuers, who drowned not were killed with poles & shot with muskets.

SOURCE 8.33: Picture from 1645; we do not know if the artist was an eyewitness

**B** We were locked up, 100 men and children in Loughgall church. Many were sore, tortured by strangling and half hanging … then driven like hogs six miles to the River Bann in Portadown … pushed onto the bridge, stripped naked and then forced by pikes into the river … those that did not drown were shot by the rebels as they tried to swim ashore …

SOURCE 8.34: Eyewitness description by William Clarke, 1641 Depositions

1  Examine the writing on the illustration. Is there any letter that is now written differently?
2  Are there any differences between the two accounts of the massacre? Explain your answer.
3  Which source gives the most information about the event, A or B? Say why.
4  Which source would have been the most effective in the 1600s? Give a reason.
5  Are the sources British or Irish? Explain your answer.
6  Can we trust these sources? Are they biased? Explain your answers.

# What was the long-term impact of the Ulster plantation?

The plantation not only changed Ulster, it also brought some problems.

## Undertakers broke their agreements

Many undertakers broke their agreements. They did not build proper defences and often took on Gaelic tenants. This meant that the Gaelic Irish, who were very bitter about losing their land, continued to outnumber the planters. They hated the settlers and often attacked them.

### Activity 7

Examine this source and then answer the questions below.

> Only 145 houses are built
>
> Only part of the town is built and the rest is so dirty 'that no man is able to go on it'
>
> There is no market square
>
> The walls are built of sods and filled with earth. They begin to fall apart
>
> The bulwarks [walls made of earth] are so small no cannon would fit on them
>
> The gatehouse was built only of wood and easily broken down

**SOURCE 8.35: Report on Coleraine in 1618, seven years after the plantation had started there**

1. Why, do you think, did the town remain unfinished?
2. Why is the writer of this report so worried about the town's defences?
3. What does this source tell you about the progress of the plantation?

## Religious divide

The English hoped that plantation would turn the Catholic Irish into Protestants, but that did not happen. Religion divided people in Ulster, as the settlers were Protestants and the natives were Catholic. There was also tension between the Anglican English settlers and the Presbyterian Scottish settlers.

Differences over land and religion between the native Irish and the settlers led to a Catholic Irish rebellion in 1641. Historians now reckon that about 12,000 of the 40,000 settlers were massacred in this rebellion.

### Activity 8

Examine this source and then answer the questions below.

**Key**
- Protestants
- Catholics
- Other

Northern Ireland

19% 38% 43%

Republic of Ireland

3% 5% 92%

**SOURCE 8.36: Percentage of Protestants and Catholics living in Ireland in 1991**

1. Where did most Protestants in Ireland live in 1991?
2. Why, do you think, is this the case?

## Are there still divisions?

Division between descendants of the Gaelic Irish and of the planters is still evident today. In 1922 the Northern Ireland state was established. It is part of the United Kingdom because that is what the majority of people who live there want.

Most of the descendants of Protestant settlers became **unionists**. Unionists want Northern Ireland to remain part of the UK. Most of the descendants of the Gaelic Irish became **nationalists**. Nationalists want a united and independent Ireland. Between 1968 and 1993 over 3,000 people were killed in violence between some unionists and nationalists in Northern Ireland. People refer to this violent period as **the Troubles** (see Section 12).

### Activity 9

**Plantations: A good idea or a bad one?**

1　Draw up a table with two columns. At the top of one column write 'Advantages of the Ulster Plantation for Ireland'. At the top of the other write 'Disadvantages of the Ulster Plantation for Ireland'.

2　Now fill in each column with as many ideas as you can think of.

3　Which column is longer?

4　Based on your table and information in this section, do you think that plantation was a good thing or a bad thing for Ireland? Give two reasons for your answer.

| DO YOU UNDERSTAND THESE KEY TERMS? | |
| --- | --- |
| Anglican | the Troubles |
| nationalist | unionist |
| Presbyterian | |

Chapter summary　　Weblinks　　PowerPoint summary

SOURCE 8.37: Unionists marching in Belfast

SOURCE 8.38: Nationalists marching in Belfast

## SELF-ASSESSMENT – CAN YOU?

1　Give four examples of how plantation changed life in Ulster.

2　Describe relations between the native Irish and the planters.

3　Outline the long-term impact of the Ulster plantation.

# 9 HOW TECHNOLOGY CHANGED SOCIETY

How did changes in the textile industry in the eighteenth and nineteenth centuries affect how people worked and lived?

What was the impact of the development of railways on the lives of people in Britain in the 1800s?

Milestones in information and communications technology

# HOW DID CHANGES IN THE TEXTILE INDUSTRY IN THE EIGHTEENTH AND NINETEENTH CENTURIES AFFECT HOW PEOPLE WORKED AND LIVED?

## 🎯 LEARNING INTENTIONS

**At the end of this section, you should be able to:**

◎ Explain what the term 'technological development' means

◎ Explain the term 'domestic system'

◎ Investigate how innovations impacted on the textile industry in Britain during the Industrial Revolution

◎ Analyse the impact of the steam engine in the textile industry

◎ Investigate how steam power changed the working conditions of the workers in the textile industry

◎ Outline measures that were taken to improve working conditions in the textile mills

◎ Analyse the impact of changing technology on how people lived their lives

◎ Describe the measures taken to improve the living conditions in industrial towns.

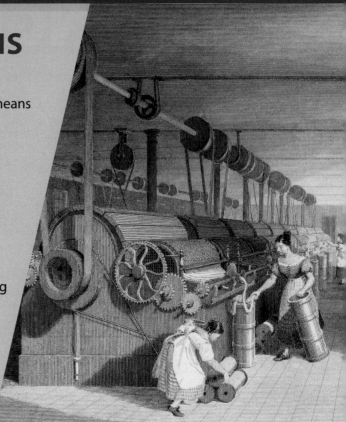

## The age of steam

This section is about the impact of technological change on the textile industry and the railways. It examines in particular how steam power transformed the textile industry and created a new type of transport called the railway. It shows how society is changed by innovations and adopts new ways of doing things. It also looks at the impact of technological change and innovation on people's lives.

Between the middle of the eighteenth century and the early nineteenth century, Britain was experiencing an industrial revolution.

Britain had all the necessary conditions for **industrialisation**:

> **Colonies** of the British Empire supplied cheap raw materials such as cotton. They also provided a market for British goods.

> The **population was growing**. As a result there were more people to work in the factories and more people to buy the goods made in the factories.

> There was a good **supply of coal and iron**. Coal was used to heat water to produce steam, and steam was used to power machines. Machines were made of iron.

**SOURCE 9.1: Steam train**

**Industrialisation**
A time when society changed from farming to manufacturing and altered the way people worked, lived and travelled.

**Colony**
A country taken over and ruled by another country.

› Britain had **inventors** who designed and made new machines. **Richard Arkwright** invented the **water frame**, which made the textile industry more efficient. **James Watt** invented a **steam engine** that was used to drive machines in the factories and to drive locomotives on the railway.

## How did textile production change?

### Domestic system

Before 1750 people made cloth by hand in their own homes in the countryside. Women used a **spinning wheel** to turn wool into thread (yarn). Men wove the thread into cloth using a **loom**. These machines were small and powered by hand. This system is called the **domestic system** or **cottage system**.

However, the domestic system was slow and the amount of cloth produced was very small. Around 1750 there was a huge increase in demand due to the growing population. This meant that new innovations had to be introduced to produce more cloth more quickly.

> **DID YOU KNOW?**
>
> The population of Britain increased because:
> - Plagues such as the Black Death disappeared
> - A wider choice of food to eat meant fewer famines
> - Medical discoveries helped people live longer.

### Innovations in the textile industry

In 1733 **John Kay**'s invention of the **flying shuttle** made it faster and easier to weave thread into cloth. This machine was twice as quick as the earlier loom. It needed three people working on spinning wheels to keep the loom supplied.

In 1764 **James Hargreaves** invented the **spinning jenny**. It was eight times quicker than the spinning wheel. This meant that thread could be mass-produced.

Both the flying shuttle and the spinning jenny were small enough to be used in a cottage and could be worked by hand.

**Innovation**
New ways of doing things (inventions).

**Mass production**
Making things on a large scale.

---

**Activity 1**

Draw a spider diagram to show the reasons why Britain had an Industrial Revolution.

**Technological developments**
Changes in the way products are made.

**SOURCE 9.2: People spinning and weaving in their home**

---

**Activity 2**

Examine this source and then answer the questions below.

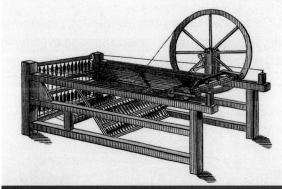

**SOURCE 9.3: Hargreaves' spinning jenny**

1 Can you explain how the spinning jenny worked?
2 Why was the spinning jenny an important invention?

In 1769 **Richard Arkwright** invented the **water frame**. The frame could spin hundreds of threads at once. These machines were too large to be used in a cottage. They had to be put in special buildings called factories. Arkwright's factory/mill was in

SOURCE 9.4: Richard Arkwright

Cromford, Derbyshire. The water frame was powered by a water wheel turned by the river outside the mill. Flowing water turned a large wheel that was connected by big belts or spindles to machines in the factory. The water frame could spin hundreds of threads at the same time. Richard Arkwright is credited with bringing in the **factory age**.

The disadvantage of using rivers to turn the wheels was that in winter the water could freeze and in summer there might be very little water due to lack of rain. If there was not enough water production would have to stop.

The machines were working twenty-four hours a day, and workers worked twelve-hour shifts. This was a huge change from working at home. In one week one operator working Arkwright's machine could produce sixty times more cloth than a whole family working at home under the domestic system. The mill was therefore able to produce a lot more cloth at a much lower cost.

Arkwright opened factories all over the country and became very wealthy. This inspired other factory owners to use similar methods and to invent other machines.

In 1779 **Samuel Crompton** invented the **spinning mule**. This invention improved spinning even further, and became very popular in the cotton mills.

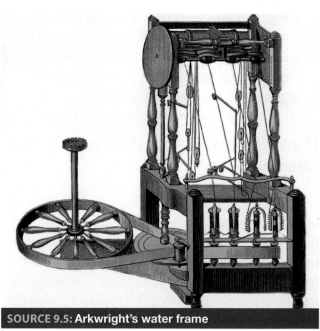
SOURCE 9.5: Arkwright's water frame

SOURCE 9.6: Cromford mill

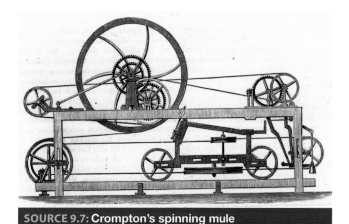
SOURCE 9.7: Crompton's spinning mule

While thread was being spun in factories, weaving was still being done in people's homes (domestic system).

## Impact of the steam engine on the textile industry

The textile industry changed completely with the invention of the **power loom** by **Edmund Cartwright**. This machine allowed cloth to be made as quickly as thread/yarn was being spun in factories. It was the first machine to be powered by steam power rather than by water. It adapted Watt's steam engine.

The steam engine's job was to turn a wheel. To do this, coal was burned to turn water in the boiler into steam. The steam escaped into the cylinder and moved the piston, which pushed up one side of the beam. This turned the wheel. When the piston reached the top of the cylinder, the steam escaped and the piston and beam went back down. Then the whole process started again. The see-saw action of the beam was used to turn the wheel.

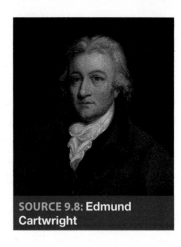

SOURCE 9.8: Edmund Cartwright

### Activity 3

Examine the source and then answer the question below.

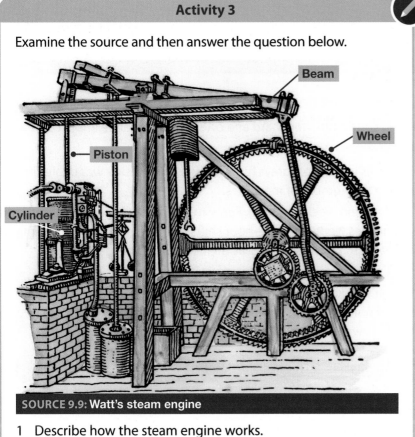

SOURCE 9.9: **Watt's steam engine**

1   Describe how the steam engine works.

> **DID YOU KNOW?**
>
> The first steam engines were used to prevent coal mines flooding. Thomas Savery invented a steam engine that created a vacuum that sucked up water from the mine.
>
> Thomas Newcomen made the steam engine more efficient by putting a piston inside the cylinder. James Watt improved this machine, which could now turn a wheel.

The effect of Watt's steam engine was incredible. It replaced water power in factories, so now factories could be located anywhere, not just beside a river. Machines could be used twenty-four hours a day, 365 days a year. This hugely increased the profits of the factory owners. By 1850 Britain's factories produced two-thirds of the world's cotton cloth.

Watt's steam engine was the most important invention of the Industrial Revolution.

Steam became the major power source of the Industrial Revolution.

SOURCE 9.10: **A cotton mill**

## The new factories

Under the domestic system people worked in their homes, women spinning yarn and men weaving on a loom. Most people's main occupation was farming and this took up most of their time.

With the new machines operating in factories people had to leave the countryside and go where the work was – in factories. People now lived in the towns that grew up around the factories. There was a dramatic change in their working conditions.

More women and children worked in the mills than men. This was because their wages were lower, so they were cheaper to employ. In some mills two-thirds of the workforce were children. Children had to work because the family needed the money, and the factory owners employed them as they were cheaper than adults. Small children were able to crawl between the moving machines to pick up cotton waste. Older children would re-tie broken threads while the machines were running – they were called piecers.

### What were working conditions like in the textile mills?

Working conditions were hard and often had a negative impact on the health of the workers.

> The mills were five storeys high and the noise inside was deafening, due to the number of machines.

> The working week was long. Some mills operated round the clock and employees worked twelve-hour shifts. In other mills they worked from 5.30 a.m. to 8 p.m. Sunday was their only day off.

> Dust was everywhere and this caused lung diseases.

> The air was kept moist, hot and damp so that the cotton threads would not break. Windows were kept closed to keep in the heat. Workers would often faint due to the heat.

---

**Activity 4**

Examine this source and then answer the questions below.

> They reached the mill about 5.30 am. The moment he entered the doors, the noise appalled him, and the stench seemed intolerable.
>
> The first task given him was to pick up the loose cotton from the floor. He was much terrified by the whirling motion and noise of the machines, and not a little affected by the dust with which he was half suffocated.
>
> Unused to the stench he soon felt sick and by constantly stooping, his back ached. He sat down but this he found was strictly forbidden. His taskmaster gave him to understand he must keep on his legs. He did so, till twelve o'clock. Blincoe suffered greatly with thirst and hunger.

SOURCE 9.11: **An extract from *A Memoir of Robert Blincoe*, John Brown, 1832, describing his first day in the mill**

1 Describe Blincoe's first day at work.

2 Blincoe wrote this account when he was an adult. He had to stop work because he became disabled. Do you think this account is reliable?

SOURCE 9.12: **Workers at the machines**

People's backs became permanently bent from the physical hardship of working the machines all day. Piecers, who had to lean over the machine while repairing threads, put severe strain on their knees and ankles and were often disabled as a result.

## Activity 5

Examine these sources and then answer the questions below.

**A** I have had frequent opportunities of seeing people coming out from the factories and occasionally attending as patients. Last summer I visited three cotton factories with Dr. Clough of Preston and Mr. Barker of Manchester and we could not remain ten minutes in the factory without gasping for breath. How it is possible for those who are doomed to remain there twelve or fifteen hours to endure it? If we take into account the heated temperature of the air, and the contamination of the air, it is a matter of astonishment to my mind, how the work people can bear the confinement for so great a length of time.

SOURCE 9.13: **Dr Ward from Manchester interviewed by Lord Kenyon's House of Lords Committee on the health of textile workers, 1819**

**B** **Whatton:** [Child labour in factories] is so moderate it can scarcely be called labour at all; and under those circumstances I should not think there would be any injury from it. **Parliamentary committee:** Have you observed any particular symptoms of disease about the children? **Whatton:** No; I cannot say that I did. **Parliamentary committee:** Do you happen to know whether or not any particular effect is produced upon a child's frame that is kept standing longer than his strength will permit, or rather, than he ought to be subjected to? **Whatton:** I am not aware of any effect.

SOURCE 9.14: **Dr Whatton from Manchester being interviewed by Lord Kenyon's House of Lords Committee on working conditions in a textile factory, 1818**

1 What does Dr Ward say about the effects of working conditions on the health of the workers?
2 What is the opinion of Dr Whatton on the effects of working conditions on the workers' health?
3 Suggest why they might have opposite views.
4 From your study of the Industrial Revolution, which opinion do you agree with? Give two reasons for your answer.

If a worker fell against a machine, there was no protection. Such accidents often resulted in lost limbs.

## Activity 6

Examine this source and then answer the questions below.

A girl named Mary Richards, who was thought remarkably handsome when she left the workhouse, and, who was not quite ten years of age, attended a drawing frame, below which, and about a foot from the floor, was a horizontal shaft, by which the frames above were turned. It happened one evening, when her apron was caught by the shaft. In an instant the poor girl was drawn by an irresistible force and dashed on the floor. She uttered the most heart-rending shrieks! Blincoe ran towards her, an agonized and helpless beholder of a scene of horror. He saw her whirled round and round with the shaft – he heard the bones of her arms, legs, thighs, etc. successively snap asunder, crushed, seemingly, to atoms, as the machinery whirled her round, and drew tighter and tighter her body within the works, her blood was scattered over the frame and streamed upon the floor, her head appeared dashed to pieces – at last, her mangled body was jammed in so fast, between the shafts and the floor, that the water being low and the wheels off the gear, it stopped the main shaft. When she was extricated, every bone was found broken – her head dreadfully crushed. She was carried off quite lifeless.

**SOURCE 9.15:** Account of an eyewitness report from Robert Blincoe, who worked in the textile mills

1  Describe, in your own words, what happened to Mary Richards.
2  What were Blincoe's feelings about the accident?

Workers were only allowed forty minutes for dinner and could have three toilet breaks a day. Discipline was harsh. Workers were not allowed talk or whistle. If you were late you were fined. Those in charge of the children were called overseers. They often beat children if they were not working fast enough or if they fell asleep.

## Activity 7

Examine the source and then answer the question below.

After I had worked for half a year I could scarcely walk. In the morning my brother and sister used to take me under each arm and run with me, a good mile, to the mill. If we were five minutes late, the overseer would take a strap and beat us black and blue. I have seen my mother weep at me sometimes, but she would not tell me why she was weeping.

**SOURCE 9.16:** Joseph Hebergam, aged seventeen, interviewed by Michael Sadler, House of Lords Committee (1832), about his work in a mill in Huddersfield

1  Many parents let their children work in these conditions. Does this mean they were cruel and didn't care about their children?

**SOURCE 9.17:** Children being beaten by overseers

### KS 👥  Activity 8

Work in pairs.

1   Make a list of all the bad points about children working in the mills.

2   Design a pamphlet to send to all employers calling on them to improve conditions for children. Choose the most important points from your list to go into the pamphlet. Be able to explain why you have chosen these points.

3   Then write a letter from an employer replying to the points you have raised.

# Improving working conditions

The situation became so bad in the mills that people began to demand new laws to improve working conditions.

## Factory Acts

**Lord Shaftesbury** was the man who did most to improve working conditions. A series of **Factory Acts** were passed by the government, which was afraid that there might be a revolution in Britain if they did not do something. There had been a revolution in France in 1789 (see Section 10).

SOURCE 9.18: **Lord Shaftesbury**

| Factory Acts | |
|---|---|
| **1833** | 〉 Children under nine could not work in factories |
| | 〉 Children aged between nine and thirteen could not work over 55 hours a week and had to attend school for two hours a day |
| | 〉 Inspectors were appointed to make sure the law was obeyed |
| **1842** | 〉 Women and children under ten could not work in the mines |
| **1844** | 〉 Women could work no more than twelve hours a day |
| | 〉 Children could work no more than six and a half hours a day |
| **1847** | 〉 Working day restricted to ten hours for women and everyone under eighteen |

## Robert Owen

SOURCE 9.19: **Robert Owen**

**Robert Owen** owned cotton mills in New Lanark in Scotland. He treated his workers well and paid them a fair wage. He felt that they would work harder as a result. He also built good houses for his workers and schools for their children. To everyone's astonishment he made large profits. Sadly, only a small minority of factory owners followed his example.

### Activity 9

Examine the source and then answer the question below.

1 Why, do you think, is the mill located in the countryside?

SOURCE 9.20: **New Lanark mills**

### Activity 10

Examine this source and then answer the questions below.

> Seventeen years ago, a number of individuals, with myself, purchased the New Lanark establishment from Mr. Dale. I found that there were 500 children, who had been taken from poor-houses, chiefly in Edinburgh, and those children were generally from the age of five and six, to seven to eight. The hours at that time were thirteen. Although these children were well fed their limbs were very generally deformed, their growth was stunted, and although one of the best schoolmasters was engaged to instruct these children regularly every night, in general they made very slow progress, even in learning the common alphabet. I came to the conclusion that the children were injured by being taken into the mills at this early age.

SOURCE 9.21: **Robert Owen tells us about his philosophy**

1 What are the main points in this document?
2 Describe what working conditions were like in the textile mills.
3 Draw a timeline showing the Factory Acts and a short note on each one.
4 How would you feel about having to work in such a mill with the strict rules and thirteen-hour days?

## How did new technology affect people's lives?

The new factory system required large numbers of workers. Towns and cities developed around the factories because people had to live close to their place of work. In 1750, 25% of the population lived in towns. By 1850 this had risen to 50%.

---

### Activity 11

Examine these sources and then answer the questions below.

SOURCE 9.22: Manchester, c.1750

SOURCE 9.23: Manchester, c.1850

1    List two changes that occurred in Manchester between 1750 and 1850.
2    During which period would you prefer to have lived in Manchester? Give three reasons for your answer.

---

## Living conditions of workers in the industrial towns and cities

Houses were built as quickly and cheaply as possible and many families lived in a single room. Records show that forty people lived in one room in a house in Liverpool in 1847. There was little furniture and the floor was usually hard earth. Factories produced a lot of **pollution**, which made conditions in nearby houses unhealthy. City streets were polluted with thick **smog**. The filthy conditions, combined with poor hygiene, led to all sorts of ill health.

There was no running water. A toilet, which was a deep hole in the ground with a wooden shed over it, was located in the front yard. It was shared by as many as forty families. There was a pump for water nearby. The water was easily contaminated by sewage. There were open drains in the middle of the street into which rubbish was thrown. Rats were everywhere. Water was carried from the polluted river for washing and cooking. This caused many diseases.

### Activity 12

Examine this source and then answer the questions below.

|            | 1750   | 1850    |
|------------|--------|---------|
| Manchester | 75,000 | 750,000 |
| Liverpool  | 35,000 | 376,000 |
| Sheffield  | 12,000 | 150,000 |
| Leeds      | 14,000 | 172,000 |

SOURCE 9.24: Growth of cities: population 1750 and 1850

1    Draw a bar graph showing growth in population in each town over the period 1750 to 1850.

2    Calculate which town had the highest percentage increase.

3    In your own words, explain why towns grew so rapidly in this period.

The diet of the working class was bread, cheese, porridge and potatoes. Many people died young as a result of their difficult living and working conditions. In Manchester in 1840 average life expectancy was just seventeen. One in five children died before the age of one.

## Disease

Diseases in the towns were mainly caused by poor sanitation. They spread rapidly due to the overcrowded conditions.

> **Typhoid** was the most common disease. It was caused by people using dirty water for drinking and cooking.

> Many people died of **tuberculosis** (TB), which was caused by living in damp conditions.

> In 1832 an outbreak of **cholera** caused 56,000 deaths. Victims became violently ill and had diarrhoea. Their nails and skin turned black. The government was worried as cholera killed both rich and poor people.

## Measures to improve conditions

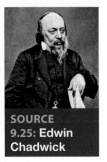

SOURCE 9.25: Edwin Chadwick

**Edwin Chadwick** was appointed by the government to investigate the causes of the cholera epidemic of 1832. In his report he said that dirty water and bad drains caused many diseases such as cholera. People put pressure on the government to change conditions. Chadwick recommended that every city should have a sewerage system and a clean water supply. This would mean raising taxes. Some of the upper class objected.

When another cholera epidemic broke out in 1848 a Public Health Act was passed. It stated that sewers and water pipes would be built. Local Boards of Health were set up to clean the streets. Gradually cities became cleaner and people's health improved greatly.

The **Agricultural Revolution** increased fresh food supplies to the cities and people's diet improved. There were also improvements in medical knowledge. For example, **Louis Pasteur** proved that germs cause disease, rather than the other way round.

### Activity 13

Examine this source and then answer the question below.

SOURCE 9.26: Death's dispensary, pollution cartoon (1866)

1 What point, do you think, is the cartoonist trying to make?

### Activity 14

Examine this source and then answer the question below.

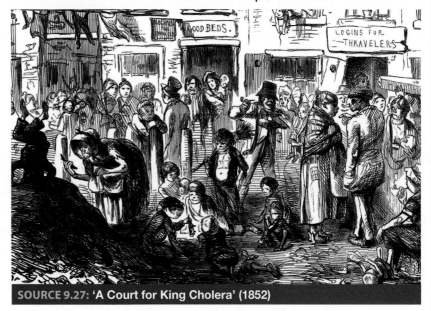

SOURCE 9.27: 'A Court for King Cholera' (1852)

1 Give three reasons why cholera would spread easily in this courtyard.

## Leisure activities

Workers' only day off was Sunday. Many of them drank to forget how hard their lives were. Gin, beer and cider were the most popular drinks. Drunkenness often led to fights breaking out. Gambling, cock-fighting and bare-knuckle boxing were other popular pastimes.

## Living conditions of the wealthy classes

Many wealthy people, such as factory owners, lived either in the suburbs or in the countryside, where they were not affected by pollution from the factories.

They lived in large houses with expensive furniture and silverware. They had butlers, maids and cooks to look after their needs. They ate fish, beef and chicken. They drank wine with their meals. Men drank port after dinner, while women drank tea.

Their children were well educated. Boys often went on to study at Cambridge or Oxford. Later they joined the family business. Girls were educated privately by tutors or governesses. They were taught good manners and needlework by their mothers.

**Activity 15**

Examine this source and then answer the question below.

SOURCE 9.28: *Gin Lane* (1751) by William Hogarth

1  Give five examples from the drawing that show the dangers of drinking too much alcohol.

### DO YOU UNDERSTAND THESE KEY TERMS?

| | | |
|---|---|---|
| colony | industrialisation | piecer |
| domestic system | innovation | steam engine |
| factory age | mass production | textile mill |

 PowerPoint summary

## SELF-ASSESSMENT – CAN YOU?

1  Compare the living and working conditions of people in the domestic system to the conditions of workers in the factory system.

2  Investigate why disease was rampant in the industrial towns.

3  Outline the measures that were taken to improve living conditions in the industrial towns.

4  Draw a timeline of innovations in the textile industry.

# WHAT WAS THE IMPACT OF THE DEVELOPMENT OF RAILWAYS ON THE LIVES OF PEOPLE IN BRITAIN IN THE 1800s?

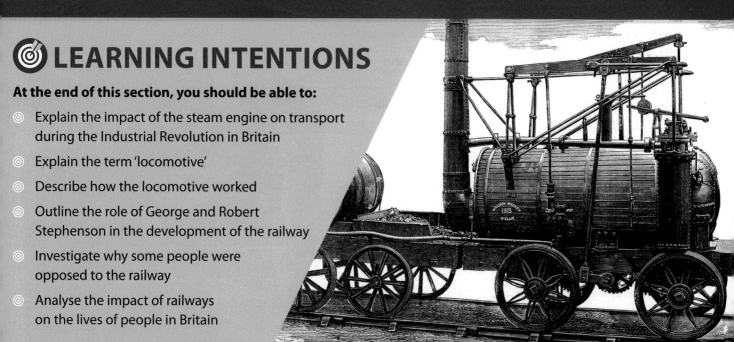

## ◎ LEARNING INTENTIONS

**At the end of this section, you should be able to:**

◎ Explain the impact of the steam engine on transport during the Industrial Revolution in Britain

◎ Explain the term 'locomotive'

◎ Describe how the locomotive worked

◎ Outline the role of George and Robert Stephenson in the development of the railway

◎ Investigate why some people were opposed to the railway

◎ Analyse the impact of railways on the lives of people in Britain

SOURCE 9.29: Richard Trevithick

## Impact of the steam engine on transport

As soon as James Watt built a steam engine that could turn a wheel, it was only a matter of time before a **locomotive** was built.

The first man to build a locomotive was **Richard Trevithick**. In 1804 his engine pulled ten tons of iron and seventy passengers for nine miles. However, it took four hours. It would have been quicker to walk.

**Locomotive**
An engine that moves along rails.

TREVITHICKS,
PORTABLE STEAM ENGINE.

Catch me who can.

Mechanical Power Subduing Animal Speed.

SOURCE 9.30: A Trevithick locomotive

# The role of George and Robert Stephenson in the development of the railway

**George Stephenson** built the first passenger steam railway in 1825. It ran between Stockton and Darlington.

The next big breakthrough came in 1829, and Britain was never the same again.

If Liverpool and Manchester could be linked together by a railway, investors in the project could make a fortune. George Stephenson built the Liverpool–Manchester railway, but if the railway was to be a success they needed a locomotive that was better than the existing ones. So they held the **Rainhill Trials** to find the best locomotive.

**Robert Stephenson** (George's son) built the *Rocket*, which was chosen as the winner. Its average speed was 25 km per hour.

SOURCE 9.31: Building the Liverpool–Manchester railway

---

**Activity 1**

In pairs, using the Internet and other sources, write a paragraph on the Rainhill Trials.

---

**Activity 2**

Examine this source and then answer the questions below.

SOURCE 9.32: Stephenson's *Rocket*

1   Do some research to find out what the letters are pointing to and how these parts contributed to the working of the locomotive (clues: coal, water, piston, rails and steam).
2   Find YouTube videos of reconstructions showing the *Rocket* in operation.

---

On 15 September 1830 the official opening of the Liverpool to Manchester railway took place. The prime minister and the Duke of Wellington were guests of honour. Huge crowds attended. However, it was not to be the best of starts. A member of parliament (MP), William Huskisson, was run over by the *Rocket* and killed. In spite of the tragedy, the opening ceremony continued; but the engine broke down. It took the Duke of Wellington six hours to make the journey to Manchester.

---

**Activity 3**

Write a newspaper article describing what happened at the official opening of the Liverpool to Manchester railway on 15 September 1830. Include an eye-catching headline; details of what happened on the opening day; details of the locomotive and how it was chosen. Also include a picture in your account.

SOURCE 9.33: Excavations for the London to Birmingham railway in the 1830s

Railway fever soon swept Britain. In 1842 there was 3,000 km of track and by 1862 there was 18,000 km. This led to a decline in the use of canals and road transport. By 1900 Britain had been transformed. Almost every village was connected to the rail network, and anyone could travel fairly easily to almost all parts of Britain. Many roads in towns today have names such as Station Lane.

## Why were some people opposed to the railways?

Not everyone was enthusiastic about the railways. Some people were afraid that:

> Hunting would be ruined
> Cows wouldn't graze within sight of the railway
> Women would miscarry at the sight of the locomotive
> Farmland, crops and buildings would be burned by sparks
> Smoke would badly affect vegetation and gardens
> Smoke and soot would get into people's houses in Liverpool and Manchester
> Their health would be affected by travelling so quickly on the train.

**Activity 4**

1 Find out whether there are any street names associated with the railway in your locality.

**Activity 5**

1 Design a poster highlighting the harmful effects of the railway.
2 Explain why each of the points you make are harmful.

# Impact of the railways on the lives of the people of Britain

The railways provided fast and cheap transport. **Heavy goods** could be transported quickly over long distances. In 1750 the journey from London to Edinburgh took two weeks by road. By 1900 it took nine hours by train.

---

### Activity 6

Examine the source and then answer the question below.

| Year | Passengers | Goods (tons) | Coal (tons) |
|------|-----------|--------------|-------------|
| 1830 | 71,951 | 1,433 | 2,360 |
| 1835 | 473,847 | 230,629 | 116,246 |

SOURCE 9.34: **Passengers and goods carried on the Liverpool–Manchester railway, 1830–35**

1 Calculate the approximate percentage increase in (a) passengers and (b) goods during the period 1830–35.

---

The success of the railways was a huge boost to the mining, iron and steel industries: one ton of coal was used by a locomotive every 100 miles.

Trade within Britain increased dramatically. Manufacturers could now sell their goods across the country, not just locally. This meant that products such as Cadbury's chocolate, Bisto gravy and Hovis bread were available nationally, and they became household names.

Unlike improvements to the roads and canals, the building of the railways did not just benefit businessmen. The railways also had a major impact on ordinary people's lives. For example:

> By 1880 there were 300,000 people working in **jobs** that depended on the railway. These included people who built the railways, ticket collectors, train drivers, firemen, guards, engineers, station masters, ticket clerks, porters, catering staff.

> Better-off workers could escape noise and pollution by moving to the suburbs and **commuting** to work.

> **Fresh food** (vegetables and dairy products) was transported every day to the cities. This improved people's diet. A better diet led to better health.

> **Fertilizers** could be taken to farms. This improved crop yields.

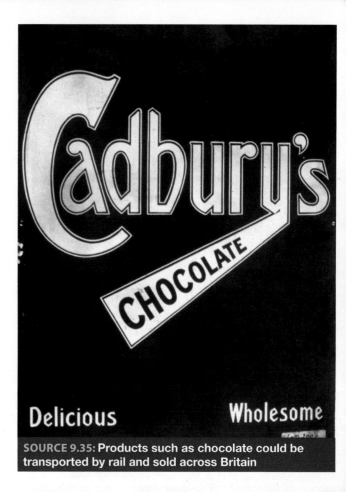

SOURCE 9.35: **Products such as chocolate could be transported by rail and sold across Britain**

---

### Activity 7

1 Use Google Images to find nineteenth-century posters advertising Cadbury's, Bisto and Hovis.

2 Write a short note on the content of one advertisement for each product.

---

### Activity 8

1 Draw a spider diagram showing the types of jobs created by the railways.

---

## Activity 9

Examine the source and then answer the questions below.

SOURCE 9.36: Brighton beach in the nineteenth century

1   Describe what is happening in the picture.
2   List three differences from a beach scene today.

> **Tourism** grew as people travelled by train to seaside resorts such as Brighton and Blackpool. Large hotels were built to accommodate tourists. Cheap third-class tickets allowed working-class people to go on day trips away from the pollution and filth of the cities. Thomas Cook organised cheap day trips to the seaside.

> Fast trains meant that **sports** clubs could play teams from other towns. The Football League was founded in 1888 with twelve teams from all over the country. Cheap rail tickets allowed supporters to travel to watch their team at away fixtures.

> Railways were also important in the development of **golf courses** such as St Andrews and Muirfield. The railways made them accessible for people living in the industrial cities.

## Activity 10

1   In groups of three or four, search online for the names of the twelve founding clubs in the Football League.

2   Choose one of the founding clubs and prepare a presentation of not more than one minute on the history of that club 1888–1914. As part of the presentation calculate the distance between your chosen club and the club that was furthest away.

› By improving communications, railways allowed **news** and ideas to spread. Newspapers were carried all over the country. People knew about political events taking place in other parts of the country, which later helped with the organisation of large demonstrations, for example by the **Chartists**.

---

### Activity 11

1. In groups of three or four, find out who the Chartists were; what their aims were; how they tried to achieve their aims; and how successful or otherwise they were.

2. Assign a role to each member of the group. Then make a presentation to the class lasting no more than one minute. You may use digital, PowerPoint, etc. in your presentation.

---

### Activity 12

Examine the source and then answer the question below.

> All the stagecoaches have stopped running. The canals have reduced their prices by 30%. Goods are delivered in Manchester the same day they arrive in Liverpool. By canal it took three days. The savings to manufacturers in Manchester, in the transporting of cotton alone, has been £20,000 a year. Coal pits have been sunk and factories have been built along the railway, giving greater employment to the poor. The transportation of milk and garden produce is easier. Residents along the line can use the railways to attend business in Liverpool and Manchester with ease and little expense. No inconvenience is felt by residents from smoke or noise. The value of land on the line has gone up because of the railway. It is much sought after for building.

**SOURCE 9.37:** *Annual Register*, 1832

1. Outline the main benefits of the Liverpool to Manchester railway, according to this source.

---

### DID YOU KNOW?

Because trains running regularly between cities had to follow a reliable timetable, local time was abandoned and eventually all of Britain was using Greenwich Mean Time. Before then, Bristol had been eleven minutes behind London. Timetables would have been too complicated if local time had continued to be used.

---

### Activity 13

1. If this is the answer, what is the question? Make up a question that can only be answered by a word on this list:
   - Stockton to Darlington
   - Coal
   - George and Robert Stephenson
   - *Rocket*
   - 1830
   - Brighton and Blackpool

---

### DO YOU UNDERSTAND THESE KEY TERMS?

| | |
|---|---|
| commuting | *Rocket* |
| heavy goods | tourism |
| locomotive | |

 PowerPoint summary

---

### SELF-ASSESSMENT – CAN YOU?

1. Analyse how railways transformed people's lives in Britain.

2. Explain the role that railways played in the Industrial Revolution.

# MILESTONES IN INFORMATION AND COMMUNICATIONS TECHNOLOGY

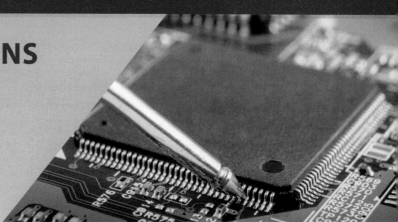

## 🎯 LEARNING INTENTIONS

**At the end of this section, you should be able to:**

◎ Describe developments in communications technology from the 1800s

◎ Assess the impact of technological developments.

## What is information and communications technology?

**Communications** refers to the process of sending or transmitting a message from one person to another. There were very few practical improvements in the process from Roman times until the nineteenth century.

For centuries the main form of communication was the **letter**.

> The time it took a letter to reach its destination depended on the distance involved, the weather, the road network, the availability of a messenger with good horses, etc.

> In 1840 a letter from London would take about twelve days to reach New York or seventy-three days to get to Sydney.

Since the nineteenth century, various inventions (discussed below) have improved the communications process. Today we talk about **ICT (information and communications technology)** because computers and other electronic devices are used for both communications and the storage and retrieval of information or **data**. As technology has developed, it has contributed to social and political change.

## Telegraph

> 1816: The **telegraph** was invented. It sent messages using electrical cables.

> 1836: A new type of message called a **telegram** was invented – in effect a letter sent by telegraph.

> 1837: **Samuel Morse** developed a telegraph system that allowed messages to be sent in a code known as **Morse code**. Each letter of the alphabet is represented by short and/or long sounds.

**SOURCE 9.38: Interior of General Post Office, Lombard Street, London by Augustus Wall Callcott (1809)**

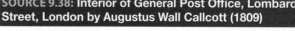

**SOURCE 9.39: Morse key**

A device called a Morse key is used to tap out messages in the code.

〉 1858: **Cables** were laid under the oceans to connect countries. The first cable linking Europe and America was from **Valentia Island** in Co. Kerry to **Newfoundland** in Canada.

〉 1866: The telegraph system from the USA to the UK opened. Laying cables was a slow process and the countries in the Pacific were not linked until 1902.

The telegraph speeded up communications and messages and news of major events could be received in a matter of minutes throughout the world.

### Activity 1

1 What advantages did Morse code have over sending a message in the post?

2 Find a copy of the Morse code. In pairs, use the code to send messages to each other.

3 What difficulties are there with communicating by Morse code?

## Radio

〉 Late 1880s: **Heinrich Hertz** proved that electrical waves could be sent and received. This was called **wireless** telegraphy. It had the great advantage that it did not require cables.

〉 1906: The first human voice was sent by **radio** (as it was now called) in Massachusetts, USA.

〉 1907: The first transatlantic wireless station was set up at Clifden, Co. Galway by one of the early pioneers of radio, **Guglielmo Marconi**.

〉 1912: The *Titanic* used wireless to contact neighbouring ships when it was sinking.

〉 1920s: Radio stations were set up throughout Europe and North America broadcasting news programmes and music. The **BBC** was established in Britain in 1922. Ireland's first radio station, **2RN**, was set up in 1926.

〉 1930s: Radio sets became cheaper and very common.

### Activity 2

Examine the source and then answer the questions below.

SOURCE 9.40: Listening to a radio, 1930

1 Comment on the radio shown in the picture.

2 Do you think this picture was used in an advertisement? Give evidence from the photograph.

3 What does the picture suggest about the role of women in 1930?

› **World War II:** The use of radios in tanks and planes revolutionised fighting. Tanks could ask for air support against targets and communicate with each other on the battlefield. Portable radio sets using batteries allowed soldiers to communicate on the battlefield.

› 1947: The **transistor** was developed. These devices control the flow of an electrical current. They greatly reduced the size of radios.

› 1995: Another major technological improvement came with the introduction of **digital** radio sets.

# Television

› 1926: **John Logie Baird** made the first broadcast on a television (TV).

› 1927: **Philo Taylor Farnsworth** broadcast the first TV pictures using a cathode ray tube. Called **electronic television**, this version of the TV would be the standard one adopted.

› 1930s and 1940s: The early sets were very expensive and very few sets were sold before World War II. There was a huge increase in TV ownership after the war when the cost of TVs began to fall dramatically.

› 1953: First **colour** broadcast (although most home TV sets remained black and white until the late 1960s).

› 1961: First broadcast by RTÉ, then known as **Telefís Éireann**.

› 1962: First **satellite** TV broadcast. This development enabled viewers to watch events or programmes from other countries.

› 1972: First **video recorder** introduced. This device allowed users to watch video cassettes and to record TV programmes.

› 1997: First **flat-screen TV** introduced by Panasonic.

TV caused a dramatic change in communications and entertainment. It became a centre of family life in the evenings. News events from around the world could be watched at home. TV stars became household names.

## Activity 3

Examine the source and then answer the questions below.

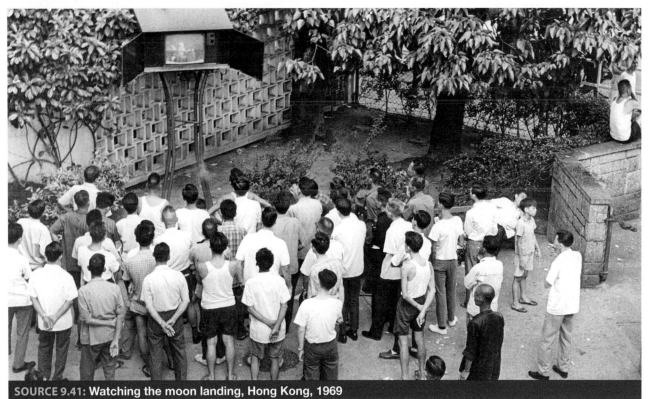

SOURCE 9.41: Watching the moon landing, Hong Kong, 1969

1 Describe what you can see in the photograph.
2 What does the picture suggest about television ownership in Hong Kong in 1969?

## Telephone

> 1876: **Alexander Graham Bell** with the help of **Thomas Watson** invented the telephone, a device that allowed the human voice to be transmitted over long distances.

> 1877: The first **telephone exchange** opened in Berlin. This was a centre where telephone calls could be connected between two different telephones. Telephone poles were set up to link cities.

> 1915: The first call was made between the western (San Francisco) and eastern (New York) coasts of the USA.

> 1920s: After World War I telephone ownership increased greatly. People dialled the number on a round dial on the front of the phone.

> 1927: The laying of telephone **cables** under the Atlantic Ocean allowed international calls to be made between Europe and the USA.

The widespread use of the phone saw a revolution in everyday life for ordinary people, who could now communicate cheaply and conveniently with each other.

### Mobile phone

> 1973: First call made on a handheld mobile phone.

> 1983: The first generation, **1G**, of mobile phones began to be used commercially in Japan. Their use soon spread to Europe and America. The phones were very large with a very short battery life.

> 1991: **2G** phones were launched in Finland. These phones allowed the first Short Message Service **(SMS)** or text messages to be sent.

> 2001: **3G** phones were introduced in Japan. Users could now send pictures and browse the Internet. These phones were known as **smartphones**.

> 2009: **4G** phones were introduced. They allowed for quicker Internet access and greater data downloads. Watching TV and videos on phones became common.

> Mobile phone usage grew dramatically and by 2017 there were over 44 billion mobile phones worldwide.

SOURCE 9.42: **New Siemens phone, 1929**

### Activity 4

Examine the source and answer the question below.

SOURCE 9.43: **1G phone – notice how big it is**

1 Comment on the mobile phone shown in the picture.

### DID YOU KNOW?

The introduction of the **Apple iPhone** in 2007 was a major development in mobile phone technology. It used **touch-screen technology** for the first time and came with an **in-built camera**. Its introduction changed the nature of mobile phones. Rival companies soon began introducing similar types of phones, using the **Android** operating system.

SOURCE 9.44: **Launch of the Apple iPhone, 2007**

## Social networks

One result of the improved technology of mobile phones has been the growth of social networks to chat with friends, to post pictures and information, and to follow world events. Companies such as Facebook, Twitter, Snapchat and Instagram have become household names. In 2017 Facebook had two billion users.

---

**Activity 5**

Examine this source and then answer the questions below.

1. Is there a public phone near where you live? Is there a need for one? Give reasons for your answer.

2. Imagine that you live in the 1960s. You do not have a telephone at home and the nearest public phone box is 500 metres from your house. Give three advantages and three disadvantages of this situation.

**SOURCE 9.45: Public phone box**

---

# Computers

The modern computer was developed during World War II. Early computers were more like calculators designed to solve complex mathematical problems and break codes. Computers have gone through stages of development called generations. Each generation has resulted in smaller computers that process information more quickly.

## First generation

> 1946: Scientists working for the US military at the University of Pennsylvania built the first general-purpose computer, **ENIAC** (Electronic Numerical Integrator and Computer). It weighed 30 tons and needed six people to operate it. It used **vacuum tubes** that were common in radios at the time.

> 1951: The first commercial computer, **UNIVAC** (universal automatic computer), was introduced.
> **Punch cards** were used to put information or data into the computer, which had a storage memory of only 1,000 words.

## Second generation – the transistor

> 1957: IBM introduced the first computer using **transistors** rather than vacuum tubes. Transistors resulted in smaller, more compact, cheaper and faster digital computers. These early computers did not have monitors (screens). Information was entered using punch cards and the results were printed out.

## Third generation – the integrated circuit

> 1960s: An important advance was the **integrated circuit** or **silicon chip** – also known as the **microchip**. This combined a number of transistors on a single piece of silicon. Their use saw the development of faster, smaller and more efficient computers, or **minicomputers** as they became known. Operators now typed in their data directly using **keyboards** and the results were displayed on **monitors**. **Operating systems** allowed the computer to run different applications at the same time.

**SOURCE 9.46: ENIAC, 1946**

## Fourth generation – the microprocessor

> 1971: Intel introduced the first **microprocessor**. A large number of very small components were implanted on a single tiny silicon chip. It is the brain of the computer, controlling all the computer's operations. This development saw a dramatic reduction in the size of computers, which also made them more affordable.

| Year | Name | Number of transistors |
|------|------|----------------------:|
| 1971 | Intel 4004 | 2,300 |
| 1982 | Intel 80286 | 134,000 |
| 1993 | Pentium Pro | 5,500,000 |
| 2002 | Pentium 4 | 55,000,000 |
| 2017 | Xeon Broadwell | 7,200,000,000 |

> 1971: The **floppy disk** was developed and it greatly improved the means of **data storage** and **transfer** between computers – a floppy could hold around one megabyte of information.

## Personal computers

The most dramatic impact of the development of the microprocessor was the growth of the personal computer (PC). Until the late 1970s computers were used only in business. A number of landmark developments saw their use spread to homes:

> 1977: The **Apple II** was the first affordable PC to be introduced.

> 1981: **IBM** PCs were launched. They used an Intel processor and the **Microsoft DOS** operating system. This soon became the standard design for PCs known as **desktops**.

> 1982: The **CD-ROM** (compact disk – read only memory) was developed. It could store millions more bytes of information (megabytes) than a floppy disk.

> 1984: **Apple Macintosh** introduced onscreen **dropdown menus** and a **mouse**. These enhancements made PCs far easier to use.

> 1985: The **Microsoft Windows** operating system was introduced and soon became the standard operating system on nearly all computers.

> 1988: The introduction of the first portable computers, or **laptops** as they became known.

### DID YOU KNOW?

The microprocessor is also known as the computer chip. The better the chip, the faster the computer, and the more applications it can run at once. The development of the microprocessor has been quite staggering as seen by the number of transistors per chip introduced by Intel between 1971 and 2017.

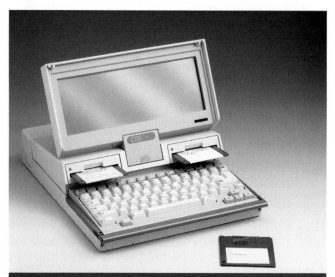

SOURCE 9.47: IBM PC with two floppy disk drives, 1980s

SOURCE 9.48: IBM laptop, 1993

> 1995: The **DVD** (digital video disk or digital versatile disk) was introduced by a number of companies. It looked the same as a CD but had a far greater storage capacity.
> 2002: The first hand-held **tablet** computer was introduced.
> 2010: Apple introduced the **iPad**.

**KS**             Activity 6

Examine these sources and then answer the questions below.

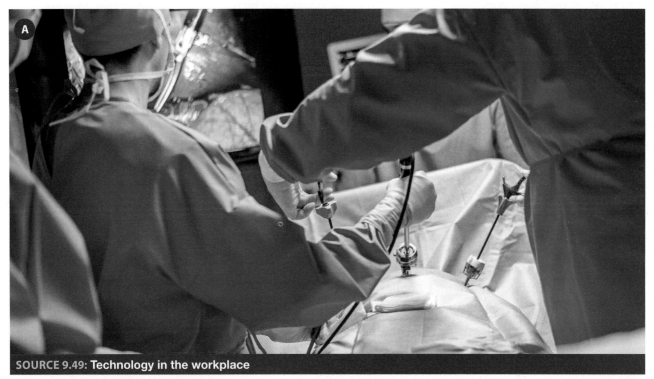

SOURCE 9.49: Technology in the workplace

SOURCE 9.50: Technology at home

1   In what ways would scenes A and B have been different (a) fifty years ago and (b) 250 years ago?
2   In pairs, discuss the advantages and disadvantages of modern technology.

**Learning Outcome** 3.11    **189**

## The Internet

〉 1960s: Originally called **ARPANET** (Advanced Research Projects Agency Network), the Internet was developed for the US military by American universities. They wanted a communications system that would survive a nuclear attack. It involved using a modem attached to a computer to transfer information down a telephone line.

〉 1990: The first **search engine** (device to search the hosts that exist on the Internet) was developed and **websites** started to come into use.

〉 1991: The **World Wide Web** was introduced. This tool, developed by the English scientist **Tim Berners-Lee**, is used by billions of people to access the Internet.

〉 1998: **Google** search engine was founded.

〉 1998: **Wi-Fi** or Wireless Local Area Network was introduced, allowing computers or phones to access the Internet from different locations without needing to be connected by a telephone line.

The Internet has revolutionised communications. Its introduction led to what is called the **Information Age** today. Nearly all aspects of life involve computers, e.g. banking, manufacturing, hospital operations. A big fear in recent years has been **cyber hacking**, where an unauthorised person breaks or hacks into a computer system. They can steal data or put in a computer virus to damage the system.

---

KS 👥　　　　　　　　　　　**Activity 7**

1　Work in groups of four to prepare and deliver a PowerPoint presentation to the class on one of the following topics:
  • Developments in the telegraph in the nineteenth century
  • How the radio changed in the twentieth century
  • Developments in phones since the late nineteenth century
  • The origin and development of the mobile phone.

Each group will need to allocate roles such as: researching information, sourcing visual images, typing up the PowerPoint, giving the presentation, taking questions from the class.

---

### DO YOU UNDERSTAND THESE KEY TERMS?

| | | |
|---|---|---|
| floppy disk | operating system | telegraph |
| integrated circuit | punch card | transistor |
| microchip | search engine | website |
| Morse code | silicon chip | |

📄 Chapter summary

📄 Weblinks

📄 PowerPoint summary

---

## SELF-ASSESSMENT – CAN YOU?

**1** Outline why the telegraph was an important development in communications.

**2** Identify the main developments in radio between 1885 and 1939.

**3** Explain how radios impacted on warfare in World War II.

**4** Examine the main developments in the telephone from 1876 until the 1960s.

**5** Describe the main events in the history of television.

**6** Outline the main generations in mobile phone development since 1973.

**7** Explain the main developments that reduced the size and increased the speed of computers.

**8** Discuss which technological development of the last two centuries has had the greatest impact on modern life, and give reasons for your choice.

# 10 REVOLUTION IN PRE-TWENTIETH-CENTURY EUROPE AND IRELAND

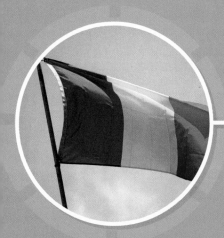

**What were the causes, course and consequences of the French Revolution?**

192

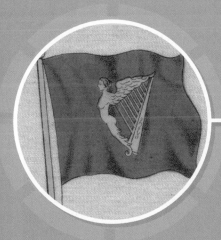

**What were the causes, course and consequences of the 1798 Rebellion?**

202

# WHAT WERE THE CAUSES, COURSE AND CONSEQUENCES OF THE FRENCH REVOLUTION?

##  LEARNING INTENTIONS

**At the end of this section, you should be able to:**

◎ Describe how France was ruled before the French Revolution

◎ Outline the causes of the French Revolution

◎ Describe the key events of the French Revolution

◎ Describe the Reign of Terror

◎ Discuss the consequences of the French Revolution.

## Rebellions and revolutions

In the eighteenth century various groups of people began to question traditional systems of government. They wanted the right to elect their own leaders. This led to a number of **rebellions** and **revolutions**. In 1789 one of the most influential events in history started – the **French Revolution**. This event saw great changes in France and led to war in Europe.

## How was France ruled before the French Revolution?

### Absolute monarch

In 1789 France was a powerful country led by **King Louis XVI** (1754–1793). He was an **absolute monarch**.

> He ruled without the aid of a parliament elected by the people.

> He made all the major decisions. He appointed his advisers.

> He believed his power came from God, a theory known as the **Divine Right of Kings**. The people of France were known as the king's **subjects**.

Louis controlled France from his beautiful palace at Versailles near Paris. A kind and generous man who loved hunting, he was popular with most French people. His wife, **Marie-Antoinette**, was not popular. She was an Austrian princess and Austria was traditionally an enemy of France.

> **Rebellion**
> An organised attempt to overthrow a ruler or government.

> **Revolution**
> The successful overthrow of a ruler or government.

> **Absolute monarch**
> Ruler who has total control over his or her country.

### Activity 1

Examine this source and then answer the question below.

**SOURCE 10.1: A painting of Louis XVI in 1779**

1 What evidence is there in the painting, in your opinion, to show that Louis was a king?

## Ancien Regime

French society was divided into three **estates**, and it had been the same way since the Middle Ages. Historians have called this the **Ancien Regime** or the Old Regime.

> The **First Estate** was made up of the bishops and priests of the Catholic Church. They numbered about 130,000. The Church ran schools and hospitals and also owned over 10 per cent of the land of France. Farmers and peasants had to pay a tax to the Church called a **tithe** (this was about one-tenth of what they produced).

> The **Second Estate** consisted of about 400,000 nobles. Most were wealthy landowners. They acted as advisers to the king, as judges or as generals in the army. They had a lot of control over the peasants who worked on their land.

> The **Third Estate** comprised 95 per cent of the population. They were also called **commoners**. The vast majority were poor workers or peasants, but there were also some rich and educated businessmen, lawyers and doctors.

This political system had been accepted in France for hundreds of years.

# What were the causes of the French Revolution?

The educated members of the Third Estate felt they should have a role in governing France and they began to demand change.

## The Enlightenment

People who called for change were influenced by the **Enlightenment** writers, such as **Voltaire** and **Jean-Jacques Rousseau**, who were read by many people. They argued that:

> The king's power came from the people rather than from God.

> The king should rule France with the help of an elected parliament.

> Religion was superstition, and decisions should be based instead on reason and science.

> The Church and the nobles were too powerful and the ordinary people of France should have a greater say in running their country.

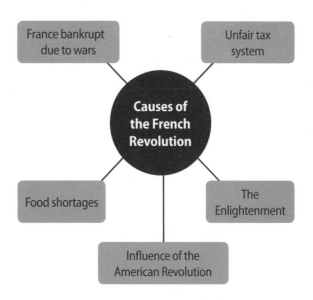

Causes of the French Revolution

- France bankrupt due to wars
- Unfair tax system
- Food shortages
- The Enlightenment
- Influence of the American Revolution

### Activity 2

Examine this source and then answer the questions below.

SOURCE 10.2: Cartoon attacking French society

1 Who do each of the figures in the cartoon represent?
2 What is the message of this cartoon?

**The Enlightenment**
An eighteenth-century movement that stressed the importance of reason and challenged many traditional ideas and institutions.

## Taxation

The **unfair tax system** was another major source of discontent. The Church did not pay any taxes but gave a gift of money to the king every year. The rich nobles did not have to pay many of the taxes that the king collected from the Third Estate. Although most peasants were poor, they also had to pay taxes to their local lord and the tithe to the Church.

## Food shortages

In the late 1780s a number of bad harvests led to a food shortage. The price of food items such as bread rose significantly. Bread was the staple diet of poor people in France.

### DID YOU KNOW?

Some historians think that an eruption of a volcano in Iceland in 1783 could have caused the bad harvests in Europe in the late 1780s. The volcano erupted for eight months and the amount of dust it threw into the atmosphere affected the weather. These historians have formed this view from reading contemporary sources.

### DID YOU KNOW?

#### American War of Independence

British settlement in America began in the early 1600s. By 1765 there were about 2.5 million people living in British America. They lived in thirteen colonies, each of which looked after its own affairs. When the British government tried to tax these colonies in order to pay for their defence against French or Indian attacks, the Americans protested. They felt that taxation should be decided by the colonists themselves, not by the British parliament in faraway London. By 1775 the two sides were at war. In 1776 the Americans passed the **Declaration of Independence**. It rejected the traditional view that the power of a ruler came from God. It stated that the power of the King of England, George III, to rule came from the people. As the king's government had treated the American people badly, they no longer agreed to be ruled by Britain. The declaration was passed on 4 July and this is why people celebrate US Independence Day on that date.

Peace negotiations eventually took place (in Paris) and in 1783 the independence of America, or the United States, was recognised by Britain.

## American War of Independence

Recent events in America had a major influence on France.

› There had been a lot of sympathy in Europe for the Americans in their struggle against the mighty British Empire. Volunteers travelled to help the Americans.

› Importantly, France came to their aid and declared war on the British. French troops and ships played a crucial role in the final American victory.

› Many French soldiers who had fought in the war were impressed by developments in America and wanted to see the same freedoms at home.

› The American view that the king's power came from the people, not from God, found a lot of support in France.

› Helping the Americans had another major impact on France. The French government had fought a number of wars in the eighteenth century. These had left the government bankrupt.

› The efforts of the French government to raise more money would lead to the French Revolution.

### Activity 3

Find out about the role that George Washington played in the American War of Independence.

**SOURCE 10.3: British forces surrender at Yorktown, 1781**

The king needed to raise money from taxation. He proposed that the nobles pay more taxes. The nobles objected and forced the king to call an **Estates General**, an elected parliament that had not met since 1614. It was made up of members from the three estates. Posing as the defenders of the people, the nobles thought that they could control this parliament and stop reform. The Third Estate, however, wanted to see reform.

## How did the revolution in France begin?

During the elections for the Estates General, calls for reform of the government of France grew. The main demands were for reform of the tax system and an end to the exemptions that nobles enjoyed.

When the Estates General met at Versailles in May 1789, the key issue was how it would vote to pass laws.

> In 1614 each estate had voted separately on an issue. The result for each estate then counted as one vote. The nobles and clergy hoped that this system would continue as they would be able to stop reform by outvoting the Third Estate two to one.

> The Third Estate wanted each member of the Estates General to have a vote. They knew that, with the help of some of the nobles and clergy who were sympathetic to them, they would then be able to introduce reforms.

When their demand for each member to have a vote was rejected, the Third Estate refused to attend the Estates General. Instead, saying they represented the people of France, they met separately and called themselves the **National Assembly**. They demanded that the king agree to a constitution for France similar to one the Americans had. The French Revolution had begun.

On 20 June 1789 the National Assembly members found the door to their meeting place locked and decided to meet instead at an indoor tennis court. Fearing that they were about to be arrested by the army, they swore that they would continue meeting until their demands were met. This event became known as the **Tennis Court Oath**.

SOURCE 10.4: **Opening of the Estates General, 1789**

**Republic**
A country that is not ruled by an unelected ruler such as a king.

### Activity 4

Examine this source and then answer the questions below.

SOURCE 10.5: *The Tennis Court Oath*, as painted in 1791 by the most famous French artist of the period, Jacques-Louis David

1   Describe the event pictured in this painting.
2   Do you think the artist approved of this event? Give reasons for your answer.

---

### DID YOU KNOW?

In 1789 the Americans passed a **constitution**. It set out the rules about how the United States would be governed. America was to be a **republic** with an elected president rather than a monarch.
It set up a **federal system of government**. Each colony became a state and looked after most of its own affairs. However, for important issues such as war and foreign affairs, a federal government was established. It was divided into three parts:

* **Congress**, which was a parliament that passed laws
* A **president**, who made sure laws were carried out and who was commander-in-chief of the army
* A **Supreme Court**, which made sure that all laws passed by the federal government or by the states followed the rules set out in the constitution.

## Activity 5

Examine this source and then answer the questions below.

The want of bread is terrible: accounts arrive every moment from the provinces of riots and disturbances. The prices reported ... five sous a pound for white bread, and three and a half to four sous for the common sort eaten by the poor ... are beyond their faculties [ability to pay] and occasion great misery. It appears plain to me that the violent friends of the commons [the revolutionaries] are not displeased at the high price of corn, which seconds their views greatly and makes any appeal to the common feeling of the people more easy and much more to their purpose than if the price was low.

Note: a sou was a small coin roughly equal to five cent.

**SOURCE 10.6: British writer Arthur Young describing conditions in France in July 1789**

1   What is the impact of the 'want of bread'?
2   What effect does the high price of bread have on the poor?
3   How has the high price of bread benefited the 'friends of the commons'?

## Activity 6

Examine this source and then answer the questions below.

In the evening a detachment with two pieces of cannon went to the [Bastille], to demand the ammunition deposited there. A flag of truce had been sent before them, which was answered from within: But nevertheless, the Governor (the Marquis de Launay) ordered the guard to fire, and several were killed. The populace, enraged at this proceeding, rushed forward to the assault, when the Governor agreed to admit a certain number, on condition that they should not commit any violence. A detachment of about forty accordingly passed the drawbridge, which was instantly drawn up, and the whole party massacred. ... A breach [hole] was soon made in the gate, and the fortress surrendered. The Governor [was] carried before the Council assembled at the Hotel de Ville, by whom the Marquis de Launay was sentenced to be beheaded, which was accordingly put in execution ... and the other prisoners were also put to death.

**SOURCE 10.7: Extract from a British newspaper describing the storming of the Bastille, July 1789**

1   From the document, why did the detachment go to the Bastille?
2   Comment on the actions of the governor of the Bastille as described in the document.
3   Using your knowledge of the work of historians, would you accept this as an accurate view of events? Give a reason for your answer.

The king gave in and ordered the other two estates to join with the Third Estate. France now had a parliament and the king was no longer an absolute monarch.

## What happened at the Bastille?

In Paris there was very strong support for the National Assembly. Rumours spread in the city that the king's troops were marching on Paris to crush the revolution. The **National Guard** was formed to defend the city.

On 14 July 1789, after capturing muskets (guns), a crowd marched to the **Bastille** prison where gunpowder was stored. This medieval fortress had been used by French kings to imprison people who criticised them. The crowd stormed the prison.

The storming of the Bastille was a very important event – a symbol of the king's power had been captured by the people. The people, not the king, now controlled France.

The news of the fall of the Bastille was celebrated throughout Europe.

**SOURCE 10.8: Storming of the Bastille**

### DID YOU KNOW?

There were only seven prisoners in the Bastille when it was stormed, one of whom was Irish. The fortress was destroyed and small pieces of it were sold as souvenirs. Every year, on 14 July, the French celebrate Bastille Day as a national holiday.

## What reforms were introduced?

Louis XVI was still on the throne, but his power was greatly reduced. The National Assembly now made the laws. It made two important decisions:

› It banned the feudal system that had existed since the Middle Ages. This ended the power of the nobles. The division of society into estates was gone. The people were equal citizens, not the king's subjects.

› It passed a law known as the **Declaration of the Rights of Man and of the Citizen**. This law granted freedoms such as freedom of religion, the right to free speech and the right to a fair trial. It was heavily influenced by the American Constitution and the ideas of Enlightenment writers.

Louis was forced to move to Paris from Versailles. The National Assembly also moved to the city.

Most French people supported the changes that were being introduced and the new society that they were creating. A new slogan – **Liberty, Equality, Fraternity** – became very popular. It reflected the aims of the revolutionaries:

› **Liberty** for people from the rule of kings
› **Equality** of treatment for all
› **Fraternity,** i.e. brotherhood or cooperation, between people.

Not everyone agreed. Many nobles had fled the violence in France. Led by the king's brother, they were organising an army and hoped to restore the old system.

### The Church

Most revolutionaries disliked the Catholic Church because it had supported the king and the nobles. Some were suspicious that it did not support the changes that had been introduced into France.

› In 1790 the National Assembly passed the **Civil Constitution of the Clergy**. This law brought the Church under the control of the government.

› Church property was seized and priests had to take an oath that they supported the revolution.

## How did France become a republic?

Most people wanted the king to remain. Others called for a republic. One person who led these calls was a lawyer from northern France, **Maximilien Robespierre** (1758–1794). He was nicknamed **'the incorruptible one'** because of his devotion to the revolution. He led a political party called the **Jacobins** and was a hero to the ordinary people of Paris.

A very religious man, Louis did not like the changes to the Catholic Church. He decided to take his family to Belgium, which was ruled by the Austrian Emperor, a brother of Marie-Antoinette. The royal family left Paris on the night of 20 June 1791 but were captured near the border at Varennes – this event became known as the **Flight to Varennes**.

For Robespierre and many others this event showed that the king was an enemy of the revolution. They strongly argued that France must become a republic with no king.

In April 1792 France declared war on Austria. Soon France was at war with most of Europe. The rulers of Europe felt threatened by the changes in France and were determined to crush the revolution.

**SOURCE 10.9: Maximilien Robespierre**

**Learning Outcome 3.3**

Many people suspected that Louis was secretly hoping for a French defeat. Revolutionaries stormed the Tuileries Palace in Paris, where the royal family lived. Mobs then broke into prisons and massacred anyone suspected of being an enemy of the revolution. **Violence** was becoming a common feature of the revolution.

The revolutionaries decided to remove Louis from the throne. On 21 September 1792 the monarchy was abolished and France became a republic.

### Execution of Louis XVI

The most important issue facing the revolutionaries was what to do with the former king, now known as citizen Louis Capet. The newly elected parliament, called the **National Convention**, decided to try him for treason.

Louis was found guilty by the Convention and sentenced to death by a small majority. Robespierre was one of those who voted for the king's execution. On 21 January he was executed by **guillotine** – an action that shocked many in Europe. In October Marie-Antoinette was also beheaded.

## What was the Reign of Terror?

The revolution faced threats at home and abroad. For example:

> The king's son had many supporters. They called him Louis XVII, and claimed he was the rightful ruler of France.

> The campaign against the Catholic Church was unpopular in some areas. A region called the Vendée was in open revolt.

> France was at war with several European countries.

SOURCE 10.10: Storming of the Tuileries Palace

**DID YOU KNOW?**

After 1789 it was decided to introduce one common method of execution – the **guillotine**. A new form of execution, it was seen as quick and humane. During the Terror, it would be nicknamed the *National Razor*. It remained the method of execution in France until the death penalty was abolished in 1981.

**Activity 7**

Examine this source and then answer the questions below.

SOURCE 10.11: Execution of King Louis XVI

1  Identify the method of execution.
2  Why are there so many soldiers present?
3  Do you think the revolutionaries were right to execute Louis XVI?

The revolutionaries believed that extreme measures were needed to defeat the enemies of the revolution.

› A **Committee of Public Safety** was set up to protect the revolution. Headed by Robespierre and his supporters, it had twelve members.

› Anyone suspected of disloyalty to the government was arrested. Robespierre's rule of France became known as the **Reign of Terror**.

› In September 1793 the **Law of Suspects** was passed. Anyone accused of being an enemy of the revolution was assumed to be guilty. It was very difficult for people to prove their innocence.

› **Revolutionary tribunals** were set up to try people suspected of treason.

**Treason**
Acting in support of a country's enemy.

› **Executions** became very common, as priests, former nobles and many ordinary people were tried and guillotined.

› In six weeks 1,400 people were executed in Paris alone. Robespierre even had other revolutionaries executed.

One of the major reasons why Robespierre was able to stay in power was the support of the poorer people of Paris. They were called the *sans-culottes*. To keep them happy, Robespierre made sure that the price of bread was kept low.

**Sans-culottes**
Name given to poor men who wore long trousers instead of the knee-breeches worn by the wealthy.

**Activity 8**

In groups of four, examine the source and answer the questions below.

> 1. Immediately after the publication of the present decree, all suspects within the territory of the Republic and still at large, shall be placed in custody.
>
> 2. The following are deemed suspects:
>
>    those who by their conduct, associations, comments or writings have shown themselves partisans [supporters] of tyranny and enemies of liberty;
>
>    those former nobles, together with husbands, wives, fathers, mothers, sons or daughters, brothers or sisters, and agents of the émigrés [nobles who had left France], who have not constantly demonstrated their devotion to the Revolution

**SOURCE 10.12: Excerpt from the Law of Suspects, September 1793**

1 When will the suspects be placed in custody?

2 Explain what you think the revolutionaries meant by the phrase 'supporters of tyranny'.

3 What does the law say about the treatment of former nobles?

4 Do you think that this law could be passed today in Ireland? Give reasons to support your answer.

Robespierre's policies were bringing success on the battlefield. A large army of over one million men was created. It defeated the Austrian army and turned the tide of the war. It crushed the rebels in the Vendée with great brutality.

With the success of France's armies, the need for the terror ended.

› Nonetheless, Robespierre was having more and more people executed.

› Members of the National Convention, including his former supporters, feared they could be next.

› On 24 July 1794 Robespierre and his followers were arrested. The next day Robespierre, his brother and other prominent supporters were executed.

› A more moderate government called the **Directory** came to power.

› Robespierre had saved the revolution but at a terrible human cost. Historians believe that up to 40,000 people were executed during the Reign of Terror.

**SOURCE 10.13: A *sans-culotte***

**Learning Outcome 3.3** 199

**SOURCE 10.14:** Napoleon Bonaparte (1807) by David

**KS** **Activity 9**

In 1793 the revolutionaries introduced a new calendar, which was used until 1805, when it was abolished.

1 Search online for the Revolutionary Calendar and find out today's date.

2 Search online for information on the Revolutionary Calendar.

3 Display your findings in a PowerPoint presentation.

## What happened under Napoleon's leadership?

The war with France's enemies continued. **Napoleon Bonaparte** (1769–1821) emerged as the most successful general.

> Under his leadership French armies conquered large parts of Europe. In 1804 he crowned himself **Emperor of France** and he was the most powerful man in Europe.

> In 1812 he made a crucial error and invaded Russia. His army was forced to retreat and most of his troops died from cold, disease and starvation.

> Three years later he was defeated at Waterloo in Belgium. The monarchy was restored, with Louis XVI's brother becoming king.

> Napoleon was exiled to a remote island in the Atlantic where he died in 1821. A controversial figure in history, he is regarded as a hero today by most French people.

**Activity 10**

1 Draw up a timeline of the main events during the French Revolution from 1789 to 1815.

**Activity 11**

Examine this source and then answer the questions below.

1 Who are the three figures in the cartoon?

2 What message, do you think, is the artist trying to convey? Present evidence to support your answer.

3 Do you think the artist was a supporter of the revolution? Explain your answer.

**SOURCE 10.15:** Cartoon drawn at the time of the French Revolution

# What were the consequences of the French Revolution?

The French Revolution is one of the most important political events in history. It divided people at the time and still divides people today.

> As a result of the revolution, the feudal system ended. The king was removed from power and later executed. A parliament elected by the people governed France.

> Throughout Europe, many people welcomed the French Revolution. They, too, wanted greater freedom. They hoped that their kings and queens would share power with their people as had happened in France.

> Some argued that the only way to do this was to use violence. Inspired by events in France, Wolfe Tone hoped to spread the French revolutionary ideals to Ireland (see the next section).

> Many rulers were afraid that the French Revolution would spread to their countries. They were determined to prevent this and imprisoned supporters of the ideals of the revolution.

> The Reign of Terror shocked ordinary people throughout Europe. For many, the violence discredited the idea that a country should be run by a government chosen by the people. They preferred the order of the rule of kings to the chaos of revolution.

> Many religious people were shocked at the treatment of the Church during the revolution and therefore supported traditional rulers.

> Wars broke out in Europe, which lasted until the defeat of Napoleon in 1815. They brought death and destruction to many parts of Europe.

> Some of the symbols we associate with France today were introduced during the revolution. For example, the tricolour flag and 'La Marseillaise' remain the French flag and national anthem. The metric system of weights and measures was also introduced during the revolution.

## DO YOU UNDERSTAND THESE KEY TERMS?

| | | |
|---|---|---|
| absolute monarch | feudal dues | National Guard |
| Ancien Regime | First Estate | Reign of Terror |
| commoner | fraternity | republic |
| Divine Right of Kings | guillotine | revolutionary tribunal |
| the Enlightenment | Jacobin | *sans-culotte* |
| | liberty | Second Estate |
| equality | National Assembly | subjects |
| Estates General | National Convention | Third Estate |

### Activity 12

Research online and find out:

1 How the tricolour became the flag of France.

2 The history of the 'Marsellaise' – the French National Anthem.

 PowerPoint summary

# SELF-ASSESSMENT – CAN YOU?

1 Outline how Louis XVI governed France before 1789.

2 Explain who the members of the First, Second and Third Estates were.

3 Explain the importance of the Tennis Court Oath.

4 Discuss two important decisions reached by the National Assembly.

5 Explain the slogan of the French Revolution.

6 Explain the importance of the Civil Constitution of the Clergy.

7 Outline the significance of the Flight to Varennes.

8 Identify why the king was removed from power in 1792 and why he was executed.

9 Examine why Robespierre and his supporters felt that it was necessary to introduce terror against the enemies of the revolution.

10 List the main actions taken against suspected enemies of the revolution.

11 Explain why the Reign of Terror ended.

12 Examine the role of Robespierre in the revolution.

13 Outline the career of Napoleon Bonaparte.

14 Investigate the main consequences of the French Revolution.

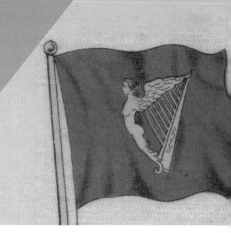

## ⊚ LEARNING INTENTIONS

**At the end of this section, you should be able to:**

◎ Describe how Ireland was governed in 1790

◎ Explain the importance of the Society of United Irishmen

◎ Explain why a rebellion broke out in Ireland in 1798

◎ Outline the main events of the 1798 Rebellion

◎ Discuss the consequences of the 1798 Rebellion.

## How was Ireland governed in 1790?

Britain ruled Ireland in 1790. An Irish parliament met in Dublin. This parliament was dominated by wealthy landlord families, called the **Protestant Ascendancy**. Most landlords had received land in Ireland in the sixteenth and seventeenth centuries. They lived in beautiful houses and made their fortune by renting land to farmers called **tenants**.

The political system was very unfair.

> Only wealthy members of the Church of Ireland could be elected as members of parliament (MPs), whereas **Catholics** made up about 75 per cent of the population.

> **Protestant Ascendancy**
> Period when Ireland was controlled by rich Protestant landowners called landlords.

> In 1793 Catholics were allowed to vote, but they were not allowed to become MPs. This was one of the few remaining **Penal Laws**. These laws had been passed earlier in the century to make sure that Catholics would not threaten British rule in Ireland.

In **Ulster**, there were a large number of **Presbyterians**. They had also suffered under some of the Penal Laws. For example, they were barred from parliament.

> Only wealthy people could vote in elections. This was unfair because the poorer people, whether Protestant or Catholic, could not vote.

### Activity 1

Examine the source and then find out the following about this building:

1  When it was built.

2  What it is used as today.

3  The very unusual feature of the building.

4  How would you know that this was an important building?

SOURCE 10.16: Irish parliament building at College Green

---

**Activity 2**

In groups of four, examine this source and then answer the questions below.

- Exclusion of Catholics from most public offices (since 1607); Presbyterians were also barred from holding public office from 1707
- Catholics were not allowed to have firearms or serve in the armed forces
- Exclusion from the legal profession and the judiciary
- Ban on Catholics and Presbyterians entering Trinity College Dublin

- Catholics were prohibited from owning a horse valued at more than £5
- Any new Catholic churches that were allowed to be built were to be made of wood, not stone, and had to be away from main roads
- 'No person of the popish religion shall publicly or in private houses teach school, or instruct youth in learning within this realm.'

**SOURCE 10.17: Examples of Penal Laws**

1   Give two examples of laws that affected both Catholics and Presbyterians.
2   What law was designed to make a future revolt against England difficult?
3   Identify two laws that affected the education of Catholics.
4   What is your group's reaction to these laws? Give examples from the source to support your answer.

---

Many people wanted to reform the Irish parliament but the Protestant Ascendancy would not share power, especially not with Catholics. Those who wanted change admired the French Revolution. In Ulster, many Presbyterians wanted to see a fairer government based on the changes introduced in France.

## What was the importance of the Society of United Irishmen?

One man inspired by events in France was a young Protestant lawyer called **Theobald Wolfe Tone** (1763–1798). He called for reform of how Ireland was governed.

**SOURCE 10.18: Wolfe Tone**

In October 1791 Tone attended a meeting in Belfast. As a result of this meeting the **Society of United Irishmen** was formed. Its members were mainly Protestants who supported the ideals of the French Revolution. Other leading figures included **Henry Joy McCracken** and **Thomas Russell**. They hoped to unite Irishmen of all religions to achieve a fairer government for Ireland through peaceful means.

When revolutionary France and Britain went to war in 1793, the British government became very suspicious of the Society of United Irishmen. In 1794 it was banned. The United Irishmen decided to continue as a secret society. **Lord Edward Fitzgerald** (1763–1798) joined and soon became one of the leaders.

The aims of the United Irishmen changed after the ban. We know this because Tone kept a detailed diary, which is now an excellent source for historians.

⟩   They wanted Ireland to have independence from Britain and to become a republic like France.
⟩   They believed violence would have to be used to achieve this aim.
⟩   They hoped to unite all Irishmen in supporting Irish freedom regardless of religion.

> **DID YOU KNOW?**
>
> Not all members of the Protestant Ascendancy opposed change. Lord Edward Fitzgerald was from one of the most powerful families in Ireland. His father was the Duke of Leinster and owned Leinster House, which is now home to the Houses of the Oireachtas.

**SOURCE 10.19: Lord Edward Fitzgerald**

## French aid

The society planned to get French help to stage a revolution in Ireland. This help would be crucial if they were to have any chance of beating the British.

In 1795 Tone was forced to leave Ireland after the British discovered he had met with a French spy. After briefly staying in America, Tone travelled to France to persuade the French to send troops to Ireland. The French, impressed by Tone's arguments, agreed to send an invasion fleet to Ireland.

A fleet of forty-three ships and 14,000 soldiers under the command of the experienced general **Lazare Hoche** left the port of Brest in Brittany in December 1796. Tone was on one of the ships. When the fleet arrived off Bantry Bay in Co. Cork a violent storm prevented the troops from landing. They were forced to return to France. Tone urged the French to send another fleet to Ireland, but they were not interested.

## Orange Order

The United Irishmen wanted to unite Irishmen of all religions. However, tensions were growing between Catholics and Protestants, especially in Ulster. In the 1790s Ireland's population was growing very quickly and there was not enough land to go around. This led to disputes over the renting of land, particularly in the densely populated county of Armagh.

Catholic tenants were prepared to pay higher rents than their Protestant neighbours. This led to violence between Catholic and Protestant farmers. Protestants formed the **Orange Order**, which grew very quickly.

Members of the Orange Order attacked and drove hundreds of Catholics from Ulster. Catholics were scared of the Orange Order and believed that the United Irishmen would defend them. Soon Catholics were joining the United Irishmen in large numbers.

> **DID YOU KNOW?**
>
> Throughout Irish history those who have wanted to defeat British rule have looked for military aid from Britain's enemies. Spain sent troops to Ireland in 1601, the French sent troops in 1796 and 1798 and the Germans sent guns in 1916.

### Activity 3

The Orange Order was set up to defend Protestants and British rule in Ireland.

SOURCE 10.20: Belfast mural celebrating the Battle of the Boyne

Do some research online to find out about the Orange Order. Identify five pieces of information about:

1. What the order commemorates.
2. What it organises on 12 July every year.

> **DID YOU KNOW?**
>
> A recent archaeological discovery revealed evidence of a refugee camp for Catholics driven from Ulster in the 1790s on the slopes of a mountain in Galway.

# Why did rebellion break out in Ireland in 1798?

The British government realised that if the French had landed in Bantry Bay, the experienced French troops would almost certainly have defeated British troops in Ireland. The British did not want to lose Ireland or have it used as a base by the French to attack England. They decided to destroy the threat posed by the United Irishmen.

> A new army called the **Yeomanry** was formed. Its members were Protestants and the government encouraged members of the new Orange Order to join.

> In 1797 the government started a reign of terror in Ulster, where the United Irishmen were strongest.

> Suspects were **flogged** (hit hard with whips).

> Others were hung until they lost consciousness – this was called **half-hanging**.

> Another cruel method of torture was the use of the **pitch-cap** – a cloth cap filled with tar was placed on a suspect's head and then set alight.

The brutality of these methods worked. Ulster was firmly under the control of the British government.

The leaders of the United Irishmen had to act or face total destruction. They also thought that French help was on the way. They set a date for the rising: 23 May 1798. Fitzgerald thought he could count on 100,000 men in the event of a revolt.

There were a large number of British spies, including two of the leaders, **Leonard McNally** and **Thomas Reynolds**. In March 1798 the leaders of the United Irishmen were arrested. Fitzgerald managed to escape arrest at first, but he was captured two months later. Betrayed by a spy, he was shot during his arrest and later died of his wounds. The government then moved its campaign of terror to Leinster, especially Co. Kildare.

 **DID YOU KNOW?**

In the late eighteenth century prisons were mainly used to hold those who were awaiting trial or punishment. Criminals were either executed or transported to a penal colony in Australia.

### Activity 4

Examine this source and then answer the questions below.

**SOURCE 10.21: A United Irishmen suspect is tortured using a technique known as half-hanging**

1 Describe what is happening in this picture.
2 Explain why the British used methods such as the one in the picture.

**Loyalist**
Supporter of the British government. Most Protestants and a large number of Catholics were loyalists.

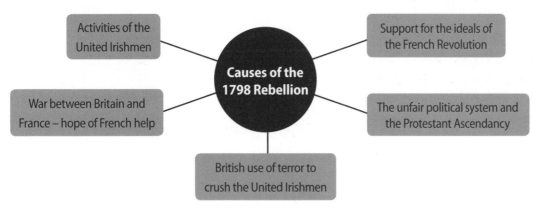

Activities of the United Irishmen

Support for the ideals of the French Revolution

**Causes of the 1798 Rebellion**

War between Britain and France – hope of French help

The unfair political system and the Protestant Ascendancy

British use of terror to crush the United Irishmen

# What were the main events of the 1798 rebellion?

With the help of information from spies, the British government easily crushed rebel plans to capture Dublin. At the end of May rebellion broke out in Counties Kildare, Meath and Carlow. The rebels were defeated by superior British forces. After battles, the rebel prisoners were often massacred.

## Wexford

The county most associated with the 1798 Rebellion is Wexford. Rebellion broke out in Wexford for two main reasons: people there were terrified by reports of massacres of rebels in neighbouring Wicklow, and there was anger at the government's extension of terror to the county.

> Led by **Father John Murphy**, the rebels captured the towns of Enniscorthy and Wexford.
> A local landlord and United Irishman, **Bagenal Harvey**, became the leader of the rebels. Copying the French Revolution, a **Committee of Public Safety** was set up to run the area controlled by the rebels.
> Though very brave in battle, the rebels lacked weapons, especially cannons.

---

**Activity 5**

In pairs, examine this source and then answer the questions below.

1  Suggest three reasons why memorials are built.
2  Are memorials useful to historians? Give five reasons for your answer.

SOURCE 10.22: **1798 memorial, Wexford. The rebels were poorly armed. They lacked guns and cannons and mainly used a spear-like weapon called a pike.**

---

> On 5 June a rebel army was defeated at **New Ross**. After the battle, the British massacred rebel prisoners. The rebels set fire to a barn at **Scullabogue** containing loyalist prisoners, including women and children.
> A further massacre of loyalist prisoners occurred on Wexford Bridge a few days later. Most of those killed, though not all, were Protestants.
> These killings shocked many people and Harvey resigned as leader of the rebels. **Fr Philip Roche** replaced him.

---

**Activity 6**

Examine this source and then answer the questions below.

SOURCE 10.23: Massacre of Protestants at Scullabogue

1  How does the image portray the rebels?
2  The image is from a nineteenth-century history of the 1798 Rebellion. Is this a reliable source?

A rebel army was defeated at Arklow and British troops pushed into Co. Wexford. On 21 June they captured the rebel headquarters after the **Battle of Vinegar Hill**. The main rebellion was over, although groups of rebels continued fighting. The leaders, including Harvey, Roche and Murphy, were captured and hanged.

---

**Activity 7**

1   Draw a timeline of the main events in Wexford during the 1798 Rebellion.

---

## Ulster

Meanwhile the remaining United Irishmen in Ulster had also staged a rebellion. **Henry Joy McCracken** attacked the town of Antrim with 6,000 men. They were defeated and McCracken was later executed.

In Co. Down, rebels led by **Henry Munro** were defeated at the **Battle of Ballynahinch**. Munro was executed. This defeat marked the end of the rebellion in Ulster.

## French aid

Much to the surprise of the British, who thought the rebellion was over, French help arrived in August. A small army of 1,000 men under the command of **General Humbert** landed at Killala in Co. Mayo. At Castlebar, they defeated a British force. Many Irishmen joined the French army as it marched east. However, at Ballinamuck, Co. Longford, Humbert surrendered to a much greater British force. The French troops were treated well but the Irish were executed.

In October a French fleet containing 3,000 soldiers, including Wolfe Tone, was captured by a British fleet off the Donegal coast. Tone was sentenced to death by hanging. When his request to be shot like a soldier was refused, he attempted to commit suicide by cutting his throat. He died of his wounds a week later.

---

**Activity 8**

Examine this source and then answer the question below.

**SOURCE 10.24: Battle of Vinegar Hill**

1   What evidence is there in this picture to explain why the British won the battle?

---

### DID YOU KNOW?

The British did not recognise the rebels as soldiers. They were viewed as traitors and thousands were executed when captured.

**SOURCE 10.25: Main battles of the 1798 Rebellion**

## Summary: Timeline of the 1798 Rebellion

| 1791 | Society of United Irishmen forms in Belfast |
|------|--------------------------------------------|
| 1794 | Society of United Irishmen is banned |
| 1796 | French attempts to land at Bantry Bay fail |
| 1797 | British government begins a reign of terror in Ulster |
| 1798 | Leader of the United Irishmen arrested |
| | Outbreak of rebellion |
| | Rebel forces capture Enniscorthy and Wexford |
| | Rebel forces defeated in Down and Antrim |
| | Battle of Vinegar Hill – decisive defeat of the rebels |
| | French force lands at Killala – defeated at Ballinamuck |
| | Wolfe Tone captured after naval battle; dies after failed suicide attempt |

## What were the consequences of the 1798 Rebellion?

The consequences of the rebellion were to be far-reaching for Ireland. Despite the aims and ideals of the United Irishmen, it brought great **death and destruction** to Ireland. The British crushed the rebellion ruthlessly.

### Human cost

Historians estimate that about 50,000 rebels faced 100,000 British troops during the 1798 Rebellion.

It is not certain how many people were killed in the 1798 Rebellion in Ireland. Both contemporary sources and modern historians disagree on the numbers. Figures range from 10,000 to 50,000, with 30,000 dead the most widely accepted figure. The vast majority were rebels and civilians who died at the hands of British troops.

### Act of Union

The British government wanted to make sure that a rebellion did not happen again and that the French would not use Ireland as a base to attack England.

> The prime minister, **William Pitt**, believed that he needed to end the separate Irish parliament in Dublin.

> In 1801 the **Act of Union** was passed and the United Kingdom of Great Britain and Ireland was created.

> The Irish parliament was no more and Irish MPs took seats in the parliament in London instead.

---

### Activity 9

Examine this source and then answer the questions below.

**Revolution in Ireland**

May 22. The affairs of Ireland have at length arrived at the most alarming and melancholy [sad] pace. After the capture of Lord Fitzgerald and the consequent developments of the plans of the United Irishmen … the government was forced to declare the metropolis [Dublin] and other places in a state of rebellion.

May 29. Several hundred rebels were killed at Saggart and Naas. In the counties of Dublin, Kildare, and Meath, the rebellion was openly supported; and several severe actions [battles] have taken place, in which, although the rebels have fought well, they were defeated with immense slaughter.

June 1. Four thousand rebels at Kildare have laid down their arms and given up their leaders, who will be hung.

June 7. The rebellion still rages in Wicklow, Carlow, and Wexford. Many of the insurgents are killed; and many inhabitants are obliged to fly [escape] to Wales for refuge.

**SOURCE 10.26: Extract from The *Columbian Sentinel* (US newspaper), 8 August 1798**

1 According to the article, what action did the government take on 22 May 1798?

2 From the article, identify four counties where the rebellion had broken out.

3 After studying the article, would you agree that the British were defeating the rebels? Give evidence to support your answer.

4 Explain why events in May and June in Ireland were being reported in an American newspaper in August.

### Religious division

> The aim of uniting Catholics and Protestants did not succeed. In reality, a major consequence of 1798 was **greater political division** between the two groups.

> Most Protestants pointed to the massacres of Protestant civilians in Wexford and worried what would happen to them if Ireland became independent. They became strong supporters of British rule in Ireland.

## Irish republicanism

The aims of Wolfe Tone inspired later generations of Irish people who wanted freedom for Ireland. Tone became known as the **'Father of Irish Republicanism'**.

> Republicans believed that the British would not leave Ireland voluntarily and that violence would have to be used to end British rule in Ireland and win Irish freedom. This is what historians call the **physical-force tradition**.

> Many see the 1798 Rebellion as the first major example of this tradition. Later Irish examples include the rebellions in 1848, 1867 and 1916 and the War of Independence.

Other Irish people who also wanted more freedom for Ireland were shocked at the violence of 1798. For that reason they opposed the use of violence to achieve political change.

> They decided that the best way to gain greater freedom was through peaceful means.

> They would send MPs to Westminster to persuade the British to agree to reforms in Ireland and greater independence. This is called **constitutional nationalism**.

> The two most popular political leaders of the nineteenth century, **Daniel O'Connell** and **Charles Stewart Parnell**, supported this view (see Section 12).

### DO YOU UNDERSTAND THESE KEY TERMS?

| | |
|---|---|
| Act of Union | Protestant Ascendancy |
| constitutional nationalism | rebellion |
| loyalist | republicanism |
| Orange Order | United Irishmen |
| physical-force tradition | yeomanry |

**Physical-force tradition**
Advocated the use of violence to remove British rule in Ireland.

### Activity 10

In 1803 Robert Emmet (1778–1803) organised another revolt in Dublin.

SOURCE 10.27: **Robert Emmet, Irish nationalist and Republican**

1   Find out more about the rebellion of Robert Emmet.
2   Show your findings to the class in a PowerPoint presentation.

Chapter summary     Weblinks     PowerPoint summary

## SELF-ASSESSMENT – CAN YOU?

1   Argue why Ireland was in need of political reform in 1798.

2   Examine the impact of the French Revolution on Ireland.

3   Explain why the Society of United Irishmen was formed.

4   Identify the main aims of the United Irishmen after the organisation was banned.

5   Outline the main events of the failed French expedition to Bantry Bay in 1796.

6   Explain the impact of disputes between Catholics and Protestants over land.

7   Explain why the leaders of the United Irishmen decided to revolt in May 1798.

8   Describe how the British were able to disrupt the United Irishmen's plans for a rebellion.

9   Describe the main events in Ulster during the 1798 Rebellion.

10  Examine the reasons why the rebels were defeated in Wexford.

11  Examine the role played by the French in the 1798 rebellion.

12  Identify and explain three important consequences of the 1798 Rebellion.

# 11 INVESTIGATION OF THE GREAT FAMINE IN IRELAND

## What was the Great Famine?

211

## Where did the Irish emigrate to?

218

## What is the significance of the Irish diaspora?

225

# WHAT WAS THE GREAT FAMINE?

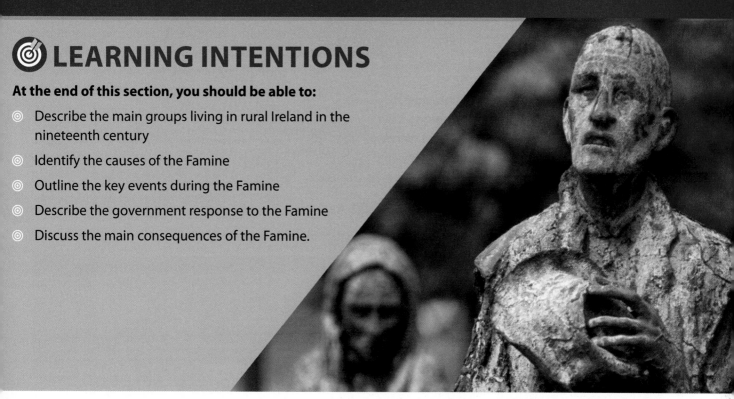

## LEARNING INTENTIONS

**At the end of this section, you should be able to:**

◎ Describe the main groups living in rural Ireland in the nineteenth century

◎ Identify the causes of the Famine

◎ Outline the key events during the Famine

◎ Describe the government response to the Famine

◎ Discuss the main consequences of the Famine.

## Who was living in rural Ireland in the nineteenth century?

Apart from the industrial northeast, Ireland depended on agriculture. Just 10 per cent of the population lived in towns and cities in the 1840s.

There were four main groups of people living in the countryside: landlords, tenant farmers, cottiers and labourers.

### Landlords

The landlords were descended from the English and Scottish settlers who had received land in the plantations (see Section 8). Ninety per cent of the land was owned by 5,000 landlords. They lived in mansions on large estates. Their main source of income came from renting their land out to tenants. Many landlords were **absentee landlords**, which meant that they lived elsewhere (usually in England) for most of the year. An **agent** collected the rent for the landlord twice a year. Any tenants who failed to pay their rent were evicted.

**Eviction**
Forcing people to leave their homes and land.

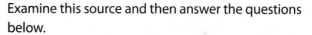

### Activity 1

Examine this source and then answer the questions below.

SOURCE 11.1: An eviction in the west of Ireland

1 Describe the eviction in this picture.
2 Imagine you were one of those being evicted. What emotions would you experience?

## Tenants

There were two types of tenant farmer.

> **Large tenant farmers:** Their farms were over 30 acres in size and they made a good living. They grew wheat and barley and had a few cattle and sheep. They usually ate potatoes, meat and milk.

> **Small tenant farmers:** They rented between 5 and 30 acres. Their land was divided among their sons (**subdivision**). Therefore, their farms were small and their income was low. They usually ate potatoes and milk.

## Cottiers

Cottiers formed the largest number of people who worked on the land. Rent was paid to farmers for one acre of land. Potatoes were grown on that plot as their only food. They mainly lived in one-roomed cabins with thatched roofs. By 1845 there were about one million cottiers and together with their families they numbered four million. They were totally dependent on the potato crop. If it failed, they faced disaster.

### Activity 2

Examine this source and then answer the questions below.

SOURCE 11.2: Interior of a cottier's cabin

1 Describe the inside of the cottier's cabin.
2 What, do you think, would it be like to live here?

## Labourers

Labourers were the poorest class. They had no land and they worked for the big farmers when extra labour was needed such as at harvest time.

# What were the causes of the Famine?

A number of factors contributed to the tragedy of the Great Famine (1845–51).

> **Rise in population:** By 1841 the population had risen to 8 million. People tended to marry young and have large families. Overpopulation meant that there were too many people for too little fertile land.

> **Subdivision:** Most small farmers divided their farms among their sons because there was no other work available. The sons, therefore, had less land and less income than their father had, which meant the people were becoming poorer.

> **Reliance on potatoes:** The cottiers depended totally on the potato as a source of food. One acre could feed a family. If the potato crop failed two years in a row it would cause famine.

> **Potato blight:** A fungal disease that had come to Ireland from Canada. This disease attacked the stalks, which turned black, and then the potatoes began to rot.

The main cause of the Famine was the **failure of the potato crop in successive years**. In **1845** the weather was warm and humid and one-third of the potato crop was lost due to potato blight. In **1846** nearly all the crop was wiped out. In **'black '47'** (1847) there was a very small crop as people had eaten the seed potatoes in desperation. **1848** was another terrible year.

**Famine**
Lack of food causing the deaths of a large number of people.

SOURCE 11.3: **Potato blight**

SOURCE 11.4: **Effects of the Famine in a small cabin. How does the artist portray the effects of starvation?**

---

## Activity 3

Examine this source and then answer the questions below.

We next went to Skibbereen. We first proceeded to Bridgetown … and there saw the dying, the living, and the dead, lying indiscriminately on the same floor, without anything between them and the cold earth save a few miserable rags upon them … not a single house out of 500 could boast of being free of death and fever, though several could be pointed out with the dead lying close to the living for the space of three or four, even six days, without any effort being made to bring bodies to an eternal resting place.

SOURCE 11.5: **James Mahony's description of the Famine in West Cork**

1  Comment on the situation in Skibbereen. Use evidence from the account to prove your point.

2  Why, do you think, were the bodies not being buried?

The cottier and labourer groups were almost wiped out. Famine fever, which was highly contagious, killed more people than starvation.

## How did the government respond to the Famine?

The government was slow to react initially, believing that a government should not intervene in economic matters. However, some attempts to relieve the Famine were eventually made. They were largely inadequate and ineffective.

### Maize

In 1845 the prime minister, Sir Robert Peel, bought £100,000 worth of maize (corn) from Canada. **Relief committees** were set up in each area to distribute the maize to the poor. It was sold at cost price to small farmers and cottiers. It helped to feed one million people.

### Public works schemes

The government did not want to give out free food as it was afraid the poor would become lazy. It set up public works schemes to enable the poor to earn money to buy food. The poor had to build roads, piers, etc. in return for a small wage. About 750,000 people worked on these schemes. However, the schemes did not address the plight of those people who were too weak to work.

### Workhouses

In 1838 **workhouses** had been introduced under the **Poor Law Act**. Ireland was divided into 130 **Poor Law Unions** and a workhouse was built in each. A tax on local landlords and big farmers, called the **poor rate**, funded the running of the local workhouse.

Workhouses were grim places and people only went there when they were desperate. On entering, families were split up and not allowed to meet. Soon the workhouses were overcrowded. Famine fever spread very quickly in these conditions.

**Workhouse**
Large building where poor people were given basic accommodation and made to work.

---

### Activity 4

Examine this source and then answer the questions below.

> … they are dying as fast as they can from 10 to 20 a day out of it there is some kind of strange fever in it and it is the opinion of the Doctor it will spread over town and country when the weather grows warm no person can be sure of their lives …

**SOURCE 11.6: Letter from Hannah Curtis, Mountmellick, to her brother John, 2 April 1846**

1 According to Curtis, what is the main cause of death?
2 What conditions does she expect will increase the death toll?
3 Rewrite this letter, adding in punctuation where appropriate to make it easier to understand.

### Activity 5

Examine this source and then answer the questions below.

**SOURCE 11.7: *At the Gate of a Workhouse* (1846)**

1 Describe the scene in the picture.
2 What word would you use to describe the expressions on their faces?
3 Imagine you are a fourteen-year-old child in the workhouse. Write a diary entry describing a typical day. Use the Internet and other sources to help you.

## Soup kitchens

The **Quakers** set up soup kitchens to give out free soup and bread to people who were starving. This saved many lives. In 1847 the government also set up soup kitchens to help those who could not be looked after in the workhouses. This was paid for by the local ratepayers. Three million people benefited from this scheme, which was very successful.

> **Quakers**
> A Protestant group who oppose violence and are very charitable.

### Activity 6

Due to extensive coverage of the Irish Famine in the newspapers, nineteen countries sent money to help feed the starving. The British Relief Association collected £400,000.

1   In pairs, research which countries sent money to Ireland. Write a paragraph on your findings.

SOURCE 11.8: Soup kitchen

## What were the main consequences of the Famine?

### Fall in population

Between 1845 and 1850 the population of Ireland decreased by two million. One million people died and one million people emigrated.

### Change in agriculture

> Landlords who had gone bankrupt as a result of the Famine were replaced by people who saw their estates as an investment. Farming changed from growing crops to raising livestock such as cattle and sheep, which was more profitable. Tenants who were no longer needed were evicted.

> Many Irish farmers were destitute and had to emigrate.

> The practice of subdivision also ended after the Famine. This meant that only the eldest child inherited the farm; the other children had to leave.

> Farm sizes increased. This was helped by the fall in population after the Famine. Bigger farms meant that farmers had a higher income.

### Emigration

Between 1845 and 1855, two million Irish people emigrated to America and Australia and 750,000 to Britain. Many were forced to move as a result of losing their land or their job. Fewer people were needed to work the land. Some landlords simply evicted their tenants, others paid for them to travel abroad.

### Activity 7

Examine this source and then answer the questions below.

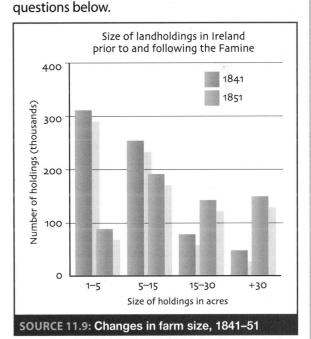

SOURCE 11.9: Changes in farm size, 1841–51

1   Describe how the Great Famine affected the size of farm holdings.

2   What size of farm decreased most in numbers?

3   Where, do you think, did those who had to leave their farms go?

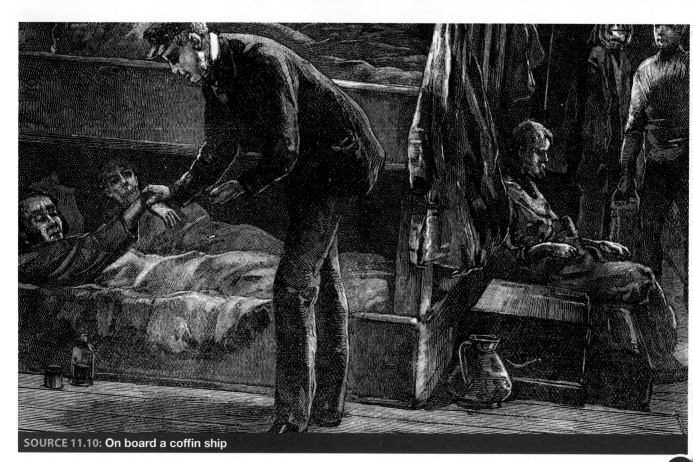

SOURCE 11.10: **On board a coffin ship**

Many people sailed to America on **coffin ships**. These were ships that were in poor condition and overcrowded. Some of these ships were so unseaworthy that they sank and drowned all on board. Thousands more people died of fever in the overcrowded conditions. When they reached America, many ships were not allowed to dock because there was fever on board.

**Steerage**
Cheapest accommodation on a passenger ship.

### Activity 8

Examine this source and then answer the questions below.

> This vessel left with 476 passengers, of whom 158 died before arrival, including the Master, mate and nine of the crew … Three days after her arrival there remained of the ship's company only the second mate, one seaman and a boy, able to do duty; all others were dead or ill in hospital.

SOURCE 11.11: **Eyewitness comment on a voyage to America**

1 Approximately what percentage of the ship's population had died before arriving in America?

2 How many crew remained after arriving in America?

### Activity 9

Examine this source and then answer the questions below.

> Hundreds of poor people, men, women and children of all ages huddled together without light, without air, wallowing in filth and breathing a fetid atmosphere, sick in body, dispirited in heart; the fevered patients lying beside the sound, by their agonised ravings disturbing those around.

SOURCE 11.12: **Eyewitness account of Stephen de Vere, who sailed in steerage in 1847**

1 Imagine you are a passenger in steerage on this ship. Write a short paragraph describing the hardship you suffered on board. Use both this source and material from the text and Source 11.10 in your answer.

## Decline in the Irish language

The Irish-speaking areas of the south and west of the country suffered most during the Famine. Many died and large numbers emigrated from these areas. This emigration continued throughout the rest of the nineteenth century.

## Anti-British feeling

The British government was blamed for the Famine by the Irish, both at home and abroad. Ships full of produce such as barley and wheat had left Ireland while the people were starving. Anger at this fact led to increasing support for groups such as the **Irish Republican Brotherhood (IRB)**. They wanted to drive the British out of Ireland using violence.

**SOURCE 11.13:** A crowd looking at 'Wanted' posters for members of the Fenian Brotherhood and Irish Republican Brotherhood, Dublin, Ireland, in the late nineteenth century

## DO YOU UNDERSTAND THESE KEY TERMS?

| | | |
|---|---|---|
| absentee landlord | cottier | soup kitchen |
| agent | famine | subdivision |
| black '47 | potato blight | tenant farmer |
| coffin ship | Quaker | workhouse |

PowerPoint summary

## SELF-ASSESSMENT – CAN YOU?

1. Outline the causes of the Famine in Ireland.
2. Comment on the various methods used by the government to deal with the Famine.
3. Analyse how the Famine affected Ireland under the following headings:

   › Irish language

   › How the Irish now viewed the British

   › The type of farming

   › Emigration.

# WHERE DID THE IRISH EMIGRATE TO?

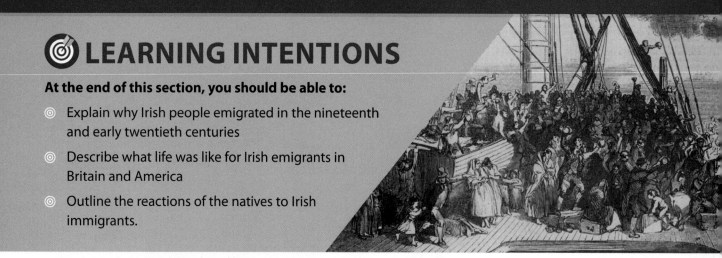

## LEARNING INTENTIONS

**At the end of this section, you should be able to:**

◎ Explain why Irish people emigrated in the nineteenth and early twentieth centuries

◎ Describe what life was like for Irish emigrants in Britain and America

◎ Outline the reactions of the natives to Irish immigrants.

## Why did Irish people emigrate?

The most important consequence of the Great Famine was that it greatly increased the rate of emigration. This high level of Irish emigration continued for over a century after the Famine. Irish people settled in many countries throughout the world.

Famine, unemployment, evictions and overpopulation were the main **push factors** for emigration; that is, they pushed or forced people to leave Ireland. Often emigration was their only option.

**Pull factors**, such as the promise of cheap land or the hope of a better life, attracted people to emigrate to another country. For them, emigration was often a deliberate choice.

Money (**remittances**) sent to Ireland by those who had already emigrated was used to pay for other members of the family to emigrate.

The two most popular destinations were the USA and Britain. Britain had been the main destination for Irish emigrants up to the time of the Famine. However, after the Famine began, the USA became the number one destination. Irish people joined English, German and Scandinavian migrants as part of the first major influx of immigrants in America.

## What was life like for emigrants to Britain?

There were two main types of emigration to Britain.

1 **Seasonal:** There was a tradition of going to Britain for short periods each year. The immigrants mainly came from the poor agricultural areas of Ulster and Connacht. Their land did not provide them with enough income. Therefore, they travelled to rural areas in England and Scotland to help with the harvests. This extra income was vital in allowing them to survive on their farms.

2 **Permanent:** Emigrants left Ireland as there were no jobs (and during the Famine because it was the only way of staying alive). They found it easy to get work in industrialised Britain as they were willing to work very hard for very long hours at low wages. Many of the most dangerous and dirtiest jobs were done by the Irish. Most of them were unskilled labourers.

**Emigrant**
Person who has left their country to live in another country.

**Immigrant**
Person who has come to live in a country from another country.

## Activity 1

Examine this source and then answer the questions below.

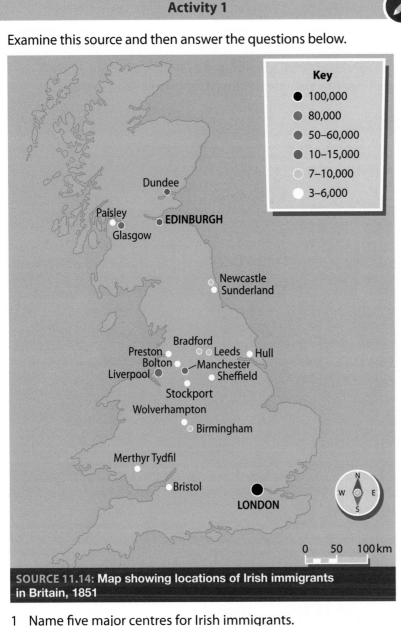

SOURCE 11.14: Map showing locations of Irish immigrants in Britain, 1851

Key
- 100,000
- 80,000
- 50–60,000
- 10–15,000
- 7–10,000
- 3–6,000

1 Name five major centres for Irish immigrants.
2 Suggest two reasons why they chose to live in these locations.
3 Why has Britain always been a popular destination for Irish emigrants?

In 1851 there were 400,000 Irish-born people living in Britain. Most of them had settled close to ports such as Liverpool, Glasgow and London. There was plenty of work in these and other industrial areas of Britain.

Irish immigrants dominated the **construction sector** in Britain. The highest-paid labourers working in Britain were the Irish navvies. Between 1750 and 1830 navvies built 3,500 miles of canals. By 1850 they were building the railways. They worked in appalling conditions and lived in huts beside the construction site. Cholera, dysentery and typhus were common, as was heavy drinking and violence. In 1845 they earned twice as much as an agricultural labourer.

Most Irish immigrants lived in filthy slums, usually in one room. They shared an outdoor water tap and toilets with many others. Overcrowding and poor sanitation led to the spread of diseases such as typhus and cholera.

## Reaction of the natives

Many British people resented Irish immigrants because they increased the demand for housing, which meant that rents were kept high. The Irish were also competing with British people for jobs. British employers hired Irish immigrants as they would work for lower wages. The native population objected to the Irish taking their jobs and keeping wages low.

## Activity 2

Examine this source and then answer the questions below.

> … a stranger to Liverpool will notice such a scene of filth and vice to parallel any part of the world …

SOURCE 11.15: *Liverpool Herald*, 17 November 1855

1 This is a reference to Irish immigrants. What are they being accused of here?
2 Comment on the attitude displayed in the quote.

## DID YOU KNOW?

Liverpool was the most popular destination for the Irish who emigrated to Britain after the Famine. However, when the natives caught diseases from the Irish immigrants it resulted in an increase in anti-Irish and anti-Catholic feelings.

SOURCE 11.16: Irish immigrants in Liverpool, 1850. Can you describe what is happening in the picture?

Religion was an issue, especially in Scotland. Some Scots claimed that their Protestant identity was being threatened by Catholic immigrants. Football clubs were (and still are) examples of the sectarian divide, with Glasgow Celtic being Catholic and Glasgow Rangers being Protestant.

**Sectarian**
Resulting from religious differences.

### Activity 3

Read the text and examine the source, and then answer the questions below.

In the nineteenth century anti-Irish and anti-Catholic feelings were stirred up in newspapers and books that claimed the Irish were 'an inferior race'.

SOURCE 11.17: 'The Irish Frankenstein' *Punch* magazine, 1882

1  How are the Irish portrayed in this source?
2  Referring to the text, explain why the Irish are portrayed in this way.
3  How, do you think, would this cartoon affect the attitude of the British population?

---

### Activity 4

Examine these sources and then answer the questions below.

**A** In our opinion, the Irish have as much right to come to our country to better their lives as the Scots and English have to go to Ireland or any other part of Britain for the same reason. Let us hear no more complaints about the influx of Irish having a bad effect on Scotland unless it is to do something about tackling the problems which cause the emigration.

SOURCE 11.18: *The Glasgow Courier*, 1830

**B** In Dumfriesshire and Galloway there are plenty of Irishmen ready to take the bread out of the mouths of our own poor. An Irishman who lives in a hovel, feeds on potatoes and neither clothes nor educates his children, can always work for less than a Scot. There are too many people who employ only the cheapest workers and do not think of the consequences.

SOURCE 11.19: *The Dumfries Courier*, 1845

1   List the main points being made in document A and in document B.
2   What is the attitude of each writer? Refer to the document when answering.
3   Why, in your opinion, is there a difference in attitude between the two documents?

## What was life like for emigrants to America?

The Industrial Revolution in America began in the early 1800s. Irish immigrants were attracted by the jobs available and the likelihood of a better standard of living. Between 1845 and 1860, 1.5 million Irish people emigrated to the United States. Irish people continued to emigrate in large numbers to the USA and by 1910 there were more people of Irish descent in New York than there were in Dublin.

**DID YOU KNOW?**

Before leaving Ireland, these emigrants had an **American wake**. Unlike the traditional funeral wake (where family, friends and neighbours gather in the house of the deceased with the body present), this social gathering was for the living. When a person left Ireland for the USA it was seen as a kind of death because it was unlikely that the emigrant would ever return.

The Irish mainly went to cities such as New York, Boston and Philadelphia. They settled in areas of these cities where there was already an Irish community for protection and support. Large numbers of very poor Irish immigrants lived in slums and tenements.

### Activity 5

Examine the source and then answer the question below.

SOURCE 11.20: **New York tenements, 1870s**

1   Imagine you are an Irish teenager who has just arrived in New York. Compare your living conditions in New York with those on your farm in Ireland.

SOURCE 11.21: Railroad workers, 1894

Many unskilled Irish women worked long hours in factories for very low wages. However, most single Irish women preferred to be maids or servants in the houses of wealthy families. This was known as **domestic service**.

By the 1860s the police force in New York was mainly Irish. As recently as 1960, 42 per cent of New York police officers were of Irish descent.

The most popular jobs for unskilled Irish men were in factories and as labourers on infrastructure projects (roads, railways, etc.). A large number of Irishmen helped build the railways to the west coast of America.

Many Irishmen worked in coal mines in Pennsylvania. Their working conditions were appalling and dangerous. A secret society of Irishmen called the **Molly Maguires** went on strike in these coal mines in 1875. They were looking for fair treatment and safer working conditions. The protest became violent and twenty suspected 'Mollies' were hanged. Their trials attracted hostile newspaper coverage and promoted anti-immigrant feelings.

## Activity 6

Examine this source and then answer the questions below.

| Year | No. of Irish immigrants |
|------|-------------------------|
| 1841–50 | 780,000 |
| 1851–60 | 914,000 |
| 1861–70 | 435,000 |
| 1871–80 | 436,000 |
| 1881–90 | 655,000 |
| 1891–1900 | 388,000 |
| 1901–10 | 399,000 |
| 1911–20 | 146,000 |
| 1921–30 | 211,000 |
| 1931–40 | 11,000 |
| 1941–50 | 19,000 |
| 1951–60 | 48,000 |
| 1961–70 | 32,000 |
| 1971–80 | 12,000 |
| 1981–90 | 32,000 |

SOURCE 11.22: Irish migrants arriving in the USA, 1841–2004

1  Draw a bar graph to show Irish emigration to the United States 1841–1930.

2  Suggest reasons why there was a dramatic decrease in immigration after 1930.

3  Why did immigration peak in the years 1841–90?

## Ellis Island

In 1892 Ellis Island was opened as a federal immigration centre. It is an island in New York harbour. Immigrants from Europe, including Ireland, were subjected to medical and mental examinations there before they could enter the USA. Anyone who failed these examinations was separated from their family and deported home. Fewer than 2 per cent of Irish immigrants were deported, but Ellis Island was still a terrible ordeal for the immigrants.

### Activity 7

Examine this source and then answer the questions below.

SOURCE 11.23: Ellis Island, 1900

1 In groups of three or four, research how immigrants were processed at Ellis Island.
2 Prepare a PowerPoint presentation to reveal your findings to the class.

### DID YOU KNOW?

Annie Moore, a seventeen-year-old Irish girl, was the very first immigrant to be processed at Ellis Island. Accompanied by her two younger brothers, she had just completed a twelve-day voyage from Cobh to New York in steerage aboard the steamship *Nevada*.
The three children were reuniting with their parents in New York. Annie was the first of more than 12 million immigrants to reach this port of entry to the USA.

### Activity 8

Examine this source and then answer the questions below.

SOURCE 11.25: The Statue of Liberty

1 Where is the Statue of Liberty?
2 Find out who presented the Statue of Liberty to the USA and when.

## Reaction of the natives

In the early years Irish men and women had a hard time finding skilled work. There was a **stigma** to being Irish and Catholic. Many businesses had a sign in the front of their shops that read 'No Irish Need Apply'. The Irish and the black populations were regarded as being inferior. Magazines such as *Puck* promoted an image of the Irish as stupid, drunken and violent. Because of the backlash against the Irish most of them lived in **ghettos** for their own protection.

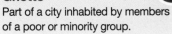

# HELP WANTED
## NO IRISH NEED APPLY

SOURCE 11.24: Boston sign, 1918

**Ghetto**
Part of a city inhabited by members of a poor or minority group.

**Stigma**
Disapproval of a particular group of people.

The fact that the Irish were willing to work for as little as fifty cents a day meant that they took jobs from the natives. This stirred up anti-Irish feelings among the American working class.

## Activity 9

Examine this source and then answer the questions below.

THE USUAL IRISH WAY OF DOING THINGS.

**SOURCE 11.26: Anti-Irish cartoon by Thomas Nast, 1871**

1 How does this cartoon depict the Irish?
2 What, do you think, was the motive behind this cartoon?

## DO YOU UNDERSTAND THESE KEY TERMS?

| | |
|---|---|
| American wake | pull factor |
| domestic service | push factor |
| Molly Maguires | remittance |

 PowerPoint summary

Despite this adverse start, the Irish quickly rose up the social ladder. This was largely because they could speak English, unlike, for example, most Italian immigrants. As they became established, some Irish, in turn, discriminated against the newer arrivals to the USA.

**Discrimination**
Treating a person or group of people unfairly.

By 1900 many Irish had become middle class. By 1946 Irish-Americans had reached the top of the social scale as many of them were highly educated. They had become the natives.

## Activity 10

Examine these sources and then answer the questions below.

A The name of 'Irish' has become identified in the minds of many, with abuse of every species of outlawry like drunk, disorderly, fighting etc.

**SOURCE 11.27: *Catholic Telegraph* in Cincinnatti, 1857**

B By 1890, being from the British Isles, the Irish were now considered acceptable and assimilable [able to adapt] to the American way of life.

**SOURCE 11.28: Extract from *The Irish Americans: A History* by Jay P. Dolan (2008)**

1 Compare A and B. What images of the Irish do they portray?
2 What brought about this change in attitude towards the Irish between 1857 and 1890?

# SELF-ASSESSMENT – CAN YOU?

1 Outline the main factors that led Irish people to emigrate during the nineteenth and early twentieth centuries.
2 Explain the challenges Irish immigrants faced in Britain.
3 Outline the types of work Irish immigrants found in the USA.
4 Describe the challenges Irish immigrants faced in the USA.

# WHAT IS THE SIGNIFICANCE OF THE IRISH DIASPORA?

## LEARNING INTENTIONS

**At the end of this section, you should be able to:**

◎ Describe the Irish diaspora

◎ Discuss the influence of Irish immigrants in Britain

◎ Discuss the influence of Irish immigrants in the USA

◎ Comment on the role of the Irish diaspora today.

## What is the Irish diaspora?

The **Irish diaspora** is the tens of millions of people living outside Ireland who come from Ireland or whose ancestors came from Ireland. It is the result of centuries of emigration.

> **Diaspora**
> Where people of an ethnic group are spread across the world through emigration.

---

### Activity 1

Examine this source and then answer the questions below.

Canada 4.7m

Great Britain 9.0m

Netherlands 0.6m

Other Europe 3.7m

Belgium 0.4m

France 1.7m

Germany 1.8m

*Atlantic Ocean*

USA 39.9m

*Pacific Ocean*

Spain 1.0m   Italy 1.3m

Asia 0.04m

Middle East 0.4m

*Pacific Ocean*

*Indian Ocean*

Australia 2.2m

Argentina 0.6m   South Africa 0.2m

New Zealand 0.2m

0   3000   6000 km

**Key**

Global Irish community   0.2m   Population in millions

**SOURCE 11.29: Map of Irish diaspora, 2016**

1   List, in rank order, the eight most popular destinations of Irish emigrants.

---

While Irish emigrants have settled across the world, the two most popular destinations were America and Britain. The Irish diaspora has had a major impact on life in these countries, politically, economically and culturally.

# What influence have Irish immigrants had in Britain?

## Irish diaspora in Britain

The 2001 British census showed that 869,000 people in Britain had been born in Ireland. It is estimated that 25 per cent of the British population has some Irish ancestry.

### Activity 2

Examine this source and then answer the questions below.

| City | % of Irish in total population |
| --- | --- |
| Liverpool | 22.3 |
| Dundee | 18.9 |
| Glasgow | 18.2 |
| Cardiff | 16.2 |
| Manchester | 13.1 |

**SOURCE 11.30: Irish proportion of population of major British cities, 1851**

1   Look at a map of Britain and find out where these cities are located.
2   Suggest why these cities have significant Irish populations.

## Economic role

A major migration of Irish people to Britain took place in the 1940s and 1950s. Britain badly needed workers during the war years to take the jobs vacated by soldiers. Half a million Irish people went to Britain to work in industry or to join the British Army. The majority remained in Britain and raised families there. As workers, they made a huge contribution in the construction, manufacturing, medical and teaching sectors.

Later in the twentieth century, a significant number of Irish immigrants worked in the teaching, nursing and IT sectors. More recent Irish immigrants have made a notable contribution to the financial services sector. Indeed, *Forbes* magazine stated in 1998, 'If you took the Irish out of the City of London, the financial services world would collapse.'

### Activity 3

Examine this source and then answer the questions below.

They don't have that inferiority complex, they know they are as good as anyone else.

**SOURCE 11.31: Comment on the Irish who arrived in Britain in the 1980s**

1   Explain what the writer means in this quote.
2   Investigate the types of jobs Irish immigrants had in 1980s Britain.

## Cultural contribution

In theatre, two Irish dramatists dominated the London scene in the late nineteenth and early twentieth centuries. Oscar Wilde specialised in comedies such as *The Importance of Being Earnest*. George Bernard Shaw was one of the most important literary figures in Europe by the 1920s. Plays such as *John Bull's Other Island* and *Pygmalion* were extremely popular. He won the Nobel Prize for Literature in 1925.

### DID YOU KNOW?

*Pygmalion* was made into a very successful film called *My Fair Lady*.

Irish musicians have enjoyed great popularity in Britain, often topping the charts and selling out concerts. And many of Britain's most successful musicians have Irish roots. For example, three of The Beatles have Irish ancestry; the Gallagher brothers of Oasis have Irish parents; and Ed Sheeran has Irish grandparents.

In TV and radio, Eamonn Andrews and Terry Wogan were very popular broadcasters in the late twentieth century. During the IRA bombing campaign of the 1980s there was a backlash against the Irish community in Britain. People like Wogan helped to make the point that not all Irish people were IRA supporters. More recently, Irish presenters such as Graham Norton, Dara Ó Briain and Laura Whitmore have had successful careers in Britain.

In sport, football clubs such as Aston Villa, Arsenal, Everton and Manchester United have a tradition of representing Irish communities in their areas. Irish greats such as Liam Brady and Dave O'Leary played for Arsenal, and Roy Keane and Denis Irwin played for Manchester United. Wayne Rooney has an Irish background and has played with Everton and Manchester United.

London holds an annual St Patrick's Day parade. It was cancelled for a period in the 1970s and 1980s due to the Troubles.

The Irish influence can even be heard in the Liverpool dialect, which is called **Scouse**.

In Scotland, the Orange Order has a large membership, especially in Glasgow. This reflects the fact that most of the Irish immigrants in Scotland come from Ulster.

### Activity 4

1  Use the internet and other sources to find out more about Oscar Wilde. Write a short paragraph on his career.
2  Write a short paragraph on the impact of Irish immigrants on British culture.

## Political influence

The Irish have a strong political presence in the UK, both in local government and at national level. Former prime ministers David Cameron and Tony Blair both had some Irish ancestry.

Traditionally, most Irish immigrants supported the Labour Party. This reflected the fact that, up to recent times, the Irish were employed in working-class jobs associated with the Labour Party.

## The Troubles

The Troubles started in Northern Ireland in 1969. In 1974 the IRA detonated bombs in two pubs in Guildford, near London. These pubs were popular with British Army personnel. Four soldiers and a civilian were killed and sixty-five others were injured. Four men were tried and convicted. However, after fifteen years the men, known as the Guildford Four, were found to have been wrongly convicted and were released from prison.

SOURCE 11.32: Roy Keane

### Activity 5

Examine this source and then answer the questions below.

> Like everybody else it has been so difficult to put one's life back on track. Many, many people have been affected by that night – not only the dead and injured and their families and friends but also the people who witnessed and helped at the scene – that one is reassured to know that there are others who understand.

SOURCE 11.33: *Surrey Advertiser* reporter Robert King on the effect of the Guildford bombing, 5 October 2014

1  How has the reporter's life been affected by the bombing?
2  Who else does he say has been affected by the bombing?
3  How would you feel towards the Irish community in Britain if you had been in Guildford that night?

In 1974 the IRA killed 21 people and injured 182 people when bombs exploded in two pubs in Birmingham. As with all the IRA bombings in Britain, there was a backlash against the Irish community there. Some people were physically assaulted. Irish pubs and community centres were attacked. People were verbally abused and threatened because they were Irish. Six men were wrongly convicted of the Birmingham bombings. Following a campaign led by the Labour MP Chris Mullin, the Birmingham Six were released after sixteen years in jail.

## What influence have Irish immigrants had in the USA?

Today 35 million people in America are entitled to call themselves Irish. They are to be found throughout the country, but there remains a large Irish community in the cities of the northeast coast such as New York and Boston. The Irish have made their way to the pinnacle of political and economic success. They have also achieved success in the arts, science, the law, religion and the army.

### Cultural contribution

A St Patrick's Day parade is held in every major US city each year. This highlights the Irish presence in the US. The largest parade occurs in New York, where over two million people take part. Many marching bands from US police and fire departments take part, reflecting the dominance of the Irish diaspora in those organisations.

**Activity 6**

Examine this source and then answer the questions below.

> I don't complain that we have a legal system that makes mistakes; that can happen anywhere in the world. What I complain about is that we lack the mechanism for owning up to mistakes.

**SOURCE 11.34: Chris Mullin MP on the release of the Birmingham Six, 4 May 1991**

1 What is Chris Mullin accusing the British legal system of not doing?
2 How would you feel if you were wrongly convicted?
3 Divide into groups and research the case of the Birmingham Six or the Guildford Four. Assign tasks to each individual in the group. Make a presentation to the class on your findings.

**SOURCE 11.35: St Patrick's Day parade in New York**

**SOURCE 11.36: Mariah Carey**

Irish-Americans have made a major impact on popular entertainment. These include actors such as Martin Sheen and Anne Hathaway; musicians and singers such as Bing Crosby, Kurt Cobain and Mariah Carey; and media personalities such as Walt Disney, Conan O'Brien and Ed Sullivan.

Some Irish-Americans have even helped to rekindle aspects of Irish culture in Ireland, for example Irish dancers and choreographers Jean Butler and Michael Flatley.

**Activity 7**

1 Take one of the Irish-Americans mentioned in this section and write a short paragraph on their career.

In literature, Irish-American writers include Eugene O'Neill (playwright), F. Scott Fitzgerald (novelist) and Edgar Allan Poe (poet). Brooklyn-born Frank McCourt won a Pulitzer Prize for his autobiographical novel *Angela's Ashes* about his childhood memories of Limerick.

SOURCE 11.37: **F. Scott Fitzgerald**

### Activity 8

1　Research the career of F. Scott Fitzgerald. Write a short paragraph on his career.

In sport, Irish emigrants brought the Irish games of hurling, Gaelic football, camogie and handball to America. Today, the North American GAA organisation is very strong, particularly in New York (see Section 20). Other Irish-American sports stars include Tom Brady (American football) and John McEnroe (tennis).

SOURCE 11.38: **John McEnroe**

Religion has always been important to the Irish-American identity and continues to play a major role in their communities. Many Irish-Americans have been leaders in the Catholic Church. An Irish-American called Francis Spellman became a cardinal and served as Archbishop of New York from 1939 to 1967. In the 1970s, 17 per cent of American Catholics were Irish and 50 per cent of bishops were of Irish descent. Irish Jesuits established Fordham University in New York, and Boston College.

SOURCE 11.39: **Cardinal Spellman**

## Political influence

**Tammany Hall** was a political group that started in New York in 1789. Run by the Democratic Party, it aimed to control New York politics. It helped immigrants, particularly Irish immigrants, to climb up the political ladder. They were enrolled as citizens so that they could vote in local elections. Each political ward (district) in the city had a **boss** who got the local vote out. It became politically corrupt as it got things done for people for an agreed price. The business community supported it as it could cut through red tape for a fee.

SOURCE 11.40: **Tammany Hall, 1830**

**Learning Outcome** 2.7　229

In the twentieth century Tammany Hall was reformed and concentrated on helping the working class. Its influence gradually began to decrease and it ceased to exist in the 1960s.

As the Irish climbed up the social ladder they began to organise themselves politically. They became strong supporters of the Democratic Party. Between 1830 and 1960, the Democrats could expect to get between 80 and 95 per cent of the Irish-American vote. Many US presidents have had Irish ancestors, but in 1960 Irish-American John F. Kennedy became the first Catholic US president.

Today, Irish-American support is divided equally between Democrats and Republicans. Ronald Reagan was an Irish-American Republican who became president in 1980. Irish-Americans are in positions of power in Congress. Paul Ryan, a Republican, became Speaker (leader) of the House of Representatives in 2015. Vice-President Mike Pence is an Irish-American.

## How did Irish-Americans get involved in the political situation in Ireland?

Irish people who had to emigrate as a result of the Famine often remained bitter about their experience. They blamed Britain for the Famine. They were willing to help any group trying to achieve Irish independence from Britain.

SOURCE 11.41: John F. Kennedy, 1962

SOURCE 11.42: Mike Pence, 2017

---

### Activity 9 ✏️

Examine this source and then answer the questions below.

> A million and a half men, women and children were carefully slain by the British government. They died of hunger in the midst of abundance which their own hands had created.

SOURCE 11.43: John Mitchel (a Protestant Irish nationalist who settled in the USA in the 1850s)

1 What point is Mitchel making here?
2 What emotion is Mitchel expressing? Quote from the text to back up your answer.

---

John Devoy was the leader of the American branch of the Irish Republican Brotherhood (IRB), which was called **Clan na Gael**. It sent money and guns to the IRB in Ireland.

During the War of Independence (see Section 12), Éamon

SOURCE 11.44: John Devoy

de Valera (who had been born in America) travelled to America as President of the Irish Republic. He wanted the US government to recognise the Irish Republic. He failed to achieve this goal, but he did manage to raise $4 million from the Irish-American community.

In the early 1970s, during the Troubles in Northern Ireland, an organisation called **Noraid** was set up in America to fund the Provisional IRA campaign. It was organised by Michael Flannery. The money was used to buy arms for the IRA. It was very successful. However, Noraid was also very supportive of the peace process in the 1990s.

In the 1980s senior Irish-American politicians such as Senator Ted Kennedy, House Speaker Tip O'Neill, Governor Hugh Carey of New York and Senator Pat Moynihan condemned American fundraising for the IRA. Their influence helped to get President Reagan to persuade British Prime Minister Margaret Thatcher to conclude the Anglo-Irish Agreement in 1985 (see Section 12).

SOURCE 11.45: Margaret Thatcher and Ronald Reagan

## DO YOU UNDERSTAND THESE KEY TERMS?

| | |
|---|---|
| Clan na Gael | Scouse |
| diaspora | Tammany Hall |
| Noraid | |

 Chapter summary   Weblinks   PowerPoint summary

# SELF-ASSESSMENT – CAN YOU?

1. Analyse the impact of Irish immigrants on the British economy.
2. Investigate the role of Irish immigrants and their descendants in American culture.
3. Write a short paragraph on the role of Tammany Hall.
4. Analyse the impact of Irish immigrants on American politics.
5. Comment on the role of Irish-Americans in Irish politics.

# 12 POLITICS AND REBELLION IN IRISH HISTORY 1823–1998

The Irish parliamentary tradition in the nineteenth century

Ireland 1911–1923

The Troubles in Northern Ireland

# THE IRISH PARLIAMENTARY TRADITION IN THE NINETEENTH CENTURY

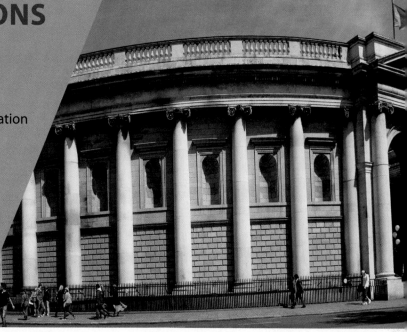

## 🎯 LEARNING INTENTIONS

**At the end of this section, you should be able to:**

◎ Explain the term 'parliamentary tradition' in the context of Irish nationalism

◎ Explain why O'Connell set up the Catholic Association and the Repeal Association

◎ Discuss the significance of O'Connell as a leader in the parliamentary tradition

◎ Describe Parnell's role in the Land Question

◎ Discuss the aims and actions of the Home Rule movement

◎ Debate the significance of Parnell as a leader in the parliamentary tradition.

## What was the parliamentary tradition in Irish nationalism?

Following the 1798 Rebellion of the United Irishmen, the British government was concerned about the situation in Ireland. It wanted to strengthen the union between Britain and Ireland and persuaded the Irish parliament to vote itself out of existence. The **Act of Union** took effect in 1801. It meant that the British parliament in Westminster passed laws for Ireland. Ireland sent 105 MPs (members of parliament) to Westminster. The laws passed in Westminster benefited the United Kingdom but sometimes did not benefit Ireland.

The first great leader in the **parliamentary tradition** in the nineteenth century was **Daniel O'Connell**. He wanted Catholics to be allowed to take seats in parliament. This was called **Catholic emancipation**. O'Connell achieved this in 1829 (see below).

**Irish parliamentary tradition**
Irish MPs in Westminster trying to persuade the British to agree to reforms in Ireland and to greater independence for the Irish.

**Irish nationalism**
Belief that the Irish should have greater control over Ireland.

---

### Activity 1

Examine this source and then answer the question below.

SOURCE 12.1: O'Connell Street, Dublin – a tale of two statues

1  In pairs, find out when the statues of Parnell and O'Connell were erected and who designed them.

SOURCE 12.2: **Houses of Parliament at Westminster, London**

O'Connell also tried to get the Act of Union repealed. He failed to do so but paved the way for the **Home Rule** movement. Its leaders included **Isaac Butt**, **Charles Stewart Parnell** and **John Redmond**. It kept Home Rule at the forefront of British politics until 1916. However, the **Easter Rising** in 1916 and its aftermath changed public opinion from supporting Home Rule to fighting for Irish independence.

Over this period, a growing minority believed that the British would not leave Ireland voluntarily and that violence would have to be used to win Irish freedom. This is known as the **physical-force tradition**.

## Who was Daniel O'Connell?

Daniel O'Connell was born in Derrynane, Co. Kerry in 1775. He was educated in France and later became a barrister. He did not support the 1798 Rebellion and was horrified by the violence he saw during it. This experience stayed with him for the rest of his life. He went on to lead Irish nationalism from the late 1820s until his death in 1847.

| The two traditions in 1900 | |
|---|---|
| **Parliamentary tradition** | Most Irish nationalists wanted a parliament in Dublin in charge of local affairs, while Ireland would still be part of the British Empire. This was called Home Rule. They wanted to achieve this by peaceful means. |
| **Physical-force tradition** | A minority of Irish nationalists wanted total independence from Britain. They were prepared to use violence to achieve this. |

### Activity 2

Examine this source and then answer the questions below.

Improvements in political institutions can be obtained by persevering in a perfectly peaceable and legal course, and cannot be obtained by forcible means.

SOURCE 12.3: **Daniel O'Connell**

1 Suggest what O'Connell meant by this statement.
2 Identify an event that convinced him that using violence was unacceptable.

## What was the Catholic Association?

In 1823 O'Connell set up the **Catholic Association** with **Richard Lawlor Shiel**. Its aim was to campaign for **Catholic emancipation**. At that time only members of the Church of England and Church of Ireland could take their seats in parliament. O'Connell wanted Catholics to have the same right to sit in parliament.

Members of the association paid one penny a month, known as **Catholic rent**. This meant that even the poorest Catholics could afford to become members. The membership grew quickly. The money was used to fund the election campaigns of Protestant candidates who were in favour of Catholic emancipation. The government tried to ban the pressure group but failed.

## What was the significance of the Clare by-election?

In 1828 the MP for Clare, Vesey Fitzgerald, resigned his seat. He supported emancipation. O'Connell decided to stand in the by-election. At that time only the **forty-shilling freeholders** had the right to vote.

> **Catholic emancipation**
> Freedom from discrimination against Catholics. It meant that Catholics would have the right to sit in parliament.

> **By-election**
> Special election held to fill a vacant seat in parliament.

> **Forty-shilling freeholders**
> Anyone who owned or rented land that was worth 40 shillings (£2) was able to vote.

SOURCE 12.4: Daniel O'Connell

SOURCE 12.5: O'Connell addressing a meeting in Co. Clare, 1828

O'Connell won, but, as a Catholic, he could not take his seat in the House of Commons at Westminster. All MPs had to take an **Oath of Supremacy** which recognised the monarch as head of the Church. Catholics could not do this. The British prime minister, the **Duke of Wellington**, was afraid that refusing to let O'Connell take his seat would cause another rebellion in Ireland. He persuaded the king, **George IV**, that Catholic emancipation had to be granted. It became law in 1829.

O'Connell took his seat in the House of Commons in 1830. The forty-shilling freeholders, however, lost their right to vote as the threshold was raised to £10. O'Connell lost a lot of his support as a result.

## How did O'Connell try to repeal the Act of Union?

Daniel O'Connell turned his attention to trying to repeal the **Act of Union**, which had abolished the Irish parliament in 1801. He wanted an Irish parliament in Dublin to be in charge of Irish affairs. Ireland would continue to be ruled by the British monarch.

British political leaders were afraid of granting repeal.

> They thought it would be a first step to Ireland regaining complete independence from Britain.

> They also feared that another country, such as France, might find it easier to use Ireland as a base to attack Britain.

In 1840 O'Connell set up the **Repeal Association**. Members paid the **Repeal rent**, which in 1843 alone amounted to £48,000. He organised **'monster meetings'** at places of historical significance in Ireland. They were called monster meetings because there would be at least 100,000 people in attendance.

O'Connell combined parliamentary pressure at Westminster with public pressure from monster meetings in Ireland to try to achieve repeal. He stated that if repeal was not granted by peaceful means, he would not be able to control the huge numbers attending these meetings. The people might then use violence instead to achieve their aims.

In 1843, at a monster meeting at the Hill of Tara, 750,000 people attended to listen to O'Connell. The government was alarmed and decided to ban the next meeting, which was to be held in Clontarf in Dublin. Fearing there would be violence, O'Connell called off the meeting.

SOURCE 12.6: O'Connell addressing a monster meeting, 1843

### Activity 3

Examine this source and then answer the questions below.

1  Investigate the reason that the Hill of Tara was chosen as a site for a monster meeting.

2  Imagine you were a reporter at this meeting. Write a short paragraph on what O'Connell said and what the atmosphere was like. Explain why this monster meeting was important.

3  What can you infer from this cartoon about the attitude in Britain to O'Connell and the Tara meeting?

SOURCE 12.7: *Punch* cartoon in response to the Tara monster meeting, 1843

## Why did the Repeal Association fail?

Monster meetings had been O'Connell's most powerful weapon, but he had shown the British government that if it banned a meeting he would back down. This weakened his position and caused unrest within the Repeal Association. A group known as the **Young Ireland** movement broke away from the association. Meanwhile O'Connell was arrested and jailed for three months.

O'Connell was seventy years of age and in poor health. He realised that the methods he had used to achieve Catholic emancipation were no longer successful. There had been support for emancipation among English politicians, but there was no support in England for repeal. He died in Genoa, Italy in 1847 and was buried in Glasnevin Cemetery.

## What was the significance of O'Connell as a leader in the parliamentary tradition?

O'Connell was the first man in Europe to use a combination of parliamentary pressure and mass meetings to achieve his aims. His non-violent methods inspired leaders all over the world. Both Mahatma Gandhi (India) and Martin Luther King (USA) were influenced by his tactics.

### Activity 4

Examine this source and then answer the questions below.

> I want to make all Europe and America know it, I want to make England feel her weakness if she refuses to give the justice the Irish require – the restoration of our parliament.
>
> **SOURCE 12.9:** O'Connell at a monster meeting in Drogheda

1 Did O'Connell make all of Europe and America aware of the fight for repeal? Illustrate your answer using evidence from the text.

2 Debate whether or not O'Connell was a significant leader in the parliamentary tradition. Use evidence from the text to support your answer.

3 Investigate whether Mahatma Gandhi and/or Martin Luther King used any of O'Connell's tactics to achieve their goals.

4 Write a short paragraph on O'Connell's campaign for repeal. Identify the reasons why it failed.

**Young Ireland**
Movement that wanted an independent Ireland and led a rebellion in 1848 that was easily defeated.

### Activity 5

Examine this source and then answer the questions below.

**SOURCE 12.8: Daniel O'Connell's grave in Glasnevin**

1 In pairs, research when the round tower was built and who designed it.

2 Find out why a round tower was chosen.

British Prime Minister William Gladstone said O'Connell was 'the greatest popular leader the world has ever seen'.

However, James Connolly, founder of the Irish Labour Party and a leader in the 1916 Rising, criticised O'Connell and accused him of siding with the wealthier class who owned property.

### Activity 6

Examine this source and then answer the questions below.

> Good God, what a brute man becomes when ignorant and oppressed. Oh Liberty! What horrors are committed in thy name ... May every virtuous revolutionary remember the horror of Wexford.
>
> **SOURCE 12.10:** O'Connell on the 1798 Rebellion

1 What words/phrases show how strongly O'Connell felt about using violence?

2 Name one political decision he made that was influenced by his horror of violence.

**Learning Outcome 2.2** 237

## Who was Charles Stewart Parnell?

**Charles Stewart Parnell** was born in 1846. He was a landlord with an estate in Avondale, Co. Wicklow. He was elected MP for Meath in 1875 and went on to lead the Irish Home Rule campaign. He died in 1891 and was buried in Glasnevin Cemetery, Dublin.

## What was the Home Rule Party?

The **Home Rule Party** was founded by **Isaac Butt** in 1873. Home Rule meant having a parliament in Dublin in charge of local affairs such as agriculture and education while Westminster would be in charge of everything else. Butt felt that laws passed by the British parliament were good for Britain but not necessarily good for Ireland.

Butt was a weak leader and was often absent from parliament as he had to work to pay off his debts. He made no impact in the House of Commons. MPs such as **Joseph Biggar** and Parnell became impatient with the lack of progress in achieving their aims.

SOURCE 12.11: **Charles Stewart Parnell**

Biggar proposed **obstructionism**. This meant holding up parliamentary business by making boring speeches that went on for hours. Parnell was one of the leading obstructionists as he felt parliament was ignoring Irish issues.

When Butt died in 1879 he was replaced by **William Shaw**. A general election in 1880 returned a majority of Home Rule MPs who supported Parnell. He was then elected leader of the Home Rule Party.

---

**Activity 7**

1 Investigate the reaction of British MPs to obstructionism.

---

SOURCE 12.12: **Joseph Biggar**

---

**Activity 8**

Examine this source and then answer the question below.

SOURCE 12.13: Isaac Butt

1 Explain why Butt was a weak leader.

---

## What was the Land League?

Initially, Parnell focused his energy on the **Land Question**, which concerned the relationship between landlords and tenant farmers. To get support for Home Rule from the tenants, he first had to improve their conditions.

---

**Activity 9**

Examine this source and then answer the question below.

SOURCE 12.14: **Parnell making an open-air speech, 1880**

1 Why did Parnell become involved with the Land Question?

---

In the **New Departure** he united tenants, members of the IRB and Home Rulers to fight for improved conditions for the Irish tenants. They set up the **Land League** to get the **three Fs** – **fair rent**, **fixity of tenure** (as long as they paid the rent they could not be evicted) and **free sale** (if their land was sold they would get compensation for any improvements) and eventually to become owners of their farms.

Parnell was leader of the Land League. He combined a mass movement in Ireland with political pressure at Westminster to try to improve conditions for the tenants. He was afraid that violence during evictions would damage the possibility of Home Rule.

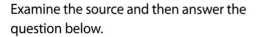

> ### Activity 10
>
> Examine the source and then answer the question below.
>
> > When a man takes a farm from which another has been evicted you must shun him on the roadside when you meet him, you must shun him in the streets of the town – you must shun him in the shop.
> >
> > **SOURCE 12.15:** Parnell's advice to tenants on how to treat a person who took an evicted tenant's land
>
> 1  Why would violence damage the possibility of Home Rule?

This policy of isolating 'land grabbers' was very effective and violence decreased as a result. It was called **boycotting** after a Mayo land agent called Captain Charles Boycott.

In 1881 **William Gladstone**, the British prime minister, passed a Land Act. This Act granted the three Fs. It also gave money to allow tenants to buy their land. Parnell felt that the Land Question was solved and he could concentrate on Home Rule.

> ### Activity 11
>
> 1  Using the Internet and any other sources, research the career of Captain Boycott. Write a paragraph on his life.
> 2  Imagine that you were being boycotted. Describe a typical day in your life under the following headings: My work on the farm. What happened when I went to town. My feelings about the boycott.

> **New Departure**
> Attempt to unite all Irish nationalists (parliamentary tradition and physical-force tradition).

> **IRB**
> The Irish Republican Brotherhood was set up in 1858 to get independence from Britain by violent means. They had staged an unsuccessful rebellion in 1867.

## How did Parnell create a modern, disciplined political party?

In 1882 Parnell set up the **Irish National League**. Its main aim was to work for Home Rule. Parnell was in complete control of the party.

Between 1882 and 1885 he concentrated on building up the Home Rule Party. His lieutenants in Ireland were **William O'Brien** and **Timothy Healy**.

> They built up more than 1,000 branches in the country.

> Many of the branches had clergy as chairmen. They held conventions to choose their candidates for election.

> Money was also raised for candidates' election expenses and to support their MPs when they were in parliament (MPs did not get paid until 1911).

> At Westminster, Parnell introduced a party pledge. MPs had to swear loyalty to Parnell. If an MP broke the pledge he had to resign his seat. This ensured Parnell had a disciplined, united party.

Parnell had created the first modern united political party in the House of Commons.

**SOURCE 12.16:** William O'Brien

## What happened at the 1885 general election?

The 1884 **Third Reform Act** more than trebled the number of voters in Ireland. Most of those who got the vote were tenant farmers. They would vote for Parnell because of his role in the Land Question.

Parnell joined with the Conservative Party to bring down the Liberal government under Gladstone. While in government, the Conservatives brought in the 1885 **Ashbourne Land Act** to keep Parnell's support. The Act set up a fund to help tenants buy their land.

Parnell, knowing that he was going to win more seats in the upcoming general election, tried to ensure that he would hold the **balance of power** in the new parliament. He encouraged Irish people living in Britain to vote for the Conservatives as he wanted to reduce the Liberals' majority. If the Conservatives and Liberals each had a similar number of seats, then the Home Rule Party would be able to decide which party got into government. The price of Parnell's support would be Home Rule.

When the results of the 1885 election were announced the Liberals had eighty-six seats more than the Conservatives. Parnell, with eighty-six seats, was in a strong position but only capable of giving the Liberals power.

**Unionists** were afraid that Parnell would win Home Rule. They felt that a parliament in Dublin would discriminate against them. Therefore, they had also organised themselves for the election. They won eighteen seats (sixteen in the north-east of Ulster and two in Trinity College, Dublin).

The success of the Home Rule Party in most of Ireland made Gladstone realise that Home Rule could no longer be ignored. On 17 December 1885 Gladstone's son Herbert stated that his father had been converted to Home Rule. This example of 'kite-flying', where an idea is put forward (usually in the media) to test the reaction of others, became known as the **Hawarden Kite** after Gladstone's home, Hawarden Castle.

The Conservatives declared that they were not in favour of granting Home Rule. They now supported the unionists. The Home Rule Party supported the Liberals in the **Liberal Alliance** and Gladstone became prime minister.

> ### DID YOU KNOW?
>
> **Phoenix Park murders**
> On 6 May 1882 the newly appointed Chief Secretary for Ireland, Lord Frederick Cavendish, and his under-secretary, Thomas H. Burke, were murdered by the Invincibles, a terrorist group, while walking in the Phoenix Park, Dublin. Public anger at this assassination helped Parnell to impose discipline on the nationalist movement and channel support towards a non-violent, parliamentary campaign for Home Rule.

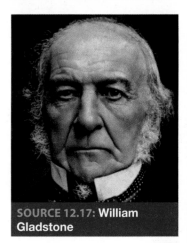

SOURCE 12.17: William Gladstone

**Unionists**
Protestants, mainly in Ulster, who opposed Home Rule.

## What was the First Home Rule Bill?

The terms of the 1886 Home Rule Bill were:

> There would be a parliament in Dublin dealing with local affairs such as agriculture and education.
> The Westminster parliament would deal with matters such as defence, trade, war and peace.
> No Irish MPs would have a seat at Westminster.

The Bill was defeated: 341 votes against and 311 votes for. There were two main reasons for its defeat.

1. The Conservative Party opposed Home Rule. They stated that they were supporting the rights of Ulster unionists. If Home Rule was passed, the unionists would be discriminated against.

2. A group within the Liberal Party opposed Home Rule. The Liberal Unionists, led by Joseph Chamberlain, feared that Home Rule would cause the break-up of the British Empire. Ninety-three members of the Liberal Party supported Chamberlain.

Gladstone resigned and another election was called. The Conservatives won the 1886 general election and were in power for most of the next twenty years. There was no possibility of Home Rule during that period.

## Activity 12

Examine this source and then answer the question below.

SOURCE 12.18: Irish MPs in Westminster (Parnell standing), 1886

1  Apart from the fact that he is standing, how does the artist convey that Parnell is the leader?

## What allegations did *The Times* publish about Parnell?

*The Times* newspaper claimed that Parnell had supported the Phoenix Park murders and published a letter that appeared to be from Parnell as evidence. Parnell claimed that the letter was a forgery. A commission was set up to investigate the allegations. **Richard Pigott**, a journalist, confessed that he had forged the letter. Parnell was cleared. This event made him more popular than ever in Ireland and also strengthened the Liberal Alliance.

## What caused the split in the Home Rule Party?

In December 1889 Captain William O'Shea filed for divorce from his wife, Katharine. He accused her of having a long-term sexual relationship with Parnell and named Parnell as co-respondent in the case. Parnell did not contest the case as he wanted the divorce to go through as quickly as possible so that he could marry Katharine. The couple married in 1891.

**Co-respondent**
Person alleged to have committed adultery with the main respondent in a divorce case.

## Activity 13

Examine this source and then answer the questions below.

> May 15, 1882
> Dear Sir
> I am not surprised at your friend's anger, but he and you should know that to denounce the murders was the only course given to us. But you can tell him and all the others concerned that though I regret the accident of Lord F. Cavendish's death, I cannot admit that Burke got no more than his [just desserts].

SOURCE 12.19: **Extract from letter, allegedly from Parnell, in *The Times***

1  Identify the points the writer is making in this letter.

2  Suggest what motivated someone to forge this letter.

3  In pairs, investigate the reasons why *The Times* would publish this letter.

## Activity 14

1. Using sources such as the Internet, write a short paragraph on Captain O'Shea.
2. In your opinion, what type of person was he? Provide evidence from your research.

SOURCE 12.20: **Katharine O'Shea**

News of Parnell's relationship with a married woman caused a huge public scandal. The Catholic bishops were shocked and said that he should resign as leader of the Home Rule Party. Gladstone knew that a majority of Liberals would not accept an alliance with a party whose leader was involved with another man's wife. He said he would no longer support Home Rule if Parnell remained as party leader. Parnell refused to resign.

A party meeting was held in Committee Room 15 at Westminster. The debate lasted six days and was very bitter. Parnell continually refused to resign, even temporarily. Eventually, fifty-four MPs left the room under the leadership of **Justin McCarthy**, leaving Parnell with thirty-one supporters. The Home Rule Party was split.

## Activity 15

Examine this source and then answer the question below.

SOURCE 12.21: **Meeting in Committee Room 15**

1. Using both the text and this source, explain what is happening in the picture.

In by-elections there were Parnellite and Anti-Parnellite candidates. These contests were very bitter. Parnell was attacked at meetings by angry crowds. The Anti-Parnellites won every by-election. In desperation, Parnell appealed to the IRB for support.

Parnell caught pneumonia during an election meeting and it led to his death on 6 October 1891. His funeral was one of the largest ever seen in Ireland. Members of the GAA provided a guard of honour.

## Activity 16

Examine this source and then answer the questions below.

In God's name, let him retire quietly with good grace from the leadership. If Parnell does not step down the alliance with the Liberal Party will disintegrate. The Irish Parliamentary Party [Home Rule Party] will be seriously damaged, if not wholly broken up.

SOURCE 12.22: **Telegram from Archbishop Croke of Cashel to Justin McCarthy MP before the meeting of the Home Rule Party**

1. What is Archbishop Croke's advice?
2. What does he believe will happen if his advice is not taken?
3. What is the significance of sending a telegram rather than a letter?
4. Using the Internet and other sources, find out in what other area Archbishop Croke was an important figure.

# What was the significance of Parnell as a leader in the parliamentary tradition?

Parnell achieved a lot in a short political career.

> He became leader of the Home Rule Party.

> He helped tenants improve their conditions on the land and also to buy their farms.

> He created the first modern united political party in Westminster.

> When the Home Rule Party held county conventions to pick candidates for the election, it showed the ordinary people democracy at work.

> He built up huge support for Home Rule in Ireland and persuaded the Liberal Party under Gladstone to support Home Rule.

However, there were negative aspects to Parnell's leadership. He was prepared to sacrifice everything for his love of Katharine O'Shea. By refusing to step aside even temporarily when news of their affair became public, he caused a split in the Home Rule Party. It would take ten years to heal that split.

### Activity 17

1   Divide into groups.
    (a) Debate whether Parnell was a significant parliamentary leader and (b) identify the similarities between O'Connell and Parnell as parliamentary leaders.

2   Draw a timeline showing the key events in Parnell's campaign for Home Rule and write a short note on each event.

## DO YOU UNDERSTAND THESE KEY TERMS?

| | | |
|---|---|---|
| balance of power | forty-shilling freeholder | New Departure |
| boycott | Home Rule | Oath of Supremacy |
| by-election | kite-flying | obstructionism |
| Catholic emancipation | Land League | parliamentary tradition |
| Catholic rent | Land Question | repeal rent |
| fixity of tenure | monster meeting | Young Ireland |

PowerPoint summary

# SELF-ASSESSMENT – CAN YOU?

1   Describe the main differences between the parliamentary tradition and the physical-force tradition in Irish nationalism.

2   Explain why O'Connell set up the Catholic Association.

3   Describe how O'Connell tried to repeal the Act of Union.

4   Identify the reasons why British politicians opposed repealing the Act of Union.

5   Describe how the government reacted to the monster meetings.

6   Explain why the Repeal Association failed.

7   Name the person who founded the Home Rule Party and list its aims.

8   Describe how Parnell created a modern, disciplined political party.

9   Explain the impact of the 1885 election results.

10  List the main terms of the First Home Rule Bill.

11  Explain why the First Home Rule Bill was defeated.

12  Describe the allegations about Parnell published by *The Times*.

# IRELAND 1911–1923

## LEARNING INTENTIONS

**At the end of this section, you should be able to:**

◎ Discuss the different strands of nationalism and the position of unionism at the start of the 1900s

◎ Explain why there was increasing support for Home Rule and why unionists opposed Home Rule.

◎ Outline the key events during the Home Rule crisis 1912–14 and the reactions of nationalists and unionists.

◎ Discuss the split in the Irish Volunteers

◎ Describe the key events of Easter 1916

◎ Analyse why the Rising was a turning point in Irish history

◎ Explain the rise of Sinn Féin

◎ Describe the key events of the War of Independence

◎ Outline how the Anglo-Irish Treaty was negotiated and its terms

◎ Describe the key events of the Civil War

◎ Recognise the significance of the Government of Ireland Act 1920

◎ Discuss how unionists governed Northern Ireland in the 1920s

◎ Outline examples of sectarianism in Northern Ireland in the 1920s.

## What was the position of nationalism at the start of the twentieth century?

The majority of nationalists were Catholics and they wanted **Home Rule**.

Nationalists felt that they were being ruled badly from Westminster. Laws were being passed in Britain for its benefit without any regard to their effect on Ireland. **John Redmond** was leader of the Home Rule Party, which had about eighty MPs in the House of Commons.

### Irish Republican Brotherhood (IRB)

A small number of extreme nationalists wanted Ireland to become a **republic**. This meant complete independence from Britain. They belonged to the IRB, a secret organisation that was prepared to use violence to win independence. However, they had very little hope of achieving this because they had very little public support.

SOURCE 12.23: John Redmond

# What is cultural nationalism?

**Cultural nationalists** wanted to stop Irish culture being replaced by English culture. The Irish language was in decline and most people spoke English. Several factors lay behind this shift.

> The Famine had hit the Gaelic-speaking areas hardest as many people had died or emigrated.

> Parents encouraged their children to learn English because they would need it if they emigrated to America.

> National schools used English as the language for teaching.

English games such as soccer and rugby had become very popular. As a result fewer people were playing hurling and Gaelic football. This process is called **anglicisation**.

Cultural nationalists were afraid that there would soon be little difference between English and Irish people. If that happened, they believed that Irish people would not be able to claim the right to rule themselves. Therefore, organisations such as the GAA and Gaelic League were set up in the late nineteenth century to promote and develop Irish culture.

## Gaelic Athletic Association (GAA)

Michael Cusack set up the GAA in Thurles in 1884. It aimed to revive Irish games such as hurling and Gaelic football.

For more on the GAA, see Section 20.

**Anglicisation**
Spread of English language and culture.

## Gaelic League

Douglas Hyde and Eoin MacNeill set up the Gaelic League in 1893 to stop the decline in the Irish language. It trained teachers called **timirí**, who went all over the country teaching the Irish language. It set up an Irish newspaper called ***An Claidheamh Soluis*** (*The Sword of Light*). It also encouraged Irish dancing and music.

The Gaelic League did succeed in slowing the decline in the Irish language. It also attracted people who wanted to lessen British political influence in Ireland; people who felt that the Irish language could be protected only by an Irish government. Its members included Patrick Pearse and Thomas MacDonagh, who went on to become leaders in the 1916 Rising.

A side-effect of cultural nationalism was an increase in support for the IRB.

### Activity 1

1  How successful was the Gaelic League in promoting the Irish language? Provide three examples of the Irish language movement's influence on Ireland today.

SOURCE 12.24: **Douglas Hyde and Eoin MacNeill**

# What was the position of unionism at the start of the twentieth century?

The majority of unionists were Protestants. They supported the union with Britain and did not want Home Rule. They were a small minority in most of the country except in the northeast of Ulster, where they had a large majority. The Unionist Party represented them in Westminster. Their leaders were **Edward Carson** and **James Craig**.

> Unionists opposed Home Rule because they thought that an Irish parliament in Dublin would favour the Catholic population. Catholics would have a large majority in any Irish parliament and Protestants were afraid that they would be discriminated against because of their religion. They used the slogan 'Home Rule is Rome Rule'.

> The industries in northeast Ulster, such as shipbuilding and linen, needed to maintain free access to the British market. In other words, their products could be sent for sale in Britain without any extra taxes being added to them. If there was a Home Rule parliament in Dublin, there was a danger that would no longer be the case.

| Activity 2 |  |
|---|---|

1  Why would the Protestant majority in northeast Ulster be opposed to Home Rule?

The UK's Conservative Party was against Home Rule. It had been in government in Britain for most of the time from 1886 to 1905, effectively removing the possibility of Home Rule during that period.

# What led to the passing of the Home Rule Bill 1912–14?

In 1909 there were two main parties at Westminster:

> The Liberal Party, led by Prime Minister Herbert Asquith

> The Conservative Party (Tories), led by Andrew Bonar Law.

When the Liberals tried to increase taxes on the rich, the plan was defeated by the Conservatives in the House of Lords, where they had a majority. Asquith immediately called a general election.

> **Unionism**
> Belief that Ireland should remain united with Britain.

SOURCE 12.25: Edward Carson

**DID YOU KNOW?**

The British parliament at Westminster comprises the **House of Commons** and the **House of Lords.** They share the task of making and shaping laws. The UK public elects 650 members of parliament (MPs) to represent them in the House of Commons. There are about 800 members of the House of Lords, the majority of whom were appointed by the British monarch.

The Liberal Party needed the support of the Home Rule Party after the election in order to stay in government. Redmond demanded Home Rule as the price of his support.

Asquith passed the **Parliament Act** in 1911 to end the **veto** of the House of Lords. A bill could be rejected twice by the Lords, but it would become law the third time. Therefore, the Home Rule Bill that was passed by the House of Commons in 1912 would become law in 1914.

The Home Rule Bill 1912–14 was known as the **Third Home Rule Bill**.

## Unionist reaction

Unionists were very disappointed. Led by Carson and Craig, they organised **protest marches**. They got people to sign the **Solemn League and Covenant** in 1912. This pledge, commonly known as the **Ulster Covenant**, stated that they would use every means, including violence, to prevent Home Rule.

**Veto**
Power to reject something.

### Activity 3

1   Imagine that you have just got home from attending a protest march. Write an entry in your diary, explaining the reasons for the march and why you went. Say what your feelings were during the march.

SOURCE 12.26: Belfast protests, 1912

The **UVF (Ulster Volunteer Force)** was set up to train men to resist Home Rule by violence if necessary. By 1914 it had 100,000 men. Guns and ammunition were landed at Larne, Co. Antrim.

## Nationalist reaction

Nationalists were delighted that Home Rule would soon become law. However, they were worried that the unionist reaction would force the British government to back down. They formed the **Irish Volunteers** in 1913. Led by Eoin MacNeill, their aim was to ensure that Home Rule would be granted.

The IRB hoped to trick the Volunteers into fighting for complete independence (i.e. an Irish republic). They landed arms at Howth, Co. Dublin.

## Threat of civil war

These unionist and nationalist reactions are referred to as the **Home Rule Crisis 1912–14**. It resulted in two armed forces in Ireland, the UVF and the Irish Volunteers, and a very real threat of **civil war**.

Asquith persuaded Redmond to accept **partition**. This would allow a section of Ulster to opt out of Home Rule and remain fully united with Britain. However, Redmond and Carson could not agree how many counties in Ulster could opt out. Carson wanted six but Redmond would agree to only the four with unionist majorities (Derry, Antrim, Armagh and Down).

The crisis ended with the outbreak of World War I in 1914 and the decision to postpone Home Rule from coming into effect until after the war.

| Activity 4 |
| --- |

Examine this source and then answer the question below.

SOURCE 12.27: **Erskine and Molly Childers on the *Asgard*, which landed guns at Howth**

1   Using the Internet and other sources, research the life of Erskine Childers. Write a paragraph on his career.

**Civil war**
War fought between groups within the same country.

**Partition**
Dividing a country into two parts.

# Commemoration

In 1966 the fiftieth anniversary of the Rising was celebrated. Many of the veterans were still alive. An RTÉ series, *The Insurrection*, portrayed the rebels as heroes.

However, the Troubles in the North led to a change of attitude. It was impossible to praise an armed revolt in 1916 on the one hand and condemn the IRA campaign in the North on the other. Therefore in 2016 the commemoration was inclusive and respectful of all traditions. This was true of all commemorative events in the 'decade of centenaries', which commemorated the Home Rule Bill of 1912 and the 1916 Rising, as well as the Battle of the Somme.

**Commemoration**
Public act of remembrance of an historically significant event or person.

# Why was there a split in the Volunteers?

When World War I began in August 1914 it was decided to postpone Home Rule until after the war. John Redmond and Edward Carson both urged their supporters to join the British Army. Many members of the UVF joined the army and fought in the war. The Irish Volunteers, however, were split on the issue. The majority (170,000) supported Redmond. They became known as the **National Volunteers** and thousands fought in the war. The remaining 11,000, led by Eoin MacNeill, disagreed. They kept the name **Irish Volunteers**. Their aim was to remain in Ireland to make sure that the British government did not break its promise of granting Home Rule.

## Activity 5

Examine this source and then answer the question below.

SOURCE 12.28: **Irish Volunteers, 1914**

1 What do you notice about the clothes of the Volunteers?

# What led to the 1916 Rising?

The IRB saw that Britain's attention was focused on the war at the Western Front. They adopted the slogan 'England's difficulty is Ireland's opportunity'. In other words, the war had presented an opportunity to have a rebellion in Ireland in an effort to achieve independence. It began to plan for a rising.

In 1915 a **military council** was set up to plan for a rising. **Patrick Pearse**, **Thomas Clarke** and **Joseph Plunkett** were members. When they heard that **James Connolly** was also planning a rebellion with the **Irish Citizen Army**, Connolly was asked to join.

**Western Front**
Trenches in France that stretched from the English Channel to the Swiss border.

**Rising**
Armed rebellion against the ruling power.

### DID YOU KNOW?

SOURCE 12.29: **James Connolly**

James Connolly had founded the **Irish Citizen Army (ICA)** to protect workers from attacks by the police during the 1913 Lockout (a bitter and violent industrial dispute that saw up to 20,000 workers locked out of their places of employment for months). In 1916 Connolly was going to use the ICA to fight for a socialist republic.

SOURCE 12.30: **Thomas Clarke**

**Socialism**
System that promotes equality among citizens through shared ownership of land and industry.

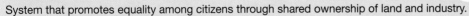

The IRB needed arms for the rising. It sent **Roger Casement** to Germany to buy guns and to ask for German support. A ship called the *Aud* set sail for Ireland with guns on board. It was to arrive off the Kerry coast at the start of the rising, which was planned for Sunday 23 April 1916. However, the *Aud* arrived on Good Friday, 21 April, and was captured by the British.

The IRB, which had only a few hundred members, realised that the support of the Irish Volunteers would be required for a successful rising. However, MacNeill, leader of the Irish Volunteers, was known to be against an armed rebellion. Unknown to MacNeill, many of his fellow leaders were also IRB members.

The IRB decided to trick MacNeill. Joseph Plunkett forged a document (called the **Castle Document**), which stated that the government was going to arrest the leaders of the Irish Volunteers. MacNeill felt obliged to take action and told his members to get ready to resist such a move by mobilising on Sunday 23 April.

When MacNeill discovered the Castle Document was a fake, and learned about the capture of the *Aud*, he cancelled the plans for fighting. This order was published in the Sunday newspapers. It ended any hope of a countrywide rebellion.

The military council met on Easter Sunday and decided to go ahead with the rising the next day, despite the fact that it now had no hope of success. They were influenced by the idea of **blood sacrifice** – they felt that their deaths would inspire others to fight for Ireland's freedom.

SOURCE 12.31:
**Roger Casement**

SOURCE 12.32:
**Joseph Plunkett**

## What were the key events of Easter week?

On Easter Monday, 24 April 1916, the Irish Volunteers and the Irish Citizen Army (1,500 participants in total) took over key buildings in Dublin city centre. These included the Four Courts, Jacob's biscuit factory and Boland's Mills. Their headquarters was the GPO (General Post Office).

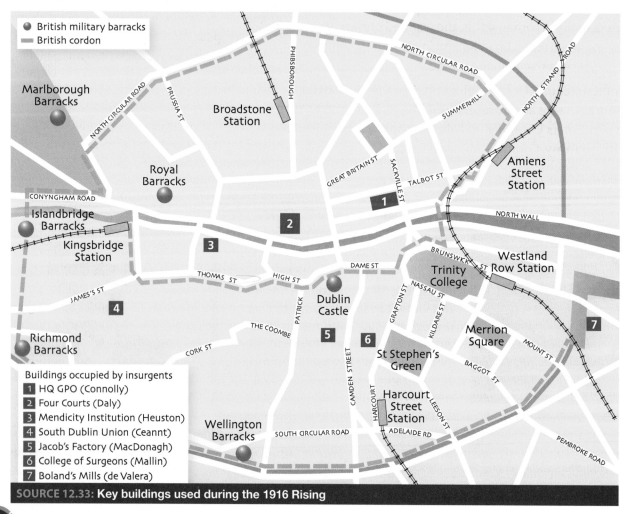

Buildings occupied by insurgents
1. HQ GPO (Connolly)
2. Four Courts (Daly)
3. Mendicity Institution (Heuston)
4. South Dublin Union (Ceannt)
5. Jacob's Factory (MacDonagh)
6. College of Surgeons (Mallin)
7. Boland's Mills (de Valera)

SOURCE 12.33: **Key buildings used during the 1916 Rising**

Patrick Pearse read the **Proclamation** on the steps of the GPO to puzzled onlookers. This statement declared the creation of a republic. It was signed by the seven members of the military council:

Patrick Pearse

Thomas Clarke

Éamonn Ceannt

Thomas MacDonagh

Joseph Plunkett

James Connolly

Seán MacDiarmada

The British authorities were caught by surprise. On Tuesday 25 April martial law was declared and **General Sir John Maxwell** was put in charge. He said he would teach 'those infernal fellows a lesson they would not soon forget. I am going to ensure that there will be no treason for a hundred years.'

**Martial law**
When the army takes control of law and order.

**Activity 6**

1   In groups of four, use the Internet and other sources to research the life of one of the signatories of the Proclamation. Make a presentation of your findings to the class.

British troops surrounded the city centre. At first they concentrated their attack on the GPO. On Wednesday the gunship *Helga* came up the River Liffey and began to fire explosive shells at Liberty Hall.

SOURCE 12.34: **Patrick Pearse**

Pearse evacuated the GPO on Friday as it was on fire. The rebels retreated to some houses in nearby Moore Street. The following day, Saturday 29 April, Pearse surrendered and sent orders to all the other Volunteer units to surrender.

## Why did the Rising fail?

> The British Army could concentrate their forces in Dublin as there was no countrywide rebellion.
> The rebels' tactic of taking over key buildings in the city centre made it easy for the British Army to surround them.
> The British Army greatly outnumbered the rebels. They were also better armed and better trained.

## What was the impact of the Rising?

The immediate effects of the Rising included:

> Loss of life: 450 people were dead, 300 of whom were civilians
> Damage to property: €3 million worth of damage in Dublin city centre
> Arrests: more than 3,000 people were arrested; many were sent to prisons in England or to Frongoch internment camp in Wales

**Internment**
Putting people in prison for political reasons, without trial.

> Public anger over needless deaths and the destruction of the city centre. People had also lost a week's wages as they were unable to go to work.

Fourteen leaders of the Rising, including the seven signatories of the Proclamation, were executed at **Kilmainham Gaol**.

The executions, especially that of the badly wounded Connolly, gradually changed public opinion, as did the large-scale programme of arresting and imprisoning suspects, the vast majority of whom were innocent.

The British stopped the executions, but it was too late. Most people would no longer be content with Home Rule; they wanted total independence from Britain, an Irish Republic. Historians agree that this was a turning point in Irish history.

**Activity 7**

1   Draw a timeline of the events of the 1916 Rising from 21 to 29 April.
2   Write a short note on each event.

## Increased support for Sinn Féin

One of the most important impacts of the 1916 Rising was the increase in support for **Sinn Féin**. Sinn Féin had been set up by **Arthur Griffith** in 1905. It wanted independence from Britain rather than Home Rule, and it wanted to achieve it by peaceful means.

Until 1916 the party had very little support. However, the British wrongly labelled the 1916 Rising a 'Sinn Féin rebellion'. Therefore, although Sinn Féin had not taken part in the Rising, it benefited most from the change in public opinion after the Rising. By 1917 most nationalists wanted more than Home Rule and they joined Sinn Féin.

The release of prisoners and those who had been interned in Wales further boosted support for Sinn Féin. The returning survivors of the Rising, such as **Éamon de Valera** and **Michael Collins**, were seen as heroes by the Irish people. Griffith stepped aside as leader of Sinn Féin and was replaced by de Valera. The party now supported the use of physical force to achieve independence.

Its growing support was evident when Sinn Féin won four by-elections for vacant Westminster seats.

## What was the outcome of the 1918 general election?

World War I ended in November 1918 and a general election was called. Many people voted for Sinn Féin as it was seen as a young and dynamic party. The Home Rule Party was viewed as old and tired.

Sinn Féin won seventy-three seats while the Home Rule Party won six. It was clear that Sinn Féin was now the party of nationalist Ireland. The Unionist Party won twenty-six seats and would play a major role in the coming years.

| Party | Seats before | Seats after |
|---|---|---|
| Home Rule | 78 | 6 |
| Sinn Féin | 7 | 73 |
| Unionists | 16 | 26 |

SOURCE 12.36: **Outcome of the 1918 general election**

SOURCE 12.35: **Arthur Griffith**

## The First Dáil

Sinn Féin MPs refused to take their seats at Westminster. Instead, they met at the **Mansion House** in Dublin on 21 January 1919. There were only twenty-seven of the elected MPs present because the others were in prison. Those present declared Ireland's independence. They were the parliament of the **Irish Republic**. They called it the **Dáil** and themselves **TDs (Teachta Dála)** rather than MPs.

The Dáil met again in April to set up a government. Éamon de Valera was elected president, and government ministers included Arthur Griffith (Home Affairs) and Michael Collins (Finance). The new government set up Sinn Féin courts to replace British courts.

Many local councils supported the Dáil instead of the British government.

Collins organised a loan of £350,000, which paid for weapons and the running of the government. Meanwhile, de Valera went to America, where he raised $4 million for the new government.

SOURCE 12.37: Members of the First Dáil, 1919

## What was the War of Independence?

The first shots of the **War of Independence** were fired on 21 January 1919 – the same day that the First Dáil met in the Mansion House. **Dan Breen** and **Seán Treacy** were the leaders of a group of Volunteers who killed two **RIC (Royal Irish Constabulary)** policemen in Soloheadbeg, Co. Tipperary.

Many Volunteers believed that Irish freedom could be achieved only by violence. They now referred to themselves as the **IRA (Irish Republican Army)**. RIC barracks in rural areas were attacked in order to get weapons. As a result, the RIC retreated to the towns and the IRA took control of the countryside.

### Michael Collins

Collins was Director of Intelligence in the IRA. He set up a **network of spies** throughout the country, including railway and office workers. His most important spies were in the British headquarters at Dublin Castle. He also set up a **group of assassins** called the **'Squad'**. They executed British spies to prevent the British finding out the IRA's plans.

### Guerrilla warfare

**Guerrilla warfare** involved the IRA using hit-and-run tactics against the British forces. This meant ambushing British convoys of lorries, then escaping into the countryside. They knew the local countryside well, which meant they could disappear very quickly. As they did not wear uniforms, they could hide among the ordinary people. Many people provided safe houses for them.

 **Activity 8**

Examine this source and then answer the questions below.

## POLICE NOTICE.

# £1000 REWARD

### WANTED FOR MURDER IN IRELAND.

## DANIEL BREEN

(calls himself Commandant of the Third Tipperary Brigade).

Age 27, 5 feet 7 inches in height, bronzed complexion, dark hair (long in front), grey eyes, short cocked nose, stout build, weight about 12 stone, clean shaven; sulky bulldog appearance; looks rather like a blacksmith coming from work; wears cap pulled well down over face.

SOURCE 12.38: Wanted poster for Dan Breen

1   In pairs, discuss the text of the poster. What does it suggest about the writer's attitude to Breen?

2   Does the reward (worth more than €55,000 today) offered for Breen surprise you? Give a reason for your answer.

It was very difficult for the British to capture them, which led to frustration. The British retaliated with acts of terror against the local population such as burning their houses. Such actions in turn increased support for the IRA.

Some of the most famous local commanders were Dan Breen (Tipperary) and **Tom Barry** (West Cork). Towards the end of 1920, the IRA formed **flying columns**. These were groups of up to thirty full-time Volunteers. They moved from place to place to help local commanders set up ambushes.

The most famous ambush happened on 28 November 1920, when Tom Barry and the West Cork Brigade ambushed and killed seventeen Auxiliaries (see below) in Kilmichael.

### Activity 9

1   Find and download a picture of the ambush site. Why was this site chosen, do you think?

## Black and Tans

By the early months of 1920 the RIC was helpless. The British recruited extra police to reinforce the RIC. These men, who were ex-soldiers, were known as the **Black and Tans** because they wore army khaki trousers and RIC dark green jackets.

In July ex-army officers were recruited to form the **Auxiliaries**. Both the Black and Tans and the Auxiliaries were involved in destroying property, including the burning of towns such as Balbriggan in Co. Dublin and Cork city. The latter was revenge for an IRA ambush near Cork. This further increased support for the IRA and Sinn Féin.

SOURCE 12.39: Members of the Irish delegation: Robert Barton, Arthur Griffith, Michael Collins and George Gavan Duffy, 1921

## Bloody Sunday

On the morning of 21 November 1920 the Squad killed thirteen British spies. That afternoon the Auxiliaries went to Croke Park looking for the killers. Dublin and Tipperary were playing a football match. The Auxiliaries opened fire on the crowd in retaliation for what had happened earlier that day. Fourteen people were killed. This violent day was called **Bloody Sunday**.

## What was the Truce?

Several factors combined to end the War of Independence.

> On 25 May 1921 the IRA burned the Custom House in Dublin, but lost eighty men in the process.

> The war had reached a stalemate. Both sides were exhausted. The IRA could not beat the British forces. Neither could the British defeat the IRA.

> People in Britain were embarrassed by the behaviour of the British forces in Ireland.

> The IRA was short of guns and ammunition.

On 11 July 1921 a Truce was agreed to allow the two sides to negotiate the terms of an agreement.

### Activity 10

1   Draw a timeline of the main events of the War of Independence and write a short note on each event.

## How was the Anglo-Irish Treaty negotiated?

A delegation led by Arthur Griffith and including Michael Collins went to London in October to negotiate a treaty with Britain. Surprisingly, Éamon de Valera decided not to go. He felt it would be better if he stayed in Dublin so that the delegation could consult him before agreeing anything. The British side was led by Prime Minister **David Lloyd George**.

**Delegation**
Group of people sent to represent a larger group of people.

## Activity 11

Examine this source and then answer the questions below.

> De Valera stayed behind in Dublin … he thought his absence from the negotiations would buy the Irish delegates time for reflection at the crucial moment. William Cosgrave, later to become the first prime minister of the Irish Free State, argued in the [Dáil], it was a pity to have 'their best player among the reserves'.

**SOURCE 12.40: Extract from *A Short History of Ireland* by John O'Beirne Ranelagh**

1  Explain what Cosgrave meant by the statement 'their best player among the reserves'.

### Aims of the Irish delegation:

> To set up a republic so that Ireland would be completely independent of Britain

> To bring an end to partition and create a united Ireland.

### Aims of the British delegation:

> To protect Northern Ireland so that the unionists would not revolt

> To make sure Ireland stayed in the British Commonwealth otherwise it might encourage other dominions to leave.

**SOURCE 12.41: David Lloyd George**

The talks dragged on and finally, on 5 December, Lloyd George issued an **ultimatum**. The delegates had to accept the final terms or an 'immediate and terrible' war would follow within three days.

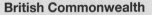

**British Commonwealth**
Grouping of countries that had been colonies of the British Empire.

**Dominion**
Country in the Commonwealth that rules itself but retains the British monarch as head of state.

## What were the terms of the Treaty?

> Ireland (twenty-six counties) would be called the **Irish Free State**.
> A **Boundary Commission** would be set up to decide the boundary between the Irish Free State and Northern Ireland. Each state would have a representative and there would be an independent chairperson.
> The Free State would be part of the British Commonwealth, not a republic. This is called **dominion status**. This meant the king would be head of state and the TDs would have to take an oath of loyalty to the king.
> A **governor-general** would be appointed as the representative of the king in Ireland.
> British forces would withdraw from the Free State, but would keep **three naval ports**: Lough Swilly, Cobh and Berehaven.

In the negotiations Lloyd George had promised that the Boundary Commission would recommend that any area of Northern Ireland that had a nationalist majority (e.g. Co. Tyrone) would be allowed join the Free State.

Collins reluctantly signed the treaty on 6 December 1921. He knew that if he didn't sign, war would recommence and that, as they had very few weapons left, the IRA would not win against much better-equipped British soldiers.

## Activity 12

Examine this source and then answer the questions below.

> Think – what have I got for Ireland? Something which she has wanted these past seven hundred years. Will anyone be satisfied at the bargain? Will anyone? I tell you this – early this morning I signed my death warrant.

**SOURCE 12.42: Michael Collins, 6 December 1921**

1  What had Collins 'got for Ireland'?
2  Why did Collins believe that he had signed his 'death warrant' when he signed the Treaty?

## What was the reaction to the Treaty?

Most people in Ireland accepted the Treaty as they were relieved that the fighting had come to an end. However, both Sinn Féin and the IRA were split down the middle. De Valera felt that he should have been consulted before the Treaty was signed. The Dáil met to discuss the Treaty. The debates lasted until 7 January 1922 and many of the exchanges were passionate and bitter.

### Arguments in favour:

› The Treaty gave Ireland more independence than Home Rule would have done.

› Collins stated, 'It was a stepping stone to greater independence.'

› The IRA would be beaten if the war started again.

### Arguments against:

› The Free State was not a republic, which was what they had fought for.

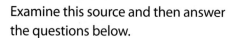

**SOURCE 12.43: Anglo-Irish Treaty, December 1921, signature page**

› Republicans could not swear an oath of loyalty to the king.

› Britain would interfere in Irish affairs as it was so close and the king would be head of state.

On 7 January the Dáil voted: sixty-four TDs were for the Treaty and fifty-seven were against. De Valera and the anti-Treaty side left the Dáil. Griffith replaced de Valera as president.

## What factors led to the Civil War?

The Treaty caused much division and bitterness throughout the country. The IRA split into two military groups:

› **Free State Army** – the pro-Treaty side

› **Irregulars** – a large anti-Treaty group who agreed with **Liam Lynch** when he said, 'We have declared for an Irish Republic and will not live under any other law.'

As British forces vacated their barracks, either the Free State Army or the Irregulars took them over.

Then, led by **Rory O'Connor**, the Irregulars took over the **Four Courts** and established a headquarters there in April 1922. At first, Collins did nothing as he was trying to avoid a civil war. However, two events caused him to act:

› Success in the general election in June (pro-Treaty: 58 seats; anti-Treaty: 36 seats)

› General O'Connell of the Free State Army was kidnapped by the forces in the Four Courts.

Collins could no longer avoid going to war against his former colleagues.

---

### Activity 13

Examine these sources and then answer the questions below.

> We who stand by the Republic still will, I presume, rebel against the new government that would be set up if this Treaty is passed.
>
> **SOURCE 12.44: Liam Mellows TD, 17 December 1921**

> … we have not been able to drive the enemy from anything but a fairly good-sized police barracks …
>
> **SOURCE 12.45: Richard Mulcahy TD, 22 December 1921**

1 Was Mellows pro-Treaty or anti-Treaty? Explain your answer.

2 What point is Mulcahy making?

3 Do you think Mulcahy was pro-Treaty or anti-Treaty?

### Activity 14

Examine this source and then answer the questions below.

> We have brought back the flag; we have brought back the evacuation of Ireland after 700 years by British troops, and the formation of an Irish army … We have brought back to Ireland equality with England, equality with all the nations which form that Commonwealth, and an equal voice in the direction of foreign affairs in peace and war.
>
> **SOURCE 12.46: Arthur Griffith TD, 19 December 1921**

1 List the points that Griffith makes in favour of accepting the Treaty.

2 What percentage of TDs voted for and voted against the Treaty?

3 Would you have voted for or against the Treaty? Give reasons for your answer.

# What were the key events of the Civil War?

On 28 June 1922 Collins bombarded the Four Courts with artillery borrowed from the British. This was the start of the **Civil War**. The Irregulars surrendered two days later. A week later they had been driven out of Dublin.

Under pressure from the Free State Army, the Irregulars retreated to Munster. They set up the **Munster Republic**. Led by Liam Lynch, they used guerrilla tactics against the Free State Army, as they had once done against the British. However, as the Free State soldiers knew the countryside they gradually took control of Munster.

On 12 August 1922 Arthur Griffith died of a stroke. Ten days later Michael Collins was killed in an ambush at Béal na Bláth, Co. Cork. Collins' death was a huge blow to the country as a whole. **William Cosgrave** became head of the Free State government.

Cosgrave's government brought in tough new measures to tackle the Irregulars.

› **Kevin O'Higgins** introduced a Special Powers Act. It included the death penalty for carrying a gun. **Erskine Childers** was executed as a result.
› When a pro-Treaty TD, **Sean Hales**, was murdered, four Irregulars were executed in prison.
› Liam Lynch, the leader of the Irregulars, was killed in the Comeragh mountains.

The Irregulars surrendered in May 1923.

SOURCE 12.47: **Four Courts under attack during the Civil War**

## Activity 15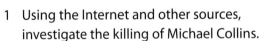

1 Using the Internet and other sources, investigate the killing of Michael Collins.
2 Write a report on the various theories about his death.

## Activity 16

Examine this source and then answer the questions below.

> Ah, curse the time, and sad the loss my heart to crucify,
> that an Irish son, with a rebel gun, shot down my laughing boy.
> Oh, had he died by Pearse's side, or in the GPO,
> killed by an English bullet from the rifle of the foe,
> or forcibly fed while Ashe lay dead in the dungeons of Mountjoy,
> I'd have cried with pride at the way he died, my own dear laughing boy.

SOURCE 12.48: **Extract from a ballad written by Brendan Behan, 1936**

1 Who, do you think, is the 'laughing boy'?
2 Suggest why the speaker is sad.
3 Why would he have 'cried with pride' if the 'laughing boy' had died another way?
4 What, do you think, is Behan's opinion of the 'laughing boy'?

# What was the impact of the Civil War?

The immediate effects of the Civil War included:

› Loss of life: More than 1,000 people had died
› Lasting divisions: families were divided and in some cases brother had fought against brother.

It took years for the country and the economy to recover.

Meanwhile Sinn Féin split into two parties:

› **Cumann na nGaedheal** (later Fine Gael) was the pro-Treaty party
› **Fianna Fáil** was the anti-Treaty party.

These became the two main political parties in the state and there was deep bitterness between the two sides for years to come.

## How was Northern Ireland established?

Northern Ireland was created by the Government of Ireland Act 1920. It was still part of the United Kingdom and was represented by twelve MPs in Westminster, but local affairs such as education and local government were controlled by a Northern Ireland parliament. As the unionists had a large majority in Northern Ireland, they were permanently in government.

Nationalists were represented by either Sinn Féin or the Nationalist Party (the old Home Rule Party). They did not want to be part of the Northern Ireland state. They wanted to be part of the Irish Free State. As a result they were hostile to the Northern Ireland state.

 **DID YOU KNOW?**

The Government of Ireland Act divided Ireland into two: Northern Ireland (six counties) and southern Ireland (twenty-six counties).

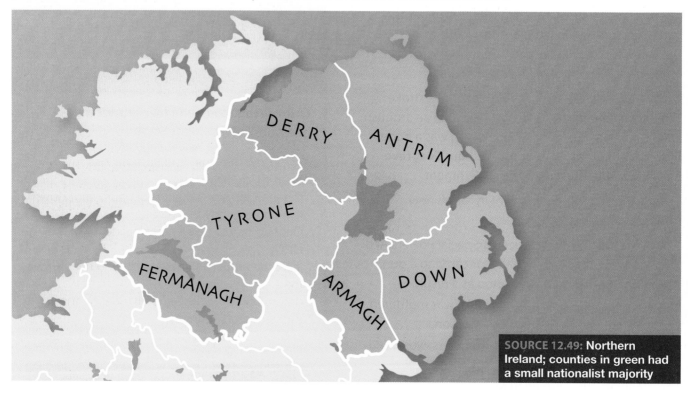

SOURCE 12.49: **Northern Ireland; counties in green had a small nationalist majority**

## How did the unionists rule Northern Ireland?

**James Craig (Lord Craigavon)** became Prime Minister of Northern Ireland. He knew that the nationalists wanted to join the Irish Free State and saw them as a threat to the existence of Northern Ireland.

### Activity 17

Examine this source and then answer the questions below.

If a man is a Roman Catholic, if he is fitted for the job, provided he is loyal to the core, he has as good a chance of appointment as anybody else … there are ways of discovering whether a man is heart and soul in carrying out the intention of the Act of 1920, which was given to the Ulster people in order to save them from being swallowed up in a Dublin Parliament. Therefore, it is undoubtedly our duty and our privilege, and always will be, to see that those appointed by us possess the most unimpeachable loyalty to the King and Constitution. That is my whole object in carrying on a Protestant Government for a Protestant people.

SOURCE 12.50: **James Craig, speaking during a Westminster debate on Northern Ireland, 21 November 1934**

1 What is the prime minister of Northern Ireland saying here about employment opportunities in the Northern Ireland public service?
2 In your opinion, is his argument justified?
3 Comment on the phrase 'a Protestant Government for a Protestant people'.

In general, the unionist government treated the Catholic population of Northern Ireland badly. Such discrimination is called **sectarianism**. For example:

> In 1922 the Northern Ireland parliament passed the **Special Powers Act**. It enabled the government to outlaw the IRA and target the nationalist community. Suspected IRA members were imprisoned without trial (internment).

> The **RUC (Royal Ulster Constabulary)** was largely a Protestant police force. It was helped by the **B-Specials**, a part-time reserve police force that was almost entirely Protestant. The B-Specials treated nationalists very harshly.

> **Gerrymandering** (rearranging the borders of local electoral wards) ensured that the unionists had a majority of seats, even where the nationalists had a majority of the voters. In Derry, for example, nationalists had twice the number of voters but gerrymandering ensured that the unionists had a majority on the city council.

> As unionists dominated local councils they controlled public **housing** policy. They gave houses to Protestants rather than Catholics.

> Catholics also found it harder to get jobs, both in the civil service and in private companies. At Harland and Wolff (Belfast's very successful shipyard), thousands of Catholic workers lost their jobs in 1920. This led to high **unemployment** among Catholics.

The discrimination against Catholics was the root cause of the Troubles in Northern Ireland later in the century (see the next section).

SOURCE 12.51: James Craig

**Electoral ward**
Area or district used for elections; each ward elects its own representatives to the local council.

**Activity 18**

1 In pairs, find out how many unionists and how many nationalists were on Derry city council in the 1920s.

**DID YOU KNOW?**

The Northern Ireland parliament needed a home. A large site, the Stormont Estate, on the eastern edge of Belfast was chosen and plans were agreed. Parliament Buildings (commonly referred to as Stormont) opened in 1932 and is used today by the Northern Ireland Assembly.

SOURCE 12.52: Stormont, the home of the Northern Ireland Assembly

**SOURCE 12.53:** Harland and Wolff shipyard, Belfast

## DO YOU UNDERSTAND THESE KEY TERMS?

| | | |
|---|---|---|
| Commonwealth | guerrilla warfare | Proclamation |
| conscription | Home Rule Crisis | sectarianism |
| cultural nationalist | Irish Citizen Army | Stormont |
| dominion | Irish Volunteers | Ulster Covenant |
| flying column | Irregulars | UVF |
| GAA | Munster Republic | War of Independence |
| Gaelic League | National Volunteers | |
| gerrymandering | partition | |

 PowerPoint summary

## SELF-ASSESSMENT – CAN YOU?

1. Discuss the opposing views of nationalism at the beginning of the twentieth century.

2. Explain why Irish culture was in decline in the late 1800s.

3. Outline the political impact of cultural nationalism.

4. Explain why unionists opposed Home Rule and describe how they opposed the Third Home Rule Bill.

5. Explain why Ireland was on the brink of civil war in 1914.

6. Explain why there was a split in the Irish Volunteers in 1914.

7. Describe the IRB's plan for the 1916 Rising.

8. Explain why historians view the Rising as a turning point in Irish history.

9. Explain why Sinn Féin won the 1918 election.

10. Outline why the First Dáil was set up and describe its role.

11. Summarise the key events of the War of Independence and explain the impact of the war.

12. Explain the terms and impact of the Government of Ireland Act.

13. Outline the terms of the Treaty and summarise the reactions to the Treaty.

14. Outline the key events of the Civil War and summarise the impact of the war.

15. Describe how nationalists felt about partition.

16. Describe how unionists governed Northern Ireland.

17. Comment on how Catholics experienced discrimination, giving four examples.

# THE TROUBLES IN NORTHERN IRELAND

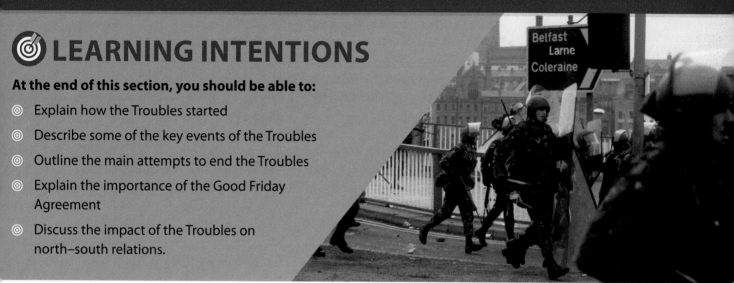

## 🎯 LEARNING INTENTIONS

**At the end of this section, you should be able to:**

◎ Explain how the Troubles started

◎ Describe some of the key events of the Troubles

◎ Outline the main attempts to end the Troubles

◎ Explain the importance of the Good Friday Agreement

◎ Discuss the impact of the Troubles on north–south relations.

## What was the background to the Troubles?

**The Troubles**
The conflict in Northern Ireland 1969–98.

The unionists were permanently in government in the Northern Ireland state set up in 1920. They had a 3:1 majority in seats. Unionists saw nationalists as a threat to Northern Ireland and discriminated against them in all areas of life.

However, by 1963 change seemed to be on the way. **Terence O'Neill** became prime minister and wanted to end discrimination against nationalists. O'Neill was the first Northern Ireland prime minister to meet with the taoiseach, **Seán Lemass**. Extreme unionists such as Ian Paisley objected to O'Neill's soft approach to nationalists and were alarmed by the meeting with Lemass.

SOURCE 12.54: Terence O'Neill (left) and Seán Lemass (right)

In the end, O'Neill did very little to end discrimination. Nationalists were disappointed and set up the **Northern Ireland Civil Rights Association (NICRA)** in 1967. It was modelled on the black civil rights movement in the USA. Its leaders were **John Hume**, **Gerry Fitt** and **Bernadette Devlin**.

NICRA's main aims were:

❯ One person, one vote in local elections

❯ An end to discrimination in jobs and housing.

Peaceful marches were held to highlight these aims. **Loyalists** organised counter-demonstrations, which led to violence.

**Loyalists**
Extreme unionists who were prepared to use violent methods to keep Northern Ireland British.

SOURCE 12.55: John Hume

SOURCE 12.56: Burntollet

Peaceful marchers at **Burntollet** were attacked by a loyalist mob and the **RUC** did little to protect them. TV showed these pictures all over the world. This embarrassed the British government.

Britain forced the unionists to give civil rights to nationalists in areas such as local elections and housing. O'Neill resigned in 1969 as he was blamed by his party for accepting these reforms.

## When did the Troubles begin?

The Troubles began in August 1969. A march by the **Apprentice Boys** in Derry caused rioting in the nationalist Bogside area of the city. The nationalists blocked off the Bogside and fighting broke out between the police and the nationalists. This was called the **Battle of the Bogside**.

> **RUC**
> Royal Ulster Constabulary, police force of Northern Ireland 1922–2001.

> **Apprentice Boys**
> Society that commemorates the 1689 siege of Derry, in which Protestants shut the gates against the Jacobite (Catholic) army and held out until the siege was lifted by the arrival of English ships.

### Activity 1

Examine this source and then answer the questions below.

> … the Irish government can no longer stand by and see innocent people injured and perhaps worse.

SOURCE 12.57: Taoiseach Jack Lynch, responding to the violent scenes in Derry

1   What did Lynch mean by this statement?
2   In your opinion, how would the unionists react to such a speech?

Meanwhile in Belfast, Catholics were burned out of their houses by loyalist mobs. Many fled south to the Irish Republic.

Northern Ireland was on the brink of civil war. As the RUC was unable to cope, the **British Army** was sent in. Initially, it protected nationalist areas from attacks by loyalists.

SOURCE 12.58: Burnt-out houses, Belfast

# What caused the rise in paramilitary violence?

The IRA had not defended nationalist areas from loyalist attacks. This caused a split in the organisation.

> The **Official IRA** wanted to use peaceful means to achieve its aims. It was socialist.

> The **Provisional IRA** favoured using violence to get a united Ireland. Its political wing was **Sinn Féin**.

The Provisional IRA started a bombing campaign and began shooting at British soldiers. The British Army reacted to these shootings by being heavy-handed when searching Catholic homes. This turned Catholics against the British Army.

On the loyalist side, two paramilitary groups – the **UVF (Ulster Volunteer Force)** and **UDA (Ulster Defence Association)** – began to attack Catholics. The death toll rose dramatically.

## Internment

Northern Ireland Prime Minister **Brian Faulkner** introduced **internment** in 1971. Over 300 people were interned. It may have been introduced to try to stop the violence, but as all those interned were nationalists, it led to a massive increase in violence and also greatly increased support for the IRA.

# Why was Bloody Sunday a key event?

On 30 January 1972 a march protesting against internment took place in Derry. The British Army's **Parachute Regiment** shot dead thirteen unarmed Catholics. This event became known as **Bloody Sunday**.

**Paramilitary**
Illegal group that acts like an army.

SOURCE 12.59: **Brian Faulkner**

---

**Activity 2**

Examine this source and then answer the questions below.

1 This photo shows Fr Edward Daly waving a white handkerchief. Why, do you think, was a priest doing this?

2 What does this picture tell you about Bloody Sunday?

SOURCE 12.60: **Bloody Sunday, Derry, 1972**

Bloody Sunday caused outrage among the nationalist community. There was a huge increase in violence in Northern Ireland. In Dublin, the British embassy was burned by an angry crowd.

---

### Activity 3

Examine these sources and then answer the questions below.

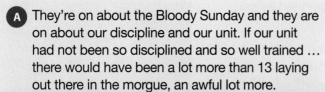

**A** They're on about the Bloody Sunday and they are on about our discipline and our unit. If our unit had not been so disciplined and so well trained … there would have been a lot more than 13 laying out there in the morgue, an awful lot more.

SOURCE 12.61: **Soldier of the Parachute Regiment page 2, transcript of *This Week* programme, 3 February 1972**

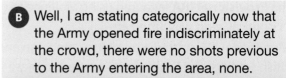

**B** Well, I am stating categorically now that the Army opened fire indiscriminately at the crowd, there were no shots previous to the Army entering the area, none.

SOURCE 12.62: **James Chapman (retired British soldier living in Derry) page 2, transcript of *This Week* programme, 3 February 1972**

1. What were the main points made by the soldier in document A?
2. What was his attitude to Bloody Sunday? Use evidence from the document to support your answer.
3. What did Chapman say about Bloody Sunday (document B)?
4. Why, do you think, are there different versions of what happened on Bloody Sunday?
5. Which statement is more useful in giving us information about what actually happened on Bloody Sunday? Give reasons for your answer.

---

The situation was out of control. The British government closed the Stormont parliament and ruled Northern Ireland directly from Westminster. This is known as **direct rule**. **William Whitelaw** became the first Secretary of State for Northern Ireland. However, the violence continued.

**Direct rule**
Rule by the central (national) government.

## What was the Sunningdale Agreement?

The British government saw that **power-sharing** was the only solution to stop the violence. In 1973 it began talks with the Unionist Party, the Alliance Party and the SDLP. At that time the **Alliance Party** (formed in 1970) represented moderate unionism. The **SDLP** (Social Democratic and Labour Party, formed in 1970) is a nationalist party that has always been opposed to violence.

SOURCE 12.63: **William Whitelaw**

**Power-sharing**
Groups from opposing sides taking part in government together.

In December 1973 the **Sunningdale Agreement** was signed by British Prime Minister **Ted Heath**, Taoiseach **Liam Cosgrave** and the leaders of the Northern Ireland parties. It set up two bodies.

> **Power-sharing executive:** A government involving the Unionist Party, the Alliance Party and the SDLP. **Brian Faulkner** (Unionist Party leader) was prime minister and **Gerry Fitt** (SDLP leader) was deputy prime minister.

> **Council of Ireland:** A group to advise on policies in Northern Ireland. It consisted of politicians from Northern Ireland and the Irish Republic.

## Opposition

Ian Paisley's party, the **Democratic Unionist Party** (DUP, formed in 1971), bitterly opposed the idea of power-sharing. The DUP did not want politicians from the Irish Republic to have any say in Northern Ireland's affairs.

Unionist workers staged a series of **strikes** in protest at the agreement. These were organised by the **Ulster Workers' Council**. They paralysed Northern Ireland's economy.

This opposition brought about the fall of the power-sharing executive after only five months. Direct Rule was brought back. Violence continued throughout the 1970s.

## Why were the hunger strikes a key event?

IRA prisoners were treated as **political prisoners**. As such, they did not have to wear prison clothes. However, this concession was removed in 1976. The IRA prisoners in the Maze prison (often known as the H Blocks) wanted their political status reinstated. They refused to wear prison clothing and wore blankets instead (the **blanket protest**). They smeared their cell walls with excrement (the **dirty protest**).

### Activity 4

Examine this source and then answer the questions below.

SOURCE 12.64: **Excrement-smeared walls in the Maze prison**

1. In your opinion, what would it feel like to live in those conditions?
2. What can you infer from this source about the determination of the prisoners?

When this did not work, other prisoners decided to go on **hunger strike** in 1980. This ended after fifty-three days when strikers believed that their demands had been met. When it became clear that this was not the case, a second strike began. **Bobby Sands** led the strike. British Prime Minister **Margaret Thatcher** was determined not to give in. After sixty-six days, Sands died. Nine other prisoners also died on hunger strike.

### Activity 5

1. Find out the names of the other hunger strikers who died.

**Hunger strike**
Refusal to eat, as a way of protest.

SOURCE 12.65: **Funeral of Bobby Sands**

Eventually the hunger strikes were called off without the IRA getting political status. However, the publicity attracted a huge increase in support for the IRA. The IRA also got increased financial backing from America through **Noraid**. The money was used to buy guns and bomb-making equipment.

**Noraid**
Fundraising body in the USA that supported the fight for a united Ireland.

## What was the Anglo-Irish Agreement 1985?

The violence continued and the British and Irish governments continued to look for a solution. Eventually Taoiseach **Garret FitzGerald** persuaded Thatcher to agree that the Irish government should be involved in helping to bring about peace.

**Main terms of the Anglo-Irish (Hillsborough) Agreement:**

> The Irish Republic agreed that the reunification of Ireland could come about only when a majority of the people of Northern Ireland voted for it.

> The Irish Republic had a role in the internal affairs of Northern Ireland for the first time.

> The Irish government promised to strengthen security at the border to prevent IRA members escaping to the Irish Republic.

SOURCE 12.66: Garret FitzGerald and Margaret Thatcher sign the Anglo-Irish Agreement, 1985

Despite objections from the DUP, the British government held firm and the agreement stood. It laid the foundation for further progress towards peace in Northern Ireland. It also played a role in bringing about the IRA ceasefire in 1994.

| Activity 6 |
| --- |

Examine this source and then answer the question below.

Where do the terrorists operate from? From the Irish Republic! That's where they come from! Where do the terrorists return to for sanctuary? To the Irish Republic! And yet Mrs Thatcher tells us that that Republic must have some say in our Province. We say never, never, never, never!

SOURCE 12.67: Ian Paisley (DUP) in a speech about the 1985 Anglo-Irish Agreement

1   What are Paisley's main points about the Anglo-Irish Agreement?

## Activity 7

Examine these sources and then answer the questions below.

**A** Documents released by the National Archives in Dublin under the 30-year rule show the taoiseach urged Mrs Thatcher to stick with the treaty despite the much deeper than anticipated Unionist opposition. At the same time, she pressured him to get visible evidence of beefed up border security on the Irish side. 'The Unionist reaction is very much more serious than I had thought,' Mrs Thatcher said. 'I have been told: you are treacherous, you have betrayed us, etc. I have got to reassure the Unionists and fast.'

SOURCE 12.68: *Irish Independent*, 30 December 2015

**B** I started from the need for greater security, which was imperative. If this meant making limited political concession to the South, much as I disliked this kind of bargaining, I had to contemplate it.

SOURCE 12.69: **Extract from Thatcher's autobiography, *The Downing Street Years* (1993)**

1   What does document A tell us about reactions to the Anglo-Irish Agreement?
2   What did Thatcher urge FitzGerald to do?
3   How useful is document A? Give reasons for your answer.
4   Why did Thatcher give a 'political concession to the South' (document B)?
5   Compare documents A and B. What is the difference in emotion in the two documents? Give reasons for your answer.

# What was the Downing Street Declaration 1993?

This agreement was between British Prime Minister **John Major** and Taoiseach **Albert Reynolds**.

**Main terms of the Downing Street Declaration:**

〉 The Irish government agreed that Irish unity could take place only with the consent of the people of Northern Ireland.

〉 The British government said that it would not prevent Irish unity if the people of Northern Ireland voted for it.

This declaration helped the cause of peace. In 1994 the IRA declared a ceasefire.

SOURCE 12.70: **John Major and Albert Reynolds, 1993**

## What was the Good Friday Agreement 1998?

The Labour Party won the 1997 British general election. Its leader, **Tony Blair**, wanted to achieve peace in Northern Ireland. **David Trimble**, leader of the Ulster Unionist Party (UUP), was willing to talk to republicans. Through talks with **John Hume** (SDLP), **Gerry Adams** (Sinn Féin), Taoiseach **Bertie Ahern** and others they reached an agreement on Good Friday 1998.

**Main terms of the Good Friday Agreement:**

> The people of Northern Ireland would elect an assembly.

> The assembly would elect a power-sharing executive (the main nationalist and unionist parties would share power).

> Articles 2 and 3 of the Irish Constitution, which claimed control over the whole island of Ireland, would be removed (after a referendum).

There was a dramatic decrease in violence. In 2007 the IRA finally put its weapons 'beyond use'.

SOURCE 12.71: Bertie Ahern, US Senator George Mitchell and Tony Blair, Good Friday 1998

**Activity 8**

1  In pairs, discuss what the phrase 'putting weapons beyond use' means.

SOURCE 12.72: Ian Paisley and Martin McGuinness led the executive in 2007/8

The **Northern Ireland Assembly** was established in 1998. The **Northern Ireland Executive** was established in 1999 and led by First Minister **David Trimble** (UUP) and Deputy First Minister **Seamus Mallon** (SDLP).

# What role has the Republic of Ireland had in the internal affairs of Northern Ireland since 1973?

From 1973 onwards the Irish government had an increasing role in the internal affairs of Northern Ireland. This is shown by the improving relationship with Britain between 1973 and 1998. The Irish government was involved in the negotiations for each of the agreements that sought a solution to the Troubles during this period:

> 1973 Sunningdale Agreement
> 1985 Anglo-Irish Agreement
> 1993 Downing Street Declaration
> 1998 Good Friday Agreement.

Gradually the unionist community accepted that the Irish Republic had a role in the internal affairs of Northern Ireland.

Public opinion in the south also changed. In the early years of the Troubles people felt that partition was the cause of the problems in Northern Ireland. However, by the 1990s people realised that the solution had to be found in the two communities of Northern Ireland itself.

**Activity 9**

1 Draw a timeline showing the key events in Northern Ireland during the period 1969–98. Write a short note on each key event.

---

**DO YOU UNDERSTAND THESE KEY TERMS?**

| | | |
|---|---|---|
| Apprentice Boys | internment | paramilitary |
| Bloody Sunday | loyalist | power-sharing |
| direct rule | NICRA | RUC |
| hunger strike | Noraid | |

 Chapter summary     Weblinks    PowerPoint summary

---

## SELF-ASSESSMENT – CAN YOU?

1 Outline the background to the Troubles.

2 Explain what Terence O'Neill sought to do as prime minister of Northern Ireland.

3 Explain why the Troubles began.

4 Outline what caused the split in the IRA.

5 Describe the effect of the introduction of internment.

6 Explain why Bloody Sunday was such a key event.

7 Analyse the success or otherwise of the Sunningdale Agreement.

8 Explain why the hunger strikes were a key event.

9 Discuss the importance of the Anglo-Irish Agreement.

10 Explain the significance of the Downing Street Declaration.

11 Describe the impact of the Good Friday Agreement.

12 Explain how the Troubles affected relations between the British and Irish governments.

13 Analyse the role of the Republic of Ireland in the internal affairs of Northern Ireland 1968–98.

14 Outline how public opinion in the Irish Republic changed during the Troubles.

# 13 WOMEN IN IRISH SOCIETY IN THE TWENTIETH CENTURY

What was life like for women in the early 1900s?

271

What part did women play in Irish politics 1912–23?

275

What was life like for women after Irish independence?

278

# WHAT WAS LIFE LIKE FOR WOMEN IN THE EARLY 1900s?

## 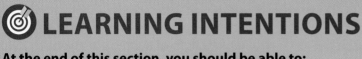 LEARNING INTENTIONS

**At the end of this section, you should be able to:**

◎ Describe the differences between boys' and girls' education

◎ Outline the types of work women did

◎ Discuss attitudes towards the role of women

◎ Explain how women got the vote.

## Were women educated?

Girls and boys were treated differently when it came to education. It was common for girls to be kept at home from school to look after younger brothers and sisters.

Everyone had to pay a fee to go to secondary school and most schools were single sex. Those girls whose parents could afford to send them to secondary school often got an inferior education to that offered to boys. Many girls' schools did not teach science or higher level maths, which made it difficult for girls to get work in these areas.

 **DID YOU KNOW?**

Until the 1960s very few women attended university. Although Irish women could study and get a degree at the Royal University by the 1880s, they were not allowed to attend Trinity College, Dublin, until 1904. Even then most parents believed that their daughters would get married and have husbands to look after them, so they did not need to train for a career.

**SOURCE 13.1: Girls of the Ursuline Convent, Waterford, 1908**

# What work did women do?

Everyday life for most men and women in the early 1900s was a hard grind. Very few homes had electricity and nearly all work was manual (done by hand). Women worked for long hours on farms, in small shops, in factories, sewing or taking in washing. It was accepted by almost everyone that women's role in society was different from men's.

## Activity 1

Examine this source and then discuss the questions below.

### 1901 Census

| | | |
|---|---|---|
| 1 | Professional | 32,675 |
| 2 | Domestic servants | 193,331 |
| 3 | Commercial | 5,026 |
| 4 | Agricultural workers | 85,587 |
| 5 | Industrial workers | 233,256 |
| 6 | Indefinite and non-productive* | 1,708,861 |

\* Women who worked in the home or in the family business. Most farms and family businesses were family run.

**SOURCE 13.2: Occupations of women, 1901**

1  What was the most popular type of work, apart from category 6?

2  Why did so many women work as domestic servants, do you think?

3  What percentage of female workers were industrial workers? In what part of Ireland is it likely that most of them lived?

4  Which category includes the highest number of women? Suggest what these women did.

5  Which of these categories would most women be in today, do you think?

6  Is this a reliable source, do you think? Explain why/why not.

## What roles were women expected to play in Irish life?

It was believed that women were not as intelligent as men and that they were born with certain qualities that made them more suited to minding children and doing housework. Their main role was to be a good mother and homemaker.

Very few middle- or upper-class women worked outside the home. Most husbands would have seen it as a bad reflection on them if their wife went out to work. People would say that he could not provide for her.

## Activity 2

Examine these sources and then answer the questions below.

**A** It seems plain enough that allowing to women the right of suffrage is against the Catholic ideal of the unity of domestic [home] life ... while the wife has her well recognised sphere of influence and authority in the domestic circle, the final word ... rests with the husband for he is the head of the wife as Christ is of the Church.

**SOURCE 13.3: Extract from an article written by a Catholic priest, Fr David Barry, 1909**

**Suffrage**
The right to vote.

**B** 'Woman's proper and ideal sphere [place] is in the home.'

**SOURCE 13.4: Senator Michael Comyn voicing his support for the exclusion of women from certain types of work, 1935**

1  What is meant by the phrase 'the unity of domestic life' in A?

2  Why is Fr Barry against giving women the right to vote?

3  In what way are the two quotes similar in their views on women?

**SOURCE 13.5: Factory workers, Belfast, 1918**

SOURCE 13.6: A city street in the 1900s. Note the way the women are dressed.

## Social behaviour

Women's behaviour in society was strictly controlled. Up until World War I (1914–18) it was not considered proper for a woman to smoke in public or to go into a public house. Some bars had special areas called 'snugs' where 'respectable' women could have a drink.

It was also the norm for middle-class girls to have a **chaperone** if they were meeting a young man. There was no question of even kissing your boyfriend until you were engaged to be married!

**Chaperone**
Person, usually an older woman, who accompanied an unmarried girl when she went out.

**Franchise**
The right to vote.

# Did women have the right to vote?

In 1900 women did not have the right to vote for members of parliament or to become a member of parliament. Ireland's biggest political party, the **Home Rule Party**, did not even allow female members.

One of the big political debates in the early 1900s was whether women should have **suffrage**, which is the right to vote.

The **suffragette movement** fought for women's rights to vote and to sit in Westminster. In Ireland, the group that led the campaign for women's suffrage was the **Irish Women's Franchise League (IWFL)**.

One of the founders of the IWFL was **Hanna Sheehy-Skeffington**. She came from a political family and had been to university. She and other women were angry that they were not allowed to vote, even though men who could neither read nor write were. They heckled politicians and threw bricks through the windows of the places where politicians were meeting.

All women over the age of twenty-one were given the right to vote in the new Irish Free State in 1922.

SOURCE 13.7: Hanna Sheehy-Skeffington lost her job as a teacher in 1913 as a result of her IWFL activities.

**Learning Outcome** 2.9 · 273

KS                              **Activity 3**

Examine these sources and then answer the questions below.

**A**

# THE
# IRISH CITIZEN

AUGUST 15, 1914 - ONE PENNY

## VOTES FOR WOMEN
## NOW!
## DAMN
## YOUR WAR!

SOURCE 13.8: Newspaper headline from 1914

SOURCE 13.9: Poster from 1909

1   Is the newspaper headline for or against women getting the vote?
2   Which war is referred to in A?
3   Is the poster (B) for or against women getting the vote? Give reasons for your answer.

**DO YOU UNDERSTAND THESE KEY TERMS?**

| | |
|---|---|
| chaperone | Irish Women's Franchise League |
| domestic service | suffrage |
| franchise | suffragette movement |

PowerPoint summary

## SELF-ASSESSMENT – CAN YOU?

1  Explain, giving two reasons, why girls often had an inferior education to boys.

2  Outline where most women worked in the early 1900s.

3  Give two reasons why people were against giving women the vote in 1900.

4  Explain what the Irish Women's Franchise League was and who set it up.

5  Identify two pieces of information from this section that reveal the general attitude to women in the 1900s and explain how they do this.

# WHAT PART DID WOMEN PLAY IN IRISH POLITICS 1912–23?

## 🎯 LEARNING INTENTIONS

**At the end of this section, you should be able to:**

◎ Explain how women came to play an active role in Irish politics

◎ Outline women's contribution during the Revolutionary Era

◎ Describe women's involvement in trade unionism.

## Were women involved in politics?

Women were very active in all the political movements of the Irish Revolutionary Era. **Sinn Féin** was the first Irish political party to admit women as full members. In 1912 **Jenny Wyse Power** became its vice-president and the party put forward two women candidates in the 1918 general election. One of these, **Countess Markievicz** (1868–1927), was elected to the first Dáil. When Sinn Féin set up an Irish government in 1919 she was appointed Minister for Labour. She was the first woman elected to the British parliament, although she did not take her seat.

SOURCE 13.10: **Constance Markievicz, the first female minister in Western Europe**

## Were women involved in revolutions?

In the 1916 Rising and later War of Independence (1919–21) women acted as messengers, spies and nurses for the rebels. They wrote regularly for nationalist newspapers and fundraised for nationalist causes. They provided safe houses and shelter for those hiding from the Black and Tans.

### 🔍 DID YOU KNOW?

The period in Irish politics from 1912 to 1923 is often called the **Revolutionary Era.** This is because there was so much political change in Ireland during this time. For example, workers were fighting for their right to have trade unions; nationalists wanted more independence from Britain; unionists were determined to keep Ireland part of Britain.

### Activity 1 ✏️

Examine this source and then answer the question below.

SOURCE 13.11: **Supporters pose with an Irish tricolour to publicise a republican meeting, June 1916**

1 Write down two things you find interesting in this photo.

Some women also fought as soldiers. They were members of:

> **Cumann na mBan:** female version of the Irish Volunteers, set up in 1914
> **Irish Citizen Army (ICA):** trade union army of men and women who defended workers' protest meetings. Countess Markievicz and other ICA female members fought side by side with the male rebels in the 1916 Rising.

---

### Activity 2

Examine the source and then answer the question below.

SOURCE 13.12: Ulster women mobilise against Home Rule, 1912

1   What do you notice about all the women in the photograph?

---

## Were women involved in unionism?

Women were also politically active on the unionist side. The **Ulster Women's Unionist Council** was formed in 1911. By 1913 it had over 100,000 members who vowed to 'stand by our husbands, our brothers and our sons … in defending our liberties against the tyranny of Home Rule'. In 1912, 234,046 Ulster women signed an agreement stating they would fight to the death against anyone who tried to weaken the link between Ireland and the rest of Britain.

**Unionists**
People who wanted Ireland to remain under British rule.

# Were women involved in trade unions?

**Delia Larkin** and **Rosie Hackett** set up a women's trade union called the **Irish Women Workers' Union (IWWU)**. They fought for better working conditions for female workers. They also campaigned for better education and living conditions for women.

Larkin set up a library, literacy classes and Irish language classes for working-class women at Liberty Hall in Dublin. In 1913 she wrote, 'Tenements are one of the greatest causes which help to make drunken slaves of the women who live there.'

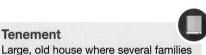

**Tenement**
Large, old house where several families rented rooms.

SOURCE 13.13: Members of the IWWU, c.1920; Delia Larkin is seated (circled)

### DO YOU UNDERSTAND THESE KEY TERMS?

Cumann na mBan

Revolutionary Era

tenement

unionism

PowerPoint summary

## DID YOU KNOW?

A bridge over the River Liffey in Dublin is named after Rosie Hackett. It commemorates her roles in both the 1916 Rising and the trade union movement.

SOURCE 13.14: The Rosie Hackett Bridge, Dublin

# SELF-ASSESSMENT – CAN YOU?

1. Outline the roles that women played in the 1916 Rising and the War of Independence.

2. Explain what the Irish Citizen Army was.

3. Name the woman who became a minister in the first Dáil.

4. Explain what the Irish Women Workers' Union was.

5. Give two reasons why Delia Larkin is important in history.

6. Debate whether it is important to commemorate people such as Rosie Hackett, giving reasons for your views.

7. Explain what the Ulster Women's Unionist Council was.

Learning Outcome 2.9

# WHAT WAS LIFE LIKE FOR WOMEN AFTER IRISH INDEPENDENCE?

## 🎯 LEARNING INTENTIONS

**At the end of this section, you should be able to:**

◎ Describe how life changed for Irish women when they got the vote

◎ Outline other improvements for women during the twentieth century.

## Did life change for women when they got the vote?

When the Irish Free State was set up in 1922 all men and women over the age of twenty-one years got the right to vote. At long last women could vote on the same terms as men.

---

**KS** **👥**                          **Activity 1**

Examine these sources and then discuss the questions on the next page.

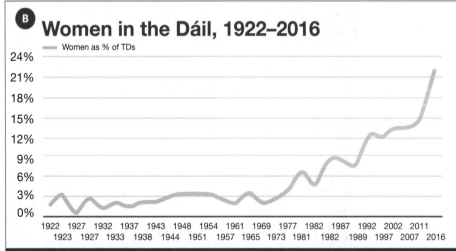

**A** Between 1922 and 1970 there was an average of four female TDs in the Dáil out of a total of 166 members. After Countess Markievicz in 1918 there were no other female ministers until 1979, when Máire Geoghegan-Quinn was appointed.

**SOURCE 13.15: Oireachtas figures**

**B** **Women in the Dáil, 1922–2016**

Women as % of TDs

24% 21% 18% 15% 12% 9% 6% 3% 0%

1922 1927 1932 1937 1943 1948 1954 1961 1969 1977 1982 1987 1992 2002 2011
1923 1927 1933 1938 1944 1951 1957 1965 1973 1981 1982 1989 1997 2007 2016

**SOURCE 13.16: Central Statistics Office**

**C** In 1932 the Irish government introduced a 'marriage bar' that required female National School teachers to retire when they got married. It was later extended to female workers in other areas of the public service, who then also had to give up their jobs when they married. The marriage bar finally ended on 31 July 1973.

**SOURCE 13.17: The terms of the 'marriage bar'**

**D**

| 1927 | Juries Act prevented women from sitting on juries |
|------|---------------------------------------------------|
| 1929 | Censorship of Publications Act banned the publication of any information on contraception |
| 1932 | Marriage bar introduced, forcing women teachers to give up their jobs when they got married |
| 1935 | Criminal Law Amendment Act made sale of contraceptives illegal<br>Marriage bar extended to Civil Service |
| 1936 | Conditions of Employment Act limited number of women working in industry |

**SOURCE 13.18: Acts of parliament relating to women passed in the 1920s and 1930s**

**E** '… by her life within the home, woman gives to the State a support without which the common good cannot be achieved.'
' … mothers shall not be obliged by economic necessity to engage in labour to the neglect of their duties in the home.'

**SOURCE 13.19: Extracts from the 1937 Irish Constitution**

**F**

| 1990 | Mary Robinson became the first woman to be President of Ireland |
|------|---------------------------------------------------------------|
| 1997 | Mary McAleese became President of Ireland |

**SOURCE 13.20: Female Presidents of Ireland**

1 Which of the sources A–F are primary? Which are secondary? Explain why.

2 Looking at A and B, what was the average number of women in the Dáil between 1922 and 1970? What percentages of women were elected to the Dáil in 1987 and 2011? Do both sources agree with each other?

3 Summarise in one sentence the basic point that A and B are making.

4 As D shows, supplying information on contraception and selling contraceptives were forbidden in Ireland. Suggest why this policy affected women more than men.

5 In 1936 Irish industries were discouraged from taking on too many women. Suggest why this law might have been passed.

6 Do you think many women voted against the 1937 Constitution? Explain your answer.

7 Would you say that women became more or less equal to men between 1922 and 2000? Give three pieces of evidence from the above sources to support your answer.

8 Did women get more involved in Irish political life? Give one piece of evidence from these sources that supports the view that they did and one piece of evidence that shows us they did not.

## How has life improved for women?

Women's lives began to improve from the 1960s. There were three main reasons for this:

1 The coming of **electricity** to every home in Ireland

2 The **Irish economy** improved during the 1960s

3 The **Irish Women's Liberation Movement (IWLM)**.

**Activity 2**

Examine this source and then answer the questions below.

**SOURCE 13.21: Magazine advertisement from 1956**

1 Describe how the women are dressed. Would most women in the 1950s have dressed like this in their kitchen, do you think? Give a reason for your answer.

2 Do women dress like this now to do housework? Give a reason for your answer.

3 What can ads like this one tell us about the past? Suggest one example.

4 Why should historians be careful about using ads for information?

5 Some people say that inventions such as the washing machine and dishwasher brought the biggest change to women's lives in the twentieth century. Why would people say this, do you think?

**Learning Outcome 2.9** **279**

## Electricity

Towns in Ireland began to be linked up to electricity in the 1920s. In 1946 the **rural electrification scheme** began. Three million electricity poles were put up, bringing electricity to every home in rural Ireland by 1964. Electricity transformed life for everyone.

Electricity brought enormous changes to the way women lived. Women had always washed and ironed clothes by hand. Stone or concrete floors had to be scrubbed. In most homes water had to be brought in from an outside pump or well as there was no running water.

In the 1960s people started to use washing machines and electric cookers. In the 1980s vacuum cleaners and dryers became common. These appliances freed up women to go out to work or do other things. It was a revolution for women.

Some people were afraid of the arrival of electricity.

> I was 6 or 7 when the candles were snuffed, the paraffin lamp quenched and the electric switch thrown for the first time in our house in very rural Kilkenny. My grandfather, whose house I grew up in, was adamant that no wires would ever connect him to a central generating station. His fear was that some, to quote himself, madman would drop a bomb on Shannon and 'we would all be blown up in our own beds'.

SOURCE 13.22: Documentary maker Joe Kearney recalls his grandfather's views of electricity (RTÉ Documentary On One: Then There Was Light, 5 November 2016)

**Electrification**
Connecting an area with a supply of electricity.

## Irish economy

In the 1960s there was a boom in the Irish economy. New multinational companies began to set up in Ireland and employ Irish workers. After Ireland joined the **EEC** (now the European Union) in 1973, the Irish export trade grew. More jobs were created and women were needed for the labour market.

Education opportunities also improved when free secondary education was introduced in 1967. Women became better educated and began to demand equal treatment.

**EEC**
European Economic Community, set up in 1957.

## Irish Women's Liberation Movement (IWLM)

In the USA a new women's liberation movement demanded equal rights for men and women in every area of life. In Ireland this group became known as 'Women's Libbers'.

They won an end to the marriage bar and got laws passed ending discrimination in jobs on grounds of gender. The Employment Equality Act of 1977 meant that men and women doing the same job would get equal pay. Job advertisements for just men or just women were not allowed.

Attitudes towards women working changed more slowly. It was not until the 1980s that it really became acceptable for married women to go out to work.

SOURCE 13.23: Feminists demonstrating, 1972

## How did social attitudes change?

Examine these sources and then answer the questions below.

SOURCE 13.24: Veronica Lake, 1942

SOURCE 13.25: Muriel Day, 1969

1　Choose three words to describe the actress in A. Does she look happy, shy, strong …?
2　What can an image like this tell us about life in the 1940s? Give two examples.
3　What is the main difference in clothing between the two pictures?

Attitudes changed after World War II. Women gradually
gained more freedom. It became more acceptable for women
to smoke and drink in public.

The IWLM demanded more sexual freedom for women and the availability of contraceptives. On 22 May 1971 Irish women travelled by train from Dublin to Belfast to buy contraceptives, where it was legal to buy them.

SOURCE 13.26: The 'contraceptive train' at Connolly Station, Dublin

Although a law passed in 1979 allowed contraceptives to be prescribed by doctors, it was not until 1985 that they could be openly sold.

### DO YOU UNDERSTAND THESE KEY TERMS?

| | |
|---|---|
| marriage bar | women's liberation |
| rural electrification | movement |

 Chapter summary       Weblinks       PowerPoint summary

**Activity 4**

1   In your opinion, what was the most important reason why women's lives improved after the 1960s? Give a reason for your answer. Contribute to a class debate on this topic.

## SELF-ASSESSMENT – CAN YOU?

1   Describe the Rural Electrification Scheme and explain why it was so important for women.

2   Explain what the 'marriage bar' was and how it affected women, and say when it was removed.

3   Give two reasons why women's lives in the workplace have improved since 1970.

4   List three main reasons why women's lives improved in the twentieth century.

5   Name the first female president of Ireland.

# 14

# LIFE IN A COMMUNIST AND FASCIST STATE

**What was life like in Stalin's Russia?**

284

**What was life like in Hitler's Germany?**

289

# WHAT WAS LIFE LIKE IN STALIN'S RUSSIA?

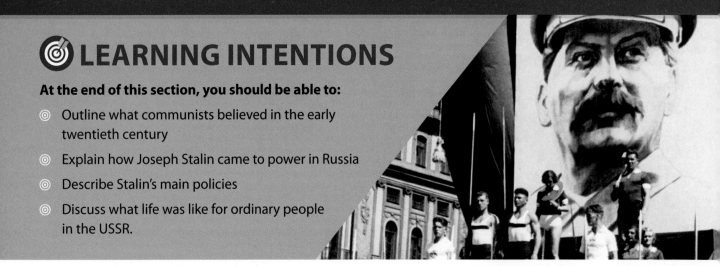

## 🎯 LEARNING INTENTIONS

**At the end of this section, you should be able to:**

◎ Outline what communists believed in the early twentieth century

◎ Explain how Joseph Stalin came to power in Russia

◎ Describe Stalin's main policies

◎ Discuss what life was like for ordinary people in the USSR.

## What did communists believe?

**Communism** is an idea that came from the writings of the German economist **Karl Marx**. It became an important political movement in the years before World War I. Followers of Marx became known as communists.

### Main features of communism

> **Opposition to capitalism:** Communists were strongly critical of the gulf that existed between the rich people and the ordinary people. They argued that the economic system, capitalism, exploited the ordinary workers who made up the majority of the population.

> **Creation of a classless society:** Communists believed that a **revolution** was needed to create a country where everyone would be **equal**. Such a society would have no social classes. They argued that after the revolution a **dictatorship** of the **Communist Party** was needed to achieve this classless society.

> **Shared ownership:** In a classless society there could be no private businesses. Instead, goods and services would be produced and supplied by government-run companies. Society as a whole would own these companies. The **wealth would be shared** by all citizens.

> **No religion:** Communists believed religion had no place in society.

> They also called for **international cooperation among workers** to achieve this goal.

SOURCE 14.1: Karl Marx

**Capitalism**
System in which businesses are owned by individuals and run for profit.

| Activity 1 |
| --- |
| 1  Write down any features of communism that you find appealing, and any features that you find unappealing. |
| 2  What problems might someone living in a communist country encounter? |

## Russian Revolution

In 1917 the world's first communist revolution occurred in Russia, or the **USSR** as it became known. The **Bolsheviks**, led by **Vladimir Lenin** (1870–1924), seized power. Lenin promised to set up the first country to be run by workers and peasants. He made it clear that he was not going to share power with other parties and only his **Communist Party** would be allowed.

A bloody civil war followed, and by 1920 the communists had won the war. The economy was in ruins and there was widespread famine. Lenin's economic policies – where the government took control of industry and agriculture – had failed. In response he allowed small businesses to operate without government control.

## How did Stalin come to power in the USSR?

**Joseph Stalin** (1878–1953) was born to a very poor family in Gori in Georgia. His real name was Joseph Vissarionovich Djugashvili. A loyal supporter of Lenin, he adopted the revolutionary name Stalin: the **man of steel**. Stalin was appointed **General Secretary of the Communist Party** in 1922. He used this role to appoint his supporters to senior positions in the party throughout the USSR. In 1924 Lenin died. Stalin gradually defeated his rivals to become the new dictator of the country by 1928. His main rival, **Leon Trotsky**, was forced into exile.

## What policies did Stalin introduce?

In 1928 Stalin introduced **Five Year Plans** to rapidly industrialise and modernise the USSR. All economic decisions were to be made by the government.

> **New towns** were built containing **large factories**. **Magnitogorsk** was built around the largest steel works in the world.

> **Heavy industry** was promoted. Coal, iron and steel production increased dramatically.

> **Bolshevik**
> Russian word meaning majority. Name given to the supporters of Lenin and his communist ideas.

### Activity 2

SOURCE 14.2: **Vladimir Lenin.** Lenin came to power in the October Revolution in 1917.

In groups of four, research the October Revolution. Base your research on these topics:

1 Lenin's life before 1917.

2 The causes of the revolution.

3 The main events during the revolution.

Show your findings to the class in a PowerPoint presentation.

SOURCE 14.3: **Joseph Stalin**

🔍 **DID YOU KNOW?**

USSR stands for the **Union of Soviet Socialist Republics. A soviet** was a workers' and soldiers' council that controlled the cities in Russia during the Russian Revolution. The USSR was also referred to by a number of other names, including the Soviet Union or Russia (as Russia was the largest part of the USSR).

> Massive **building projects** were undertaken, for example, canals and dams were constructed.

> Small farms were joined together to create larger farms called **collectives**. Stalin hoped that these larger farms would produce more food to feed the growing population in the towns.

As in Hitler's Germany, **indoctrinating young people** was another important policy for Stalin. Schools were tightly controlled, with history textbooks rewritten to promote Stalin. At the age of fourteen, boys and girls were expected to join the communist youth organisation **Komsomol** (Young Communist League). Members were taught the values of the Communist Party and a strong emphasis was placed on physical education and sport.

As the **Great Depression** spread in the USA and Western Europe, many people lost their jobs. They looked at what was happening in the USSR, where workers had jobs and apartments. On the surface, Stalin was creating a fairer and happier society. Communism seemed to work. Western visitors were impressed by what they saw, but it was largely an illusion.

## What was life like for ordinary people in the USSR?

There were some **improvements** for ordinary people.

> Workers had access to a job and a flat. Schools and health care were free. Many diseases, such as typhus, cholera and malaria, were tackled.

> Women enjoyed greater equality in society. This meant that careers as doctors, teachers and engineers, etc., were opened to them. Crèches and day-care centres were set up so that mothers could work.

However, Stalin used **propaganda** to promote his changes and **terror** to control his people on a scale that had rarely been witnessed before.

**Propaganda**
Information (often false) that is circulated to persuade people to take a particular view on an issue.

**DID YOU KNOW?**

Stalin would later dedicate Soviet industry to defeating Nazi Germany. The USSR's ability to produce tanks and planes was far greater than Germany's. This gave the Allies an important advantage during World War II.

**Activity 3**

Examine this source and then answer the questions below.

СПАСИБО
РОДНОМУ СТАЛИНУ
ЗА СЧАСТЛИВОЕ ДЕТСТВО!

**SOURCE 14.4:** 'Thanks to Beloved Stalin for our happy childhood!'

1 How is Stalin presented in this poster?
2 What, do you think, was the purpose of this poster?

Propaganda gave the impression of a contented and loyal population.

› Newspapers, radio, cinema, writers and artists were all tightly controlled. No criticism was tolerated.

› Stalin was portrayed as a great leader following in the footsteps of Lenin.

› Towns such as **Stalingrad** were named in his honour and statues of him were put up throughout the USSR.

› All the communist parties in Europe took direction from Moscow and they said how great things were in the USSR.

His police force, the **NKVD**, kept a very close eye on the people. Anybody, whether guilty or innocent, could be arrested at any time, anywhere. Informers were everywhere and even children were encouraged to report on their parents.

### DID YOU KNOW?

The English novelist **George Orwell** was a critic of Stalin and his regime. He wrote a famous book *Animal Farm*, which was critical of Stalin's rule of the USSR.

Anyone who was suspected of opposing Stalin's policies was executed or sent to vast prison camps called the **Gulag**.

› Prisoners were used as slaves. Millions died in the camps, where conditions were extremely harsh.

› Many of the great building projects, such as the Moscow underground, were built using slave labour.

Peasants were not happy with Stalin's proposed agricultural reforms and resisted them.

› To defeat this opposition Stalin created a man-made famine, especially in Ukraine.

› Historians estimate that 7 million people died as a result. Today this famine is called the **Holodomor** in Ukraine (see Section 16).

› A further 5 million wealthier farmers called **kulaks** were killed or sent to camps.

In an event known as the **Great Purge**, Stalin had hundreds of thousands of members of the Communist Party shot. Many had been allies of Trotsky. Most leading generals were also killed.

By 1939 the USSR was a modern industrial country and was one of the most powerful countries in the world. However, these improvements came at a terrible cost. Historians are not sure how many people were killed as a result of Stalin's policies, but it is estimated to be about 20 million.

## Activity 4

Examine this source and then answer the questions below.

**The Gulag**
The Soviet system of forced labour camps was first established in 1919 … but it was not until the early 1930s that the camp population reached significant numbers. By 1934 the Gulag, or Main Directorate for Corrective Labor Camps, had several million inmates. Prisoners included murderers, thieves, and other common criminals—along with political and religious prisoners.

The Gulag, whose camps were located mainly in remote regions of Siberia and the Far North, made significant contributions to the Soviet economy … Gulag prisoners constructed the White Sea–Baltic Canal, the Moscow–Volga Canal, the Baikal–Amur main railroad line, numerous hydroelectric stations … Gulag manpower was also used for … the mining of coal, copper, and gold.

Conditions in the camps were extremely harsh. Prisoners received inadequate food rations and insufficient clothing, which made it difficult to endure the severe weather and the long working hours … As a result, the death rate from exhaustion and disease in the camps was high.

**SOURCE 14.5: Article from 'Revelations from the Russian Archives' (US Library of Congress)**

1 What types of prisoners were sent to the Gulag, according to this source?

2 Outline the contribution of Gulag inmates to the Soviet economy.

3 Describe conditions in the Gulag.

4 Do you think this article is a reliable source about life in the Gulag?

## Activity 5

1   Work in groups of four to prepare and deliver a PowerPoint presentation to the class on one of the following topics:
   - The industrialisation of the USSR
   - The policy of collectivisation and its consequences
   - The Gulag
   - The Great Purge.

Each group will need to allocate roles such as: researching information, sourcing visual images, typing up the PowerPoint, giving the presentation, taking questions from the class.

### DO YOU UNDERSTAND THESE KEY TERMS?

| | | |
|---|---|---|
| Bolshevik | Gulag | NKVD |
| collective | Holodomor | propaganda |
| Five Year Plan | Komsomol | USSR |
| Great Purge | kulak | |

PowerPoint summary

## Activity 6

Examine the two photographs and answer the questions below.

SOURCE 14.6: Two pictures of the same event in 1937. One picture was published in 1937, the other after 1940.

1   Who is the most important person in each photograph, in your view? Explain your answer.
2   Why, do you think, was the man on the right removed from Picture B?
3   What do these sources tell you about the reliability of pictures as evidence for historians?

## SELF-ASSESSMENT – CAN YOU?

1  Identify four features of communism.

2  Explain what the Russian Revolution was.

3  Describe how Stalin became the dictator of the USSR.

4  Comment on the main economic policies Stalin introduced as ruler of the USSR.

5  Explain the role propaganda played in the USSR under Stalin.

6  List three examples of how Stalin used terror to control the Soviet people.

7  Outline the benefits of Stalin's policies for the Soviet people.

8  Illustrate how young people were indoctrinated in the USSR.

9  Discuss the view that Stalin's policies brought benefits to the USSR but at a terrible human cost.

# WHAT WAS LIFE LIKE IN HITLER'S GERMANY?

## ⊚ LEARNING INTENTIONS

**At the end of this section, you should be able to:**

◎ Outline what fascists believed in the early twentieth century

◎ Explain how Adolf Hitler came to power in Germany

◎ Describe the main features of Nazi Germany

◎ Discuss what life was like for Jewish people in 1930s Germany.

## What did fascists believe?

**Fascism** is a political idea that developed after World War I (1914–18). The man most associated with the development of this idea was an Italian, **Benito Mussolini** (1883–1945). He became the ruler of Italy in 1922.

### Main features of fascism

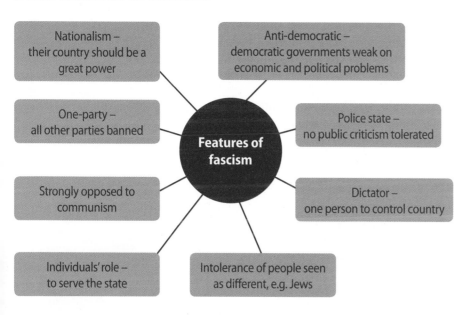

- Nationalism – their country should be a great power
- Anti-democratic – democratic governments weak on economic and political problems
- One-party – all other parties banned
- Police state – no public criticism tolerated
- **Features of fascism**
- Strongly opposed to communism
- Dictator – one person to control country
- Individuals' role – to serve the state
- Intolerance of people seen as different, e.g. Jews

**Activity 1**

SOURCE 14.7: Benito Mussolini

1 Find out about the career of Mussolini. Identify six facts that particularly interest you.

In 1933 **Adolf Hitler** came to power and he set about putting fascist ideas into practice in Germany.

**Activity 2**

1 Write down any features of fascism that you find appealing, and any features that you find unappealing.

2 What problems might someone living in a fascist country encounter?

## What were Adolf Hitler's aims?

Adolf Hitler was born in Braunau am Inn, Austria, in 1889. He joined the German army when World War I broke out. Hitler was shocked by Germany's defeat in World War I. He refused to support the democratic government called the **Weimar Republic** formed as a result of the defeat.

In 1920 Hitler became the leader of the **National Socialist German Workers' Party (NSDAP)**. It was nicknamed the **Nazi Party**.

Hitler copied a lot of ideas from Mussolini's Fascist Party. He surrounded himself with brown-shirted followers who guarded political meetings and attacked political opponents. A smaller group, called the **Schutzstaffel (SS)**, was formed to act as a personal bodyguard for Hitler.

Hitler was known as **Der Führer** (the leader) and his followers saluted each other with a right-arm salute.

In 1923 Hitler attempted to seize power in the **Beer Hall Putsch**, but this was easily defeated. While in prison he wrote a book called *Mein Kampf* (*My Struggle*), which set out his political views.

> He believed that the Germans were the **master race** and that other peoples were inferior. He wanted to remove the Jewish people from Germany.

> He was strongly opposed to communism. He also hated the democratic government of Germany. He called for a dictatorship where one man (himself) would rule Germany.

> He wanted to make Germany a strong power and overturn the Treaty of Versailles.

## How did Hitler come to power?

In 1929 the **Wall Street Crash** in America led to an economic decline both in the USA and in Europe. Known as the **Great Depression**, it had a dramatic impact on Germany.

> By 1932 nearly 6 million Germans were unemployed. There was political chaos as Germans lost faith in the democratic government. Millions turned to Hitler's party.

> Most Germans also agreed with Hitler's wish to tear up the Treaty of Versailles which had been imposed on a defeated Germany after World War I.

> Hitler wanted to make Germany a great power again. This aim was supported by nearly all Germans.

> In the election of July 1932 the Nazi Party became the largest party in the German parliament.

> On 30 January 1933 **President Hindenburg** appointed Hitler the **chancellor** (prime minister) of Germany.

### Activity 3

1 Find out five terms of the Treaty of Versailles that affected Germany.
2 Name three of the countries that negotiated the treaty.
3 From your research, do you think the treaty was too harsh on Germany? Explain your answer.

**Weimar Republic**
Name given to the period of German history between 1918 and 1933.

SOURCE 14.8: Adolf Hitler

**SS**
Schutzstaffel, a unit of the Nazi party that operated as a special security force.

**Master race**
Group of people believed to be superior to others.

**Great Depression**
A period of high unemployment in the 1930s in America and Europe.

SOURCE 14.9: Hitler addressing a crowd in 1934; he had a gift for oratory

# How did Hitler establish a dictatorship?

Hitler and his party wasted little time taking control of Germany.

> The Nazis brought the police under their control. The Brownshirts were free to terrorise political opponents.

> A secret police, known as the **Gestapo**, was set up to keep an eye on the population.

> In February 1933 the German parliament building, the **Reichstag**, was set on fire. Hitler passed a law that gave the police wide powers of arrest and imprisonment without trial.

> The Communist Party was blamed for the fire and over 10,000 people were arrested.

> In March 1933 the German parliament passed a law called the **Enabling Act**. This gave Hitler the power to pass laws without getting them approved by parliament. He was now a dictator.

> He then acted swiftly to crush democracy. A wave of terror followed. All political parties and trade unions were banned by the summer of 1933.

> Hitler and the Nazis were in total control of Germany. In 1934 he executed the leadership of the Brownshirts as he believed they were plotting to overthrow him.

## Concentration camps

> The first **concentration camp** was set up at **Dachau** near Munich in 1933. More were soon established throughout Germany.

> The SS, led by **Heinrich Himmler** (1900–1945), was given control of the camps.

> Political opponents, criminals and, later, Jews were imprisoned in the camps.

> Conditions were harsh and the prisoners were at the mercy of their guards. Torture was common.

> The camp population was quite small before World War II. Nonetheless the fear of being sent to a camp was an important way in which the Nazis controlled the German people.

**Concentration camps**
Prisons used for political prisoners and later the Jews of Europe.

---

**Activity 4**

Examine this source and then answer the questions below.

SOURCE 14.10: **Entrance to Dachau concentration camp**

1 The German words on the gate are 'Arbeit macht frei'. Find out what these words mean.

2 These words were also displayed at other concentration camps. Suggest why the Nazis chose this slogan.

3 Imagine you were a Nazi opponent sent to Dachau. How would this slogan make you feel?

---

**Activity 5**

Examine the source and then answer the question below.

> He was holding us under a hypnotic spell. I forgot everything but the man … then, glancing round, I saw that the magnetism was holding these thousands as one.

SOURCE 14.11: **An observer describing one of Hitler's speeches**

1 Describe the impact Hitler had on those who heard him speak.

# What were the main features of life in Nazi Germany?

Having established a dictatorship, Hitler's aim was to bring all aspects of German life under Nazi control. Hitler was popular with most Germans. Thanks to his successful economic and foreign policies, they were prepared to accept the loss of basic human rights, the terror and the camps.

The message the Nazis preached of a **people's community** inspired many Germans. In such a community, all Germans were equal and were working together to make Germany a great nation.

## Employment

Hitler turned the Germany economy around, solving the unemployment problem and ending the hardship of the early 1930s.

> Public works schemes employed thousands of people to build motorways, railroads and dams.

> A massive amount of money was spent on new weapons, which meant that more workers were employed to build them.

By 1937 Germany had a labour shortage – it did not have enough workers to fill available jobs.

All trade unions were banned and workers had to join the Nazi-controlled **German Labour Front**. Strikes were outlawed. To win over the ordinary workers an organisation called **Strength Through Joy** provided cheap holidays. Skiing in the Bavarian Alps and cruising in the Norwegian fjords or the Mediterranean were very popular with ordinary Germans.

The Nazis also proposed a project by which ordinary Germans could save to buy a car. This car was called a **Volkswagen** (the people's car). Although millions of Germans saved for the car, none were actually delivered by the time war broke out in 1939.

### Activity 6

One of the cruise liners built for the Strength Through Joy organisation was the *Wilhelm Gustloff*. On 30 January 1945 it was sunk by a Russian submarine.

1  Research this event online and find out four facts about the sinking of the ship.

### DID YOU KNOW?

Hitler talked about creating a **Third Reich** (empire). The First Reich or Holy Roman Empire ended in 1806. The Second Reich lasted from 1871 until 1918.

### Activity 7

Examine the source and answer the question below.

SOURCE 14.12: **1938 advertisement for Volkswagen**

1  What is the message of this advertisement?

## Propaganda

**Propaganda** played a very important role in life in Nazi Germany.

> Under the direction of the Minister of Propaganda, **Joseph Goebbels** (1897–1945), the Nazis were very successful at getting their message across to the German people. Hitler was promoted as the leader who could do no wrong, the man leading Germany to greatness.

> One popular slogan was **'Ein Volk, ein Reich, ein Führer!'** (One People, one Empire, one Leader!).

> All German newspapers were expected to support the actions of Hitler. If they did not, they were closed down.

> Goebbels even had cheap radio sets made so that the Nazi message could be spread into every home in Germany.

> The Nazi flag, the **swastika**, was displayed throughout towns and villages in Germany.

> Parades and rallies were organised. The most famous was held at **Nuremberg** every year.

## Young people

Hitler was determined that young people would be loyal to the new government. He introduced policies designed to indoctrinate the young into supporting the Nazis.

> In schools, the teaching of history was changed to reflect Nazi views.

> Teachers had to give the Nazi salute to their classes. If they criticised the regime they could lose their jobs.

> The Nazis made it compulsory for all boys and girls to become members of Nazi-controlled youth groups.

> At the age of fourteen, boys joined the **Hitler Youth** and girls became members of the **League of German Maidens**.

> Boys were trained to be the future soldiers of Germany while girls were expected to become good mothers.

SOURCE 14.14: **Joseph Goebbels**

**Indoctrination**
Policy of getting people to believe a particular message or viewpoint.

## DID YOU KNOW?

The Hitler Youth became the largest youth organisation in the world.

### Activity 8

Examine the source and answer the questions below.

All subjects – German language, History, Geography, Chemistry and Mathematics – must concentrate on military subjects, the glorification of military service and of German heroes and leaders and the strength of a rebuilt Germany.

Chemistry will develop a knowledge of chemical warfare, explosives etc, while Mathematics will help the young to understand artillery, calculations, ballistics.

SOURCE 14.13: **A German newspaper describing the school curriculum in 1939**

1 According to the newspaper, what must all subjects concentrate on?

2 Outline your views on the Nazi curriculum.

3 Do you think that newspapers printed in Nazi Germany are reliable sources for historians? Explain your answer.

SOURCE 14.15: **'Hitler is building up. Help out. Buy German goods'**

## Activity 9

In groups of four, examine this source and then answer the questions below.

**Law on the Hitler Youth (December 1, 1936)**
The future of the German Nation depends upon its youth, and German youth shall have to be prepared for its future duties.

Therefore the Government of the Reich has prepared the following law which is being published herewith:
1. All of the German youth in the Reich is organized within the Hitler Youth.
2. The German Youth besides being reared within the family and school, shall be educated physically, intellectually, and morally in the spirit of National Socialism to serve the people and community, through the Hitler Youth.
3. The task of educating the German Youth through the Hitler Youth is being entrusted to the Reich Leader of German Youth in the NSDAP. He is the 'Youth Leader of the German Reich'. The position of his office is that of a higher governmental Agency... and is directly responsible to the Fuehrer and the Chancellor of the Reich.

Berlin, 1 December 1936

The Fuehrer and Chancellor of the Reich
Adolf Hitler

**SOURCE 14.16:** 1946 translation of a law setting out the role and leadership of the Hitler Youth, published online

1. What is the date of this law and who is responsible for it?
2. What, according to the document, does the future of the German nation depend on?
3. From the document, what was the function of the Hitler Youth?
4. What evidence is there in the document that the Reich Leader of German Youth had an important job?
5. Is this a primary or a secondary source? Explain your answer.

### Women

The Nazis had a very traditional view of the role of women in society.

› They regarded a woman's place as being in the home.

› They encouraged married women to leave the workforce. Propaganda spread the message that a woman's role was supporting her husband and minding her children.

› Women found it more difficult to go to university and, for example, fewer and fewer women became doctors.

› During World War II the Nazis had to reverse these policies and by 1944 over half of the workforce were women.

## What was life like for Jewish people in Germany?

The Nazis taught the Germans to think of themselves as superior to other races. They were the master race or the **Aryans**. They said that the Jews were the enemies of the master race. Hitler also blamed the Jews for Germany's defeat in World War I and for many of Germany's problems after the war, especially the growth of communism.

Jewish people made up less than one per cent of the German population, about 500,000 people. They were very successful in business, medicine and law. Many of the best professors in German universities were Jewish. Most Jews felt themselves to be German and were dismayed by the policies of the new government.

The Nazis made **anti-Semitism** official government policy. At first the main aim of the Nazis was to get the Jews to leave Germany.

› In 1933 a boycott of Jewish shops was organised.
› Laws were passed that banned Jews from working for the government.
› Anti-Jewish signs were put up throughout the country.
› Many Jews were forced to sell their businesses to non-Jews at a fraction of their value.
› Jewish doctors were allowed to treat only Jewish patients.

**Anti-Semitism**
Hatred of and discrimination against Jewish people.

### Nuremberg Laws

In 1935 the **Nuremberg Laws** were passed.

› A person with three Jewish grandparents was classified as Jewish even if he or she was now Christian.
› The laws made it illegal for Germans and Jews to marry or to have sexual relations with each other.

> Jewish people in Germany were now second-class citizens.
> These laws were later used as the basis for deciding who was to be murdered in the Holocaust (see Section 16).

## Kristallnacht

A terrible example of anti-Semitism took place in November 1938. When a German diplomat in Paris was shot by a Jewish student, the Nazis decided to take revenge on the Jewish community in Germany.

> On the night of 9/10 November, Jews throughout Germany were attacked by the Brownshirts.
> Ninety-one Jews were murdered and over 30,000 were arrested and sent to concentration camps.
> Every synagogue (Jewish place of worship) in Germany was destroyed. Jewish property and shops were damaged.
> To add insult to injury the Jewish community was then fined one billion marks for the murder of the German diplomat.
> The event was called **Kristallnacht** (the night of broken glass). Over 80,000 Jews left Germany in the following month.

SOURCE 14.17: Synagogue destroyed during Kristallnacht

### Activity 10

Search online for a recording of Susan Warsinger's account of her experience of Kristallnacht.

1 In groups of four discuss your reaction to what you have heard. You can use the transcript of the recording to help you.

### DO YOU UNDERSTAND THESE KEY TERMS?

| | | |
|---|---|---|
| anti-Semitism | Führer | Nuremberg Laws |
| Aryan | Gestapo | Reichstag |
| Beer Hall Putsch | Great Depression | Schutzstaffel (SS) |
| Brownshirt | Hitler Youth | Strength Through Joy |
| chancellor | Kristallnacht | Third Reich |
| concentration camp | League of German Maidens | Wall Street Crash |
| demilitarised zone | master race | Weimar Republic |
| fascism | Nazi Party | |

Chapter summary    Weblinks    PowerPoint summary

## SELF-ASSESSMENT – CAN YOU?

1 Identify four features of fascism.

2 Outline how Hitler came to power in Germany in 1933.

3 Explain how the Nazis established a dictatorship in Germany.

4 Provide evidence for the view that Hitler was a popular figure in Germany in the 1930s.

5 Describe the economic policies the Nazis introduced.

6 Illustrate what life was like for workers in Germany under the Nazis.

7 Discuss how the Nazis tried to control the young people of Germany.

8 Examine the role of women in Nazi Germany.

9 Identify the main actions the Nazis took against Jewish people before 1938.

10 Explain the importance of Kristallnacht.

Learning Outcome 3.9   

# 15 THE CAUSES AND IMPACT OF WORLD WAR II

## What factors led to World War II?

## What happened during World War II?

## What were the consequences of World War II?

## How did World War II affect Irish people?

# WHAT FACTORS LED TO WORLD WAR II?

## LEARNING INTENTIONS

**At the end of this section, you should be able to:**

◎ Explain Hitler's idea of a Greater Germany

◎ Describe how Hitler broke the Treaty of Versailles

◎ Discuss the policy of appeasement

◎ Outline the factors that led to war breaking out in September 1939.

## What was Hitler's idea of a Greater Germany?

The actions of **Adolf Hitler**, leader of the fascist Nazi Party and dictator of Germany, were the main cause of World War II.

〉 He wanted to make Germany a major military power again.

〉 He aimed to unite all German speakers living outside Germany into a **Greater Germany**.

〉 He planned to create a German Empire in Eastern Europe by taking land from Poland and Russia. He called this *Lebensraum* (living space) because he intended to settle these lands with Germans.

### 🔍 DID YOU KNOW?

The Austrians spoke German and there were large numbers of Germans in Czechoslovakia, Poland, Romania and Hungary. Most had originally been part of the Austrian Empire that collapsed at the end of World War I.

## What was appeasement?

Hitler believed that he would be able to achieve his aims because the French and British wanted to avoid another war. The memories of the slaughter of World War I were strong and French and British people did not want to return to war.

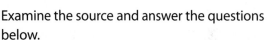

**Activity 1**

Examine the source and answer the questions below.

SOURCE 15.1: Hitler, 1936

1  What is the name of the Nazi symbol on Hitler's armband?

2  What image of Hitler is the photograph designed to portray?

**Activity 2**

After World War I the League of Nations had been set up to preserve world peace.

Research the League of Nations online and answer the following questions:

1  What was the principle of collective security?

2  Evaluate whether or not the organisation was successful in preserving world peace.

The French were very worried by Hitler but felt too weak to take action alone. France would not act without British support. The British felt that the Treaty of Versailles had been too harsh on the Germans. In 1937 there was a new prime minister in Britain, **Neville Chamberlain**. He believed in **diplomacy**. He thought that by negotiating with Hitler he could prevent war. This policy was called **appeasement**. Hitler saw it as weakness and took advantage of the British wish to avoid war.

**Diplomacy**
Negotiations between countries.

**Appeasement**
Giving in to another's demands in order to keep the peace.

## How did Hitler break the Treaty of Versailles?

### Rearmament

Hitler started by removing the limits the Treaty of Versailles had placed on the German army. In 1935 he increased the size of the German army and navy and created an air force called the **Luftwaffe**. Britain and France protested but took few steps to prevent Hitler from rearming.

### Rhineland

In March 1936 German troops crossed the River Rhine and reoccupied the **Rhineland**. The soldiers were greeted by cheering crowds. Again, the French and British did nothing except protest at Hitler's actions.

Hitler's major gamble in breaking the Treaty of Versailles had paid off. He was now prepared to take more risks. A few months later he formed an alliance with the Italian fascist dictator **Benito Mussolini** that was known as the **Rome–Berlin Axis**.

SOURCE 15.2: Neville Chamberlain

---

**Activity 3**

Examine this source and then answer the question below.

SOURCE 15.3: German occupation of Austria, 1938

1 In your opinion, does this action have popular approval? Give reasons for your answer.

## Austria

Hitler's next target was the land of his birth, **Austria**.

> Hitler threatened to invade and the chancellor (prime minister) resigned. He was replaced by the leader of the Austrian Nazis. German troops were then 'invited in' to restore order.

> Greeted by jubilant crowds, Hitler proclaimed that Austria would become a province of Germany. This event became known as the **Anschluss**. The word means joining together.

> Britain and France did not take any action, even though Hitler's act was forbidden by the Treaty of Versailles. The British felt that they could not go to war over a union between two German-speaking nations.

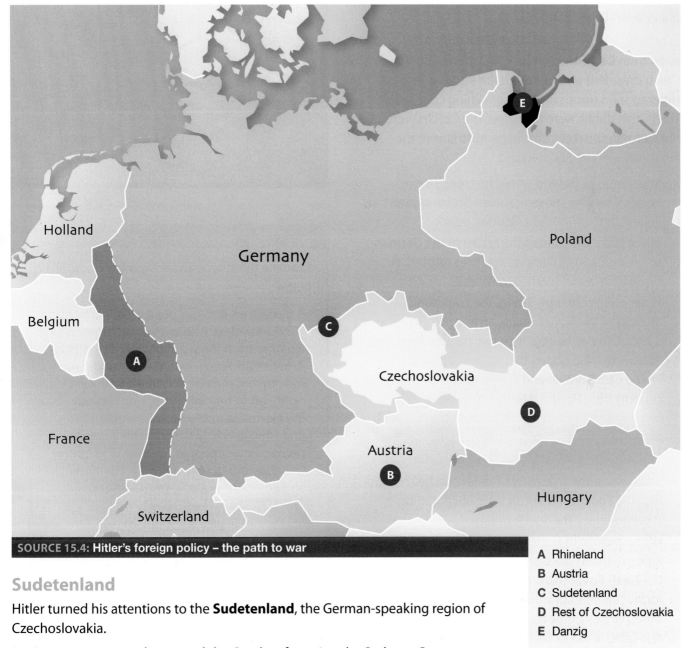

**SOURCE 15.4: Hitler's foreign policy – the path to war**

A Rhineland
B Austria
C Sudetenland
D Rest of Czechoslovakia
E Danzig

## Sudetenland

Hitler turned his attentions to the **Sudetenland**, the German-speaking region of Czechoslovakia.

> German propaganda accused the Czechs of treating the Sudeten Germans very badly. The crisis worsened as fears of a German attack on Czechoslovakia grew.

> Chamberlain flew to Germany twice to negotiate with Hitler. Just as it seemed war was about to break out, Mussolini suggested a conference of Britain, France, Italy and Germany.

> This took place at Munich in September 1938. Amazingly, Czechoslovakia was not invited to the **Munich Conference**.

> The parties agreed to German demands and the Czechs were forced to hand over the Sudetenland to Germany. Hitler promised that this was his final demand.

> Chamberlain said that he had brought back peace with honour, and he was welcomed home by cheering crowds. Unfortunately war had only been delayed.

## How did war break out in September 1939?

In March 1939 Hitler encouraged the Slovaks to break away from **Czechoslovakia**. Hitler then bullied the Czech president on a visit to Berlin into allowing Hitler to send troops into the remaining Czech lands. The British public were outraged. The Czechs were not German speakers, unlike the Austrians or the inhabitants of the Sudetenland.

> Knowing that **Poland** would be Hitler's next target, Chamberlain guaranteed British support to Poland in the event of a German attack.

> When Hitler demanded the return of the German-speaking town of **Danzig**, the Poles refused. A German invasion seemed inevitable.

> Hitler offered **Joseph Stalin**, the communist dictator of the Soviet Union, an alliance. He wanted **Soviet neutrality** when he attacked Poland. He also hoped that such an alliance would cause Britain and France to withdraw their support from Poland if Germany invaded.

**Neutrality**
Policy of not taking a side in a dispute.

> Stalin was a sworn enemy of Hitler and he thought that the French and British were encouraging Hitler to attack the Soviet Union.

> His suspicions of France and the UK led Stalin to agree to the alliance on 23 August 1939. Under the **Nazi–Soviet Non-Aggression Pact**, the two former enemies promised not to attack each other. Secretly they also agreed to divide Poland and other areas of Eastern Europe between them.

SOURCE 15.5 : Mussolini and Hitler in Munich, 1938

### Activity 4

Examine the source and answer the questions below.

> It transpired that our position at home and in home waters was a disadvantageous one whether from the point of view of the Navy, Army or Air Force, or anti-aircraft defence. In addition, public opinion was strongly opposed to any military action against the Germans in the demilitarised zone [the Rhineland]. Moreover, many people, perhaps most people, were saying openly that they did not see why the Germans should not re-occupy the Rhineland.

SOURCE 15.6: **Comments from the British Foreign Secretary about why the British did not take action against the German occupation of the Rhineland in 1936**

1   Identify two reasons why the British did not take action when Germany occupied the Rhineland.

2   From evidence in the source, do you think the British were right to take no action in 1936?

## Activity 5

Examine this source and then answer the questions below.

WONDER HOW LONG THE HONEYMOON WILL LAST?

**SOURCE 15.7: Cartoon on the Nazi–Soviet Non-Aggression Pact**

1   Identify the two people in the cartoon.
2   Describe how the cartoonist criticises the pact.
3   Why was the world shocked to hear about the pact?

On 1 September 1939 German troops invaded Poland. Britain and France stood by their guarantee and declared war on 3 September. World War II had started.

 **PowerPoint summary**

## Activity 6

One country you might have expected to read more about in this section is the USA. Research online to find out why the USA did not get involved in European affairs.

## Activity 7

1   Draw up a timeline from 1933 to 1939 of the main actions Hitler took that led to World War II.

### DO YOU UNDERSTAND THESE KEY TERMS?

| | |
|---|---|
| *Anschluss* | Luftwaffe |
| appeasement | neutrality |
| diplomacy | non-aggression pact |
| League of Nations | rearmament |
| *Lebensraum* | |

# SELF-ASSESSMENT – CAN YOU?

1   Outline two aims of Hitler's foreign policy.

2   Explain the action taken by Hitler in March 1936.

3   Explain the Rome–Berlin axis.

4   Examine why the British and French did not take action against Hitler until it was too late to avoid war.

5   Analyse the crisis over the Sudetenland.

6   Identify one important result of the German occupation of Czech lands in March 1939.

7   Explain why the Nazi–Soviet Non-Aggression Pact was significant.

8   Debate the statement: 'It was the actions of Adolf Hitler that led to World War II.'

# WHAT HAPPENED DURING WORLD WAR II?

## ⊚ LEARNING INTENTIONS

**At the end of this section, you should be able to:**

◎ Describe the military tactics Germany used in the war

◎ Explain how Germany defeated France

◎ Outline what happened during the Battle of Britain

◎ Describe the key events on the Eastern Front

◎ Outline the main events in the war outside Europe

◎ Describe what it was like to live in Nazi-occupied Europe

◎ Explain why the Allies won the war.

## What was World War II?

**World War II (1939–45)** was to be the bloodiest conflict in human history. It was mainly fought in Europe, Asia and North Africa. It brought death and destruction on a truly horrible scale. This section will look at the main events of the war.

---

 **Activity 1**

In groups of four, examine this source and then answer the questions below.

**Britain at war with Germany**

Britain and France are now at war with Germany. The British ultimatum [demand] expired at 11 a.m. yesterday, and France entered the war six hours later – at 5 p.m.

The first announcement that the country was at war was made by Mr Chamberlain in a statement broadcast from Downing Street …

Last night the King broadcast a call to the British people to stand calm and firm and united …

The banks will be closed today, but will reopen tomorrow. The Stock Exchange remains closed for the present. All cinemas, theatres, and other places of entertainment are to be closed until further notice. Sports gatherings, indoor or outdoor, which involve large numbers of people congregating are prohibited. Church and all other places of public worship will not be closed.

President Roosevelt, in his broadcast to the United States last night, declared, 'America will remain a neutral nation.' He disclosed that the proclamation of neutrality was already being prepared.

The German Government handed in its reply to Sir Neville Henderson [British Ambassador in Germany] twenty minutes after the expiry of the time limit. It refused to give any assurance to withdraw troops. For the rest the reply consisted of propaganda …

A joint Anglo-French declaration last night declared their intention to conduct hostilities with a firm desire to spare civilian populations and to preserve monuments to human achievement …

Eleven smaller European states have declared their neutrality …

The German armies are now invading Northern Poland from both sides of the 'Corridor', and Polish Silesia from Slovakia and German Silesia. They have also attacked from the air many towns and villages far from the fighting zone.

**SOURCE 15.8: *The Guardian*, 4 September 1939**

1 Which two countries declared war on Germany on 3 September 1939?

2 Describe how the declaration of war affected ordinary people in Britain.

3 Describe how the newspaper reports the German reply to the British demand.

4 Identify two examples of propaganda in this source.

---

On 1 September 1939 German troops crossed the border into Poland. Britain and France declared war on Germany on 3 September. World War II had started.

## Using sources from World War II

**Propaganda** is used as a weapon in war. The purposes of wartime propaganda include:

> Making the enemy look bad or evil to justify fighting them

> Raising morale so your soldiers and civilians support the war

> Making your cause look just.

All countries involved in World War II used propaganda. Newspapers, films and radio broadcasts were expected to support 'their side'.

Sometimes propaganda can be factual; at other times things are made up or facts are ignored. A victory would be praised and publicised, whereas a defeat would either not be reported or be reported in a way that played down its importance.

Propaganda posters were displayed on streets and in buildings. As sources for historians, they must be treated with caution. Similarly, relying on any newspaper source from World War II would not be advisable.

## How was Poland defeated?

The German army developed a new tactic called **blitzkrieg** (lightning war).

> **Blitzkrieg**
> German military tactics involving heavy bombing from the air and rapid tank movements on the ground. The aim was to surround enemy forces and force them to surrender.

> The German air force, the **Luftwaffe**, would destroy enemy targets on the ground.

> Then large numbers of German tanks, organised into **panzer armies**, would smash through the enemy's defences.

> Enemy troops would find themselves surrounded and be forced to surrender to the German **infantry**.

> **Panzer**
> German armoured vehicles.

> **Infantry**
> Soldiers on foot.

**Activity 2**

Examine this source and then answer the questions below.

SOURCE 15.9: British propaganda poster showing German soldiers surrendering

1  What is the message of this poster?
2  How effectively does this poster get its message across, do you think?

**DID YOU KNOW?**

The **Stuka dive bomber** was developed as an accurate ground-attack aircraft. Its unusual wings allowed it to dive at a steep angle, bomb a target accurately and then climb away quickly to escape the explosion of the bomb. It was a slow plane, however, and suffered heavy losses during the Battle of Britain.

SOURCE 15.10: Stuka dive bomber

The Poles were the first to experience this new tactic. The Polish capital, **Warsaw**, was heavily bombed. To make matters worse, Poland was also invaded in the east by the Soviets. After just three weeks Poland was defeated. The Poles later suffered terribly at the hands of both the Germans and the Soviets.

Britain and France did not attack Germany. There was so little fighting in Western Europe that the war was soon nicknamed **'the phoney war'**. This calm was shattered when Germany invaded **Denmark** and **Norway** in April 1940, and **Belgium**, **Holland** and **France** in May 1940.

## How was France defeated?

The French thought that the Germans would have great difficulty breaking through the **Maginot Line** that protected their border with Germany. Germany, however, had more daring plans.

> The Germans pretended that the main part of their invasion of France was coming through Belgium, avoiding the Maginot Line.

> The British and French rushed their troops to meet this threat.

> The Germans then sent their main force through a wooded, hilly area called the **Ardennes**. The French had left this area unprotected, believing it to be too difficult for tanks to go through.

Although the French had more and superior tanks, the Germans made better use of the tanks they had. They advanced quickly and French soldiers surrendered in large numbers.

**Italy** then entered the war on the side of Germany and attacked France. German forces entered Paris and France surrendered in June.

---

**Activity 3**

1   Research online to find out about one of the following:
    (a) The Maginot Line
    (b) The German invasion of Norway
    (c) Vichy France.

2   Identify six facts that you found interesting.

---

**KS**                          **Activity 4**

Examine this source and then answer the questions below.

SOURCE 15.11: Negotiating the terms of the French surrender, 1940

1   Describe the scene in the photograph.
2   Imagine you are a French negotiator. List three aims for the negotiation.
3   Imagine you are a German negotiator. List three aims for the negotiation.
4   Hitler ordered that the negotiations take place in the same railway carriage in which the Germans had surrendered in 1918. Suggest why he did this.

## Impact

Germany occupied the north of France, and allowed a French government to be formed in the south of the country. Called **Vichy France** after its capital at Vichy, it was led by **Marshal Pétain** – a French hero of World War I. Britain, with a new prime minister, **Winston Churchill**, was left to stand alone against the might of Nazi Germany.

The Germans had trapped the **British Expeditionary Force (BEF)** that had been sent to help the French at **Dunkirk** on the northern French coast. The British, however, had mounted a successful naval operation, called **Operation Dynamo**, which rescued over 300,000 British and French soldiers from the beaches at Dunkirk.

**Radar**
A device that uses radio waves to detect approaching planes.

## How did the British win the Battle of Britain?

The German plan to invade Britain was called **Operation Sea Lion**. For this invasion to be successful, Germany needed control of the skies, which meant defeating the **Royal Air Force (RAF)**.

> On 13 August 1940 waves of Luftwaffe planes bombed airfields and **radar** installations throughout Britain. What became known as the **Battle of Britain** had started.

> RAF pilots fought constant air battles, called **dogfights**. British Spitfires and Hurricanes fought German ME 109s and ME 110s.

> The use of newly invented radar allowed the British to predict the arrival of German attacks.

> By the middle of September the Germans, having failed to get control of the air, switched to night-time bombing of British cities. The RAF had won.

SOURCE 15.12: **Aircraft spotter, London**

Learning Outcome 3.4

## The Blitz

The bombing of London and other British cities was called the **Blitz** and it lasted until May 1941. The object of the bombing was to weaken civilian morale, and to destroy harbours and factories that made weapons. Hundreds of German bombers dropped high-explosive bombs. They also dropped **incendiaries** – bombs designed to start fires.

In London, many people went to the **Underground stations**. Conditions there were very overcrowded. A strict **blackout** was enforced so that no lights would be visible from the air, making it difficult for German bombers to locate their targets. Young children were evacuated from London to the countryside.

By the end of the Blitz, **London** had been bombed seventy-one times. Cities such as **Birmingham, Liverpool, Glasgow, Coventry** and **Belfast** were also bombed. In all, over 40,000 civilians were killed.

---

### Activity 5

Examine this source and then answer the questions below.

**Rationing**

**A** Everyone living on the home front in Britain during the war had to cope with shortages of food and clothing. Meat, sugar, butter, cheese, and eggs were all rationed, and people were encouraged to grow and eat their own vegetables and to try new recipes. Children joined in, growing vegetables at school and at home. Child health and welfare was a priority, so babies, children and expectant mothers had special allocations of milk and were given vitamins in the form of orange juice and cod liver oil. From June 1941, clothing was also rationed. This was a particular problem for parents of growing children and in 1942 the scheme was adapted so that children were allocated extra clothing coupons. However, children's shoes remained in short supply throughout the war.

**Work**

**B** During the war, many children between the ages of 14 and 17 were in full-time employment. They worked in agriculture, in offices and the major industries such as engineering, aircraft production, shipbuilding and vehicle manufacture. From 1941 all those aged between 16 and 18 were required to register for some form of national service, even if they had a full-time job. Younger children were expected to do their bit by salvaging scrap metal, paper, glass and waste food for recycling.

**Home front**
Name given to life in Britain during World War II.

**Ration coupon**
Card or stamp that allows you to buy an item.

**SOURCE 15.13: Extracts from 'Growing up in Britain in the Second World War', Imperial War Museum, available online**

1 From source A, identify six items that were rationed during World War II.
2 According to source A, what efforts were made to improve children's health?
3 From source A, what measures were passed to make sure children had clothes?
4 Describe the work carried out by 14–17-year-olds and by younger children, according to source B.
5 According to source B, why did children have to work during the war?
6 Is this a primary or a secondary source? Justify your answer.

---

## What was Operation Barbarossa?

**Red Army**
Soviet army.

Hitler next planned to attack the USSR and create a vast German empire there. He thought he would defeat the **Red Army** easily. The attack had been originally scheduled for May 1941, but it was delayed for a month when German troops invaded **Greece** and **Yugoslavia**.

The Germans assembled the largest invasion force in history. It consisted of 4 million soldiers, 3,000 planes and 3,000 tanks. The force was divided into three separate armies – Army Groups North, Centre and South. The invasion, codenamed **Operation Barbarossa**, began on the morning of 22 June 1941.

Stalin had refused to believe numerous warnings about a likely German invasion and so the Soviet forces were caught by surprise.

Although the USSR had far more tanks and planes than the Germans, the Red Army suffered defeat after defeat. The ordinary Soviet soldiers fought with great bravery but they were poorly led. By December, 4 million soldiers had been killed or captured by the Germans. The Germans surrounded **Leningrad** and were closing in on **Moscow**.

Despite their successes, the Germans found fighting in the USSR very tough:

› As the Soviets retreated they destroyed anything of use to the Germans such as factories or railway lines. This is called a **scorched earth policy**.

› The Soviets' new T34 tank proved superior to any tank the Germans had at that time.

› Rain in October turned the roads into a sea of mud that made movement very difficult.

› The Germans did not have winter clothing. As temperatures dropped to −40°C, the German army lost more men to frostbite than to fighting the Soviets. Petrol froze and tanks would not start.

› Crucially, despite their victories, the Germans were suffering heavy losses of troops, who could not be replaced. The Soviets had more men and could replace the men they had lost.

**SOURCE 15.15: German troops in Russia**

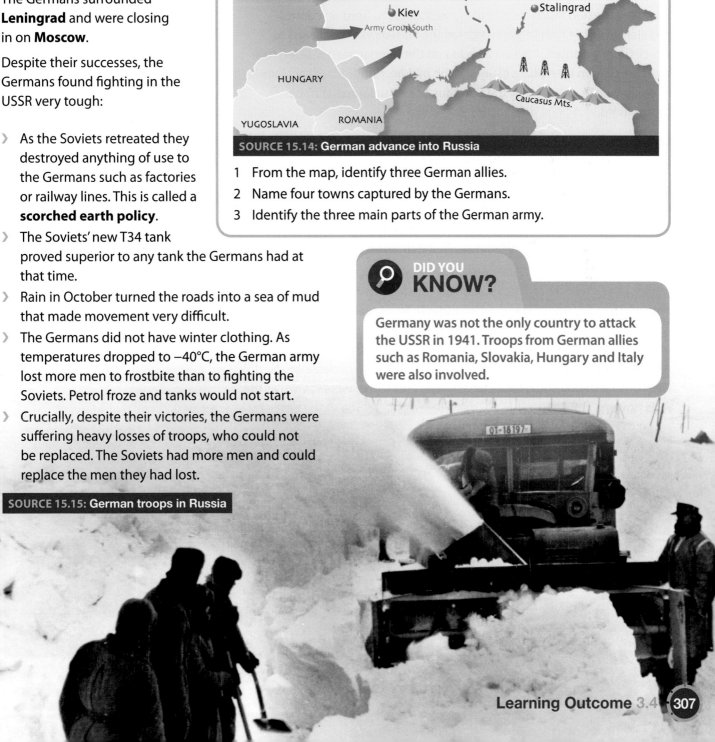

**Activity 6**

Examine this source and then answer the questions below.

Front line, 4 December 1941
German allies

SWEDEN
FINLAND
Helsinki
Stockholm
Leningrad
U S S R
Riga
Moscow
Army Group North
Smolensk
Minsk
Army Group Centre
Warsaw
Kiev
Stalingrad
Army Group South
HUNGARY
Caucasus Mts.
YUGOSLAVIA
ROMANIA

**SOURCE 15.14: German advance into Russia**

1 From the map, identify three German allies.
2 Name four towns captured by the Germans.
3 Identify the three main parts of the German army.

🔍 **DID YOU KNOW?**

Germany was not the only country to attack the USSR in 1941. Troops from German allies such as Romania, Slovakia, Hungary and Italy were also involved.

In December the Soviets launched a counter-attack. The Germans were forced to retreat and Moscow was saved.

## What was it like to live in Nazi-occupied Europe?

In the early years it looked as though the Germans were winning the war. In some countries in Western Europe (e.g. Belgium, Holland and Norway) there were small fascist parties and they welcomed the arrival of the Germans. People who supported the German occupation became known as **collaborators**.

Most people just wanted to get on with their daily lives. There was very little active opposition. As the war started to go badly for the Germans the number of **resistance** attacks began to increase, especially in France. The German response to these attacks was swift and brutal, including shooting hostages.

In Eastern Europe, the Germans viewed the civilians as inferior or subhuman. They were treated much more brutally. Resistance to German control had started in 1941 when Stalin ordered the formation of **partisans** to attack German targets. Partisan attacks and the German response led to a terrible situation for civilians caught in the middle. Hundreds of thousands of civilians were executed by the Germans and an unknown number by partisans.

## Why did war break out in Asia?

**Japan**, wanting to build an empire, had invaded China in 1937. Japan also wanted to take control of British, Dutch and French colonies in Asia. The USA put economic pressure on the Japanese to stop these actions. In response, on 7 December 1941, Japan launched a surprise attack on the main US Pacific base at **Pearl Harbor** in Hawaii. At the same time Japan attacked European colonies in Asia.

Japan's hopes that these attacks would lead to a quick victory were soon dashed. The USA, under President **Franklin D. Roosevelt**, entered the war against both Japan and Germany. Germany was now facing the might of the USA, the USSR and the British Empire, known as the **Allies**. The Allies, despite their differences, were united in the cause of defeating Nazi Germany. Germany and its allies (chiefly Italy and Japan) were known as the **Axis powers**.

### DID YOU KNOW?

The war on the Eastern Front was characterised by extreme brutality. For example, both sides treated prisoners very poorly. It can be difficult for historians to get an accurate figure of death tolls when they involve large figures. It is estimated that over 3 million or over 50 per cent of Soviet prisoners of war died in German captivity. These men died from executions, starvation and disease. There is no agreement on the numbers of Germans who died in Soviet captivity – figures between 365,000 and 1,000,000 are put forward. The Soviets did not release German prisoners until 1955 – ten years after the war ended.

**Front**
Battle line, where two opposing sides confront each other.

**Collaboration**
Helping the enemy that is occupying your country.

**Partisans**
Armed resistance group.

**SOURCE 15.16:** The main leaders during World War II (from left): Winston Churchill, Adolf Hitler, Benito Mussolini, Franklin D. Roosevelt, Joseph Stalin

# What were the main turning points of World War II?

In 1942 Germany still seemed to be winning the war. This was to change with two major defeats – one in **North Africa** and the other in the **USSR**. After that, the Allies enjoyed a number of important successes over the Germans. The Germans found themselves fighting on an increasing number of fronts against an enemy that had superior numbers of men and equipment.

## North Africa

In 1941 German troops called the **Afrika Corps** were sent to North Africa to help the Italians. The Italians had attacked British-controlled Egypt but had been defeated. By 1942 the German forces, led by **General Rommel**, had reached **El Alamein** in Egypt, where their advance was halted.

The British **Eighth Army**, under **Field Marshal Montgomery**, built up a two-to-one advantage in both tanks and men. They also had new American **Sherman tanks**, which were better than German tanks. In October Montgomery attacked the German troops with 200,000 men. The fighting was fierce, but after twelve days Rommel was defeated.

At the same time, US and British troops landed in **Algeria** and **Morocco**. The Germans were forced to retreat to **Tunisia**.

### Activity 7

Examine these sources and then answer the questions below.

**A** The whole horizon to the east spewed heavenwards in a fount of orange and blood-red flame, stabbing at the sky. The thunder of the barrage ... struck us, a tidal wave of sound; it hammered on our eardrums and whipped our shirts against our chests.

SOURCE 15.17: Australian Private James Crawford remembers the artillery barrage that began the Eighth Army's great assault

**B** Dead and mutilated bodies were to be seen wherever one looked, together with burnt-out guns, tanks and weapons of all descriptions.

SOURCE 15.18: An Australian soldier's recollection of the battle

**C** Smoke and dust covered the battlefield ... tanks engaged in single combat; in these few hours the battle of Alamein was decided.

SOURCE 15.19: Report from the German 90th Light Division

1  From source A, identify three pieces of evidence to show that the artillery barrage was very powerful.
2  How does source B reveal the horrors of war?
3  According to source C, why were the events described so important?

SOURCE 15.20: British troops and US tanks in Tunisia, 1942

## USSR

In the summer of 1942 the Germans launched a new offensive in the USSR. They advanced towards the oilfields in the south of the country. The key city in this region was **Stalingrad**. Hitler was determined to capture the city that bore the name of his enemy.

› The German **Sixth Army**, led by **General Paulus**, attacked the city. Stalin ordered that the city be defended at all costs. The Russians and Germans engaged in a bloody struggle for the city.

› Meanwhile the Soviet commander, **General Zhukov**, was secretly preparing a massive counter-attack. On 19 November 1942 the Soviets launched **Operation Uranus** and trapped the Sixth Army at Stalingrad.

› The Germans decided to supply the troops from the air but this failed.

› Conditions were horrible for the German troops as the temperature dropped to −30°C. Supplies, especially food, were very scarce.

› Disobeying Hitler, Paulus surrendered in February 1943, shattering the myth of the invincible German soldier.

› The Germans had lost an army of 300,000 men.

› The Soviet victory was the decisive turning point of the war and a massive confidence boost for the Allies.

A German offensive at **Kursk** in July 1943 was also halted by fierce Soviet resistance. The Soviets began to advance as their superior numbers of men and tanks began to tell. In 1944 they drove the Germans from the USSR and entered Poland.

## Italy

In May 1943 the war had ended in North Africa when German and Italian troops surrendered to the Allies. Allied troops then invaded Italy. Hitler's ally Mussolini was removed from power and Italy switched sides in the war. Hitler was forced to move troops to Italy to meet the Allied threat.

**DID YOU KNOW?**

One of the many errors Hitler made in the war was his refusal to allow surrounded German troops in Stalingrad to break out and retreat.

---

**Activity 8**

Examine the source and then answer the questions below.

SOURCE 15.21: German prisoners of war, Stalingrad, 1943

1 Describe the condition of the prisoners in the picture.

2 Why did the Soviets take photographs such as this, do you think?

---

**Activity 9**

Imagine that you are either a German or a Soviet soldier fighting on the Eastern Front. Describe your experiences.

---

**Activity 10**

Research online either the Battle of Kursk or the Soviet offensive of June 1944 codenamed Operation Bagration. Identify five facts that you found interesting.

---

**DID YOU KNOW?**

The Allies won the war at sea. German submarines called **U-boats** had posed a major threat to Allied shipping. By the summer of 1943 this danger was removed, partly through the breaking of the German codes.

## France

Stalin had long asked the Allies to land in France to relieve the pressure on the USSR. The plan for the invasion was developed in great secrecy. It was called **Operation Overlord**. The Allies decided to land at **Normandy**. A deception operation was carried out to persuade the Germans that the attack was going to happen near **Calais** – the closest port to Britain. It was very important for the success of the operation that the Allies kept the Germans guessing about their real intentions.

The invasion force, commanded by **General Eisenhower**, consisted of US, British and Canadian troops.

The largest armada in history was assembled for the invasion. It consisted of over 7,000 ships, including specially designed landing craft for the troops. **D-day**, the day of the invasion, was 6 June 1944. In total 156,000 soldiers were landed. They were protected by more than 10,000 planes.

Fighting in the Normandy countryside was difficult. The Germans resisted fiercely. They were helped by hedgerows and woods that gave them plenty of cover. By August, however, the main German army was destroyed at **Falaise**. Paris was then liberated and German troops were driven from France.

### Activity 11

Examine the map and then answer the questions below.

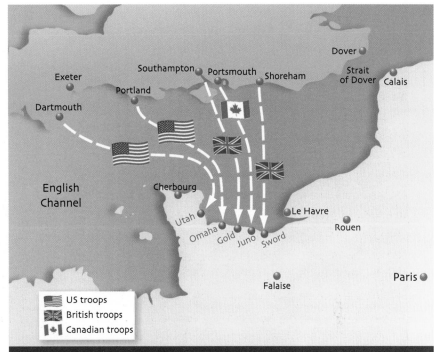

**SOURCE 15.22: Allied landings in Normandy**

1 Name three ports from which the Allied troops invaded Normandy.
2 Identify the five beaches where the Allied forces landed.
3 Looking at the map, why, do you think, did the Allies not land at Calais?

### DID YOU KNOW?

In US military planning, the day of attack is called D-day and the time H-hour. The original day of attack in Normandy was 5 June 1944, but it had to be called off because of bad weather.

### Activity 12

Examine the source and then answer the question below.

**SOURCE 15.23: Famous generals of World War II: General Eisenhower, Field Marshal Montgomery, General Rommel, General Zhukov**

1 In groups of four, research one of these generals and prepare a PowerPoint presentation to show your findings to the class.

**Activity 13**

Examine the source and then answer the question below.

SOURCE 15.24: **Dresden, 1945**

1 Describe the destruction shown in the photograph.

## The final defeat of Germany

Many Germans put their faith in new weapons such as the V2 rocket, but they made little impact.

> By 1945 Germany was in a hopeless position. Cities such as **Berlin, Hamburg** and **Dresden** had been destroyed in massive air raids involving 1,000 bombers. Over 500,000 civilians died in Allied bombings.

> German soldiers could not stop Soviet and Allied troops advancing towards Berlin from the East and the West.

> In March 1945 the Allies crossed the **River Rhine**. The following month the USSR launched a massive attack on Berlin. Millions of German refugees were also fleeing the advancing Red Army.

> On 30 April 1945, with the Soviets in the centre of Berlin, Hitler ended his life by suicide.

> His successor, **Admiral Donitz**, quickly surrendered to the Allies on 8 May 1945. This was celebrated as **VE Day** (Victory in Europe) throughout Europe.

**Refugees**
People forced to abandon their home to seek refuge elsewhere.

SOURCE 15.25: **VE Day, London**

**Learning Outcome** 3.4

# How did the Allies defeat Germany?

Historians put forward a number of reasons why the Allies defeated Germany. Here are some of the most important:

> The Germans had weak allies. The British Empire, USA and USSR were too powerful in comparison.

> American factories produced vast numbers of tanks, planes, trucks and ships for the Allies. Both the USA and USSR produced far more tanks and planes than Germany.

> The bombing of Germany was very important as it reduced the amount of military equipment the Germans could build. It also meant that the Luftwaffe was trying to stop the Allied bombers rather than helping German troops. This left the Allies with complete control of the air on both fronts.

> Hitler interfered with the decisions of his generals. For example, he refused to allow troops to retreat. As a result, hundreds of thousands of soldiers were captured or killed.

> The most important factor, however, was the Soviet Army. The Germans suffered much higher casualties on the Eastern Front than on the Western Front.

---

**Activity 14**

Read the information here and then answer the questions below.

**The July Plot**
Colonel Claus von Stauffenberg planted a bomb in Hitler's headquarters on 20 July 1944. It exploded but Hitler survived. Stauffenberg was later executed. Today he is a hero in Germany.

SOURCE 15.26: The July Plot, 1944

Research this event online to find out:
1   What was the aim of the plot?
2   What happened at Hitler's headquarters on 20 July 1944?
3   What happened to the men involved in the plot?

---

# How did the Allies defeat Japan?

After the attack on Pearl Harbor the Japanese were very successful. They conquered large parts of the French, Dutch and British Empires in Asia, including Malaysia and Indonesia. They also captured many islands in the Pacific.

The turning point of the war came at the **Battle of Midway** in June 1942. The US Navy sank four Japanese aircraft carriers. After this battle the USA adopted a policy of island-hopping. They bypassed the most heavily defended islands and attacked easier targets. The aim was to get close enough to bomb Japan.

When an island was attacked by the USA the Japanese soldiers did not surrender and inflicted a lot of casualties on the Americans. Nonetheless, by the summer of 1945, the USA was ready to invade Japan.

The US military feared that this invasion of Japan could result in the deaths of hundreds of thousands of US soldiers. They now had another option. In a top-secret project called **Operation Manhattan** scientists had developed an **atomic bomb**. US President **Harry Truman** decided that it should be used to force Japan to surrender.

In August 1945 atomic bombs were dropped on the Japanese cities of **Hiroshima** and **Nagasaki**. These bombs destroyed both cities. At Hiroshima, 90,000 people were killed instantly. The Japanese surrendered. World War II was finally over.

SOURCE 15.27: Hiroshima, 1945

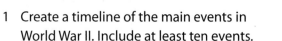

### Activity 15

1 Create a timeline of the main events in World War II. Include at least ten events.
2 Take part in a class debate on the motion: 'That the USA was right to drop atomic bombs on Hiroshima and Nagasaki.'

**DID YOU KNOW?**

The bomb dropped on Hiroshima was nicknamed Little Boy, and the Nagasaki bomb was called Fat Man.

### DO YOU UNDERSTAND THESE KEY TERMS?

| | | | |
|---|---|---|---|
| Allied powers | collaborator | Operation Sea Lion | Red Army |
| atomic bomb | D-day | Operation Uranus | scorched earth policy |
| Axis powers | Maginot Line | partisan | U-boat |
| Battle of Britain | Operation Barbarossa | phoney war | VE Day |
| Blitz | Operation Dynamo | propaganda | Vichy France |
| Blitzkrieg | Operation Manhattan | radar | |
| British Expeditionary Force | Operation Overlord | rationing | |

 PowerPoint summary

## SELF-ASSESSMENT – CAN YOU?

1 Describe what Blitzkrieg tactics involved.

2 Analyse the reasons for the defeat of France in 1940.

3 Appraise the role played by propaganda in World War II.

4 Explain why historians need to be cautious about propaganda.

5 Examine why the British won the Battle of Britain.

6 Debate the following statement, providing evidence to support your views: 'In 1941 the Germans won the battles but failed to achieve victory over the USSR.'

7 Consider the reasons why war broke out in Asia in 1941.

8 Comment on the importance of the Battle of Stalingrad.

9 Outline the main events in North Africa that led to the defeat of the Germans there in 1943.

10 Describe the main events of the Allied invasion of France in 1944.

11 Explain why the German position was hopeless by 1945.

12 Explore the reasons why the USA dropped atomic bombs on Japan.

# WHAT WERE THE CONSEQUENCES OF WORLD WAR II?

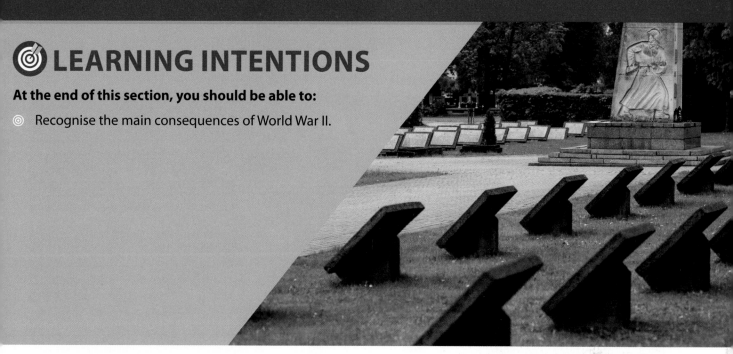

## 🎯 LEARNING INTENTIONS

**At the end of this section, you should be able to:**

◎ Recognise the main consequences of World War II.

## What were the consequences of World War II?

The most terrible war in history had a number of short-term and long-term consequences.

### Death toll

The first consequence was the terrible human tragedy. Estimates vary, but it is widely accepted by historians that up to 60 million people died as a result of the war. Most of those who died were civilians. They died as a result of being caught up in battles or bombings, or from disease or starvation.

Others were deliberately targeted in what became known as **crimes against humanity**. You will read in Section 16 that 6 million Jewish people were killed – victims of a terrifying Nazi policy called the **Final Solution**.

The USSR suffered the single highest death toll, estimated at about 26 million people. Today, because of this immense human sacrifice, the war is called the **Great Patriotic War** in Russia.

| Country | Deaths |
|---------|-----------|
| USSR | 26,000,000 |
| China | 20,000,000 |
| Germany | 7,000,000 |
| Poland | 6,000,000 |
| Japan | 3,000,000 |
| France | 600,000 |
| Italy | 500,000 |
| UK | 450,000 |
| USA | 420,000 |

**SOURCE 15.28: Deaths in World War II – selected countries**

### Activity 1

Research online and find out how World War II is remembered in Russia today.

### 🔍 DID YOU KNOW?

The USSR and China suffered many more deaths than the other main countries combined.

## Refugees

There were also millions of refugees who had been driven from their homes. For example, millions of Germans were expelled from Poland, Czechoslovakia and other countries in Eastern Europe.

---

### Activity 2

Examine this source and then answer the questions below.

SOURCE 15.29: German refugees, 1945

1  Describe the scene captured in this photograph.
2  Propose a title for this image.
3  Imagine you are one of these refugees. Write two diary entries. The first should be for the day before this photo was taken, as you prepared to leave your home. The second should describe how you feel waiting in this queue to travel to a new life in Germany or elsewhere.

---

## War crimes

The horrors of the Nazi regime were exposed by defeat in the war. Both the advancing Soviets and the Western Allies discovered concentration camps. After the war, leading Nazis were tried at Nuremberg for the crimes Germany had committed in the course of the war.

## Territorial changes

Germany lost land to Poland and the USSR. The remainder of the country was divided into four zones: one each for the USSR, UK, USA and France. The Allies were determined that Germany would never be a threat to the peace of Europe again. We will read more about the consequences of these actions in Sections 17 and 18.

**DID YOU KNOW?**

If you look at a map of Eastern Europe you will see a small part of Russia bordering northern Poland that is separated from the rest of the country. This part of German East Prussia became Russian after World War II.

SOURCE 15.30: Indians celebrate in Delhi during the declaration of Independence Day in India, 15 August 1947

## Eastern Bloc

The countries of Eastern Europe were left under Soviet domination. Communist governments were put in place that answered to Moscow. These countries were known collectively as the **Eastern Bloc**. The people of Eastern Europe were not to regain their freedom until 1989.

## Cold War

The USA and USSR were the two most powerful countries in the world. They were known as **superpowers** and they did not trust each other. A period of tension developed called the **Cold War** (see Section 17).

## Decolonisation

Britain and France had been weakened by the war and could not hold on to their large empires in Africa and Asia. Independence movements in British and French colonies became difficult to resist. In 1947 Britain granted its most important colony, India, independence. The process of colonies becoming independent states is known as **decolonisation**.

**Bloc**
Group of countries with a common political aim.

## Cooperation

Many people in Europe were determined to work together to prevent the death and destruction of another war. This feeling was very strong in the countries of the old enemies France and Germany. It led to closer European cooperation and the foundation of the **EEC (European Economic Community)** (see Section 18).

The **United Nations (UN)** was set up by fifty-one countries in 1945. Its purpose is to maintain international peace and security, to develop friendly relations among nations, to encourage cooperation to solve international problems and to promote human rights. In 2017 it had 193 member states.

---

**Activity 3**

Examine the sources and then answer the questions below.

SOURCE 15.31: The UN General Assembly

SOURCE 15.32: The UN Security Council

In pairs, find out five facts about:

1   The General Assembly of the UN
2   The Security Council of the UN.

---

**DO YOU UNDERSTAND THESE KEY TERMS?**

| | |
|---|---|
| Cold War | superpower |
| decolonisation | United Nations |
| Eastern Bloc | |

PowerPoint summary

## SELF-ASSESSMENT – CAN YOU?

1  Estimate approximately how many people died as a result of World War II.

2  Identify the main causes of death during World War II.

3  Describe four other major consequences of World War II in Europe.

4  Evaluate the impact World War II had on international relations between countries.

# HOW DID WORLD WAR II AFFECT IRISH PEOPLE?

## LEARNING INTENTIONS

**At the end of this section, you should be able to:**

◎ Explain why Ireland was neutral in World War II

◎ Describe life in Ireland during the Emergency

◎ Discuss Ireland's international relationships during the Emergency

◎ Outline Northern Ireland's role in World War II

◎ Describe the impact of World War II on Ireland, north and south.

## What was the Emergency?

The period of World War II (1939–45) was known as **the Emergency** in Ireland (Éire).

### Neutrality

When World War II began on 3 September 1939, Ireland stayed neutral. Taoiseach **Éamon de Valera** decided on **neutrality** because:

❯ Irish people did not want to fight on the side of Britain due to partition

❯ Ireland wanted to emphasise its independence from Britain

❯ Being involved in the war would result in many lives being lost and property destroyed.

An Emergency Powers Act was passed to make sure that Ireland remained neutral.

**Éire**
The Free State was renamed Éire in the 1937 Constitution.

**Neutrality**
Not taking a side in a war.

---

### Activity 1

Examine this source and then answer the question below.

SOURCE 15.33: Irish coastline during World War II

1  In pairs, discuss why the sign 'EIRE' was displayed on the Irish coastline.

---

### DID YOU KNOW?

Newspapers and radio broadcasts were censored during the Emergency so as not to favour either side. Even weather forecasts were stopped as the information might help either side in planning a bombing raid. As a result, Irish people were often unaware of what was really going on in the war.

SOURCE 15.34: Irish soldiers, 1940

## What impact did the Emergency have on daily life?

### Defence

As there was a strong possibility that Ireland would be invaded by either Germany or the Allies, the government increased the size of the Irish Army from 7,000 to 37,000 men.

A further 250,000 men joined the part-time **Local Defence Force**. Its aim was to train young people to fight if Ireland was invaded. They were poorly armed.

### Food supply

**Seán Lemass** became Minister for Supplies. There was a scarcity of imported goods such as tea because Britain restricted the amount sent to Ireland. Lemass set up **Irish Shipping**, whose ships brought essential goods from abroad. Two ships were sunk by German **U-boats** (submarines) during the war.

Rationing was introduced so that everyone got a fair share. People were given **ration books** for tea, sugar and chocolate. People found it hard to live on these rations because the amounts were so small. People got approximately one teabag per week.

### Activity 2

Examine this source and then answer the questions below.

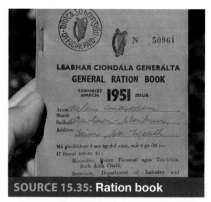

SOURCE 15.35: Ration book

1  What products were rationed?

2  Why, do you think, was rationing necessary?

## Farming

The **Compulsory Tillage Scheme** forced farmers to grow more wheat for flour. This was to make sure that everyone had enough bread. As very little fertiliser was imported after 1940, the fertility of the soil was affected and crop yields reduced.

The British depended on Ireland for imported food supplies as the German U-boats sank a lot of ships bringing food to Britain. However, Ireland received less for food exports during the war than it had in 1939.

## Fuel shortages

Gas was used for cooking in Dublin. It could be used for only a few hours each day. **Glimmer men** were appointed to make sure that people used only the amount of gas and electricity that was allowed.

Petrol was very scarce and was made available only to doctors and priests. Other people had to travel by bicycles or donkey and cart.

Trains were powered by turf as Britain needed its coal for the war effort. Trains took much longer to make a journey. It took 12 hours to travel from Dublin to Cork (about four times slower than today).

Townspeople had to cut turf for themselves in the bogs in summer. This provided them with heat in winter.

SOURCE 15.36: Queuing to buy bread

### Activity 3

Examine this source and then answer the questions below.

SOURCE 15.37: 'Glory be! The Glimmer Man!' Cartoon from *Dublin Opinion*, June 1944

1 Who were the glimmer men?
2 Why, in your opinion, is the glimmer man hiding in the oven?

SOURCE 15.38: Cut turf

## Unemployment

Due to a lack of raw materials and energy, some factories had to close. Many of those who lost their jobs went to Britain to work or joined the British Army.

## What were the threats to Irish neutrality?

The main threat to neutrality came from the IRA, which started a bombing campaign in Britain in 1939.

Several German spies came to Ireland after the IRA made contact with Germany. They were all arrested. **Hermann Görtz** arrived in Ireland in 1940 but avoided arrest for nineteen months. He was to act as a German liaison officer with the IRA. However, as he felt that he could not trust the IRA, nothing was achieved.

De Valera imprisoned over 500 IRA members in the Curragh camp. He was afraid that the British would use IRA activities as an excuse to invade Ireland.

SOURCE 15.39: Hermann Görtz

### Activity 4

Examine the source and then answer the questions below.

1 In pairs, research the role of Hermann Görtz in Ireland.
2 Write a report on your findings.

### German bombing

Despite all the rationing and hardship, neutrality remained popular among the people. It protected them from the suffering that war brought to people in other countries.

Only one German bomb did serious damage. On 30 May 1941 a bomb was dropped on the North Strand in Dublin. Twenty-seven people were killed and 300 houses were damaged. This bomb was almost certainly dropped by mistake.

### Activity 5

Examine these sources and then answer the question below.

SOURCE 15.40: North Strand, Dublin, 1941

Air raid shelters

SOURCE 15.41: Air raid shelters in O'Connell Street, Dublin

1 Which event is reflected in photograph A?
2 Describe the damage caused by the bombing.
3 What is an air raid shelter?
4 Is the air raid shelter in B located in a good position? Give reasons for your answer.

# What were relations with the Allies like?

## USA

When the USA entered the war in 1941 it wanted Ireland to join the Allies. American troops were being stationed in Northern Ireland and the USA was afraid that they would be observed by German spies from south of the border. De Valera refused to abandon neutrality.

## Britain

Britain had kept control of the ports of Lough Swilly, Berehaven and Cobh in the Anglo-Irish Treaty of 1921. However, under the Anglo-Irish Trade Agreement 1938, Ireland had got those ports back. British Prime Minister Winston Churchill wanted to use these former treaty ports as naval bases during the war in order to protect **convoys** bringing vital supplies to Britain. De Valera refused.

**Convoy**
Group of cargo ships travelling together with military protection against the enemy.

Churchill tried to persuade Ireland to enter the war on the side of the Allies. De Valera refused, despite being offered the reunification of Ireland. He felt that Churchill would not be able to deliver the six counties due to unionist opposition.

**Activity 6**

Examine this source and then answer the questions below.

> Now is your chance. Now or never. 'A Nation once again'. Am very ready to meet you at any time.

SOURCE 15.42: Secret telegram from Churchill to de Valera, December 1941

1  Explain what this telegram refers to.
2  Why, do you think, would Churchill want to keep the telegram secret?

## Irish neutrality

One of the main reasons the Allies did not invade Ireland was that Irish neutrality secretly favoured the Allies. For example:

> Allied pilots who crashed in Ireland were sent back across the border to Northern Ireland, whereas German pilots were imprisoned in the Curragh camp.
> Weather reports were secretly passed on to the Allies.
> 50,000 Irish men joined the British Army.
> When Belfast was bombed, fire brigades were sent across the border.

SOURCE 15.43: Irish recruits to the British Army, 1941

Even the British Ambassador was unaware of the pro-Allied stance of the Irish government. This was to ensure that there was no threat to Irish neutrality.

**DID YOU KNOW?**

De Valera maintained his policy of neutrality to the very end. When President Roosevelt died, he went to the US embassy to express his condolences. When Hitler died, he went to the German embassy to do the same. This annoyed the Allies.

**Learning Outcome 2.8** 323

### Activity 7

Examine these sources and then answer the questions below.

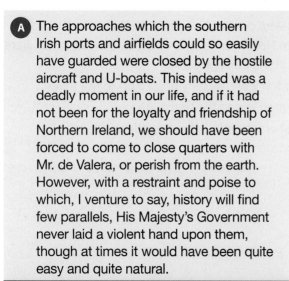

**A** The approaches which the southern Irish ports and airfields could so easily have guarded were closed by the hostile aircraft and U-boats. This indeed was a deadly moment in our life, and if it had not been for the loyalty and friendship of Northern Ireland, we should have been forced to come to close quarters with Mr. de Valera, or perish from the earth. However, with a restraint and poise to which, I venture to say, history will find few parallels, His Majesty's Government never laid a violent hand upon them, though at times it would have been quite easy and quite natural.

SOURCE 15.44: **Extract from a speech Churchill made after the war**

**B** Mr. Churchill is proud of Britain's stand alone, after France had fallen and before America entered the war. Could he not find in his heart the generosity to acknowledge that there is a small nation that stood alone not for one year or two, but for several hundred years against aggression; that endured spoliations, famine, massacres, in endless succession; that was clubbed many times into insensibility, but each time on returning to consciousness took up the fight anew; a small nation that could never be got to accept defeat and has never surrendered her soul?

SOURCE 15.45: **Extract from de Valera's reply to Churchill's speech**

**Spoliations**
Acts of plundering or theft.

1   What are the main points that Churchill is making?

2   How useful is document A?

3   How does de Valera answer Churchill's accusations?

4   How useful is document B?

5   How, do you think, did the Irish people react to de Valera's speech?

## What was the impact of World War II on Ireland?

### Impact on Éire

> Ireland avoided the destruction and loss of life that happened in the rest of Europe.

> It took many years for the Irish economy to recover as it suffered greatly during the war.

### Impact on Northern Ireland

> The war created a boom for Northern Ireland's main industries. **Harland and Wolff** produced 140 warships and 123 merchant ships. **Shorts** built 1,200 bomber aeroplanes. Belfast's textile mills supplied **linen** to make uniforms and parachutes.

> There was full employment, and the demand for workers led to increased wages.

> Food production increased by 300 per cent to meet the demand for food in Britain. Potatoes and oats were the most important crops. Cattle numbers increased by 150,000.

> Roads and ports were improved to cater for the British and US troops stationed in Northern Ireland. The Americans used Northern Ireland as a training ground for the D-day landings. The troops further boosted the Northern Irish economy.

SOURCE 15.46: **US troops in Northern Ireland**

⟩ After Germany occupied France in 1940, all ships heading to Britain went via Northern Ireland. Derry was used as a base by the Royal Navy and US Navy to patrol the Atlantic and protect convoys from attack by U-boats. This meant that vital supplies from America reached Britain. It also raised the strategic importance of Northern Ireland during the war.

---

### Activity 8

Examine this source and then answer the questions below.

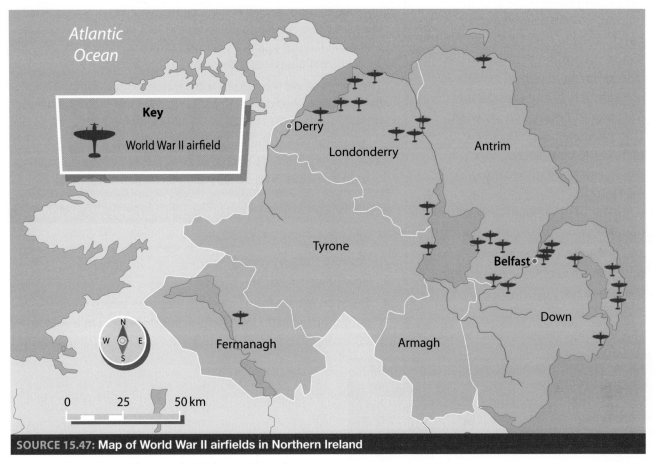

SOURCE 15.47: Map of World War II airfields in Northern Ireland

1  Where are most of the airfields located?
2  In pairs, discuss the possible reasons why airfields were located at these sites.

---

⟩ In 1939 most people in Northern Ireland felt that the war would not touch them. However, they were soon within the range of German bombers. In April and May 1941 the Luftwaffe bombed Belfast, killing 1,100 people and destroying 56,000 homes. In a gesture of goodwill, de Valera sent fire brigades from Dublin.

⟩ The Stormont government had done very little to protect Belfast from being bombed. The Prime Minister, **John Andrews**, was blamed for the poor defences. He resigned and was replaced by **Sir Basil Brooke** (Lord Brookeborough).

### Activity 9

Examine this source and then answer the question below.

SOURCE 15.48: Bombing of Belfast, 1941

1  Imagine you are the photographer who took this shot. Write a diary entry describing what you saw and how you felt.

## Impact on north–south relations

> North–south divisions widened as a result of the southern policy of neutrality.

> As part of the UK, Northern Ireland played an active part in the war. Unionists saw it as an opportunity to show their loyalty to and strengthen ties with Britain. Due to Northern Ireland's vital contribution, British support for the unionist population increased. This made the possibility of reunification less likely.

> The war brought prosperity to the Northern Ireland economy. Industrial workers and farmers benefited from improved wages and prices. This widened the north–south economic gap during the war years.

### Activity 10

Examine this source and then answer the questions below.

> … the constable looked up towards the sky. 'What's that, lad?' he asked as he tugged my sleeve and pointed upwards. I did not take time to look … I knew what it was … I shouted 'Down' and at the same time pushed him to the ground … Time seemed to stop … as the mine came swishing down … What seemed like a thousand years was in fact only a few seconds. The mine did not reach the ground but struck the spire of Trinity Street church and exploded immediately.
>
> The whole world seemed to rock, slates, bricks, earth and flying glass rained down on us. I dug my face into my arms for protection and lay for what seemed like an eternity.
>
> … by some miracle, we were still alive. We were caught in a blast of a parachute mine that had reduced a granite-built church to rubble. And devastated the surrounding area.

SOURCE 15.49: Twenty-year-old James Doherty, an air-raid warden in Belfast, 1941 from *Post 381: Memoirs of a Belfast Air Raid Warden*

1 What did the constable see?
2 How did Doherty react?
3 How powerful was the bomb?
4 This is an extract from Doherty's memoirs, which were published in 1989. How useful is this document as a source?

### DO YOU UNDERSTAND THESE KEY TERMS?

| | |
|---|---|
| Compulsory Tillage Scheme | glimmer men |
| convoy | Irish Shipping |
| the Emergency | neutrality |

 Chapter summary   Weblinks   PowerPoint summary

## SELF-ASSESSMENT – CAN YOU?

1 Explain why Ireland was neutral in World War II.

2 Outline how the war affected agriculture and industry in Ireland.

3 Explain why the Allies did not invade Ireland during the Emergency.

4 Outline the impact of World War II on Ireland.

5 Describe how the war affected agriculture and industry in Northern Ireland.

6 Describe how Northern Ireland was affected by German bombing.

7 Explain why Northern Ireland was important to the Allies.

8 Outline the impact of World War II on Northern Ireland.

9 Explain how World War II affected north–south relations.

# 16 GENOCIDE IN THE TWENTIETH CENTURY

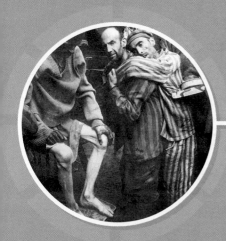

## The causes, course and consequences of the Holocaust

328

## What were the other major genocides of the twentieth century?

335

327

# THE CAUSES, COURSE AND CONSEQUENCES OF THE HOLOCAUST

## ⊙ LEARNING INTENTIONS

**At the end of this section, you should be able to:**

◎ Explain what the Holocaust was

◎ Describe how the Nazis carried out the Final Solution

◎ Discuss what happened at Auschwitz

◎ Outline the consequences of the Holocaust.

## What was the Holocaust?

**Genocide** is the mass killing or extermination of a race of people or a religious group. In the twentieth century the most famous example was the evil systematic destruction of the Jewish people in Europe, called the **Holocaust**.

> **Genocide**
> This word combines a Greek word *genos* meaning race and a Latin word *cide* meaning killing.

> **Holocaust**
> This word is of Greek origin and means burnt offering. Jews refer to the Holocaust as the **Shoah** or the calamity.

The Holocaust was guided by Nazi racial policies that regarded the Jews as subhuman and the enemy of the master race (see Section 14). The organisation responsible for the Holocaust was the **SS**, led by **Heinrich Himmler**. It ran the camps and provided the guards. It also controlled the police and the secret police or **Gestapo**, who carried out Nazi policies against the Jewish people.

SOURCE 16.1: Heinrich Himmler

## What were the ghettos?

When World War II began the Nazis spread their persecution of Jews to Poland.

> Thousands of Polish Jews were shot in mass executions.

> The rest were required to live in Jewish **ghettos** where they could be easily controlled.

> The **Decree of Identification** forced every Jew to wear a yellow Star of David.

> The most famous ghetto was the **Warsaw Ghetto**, which contained over 400,000 Jews from Warsaw and surrounding areas.

> A wall was built separating the ghetto from the rest of the city.

> Conditions there were very poor as 30 per cent of Warsaw's population was crammed into 3 per cent of the city's area. Food rations were very low and many residents slowly starved to death.

> The Nazis created ghettos elsewhere in Poland, most notably Lodz and Krakow, and later in other European cities.

### Activity 1

Examine this source and, in pairs, discuss the questions below.

SOURCE 16.2: Warsaw Ghetto, 1940

1 What was the Warsaw Ghetto?

2 Why does the old man have a star on his overcoat?

3 In pairs, take on the roles of the old man and a newspaper reporter from Ireland. The reporter should interview the man to find out about his situation.

## What was the Final Solution?

During the invasion of the USSR special SS troops called *Einsatzgruppen* rounded up and shot hundreds of thousands of Jews. It is estimated that 1.4 million had been killed by the start of 1942, mainly in the USSR.

### Activity 2

Examine the source and then answer the questions below.

SOURCE 16.3: Babi Yar massacre, Ukraine, 1941

1 Describe what is happening in the picture.

2 Find out more about the Babi Yar massacre and show your findings to the class in a PowerPoint presentation.

Despite the widespread massacres there were still large Jewish populations in the conquered territories, especially in Poland and the USSR. To address this, Hitler decided to kill the Jewish population of Europe. It was called 'the final solution of the Jewish question'. Nazi officials, led by **Reinhard Heydrich**, planned the details in January 1942 at the secret **Wannsee Conference** held near Berlin. They decided that approximately 11 million Jews would eventually be subjected to the **Final Solution**. The Nuremberg Laws (see Section 14) passed in 1935 decided who was a Jew.

Himmler was worried about the effect mass shootings were having on his men. It was decided that Jews should instead be killed in factory-like **extermination camps** specially designed for this purpose. The concentration camps developed before the war were used to terrorise opponents of the Nazi regime. The new extermination camps were designed to kill.

> Jews were placed in easily controlled ghettos.

> They were then moved from the ghettos by train to special extermination camps. For example, between July and September 1942 over 250,000 Jews were moved from the Warsaw Ghetto to **Treblinka**.

This camp was situated eighty miles northeast of Warsaw. The victims were moved by special trains.

> On arrival, the old and the young were gassed in fake shower units or gas chambers using Zyklon B gas or carbon monoxide from truck exhausts. At Treblinka an exhaust from a captured Soviet tank was used. Their bodies were then burned.

> The able-bodied were worked until they were murdered or died of disease. Some prisoners were also subjected to cruel medical experiments.

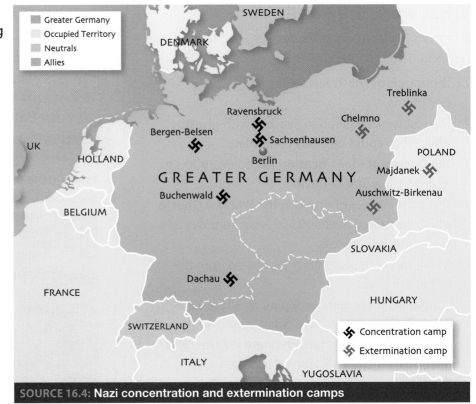

SOURCE 16.4: **Nazi concentration and extermination camps**

## Why is Auschwitz such an infamous place?

In Poland the Nazis established their largest and most infamous extermination camp at **Auschwitz** near Krakow.

> Originally a concentration camp for Polish political prisoners, Auschwitz was greatly expanded in 1941 with the addition of a much larger camp at nearby Birkenau called Auschwitz II.

> Between 1940 and 1945 **more than one million people were killed there** – the vast majority were Jews, but Poles, Roma and Russian prisoners of war were also killed.

> More people died in Auschwitz than the combined UK and US military losses during the war.

**Activity 3**

Examine the source and then answer the questions below.

SOURCE 16.5: **Auschwitz prisoners**

1  Describe the prisoners' clothes.
2  How would you describe the expressions on their faces?

> In the spring of 1943 four **gas chambers** and **crematorium complexes** were constructed. Each crematorium had forty-six ovens to burn bodies. There were electric lifts to carry bodies up to the crematoria.

> Each crematorium could handle 2,000 victims daily. Gold teeth and rings were melted down and the gold was sent back to Germany.

> Guards inspected new arrivals at the camp to determine whether or not they were fit for **forced labour**. Those who survived the initial selection were put to work in the arms factories, coal mines, farms and chemicals plant that surrounded Auschwitz.

> Most arrivals were declared unfit for work and were sent directly to the gas chambers where Zyklon B was used to kill them. Between May and July 1944 about 440,000 Hungarian Jews were deported to Auschwitz; 320,000 were gassed and the survivors were used as forced labour in the camp or at other camps in Germany or Austria.

### DID YOU KNOW?

**Zyklon B** gas was originally developed as a pesticide and insecticide to kill weeds and insects. It was first used at Auschwitz in 1941.

> SS doctors under the infamous **Josef Mengele** conducted cruel medical experiments on prisoners, especially on twins.

> When the Soviet army reached Auschwitz in January 1945 it found only 7,000 inmates. The rest had been evacuated from the camp. The march from Auschwitz in the middle of winter saw thousands die from cold or at the hands of their SS guards.

**Forced labour**
Slave labour.

SOURCE 16.6: Liberation of Auschwitz, 1945

One of the many terrible facts about the Holocaust was the **collaboration** of others in occupied Europe with the Nazi policy of extermination of the Jewish people. **Anti-Semitism** was strong in Eastern Europe, and in many instances local people helped the Germans to round up and execute Jewish people. In Western Europe local police often assisted the Germans to arrest Jews for deportation. They may or may not have known the ultimate fate of the people they arrested, but many were motivated by a hatred of the Jewish people.

---

 **Activity 4**

Examine this source and then answer the questions below.

> When we got to Auschwitz, the train stopped and they opened up the cars. Everybody had to get out. Right away they separated the women and the children to one side and the men had to go to the other side. Then we saw some men trying to whisper to us who were working around the train with striped uniforms on and their hair shaved off. They were saying, *Walk!* We couldn't figure out what that meant, but we soon found out. Anyone who was tired or felt that he couldn't walk was to go to the other side and supposedly there would be trucks that would pick them up and bring them to the camp. The people that were able to walk were to march. We got the message and we lined up to march to the camp. The other people that could not walk, or didn't want to, we never saw again. They went straight to the gas chamber.
>
> In Auschwitz they had brick barracks. Two floors, a ground floor that held about four hundred people and six hundred people upstairs. Then came the barbers and they shaved our hair off. Then they put numbers on our arm – I had number 72552. They took everything away from us. We got these pyjama-like uniforms and wooden shoes like those Dutch shoes, very uncomfortable to work with. And then we got a big speech from a man who was in charge of the block. He said, *You are going to work here. This is a work camp. There is no escape from here. The only way you can get out of here is through the chimney.*

**SOURCE 16.7: Extracts from an account by Armin Hertz, who was sent to Auschwitz in 1942**

1   According to Hertz, what was done 'Right away'?

2   Why did the men working near the train tell the new arrivals to walk?

3   What can you infer from this account about the conditions in the barracks?

4   Is this a useful source in helping you to understand what life was like in Auschwitz? Give two pieces of evidence to justify your answer.

---

## Who was Anne Frank?

The diary of a young girl, **Anne Frank**, brought home the reality of the Holocaust to millions.

> Anne was born in Germany in 1929. Her family moved to Amsterdam in 1933 to escape Nazi Germany. When Germany invaded the Netherlands in 1940, Jews lived in fear.

> The Frank family went into hiding after the Nazis began to round up Jewish people in 1942. They hid in a secret room in a house. They had to keep very quiet in case they were discovered. During this time Anne wrote a diary.

> The Franks and others stayed in this room for two years until their hiding place was raided and they were arrested.

> Anne was sent to Auschwitz and later transferred to Bergen-Belsen concentration camp, where she died of typhus in the spring of 1945.

> Anne's diary survived the war and was published in 1947. It became a bestseller and has been translated into seventy languages.

SOURCE 16.8: **Anne Frank**

# What were the consequences of the Holocaust?

## Death toll

It is estimated that up to 6 million Jews perished during the Holocaust. Jews from all over Nazi-occupied Europe were sent to the extermination camps. Centuries-old Jewish communities in Eastern Europe were wiped out by the Holocaust. It is estimated that two-thirds of Europe's pre-war Jewish population was killed, with 94 per cent of Lithuania's and 88 per cent of Poland's Jews perishing in the Holocaust.

### Activity 5

Examine this source and then answer the question below.

| Country | Jews murdered |
|---------|---------------|
| Poland | 2,900,000 |
| Ukraine | 900,000 |
| Hungary | 450,000 |
| Romania | 270,000 |
| Belarus | 245,000 |
| Lithuania | 220,000 |
| Holland | 106,000 |
| Russia | 100,000 |
| France | 90,000 |

SOURCE 16.9: Holocaust deaths – selected countries

1   Draw a bar chart showing the information in the table.

SOURCE 16.10: Symbolic graveyard built in the 1960s at the site of the Treblinka camp

## Prosecutions

After the war, Nazi leaders were prosecuted for war crimes at Nuremberg. A number were hanged. Further trials were held of SS commandants and others involved in the Holocaust. The commandant of Auschwitz, **Rudolf Hoess**, was executed at the site of his crimes in 1947. One of the main officials responsible for carrying out the Final Solution, **Adolf Eichmann**, fled to Argentina. In 1960 he was kidnapped by Israeli agents and taken to Israel. He was executed for his crimes in 1962.

SOURCE 16.11: Nuremberg trial, 1946

## Israel

Another important consequence of the Holocaust was increased sympathy and support for the creation of a homeland for the Jewish people in the 'Land of Israel'. Many Jewish refugees arrived there after the war. In 1948 the state of **Israel** was officially created. Today over 40 per cent of the world's Jewish population lives there.

 **DID YOU KNOW?**

Large numbers of Jewish refugees also went to the USA, Canada and parts of Western Europe.

---

**KS**    Activity 6

Examine this source and then answer the questions below.

1 The Yad Vashem Museum commemorates the victims of the Holocaust. Why would Israel have such a museum, do you think?

2 What impact, do you think, do these photographs have on visitors to the museum?

3 Research online to find out five other ways in which the Holocaust is commemorated.

4 Do you think it is important to commemorate the Holocaust? Explore this question in groups of four. Decide on your answer and at least four reasons to support it. Nominate a spokesperson to report your conclusions to the rest of the class.

SOURCE 16.12: **Jews murdered in the Holocaust, Yad Vashem Museum, Israel**

**Commemorate**
Remember a historically significant event or person in a public way.

---

### DO YOU UNDERSTAND THESE KEY TERMS?

| | |
|---|---|
| Anti-Semitism | forced labour |
| Decree of Identification | genocide |
| *Einsatzgruppen* | ghetto |
| extermination camp | Holocaust |
| Final Solution | Zyklon B |

 PowerPoint summary

## SELF-ASSESSMENT – CAN YOU?

1 Describe what life was like in the Warsaw Ghetto.

2 Examine the role of *Einsatzgruppen* in the USSR.

3 Demonstrate the significance of the Wannsee Conference.

4 Explain the term 'the Final Solution'.

5 Outline the process by which the Final Solution was implemented.

6 Examine the role that the Auschwitz camp had in the Holocaust.

7 Discuss the main consequences of the Holocaust.

# WHAT WERE THE OTHER MAJOR GENOCIDES OF THE TWENTIETH CENTURY?

## ⊚ LEARNING INTENTIONS

**At the end of this section, you should be able to:**

◎ Discover more about genocide in the twentieth century

◎ Understand whether the people who carried out these actions were punished for their crimes.

The Holocaust is the most tragic example of a genocide carried out in the twentieth century. Unfortunately, it is not the only one. In this section we will examine some of the most infamous.

## What was the Armenian Genocide?

In World War I the Ottoman Empire (modern-day Turkey) was allied with Germany and Austria against Britain, France and Russia. Because it bordered Russia there was a lot of fighting between the two countries. The Ottoman government was deeply suspicious of the loyalty of its Christian Armenian population. It was afraid that the Armenians would support a Russian invasion.

> In 1915 the government decided to act against its Armenian population, which numbered about 2 million people. There were massacres, destruction of villages and forced conversions of children to Islam.

> The land and property of Armenians was confiscated without compensation.

> Armenian civilians were told they were being deported to other parts of the empire. They were then forced to march hundreds of miles through desert.

> On the march they suffered extreme brutality at the hands of the soldiers escorting them. Hundreds of thousands died by execution, disease, famine and exhaustion. Historians call these events '**death marches**'.

> The survivors of the marches were held in concentration camps where the survival rate was very low.

> This terrible treatment of the Armenians continued throughout the war and until 1922.

SOURCE 16.13: **Armenians killed during the Armenian genocide of 1915**

Some of the men responsible fled to Germany after World War I. There were a few trials but no one was punished. Today, most historians call this event a **genocide** – a premeditated and systematic campaign to exterminate an entire people.

However, nobody is sure how many people died in the genocide. Some historians think it is about 1.5 million people, although this is disputed by others. They say the figure is far lower.

To this day, Turkey denies that a genocide took place at all and it is illegal to call the events a genocide in Turkey.

SOURCE 16.14: **Remembrance of the Armenian genocide of 1915**

---

**Activity 1**

Examine this source and then answer the questions below.

> Rape and beating were commonplace. Those who were not killed at once were driven through mountains and deserts without food, drink or shelter. Hundreds of thousands of Armenians eventually succumbed or were killed.

**SOURCE 16.15:** Historian David Fromkin writes about the Armenian genocide, *A Peace to End All Peace* (1989)

1   From the above account, describe the brutal treatment the Armenians suffered.

2   Find out how Armenia commemorates this event today.

---

## What was the Holodomor?

In 1932 the Soviet leader Joseph Stalin decided to deliberately start a famine in the Ukraine, which was part of the USSR. There were two main reasons for this decision:

1   He wanted to crush opposition to his policy of joining privately owned farms together to form large state-owned farms called collectives.

2   He planned to crush Ukrainian nationalism – the desire of Ukrainians to have an independent state.

Between 1932 and 1933 grain was seized and farmers and their families were left to starve. Troops and police turned the countryside into a vast prison.

Today the event is commemorated in Ukraine as the **Holodomor**. This word means 'to kill by starvation'. It is also called the **Ukrainian Terror-Famine**.

**SOURCE 16.16:** *Daily Express*, 6 August 1934

**SOURCE 16.17: A collective farm on the steppes of the Ukraine, USSR**

As with the Armenian genocide, historians disagree about the number of people who died. This is made more difficult by the absence of sources. The Soviet government denied that there was a famine and kept few records.

Nikita Khrushchev, who was a senior government official at the time, wrote: 'I can't give an exact figure because no one was keeping count. All we knew was that people were dying in enormous numbers.'

Figures for the death toll range between 2.5 million and 10 million.

Nobody was ever tried for these crimes.

SOURCE 16.18: Women walk past people dying of starvation in Ukraine in the early 1930s

---

### Activity 2

Examine this source and then answer the questions below.

> On one side, millions of starving peasants, their bodies often swollen from lack of food; on the other, soldiers, members of the police carrying out the instructions of the dictatorship of the proletariat [government of the USSR]. They had gone over the country like a swarm of locusts and taken away everything edible; they had shot or exiled thousands of peasants, sometimes whole villages; they had reduced some of the most fertile land in the world to a melancholy [sad] desert.

SOURCE 16.19: Malcolm Muggeridge, British foreign correspondent, 'War on the Peasants', *Fortnightly Review*, 1 May 1933

1   What was the condition of the peasants?
2   Describe the activities of the soldiers and secret police.
3   Explain how the actions of the soldiers and police had affected the countryside.
4   Describe your reaction on reading this source.

---

## What happened in Cambodia between 1975 and 1979?

In 1975 Pol Pot and his communist movement the Khmer Rouge came to power in Cambodia.

> Pol Pot wanted to create a classless society and believed that Cambodia should become a country of farmers.

> He targeted the educated, the religious, non-Cambodians and residents of cities, who, he believed, opposed his policies. The capital, Phnom Penh, was emptied of its residents.

> These people were forced to work on the land as part of a 're-education process'. They worked in the most brutal conditions.

> An estimated 1.5 to 2 million Cambodians died from starvation, execution, disease or overwork. Their bodies were buried in mass graves that became known as the **killing fields**.

SOURCE 16.20: Pol Pot

In 1979 Pol Pot's government was overthrown after a Vietnamese invasion. Pol Pot and the Khmer Rouge fled to a remote jungle area, where he died in 1998. He was never punished for the crimes he committed against the Cambodian people.

# What was the Rwandan genocide?

Rwanda is a small country in East Africa. Its population comprised two main peoples: the **Hutu** (the majority) and the **Tutsi** (the minority).

> In 1990 civil war broke out between the two groups. In 1994 the Hutu president of the country was killed when his plane was shot down. This event triggered a wide-scale slaughter of Tutsis throughout the country by the army, police and militias (unofficial armies).

> Roadblocks and barricades were erected throughout the country. Identity papers which stated whether a person was a Hutu or Tutsi were checked. The Tutsis were killed.

> The killings went on from April until July when a Tutsi military force defeated the government and took power. To make matters worse, over 2 million Hutu refugees fled Rwanda to neighbouring Congo.

> It is believed that between 500,000 and 800,000 people perished in the genocide.

> Although there was a small UN force in Rwanda at the time of the killings it was virtually powerless to stop the events. The reaction of the international community was too slow to save the victims.

> It is estimated that up to 1 million people actually took part in the massacres. Over 100,000 people were arrested by the new government. There were only a small number of executions.

> The United Nations established the **International Tribunal for Rwanda** to investigate crimes there. It held fifty trials and sentenced twenty-nine people to prison for their involvement in the genocide.

| Activity 3 |
| :-- |

Examine this source and then answer the questions below.

SOURCE 16.21: **Marking the twentieth anniversary of the genocide against the Tutsis in Rwanda**

1 Imagine you are a radio news reporter. Using this source, prepare a short report to inform listeners about the event taking place. Include a brief interview with one of the marchers.

2 Do you think a walk is a good way to commemorate a genocide? Give reasons for your answer.

3 Research another genocide that has taken place in the last fifty years (e.g. the genocides in East Timor, Sudan). Present two facts about this genocide to the class and provide evidence to verify this information.

# What happened at Srebrenica in 1995?

Srebrenica is a town in Bosnia that was the site of the worst mass killings in Europe since World War II.

In 1991 the country of **Yugoslavia** broke up into a number of different countries. War broke out in two of the former parts of Yugoslavia: **Croatia** and **Bosnia**. It was the war in Bosnia that was particularly brutal.

› Bosnia had a mixed population of Muslims (called Bosniaks), Serbs and Croats. When the republic declared independence war broke out between the different groups.

› The Bosnian Serbs in particular wanted to control as much of Bosnia as possible. They started to terrorise non-Serbian populations in the areas they controlled.

› The aim was to remove them from their territory. This became known as **ethnic cleansing**. The Croats and Bosniaks also did the same, but on a lesser scale.

› In July 1995 Bosnian Serb forces rounded up all male Muslims in the town of Srebrenica.

› The men were held in warehouses, farm sheds and schools. They were then transported in small groups in buses to execution sites, where they were shot.

› In all about 8,000 men and adolescents were killed.

After the war ended in the same year an International Court was established in the Hague to try those involved in this massacre and other crimes in the wars in Bosnia and Croatia. A number of men have been convicted for their part in the massacre, including the leader of the Bosnian Serbs during the war, **Radovan Karadzic**, and the commander of the Bosnian Serb army, **Ratko Mladic**.

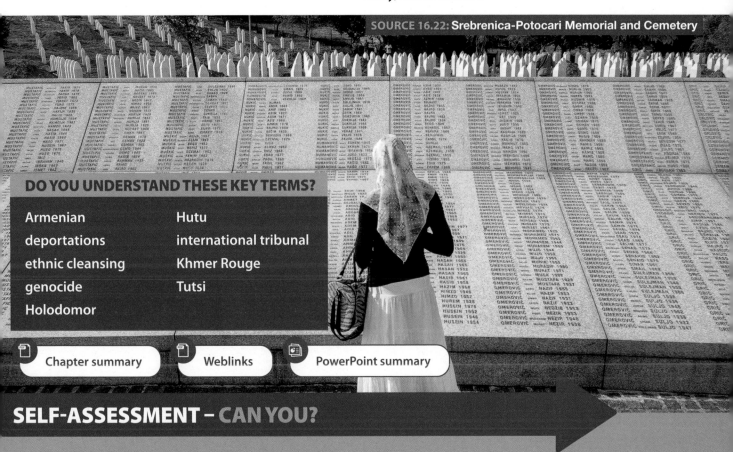

SOURCE 16.22: Srebrenica-Potocari Memorial and Cemetery

**DO YOU UNDERSTAND THESE KEY TERMS?**

| | |
|---|---|
| Armenian | Hutu |
| deportations | international tribunal |
| ethnic cleansing | Khmer Rouge |
| genocide | Tutsi |
| Holodomor | |

Chapter summary    Weblinks    PowerPoint summary

# SELF-ASSESSMENT – CAN YOU?

1 Describe how Armenians were treated during World War I.

2 Explain why Stalin decided to introduce a man-made famine in the Ukraine.

3 Identify why historians disagree about the number of people who died in the Holodomor.

4 Evaluate why nobody was ever punished for the Holodomor.

5 Describe the events in Cambodia between 1975 and 1979.

6 Investigate how the genocide in Rwanda was carried out.

7 Discuss how the perpetrators of the Rwandan genocide were punished.

8 Explain the events that occurred at Srebrenica in 1995.

# 17 THE IMPORTANCE OF THE COLD WAR IN THE TWENTIETH CENTURY

**What were the major crises during the Cold War?**

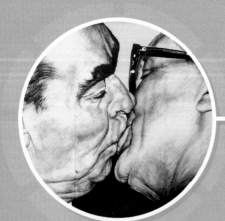

**How did the Cold War end?**

# WHAT WERE THE MAJOR CRISES DURING THE COLD WAR?

## LEARNING INTENTIONS

**At the end of this section, you should be able to:**

◎ Outline the causes of the Cold War

◎ Explain the importance of the Berlin Blockade

◎ Identify and discuss key events that affected relations between the superpowers during the 1950s and 1960s.

## What was the Cold War?

One of the consequences of **World War II** was the development of a period of tension between the USA and the USSR. They were now the world's most powerful countries and they greatly distrusted each other. Both were armed with nuclear weapons that could destroy the world. This made them more powerful than any other countries in history, which is why they became known as **superpowers**. The hostility between them continued until the 1980s. This period is known as the **Cold War**.

The two superpowers had very different views about how politics should operate and how best to run their economies.

**Superpower**
A country with great power and influence; often linked to the country's wealth and possession of nuclear weapons.

**DID YOU KNOW?**

The term Cold War was first used by a journalist in 1947. As there was no actual fighting, the Cold War never became a 'hot' war.

---

### Activity 1

Examine this source and then answer the question below.

|  | **USA – Capitalism** | **USSR – Communism** |
|---|---|---|
| **Political system** | ❯ **Democracy:** governments were chosen in free elections in which people could vote for different political parties<br><br>❯ Citizens were free to express opinions on political matters<br><br>❯ There was a **free press**, although at times people who expressed communist views were closely watched | ❯ **Dictatorship:** there were elections but only the Communist Party was allowed to hold power<br><br>❯ **Secret police** were used to spy on the people<br><br>❯ The government controlled what people watched, listened to and read; this is called **censorship** |
| **Economy** | ❯ **Capitalism:** businesses were privately owned<br><br>❯ Great poverty existed side by side with great wealth | ❯ **Socialism:** businesses were owned and managed by the government<br><br>❯ Everyone had a job, but there were severe shortages of everyday items |

**SOURCE 17.1: Cold War differences**

1  Outline two advantages and two disadvantages of living in (a) the USA and (b) the USSR.

## What were the causes of the Cold War?

The USA and USSR were allies in World War II against Germany and Japan; however, they had different views on the future of post-war Europe.

> At the **Yalta Conference** in February 1945, they disagreed on what should happen to Poland.

> The USA wanted to see free Polish elections to choose a new government.

> The USSR wanted to make sure that Poland would be a communist ally. It had been invaded twice through Poland in the twentieth century and Stalin was determined this would never happen again.

**Franklin D. Roosevelt** died in April 1945, and was replaced as US president by **Harry S. Truman** (1884–1972). USA–USSR relations grew worse.

The spread of communism in Eastern Europe alarmed the Americans. In 1945 the Soviet army controlled Eastern Europe, much of which had been devastated by the war.

> Slowly but surely, communist governments were imposed on Eastern Europeans.

> By 1948 Poland, Bulgaria, Romania, Czechoslovakia and Hungary were firmly under the control of communist governments, which were in turn controlled by the USSR.

> The Eastern Bloc countries were known as **satellite states**, as they were dominated by the USSR. All these countries were one-party states controlled by the Communist Party, with a secret police to keep an eye on those who criticised the government. The newspapers, radio and TV were controlled by the government.

> The term **'Iron Curtain'** was used to describe the division between Western and Eastern Europe.

Concerned by the growth of communism in Europe, Truman decided to act.

> In 1947 he announced the **Truman Doctrine**. He promised that the USA would give military aid to any country resisting communism.

> This policy, which aimed to stop or contain the spread of communism, was called **containment**. It became the main aim of the USA during the Cold War.

There were serious economic problems in Europe after the war.

> Communism was attractive to many people who had little food or no job. The USA realised that military aid alone was not enough to stop the spread of communism. They had to help rebuild the economy of war-torn Europe.

> In 1947 Truman's foreign minister, General George Marshall, announced massive economic aid for Europe. This became known as the **Marshall Plan**.

SOURCE 17.2: **Rebuilding Munich Cathedral, 1946**

**Satellite state**
Country controlled by a larger and more powerful country.

**DID YOU KNOW?**

'Iron Curtain' was first used by Winston Churchill in a speech in America. He used it to describe the division of Europe between the communist east and the non-communist west of Europe.

**Containment**
Policy to stop the spread of communism throughout the world

SOURCE 17.3: **Harry S. Truman**

In all the USA gave $13 billion in the form of loans and grants to the countries of Western Europe. Financial aid was also offered to the countries of Eastern Europe, but Stalin forced them to refuse it. When the USA introduced Marshall Aid to Germany, it caused the first major crisis of the Cold War, the **Berlin Blockade**.

**Activity 2**

1. In pairs, discuss the reasons why the USA opposed the spread of communism.
2. In your opinion, was the USA justified in its concerns about communism?

## What was the Berlin Blockade?

As a result of the war, Germany had been completely defeated. Its cities were destroyed, its economy was in ruins and its currency was worthless. Millions of Germans were homeless and there were over 12 million refugees.

The country had been divided into four zones after the war. The USA, Britain, France and the USSR each had a zone. The capital, Berlin, was located deep inside the Soviet zone. It had also been split into four occupation sectors.

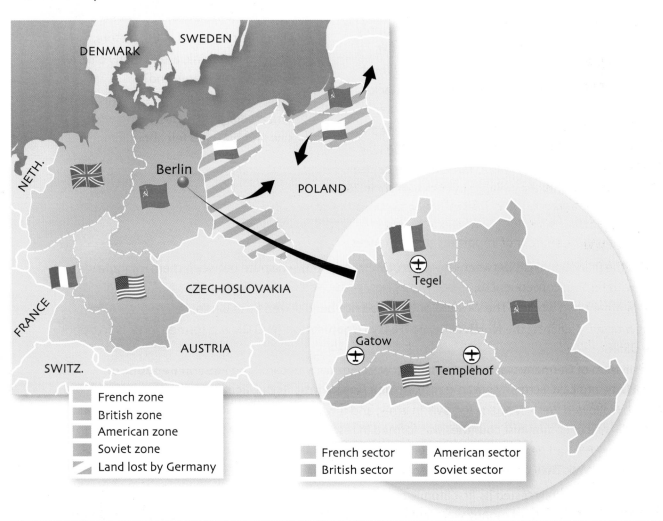

French zone
British zone
American zone
Soviet zone
Land lost by Germany

French sector · American sector
British sector · Soviet sector

**SOURCE 17.4:** The four occupation zones in Germany; Berlin was also divided into four sectors

The USSR and the USA disagreed on how to treat Germany. Stalin wanted to keep Germany weak and divided. The USA wanted to unify the four zones and rebuild the economy. No agreement was reached. So the USA persuaded the British and the French to agree to join their three zones together to form **West Germany**. At the same time, their zones in Berlin were joined together to form **West Berlin**.

In June 1948, as part of the Marshall Plan, a new currency, the **deutschmark**, was introduced into West Germany. Stalin knew that if West Berlin had the new currency, it would become much richer than the Soviet zone surrounding it.

› When the deutschmark was introduced into West Berlin, Stalin decided to drive the Allies out of Berlin.

› He ordered the closing of all road, water and rail access to the city. There was no way of travelling by land into the city. This is called a **blockade**.

› The only way in was by air. Stalin believed that the Western powers would not remain in Berlin if the land access was cut.

› Following the policy of containment, Truman was determined that the Western powers would remain in Berlin.

› Supported by the British, the USA decided to supply Berlin by air. This was known as the **Berlin Airlift**.

› British and US planes flew supplies of fuel and food into Berlin for 320 days. The Soviets did not attack the planes as they knew that it would lead to war.

› In May 1949 Stalin admitted defeat and reopened the routes into West Berlin. The Berlin Blockade was over, but the divided city was to remain at the centre of the Cold War until the collapse of communism in 1989.

> ### Activity 3
>
> Examine this source and then answer the questions below.
>
>
>
> **SOURCE 17.5: A plane landing during the Berlin Airlift**
>
> 1 Describe the crowd in the picture.
> 2 Why, do you think, are so many children watching the plane land?
> 3 Imagine you are a Berliner in this crowd. Write a diary entry describing what you saw and how you felt about it.

## Impact

The blockade had a number of important consequences.

› It was the first open crisis between the superpowers. Any future dispute between them might lead to war, with terrible consequences, as both sides now possessed nuclear weapons.

› Containment had worked. The Western powers had not been driven from Berlin.

› A new military alliance, the **North Atlantic Treaty Organisation (NATO)**, was formed in 1949 to oppose the USSR.

› The division of Germany was now permanent. West Germany became the **Federal Republic of Germany** and East Germany became the **German Democratic Republic**.

› The USA allowed West Germany to have an army, and it was admitted into NATO in 1955. The **Warsaw Pact** alliance of communist countries was formed in response to Germany joining NATO.

Although the USA had defeated the blockade of West Berlin, many Americans believed that they were losing the Cold War. They pointed to two events in 1949.

1 The USSR successfully tested its first atomic bomb. An **arms race** then developed between the USSR and the USA. Vast sums of money were later spent by both superpowers as each sought to have more and better nuclear weapons than the other.

2 Chinese communists, under the leadership of **Mao Zedong**, took control of China. Their defeated opponents fled to the island of Taiwan.

**Arms race**
Two countries competing to have a superior supply of weapons.

## What was the Korean War?

In 1950 events in Korea were to test the US determination to stop any further communist successes.

Following World War II, the Japanese colony of Korea had been divided in two along the 38th Parallel. When no agreement could be reached on reuniting the two parts, two countries were set up:

> North Korea: **People's Republic of Korea**, led by **Kim Il Sung** – supported by the USSR
> South Korea: **Republic of Korea**, led by **Syngman Rhee** – backed by the USA.

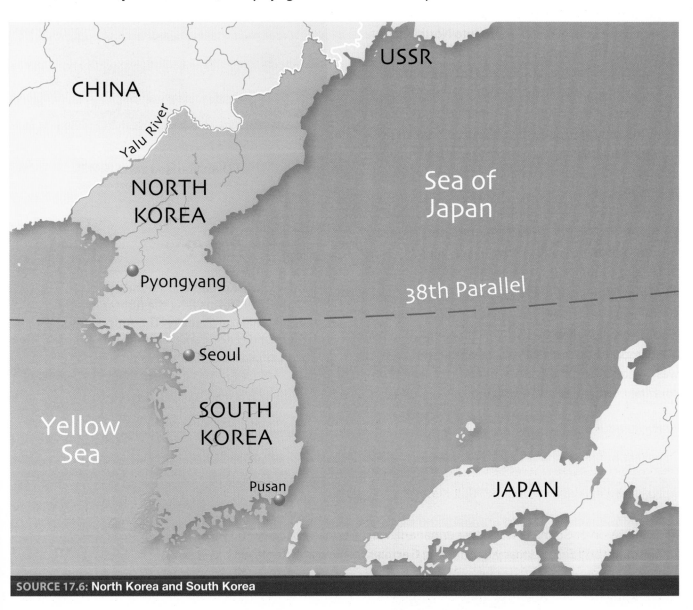

SOURCE 17.6: North Korea and South Korea

In June 1950, with Soviet support, troops from North Korea invaded South Korea. Their aim was to reunify the country under communist control. Within weeks North Korea's forces controlled the peninsula except for the city of Pusan in the very south of the country.

> Truman called on the **United Nations (UN)** to send troops to help defend South Korea against communist aggression. Luckily for Truman, the USSR was boycotting the UN's Security Council and did not veto (stop) his request.

**DID YOU KNOW?**

The **United Nations Security Council** made the most important decisions. Five countries had the power to block any action taken by the Security Council: France, China, UK, USA, USSR.

A UN military force was quickly sent to defend South Korea. Although this army contained soldiers from sixteen nations, most were American. Commanded by US General **Douglas MacArthur** (1880–1964), they completely defeated the North Koreans, who were soon in full retreat.

> UN troops then invaded North Korea and advanced quickly towards the border with China. China sent more than 300,000 troops into North Korea to attack the UN troops. They drove the UN forces back to the original border, where they were halted.

> Truman wanted to limit the war to Korea. He dismissed MacArthur, who had criticised this policy.

> Both sides now found it difficult to advance. The USSR sent military aid to both the North Koreans and the Chinese, but did not get involved in the actual fighting.

Peace talks began in November 1951 and dragged on for two years. The main reason for the slow progress was the attitude of Stalin. He was quite happy to allow the war to continue as it was a drain on US manpower and resources.

When Stalin died in 1953, the new leaders in the USSR agreed to a ceasefire. Over 2.5 million people had been killed, most of them civilians. A **demilitarised zone** was created along the pre-war border between the countries. This border still exists today.

SOURCE 17.7: General MacArthur (left) with President Truman

**Demilitarised zone (DMZ)**
Area that troops are not allowed to enter.

🔍 **DID YOU KNOW?**

During the Korean War Russian pilots in Chinese uniforms flew the fighter jets the USSR gave the Chinese. The Americans knew this but did not make it public for fear of starting a war with the USSR.

SOURCE 17.8: UN troops in Korea

## Impact

The Korean War had a number of important consequences.

> The war was a success for the US policy of containment. South Korea had been saved from communism.

> The Cold War was no longer confined to Europe. A crisis in any part of the world could lead to a clash between the two superpowers. The USA was now committed to stopping the spread of communism throughout the world.

> It set a pattern for future wars involving one of the superpowers. The other superpower would assist the country at war against the superpower but would not get directly involved. This was to avoid a war between the superpowers.

**Activity 4**

Research online and find out the following:

1 An example of a war in the 1960s in which the USSR helped the country fighting the USA

2 An example of a war in the 1980s in which the USA helped the country fighting the USSR.

# How did relations develop after Stalin's death?

After Stalin's death in 1953, **Nikita Khrushchev** (1894–1971) became the leader of the USSR. He was more moderate than Stalin. He wanted East and West to live side by side. He called this policy **peaceful coexistence**.

An improvement in relations followed until 1956. In that year Khrushchev sent troops into Hungary to crush a revolt against Soviet control. The USA did not take action as to do so would have meant war. It accepted that the USSR had control of Eastern Europe.

The arms race continued. Both countries built **missiles** that could travel thousands of miles. They were much more powerful than the bombs that destroyed Hiroshima or Nagasaki.

SOURCE 17.9: Nikita Khrushchev

**DID YOU KNOW?**

When the USSR sent the first man-made satellite into space, the USA was not just disappointed that the USSR had made this technological breakthrough; it also knew the implications for the arms race. The USSR now had a missile powerful enough to reach the USA.

**Activity 5**

1 Find out more about one of the following tests: (a) the Castle Bravo Test 1954 or (b) the Tsar Bomba 1961.

2 Present five facts about your chosen test to the class.

In 1961 Khrushchev was concerned about mass emigration of East Germans, who were leaving through West Berlin.

> He tried to force the Allies out of Berlin.

> When this failed, Soviets and the East Germans built a wall around West Berlin to stop East Germans fleeing to the West.

> Called the **Berlin Wall**, it became a symbol of division between East and West.

Both superpowers were very suspicious of each other's intentions. This suspicion was to contribute to the worst crisis of the Cold War – the Cuban Missile Crisis.

# What was the Cuban Missile Crisis?

In 1959, after a successful revolution, the communist **Fidel Castro** (1926–2016) seized power in Cuba, a near neighbour of the USA. This worried the USA, which stopped trading with Cuba. In 1961 the Americans supported an attempt to overthrow Castro, but it was defeated at the **Bay of Pigs**.

The USSR came to Castro's aid. It agreed to buy Cuba's main export: sugar. The Soviets also secretly began to install **missiles** on the island. Khrushchev wanted to protect Cuba against a US attack.

There was another reason. The Soviets boasted that they had hundreds of long-range missiles, but this was propaganda. In reality, they had very few and the USA had far more. The USSR hoped that by placing missiles with shorter ranges on Cuba, it could catch up with the USA.

The Americans soon found out what was happening. Special spy planes, called U-2s, took photographs of the missile bases. The presence of Soviet missiles so close to the USA was completely unacceptable to the Americans.

US President **John F. Kennedy** (1917–1963) set up a secret committee of senior advisers to decide what to do. Kennedy did not want the Soviets to know that he had found out about the missiles in Cuba.

SOURCE 17.10: Fidel Castro

**DID YOU KNOW?**

A feature of the Cold War was the use of propaganda. Radio, newspapers, TV and films were used to get the message across – we are the good guys and they are the bad guys!

---

## Activity 6

Examine this source and then answer the questions below.

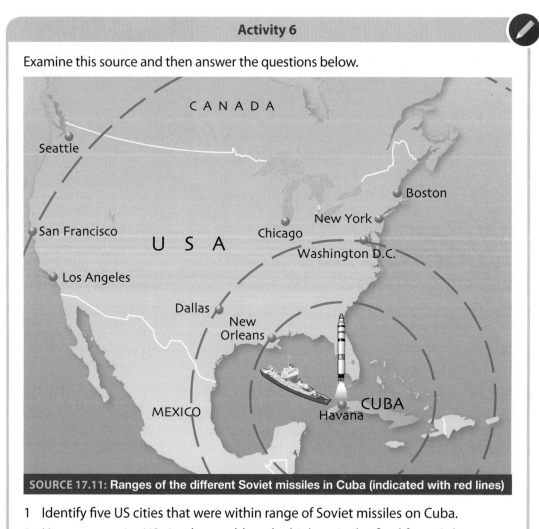

SOURCE 17.11: Ranges of the different Soviet missiles in Cuba (indicated with red lines)

1 Identify five US cities that were within range of Soviet missiles on Cuba.
2 Name one major US city that could not be hit by missiles fired from Cuba.

> Many of Kennedy's advisers wanted to attack the missile sites or invade Cuba, but Kennedy did not want a war with the USSR.
> He decided to set up a blockade to stop Soviet ships travelling to Cuba.
> He hoped that his response would allow for negotiations and prevent war.

On 22 October 1962 Kennedy went public. In a televised broadcast he told the world about the Soviet missiles. He said he was going to **quarantine** Cuba. At the same time US military forces were prepared for the possibility of war.

Throughout the world people were worried. There was **panic buying** as shop shelves emptied. World War III seemed almost certain. However, like Kennedy, Khrushchev did not want war. He ordered the Soviet ships to slow down as they approached Cuba.

The USA still needed the USSR to remove its missiles from Cuba. They reached an agreement that ended the crisis:

> The Soviets agreed to withdraw their missiles from Cuba
> The Americans promised not to attack Cuba
> Secretly the USA also agreed to withdraw its nuclear missiles from Turkey – a country that bordered the USSR.

SOURCE 17.12: John F. Kennedy

**Quarantine**
Period of forced isolation to stop the spread of a disease.

---

**Activity 7**

Examine this source and then answer the questions below.

SOURCE 17.13: **Soviet freighter with missiles is intercepted by US destroyer**

1  Describe what is happening in the photograph.
2  Is there any evidence in the picture that the Soviet vessel is carrying missiles?
3  How does this picture show how serious the Cuban Missile Crisis was?

## Impact

The Cuban Missile Crisis had some important consequences for superpower relations.

> The USA and USSR had come very close to war. They realised that they would have to cooperate in future to prevent war. A **hotline** was set up between the leaders of the two countries to improve communication in any future crisis.

> Both countries agreed to sign a treaty to stop testing nuclear weapons on land or at sea. This was called the **Partial Test Ban Treaty**.

### Activity 8

Examine this source and then answer the questions below.

1. Who are the two leaders shown in the cartoon? What countries do they represent?

2. Describe what you see happening in the cartoon. Suggest a suitable caption.

3. In your opinion, what is the attitude of the cartoonist to the crisis? Give a reason to support your answer.

4. 'The cartoon is an effective source for learning about the Cuban Missile Crisis.' Do you agree with this statement? Give reasons to support your answer.

**SOURCE 17.14: Cartoon about the Cuban Missile Crisis,** *Daily Mail,* **29 October 1962.** *Supplied by Llyfrgell Genedlaethol Cymru / National Library of Wales. Reproduced by permission of Solo Syndication*

### DO YOU UNDERSTAND THESE KEY TERMS?

| | | | |
|---|---|---|---|
| arms race | containment | Partial Test Ban Treaty | Truman Doctrine |
| Berlin Blockade | Cuban Missile Crisis | peaceful coexistence | UN Security Council |
| Berlin Wall | Iron Curtain | quarantine | Warsaw Pact |
| capitalism | Marshall Plan | satellite state | |
| censorship | NATO | space race | |

PowerPoint summary

## SELF-ASSESSMENT – CAN YOU?

1. Describe the tensions that arose between the USA and USSR in the aftermath of World War II.

2. Explain the US policy of containment.

3. Outline the main events during the Berlin Blockade.

4. List the consequences of the Berlin Blockade.

5. Suggest why the USA felt it was losing the Cold War in 1949.

6. Distinguish between the roles of the USA and of China in the Korean War.

7. Identify the consequences of the Korean War.

8. Demonstrate how relations improved between the USA and USSR after the death of Stalin.

9. Explain why a wall was built in Berlin in 1961.

10. Describe the causes of the Cuban Missile Crisis.

11. Examine the main events during the Cuban Missile Crisis.

12. Evaluate the leadership shown by President Kennedy during the Cuban Missile Crisis.

13. Illustrate how the Cuban Missile Crisis led to improved relations between the superpowers.

# HOW DID THE COLD WAR END?

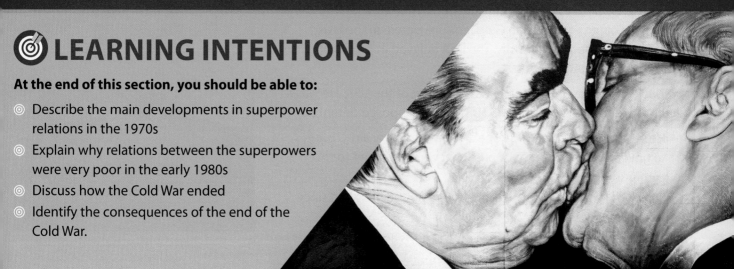

## What were the main developments in superpower relations in the 1970s?

In the early 1970s there was an improvement in superpower relations. This period of easing tensions between the two countries was known as **détente**. At the time some people called it a thaw in the Cold War.

US President **Richard Nixon** and his Soviet counterpart, **Leonid Brezhnev**, wanted to cooperate to reduce tension. One area where they aimed to do this was the arms race.

❯ In 1972 the two countries signed the Strategic Arms Limitation Treaty (**SALT I**). This treaty set limits on the number of nuclear missiles each country could develop. This was called **arms control**.

❯ Negotiations began on **SALT II** as both sides made arms control a main priority. There were crises between the two countries but neither side allowed these to interfere with increased cooperation between them.

### 🔍 DID YOU KNOW?

Superpower rivalry extended to the Olympic Games. The games were used to make a political point. Both countries competed fiercely to win the most medals at each games. In 1980 the USA boycotted the games in Moscow in protest at the Soviet invasion of Afghanistan. In 1984 the USSR boycotted the games held in Los Angeles.

### Activity 1

Examine the source and then answer the questions below.

**SOURCE 17.15: Signing of the SALT I Treaty, May 1972**

1 Identify the two men in the centre of the picture.

2 What evidence is there in the picture to show that this was an important event?

3 Why did both the USA and the USSR want pictures such as these taken, do you think?

4 Examine the painting above by Russian artist Dmitri Vrubel. Search online for the name of the painting and the names of the two communist politicians it features. Find out the title of the painting and say why you think the artist chose it. What does it tell us about the Cold War?

## Why did détente end and relations worsen?

The Soviet invasion of **Afghanistan** in 1979 considerably worsened relations. The US president, **Jimmy Carter**, was afraid that the Soviets' aim was to control the Persian Gulf. Tensions between the two countries increased significantly. The USA delayed approving the recently agreed SALT II Treaty.

In 1980 **Ronald Reagan** was elected president of the USA. He was a determined opponent of communism and he opposed détente.

> He sent more missiles to Europe and gave military aid to governments in South America that were opposed to communism.

> Relations between the superpowers had not been as bad since the Cuban Missile Crisis.

> The Soviets were worried by Reagan's actions and believed that he might be planning to attack them.

> Their fears were heightened when Reagan proposed a missile defence system to protect the United States.

> The US press called his proposal **Star Wars** after the popular film of the time. Reagan argued that a defensive system using lasers built in space could destroy Soviet missiles travelling to the USA.

> Reagan saw it as a defensive measure to protect his country. The Soviets viewed it differently. They were worried that the USA might be tempted to attack the USSR as it could now protect itself from Soviet missiles.

SOURCE 17.16: **Ronald Reagan**

## How did relations between the superpowers improve?

While Reagan's policies were seen by many as risking nuclear war, Reagan hated nuclear weapons and was willing to negotiate with the Soviets to reduce them.

In 1985 a new leader came to power in the USSR, **Mikhail Gorbachev**. Almost immediately the climate between the two countries relaxed. Gorbachev wanted to improve relations with the USA. He also wanted to introduce reforms at home.

> He talked about **glasnost** or openness – freedom of speech would be allowed.

> His main aim was **perestroika** or the restructuring of the Soviet economy. The USSR was falling further and further behind the USA in terms of wealth and the USSR could not afford to continue the expensive arms race with the USA.

SOURCE 17.17: **Mikhail Gorbachev**

Meetings between the two men went well, although Reagan refused to move on his proposed Star Wars defensive programme. However, in 1987 they signed an important treaty – the **Intermediate-Range Nuclear Forces Treaty** (**INF Treaty**). Both sides agreed to get rid of a number of nuclear missiles.

# How did the Cold War end?

In 1989 events in Eastern Europe were to lead to the end of the Cold War. The rivalry between the superpowers had started over extending Soviet control of Eastern Europe. It was the end of this control that ended the Cold War.

> Gorbachev's policy of openness saw greater freedoms in Eastern Europe.

> Both **Hungary** and **Poland** announced that they would hold free elections. These elections resulted in massive majorities for non-communist parties.

> Crucially, unlike former Soviet leaders, Gorbachev said he would not send troops to keep these countries communist.

> In 1989 Hungary announced that it would open its borders with Austria. The opening of the border saw thousands of East Germans flock to Hungary and cross the border into Austria.

> The East German government stopped travel to Hungary.

> Meanwhile East Germans took to the street at home calling for elections and freedom of travel. The East German leader wanted to use troops to stop the protests, but he was removed from power.

> At a press conference on 9 November the new government announced that travel restrictions to the West were being lifted. Thousands of East Germans flocked to the Berlin Wall to travel to West Berlin. The Berlin Wall, the great symbol of the division of the Cold War, was no more. The following year Germany was reunited as one country.

> Mass peaceful protests saw the fall of the communist government in **Czechoslovakia** in the same month as the fall of the Berlin Wall.

> Unfortunately, the year was to end with violence. The communist dictator of Romania, Nicolae Ceaușescu, refused to give up power. He was overthrown in a violent revolt and executed.

> These events have led 1989 to be called the Year of Miracles.

SOURCE 17.18: Crowds celebrate the opening of the Berlin Wall, 1989

KS 👥 **Activity 2**

1   In groups of four create a timeline of ten important events during the Cold War.

# What was the impact of the end of the Cold War on Europe?

One major impact of the end of the Cold War was the break-up of a number of countries into separate independent states.

> The USSR broke up in 1991. Fifteen independent countries were created, with Russia the most powerful. The Baltic republics of Latvia, Lithuania and Estonia gained their freedom after fifty years of Soviet occupation. Among the other newly independent countries were Belarus, Georgia and Ukraine.

> In 1991 Yugoslavia began to break apart into several newly independent countries. This process took a number of years and was accompanied by war in Croatia and Bosnia. In all, six new countries were created: Bosnia-Herzegovina, Croatia, Macedonia, Montenegro, Serbia and Slovenia.

> In 1992 Czechoslovakia became two countries with the formation of the Czech Republic and Slovakia.

## DO YOU UNDERSTAND THESE KEY TERMS?

| | |
|---|---|
| détente | perestroika |
| glasnost | SALT |
| INF Treaty | Star Wars |

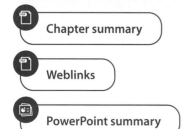

📄 Chapter summary

📄 Weblinks

📰 PowerPoint summary

## Activity 3

Examine this source and then answer the question below.

**Key**
- Former USSR
- Former satellite states
- Former Yugoslavia
- USSR-aligned until 1960

SOURCE 17.19: **Map of Europe**

1 Study this map and identify five new countries that were created as a result of the fall of communism.

## Activity 4

**Class debate**

Debate the motion 'The USA won the Cold War'.

# SELF-ASSESSMENT – CAN YOU?

1 Explain the policy of détente.

2 Identify the importance of SALT I.

3 Describe the impact of the Soviet invasion of Afghanistan on superpower relations.

4 Discuss why superpower relations were poor in the early 1980s.

5 Recognise why relations improved from 1985 onwards.

6 Explain why communism collapsed in Eastern Europe in 1989.

7 Identify the new countries created as a result of the collapse of communism.

# 18 INVESTIGATING THE EU

**What effect has the EU had on international cooperation, justice and human rights?** 356

**How did Ireland's links with Europe develop?** 363

## ⊚ LEARNING INTENTIONS

**At the end of this section, you should be able to:**

⊚ Explain why there was a movement towards European cooperation

⊚ Describe the main steps in the formation of the EEC

⊚ Outline how the EEC evolved into the EU

⊚ Discuss the impact of closer European cooperation.

## Why was there a movement towards European cooperation?

The two world wars that began in Europe in the twentieth century led many people to consider how another war could be prevented. Key to this was ending the rivalry between France and Germany. Three important political figures thought along these lines.

> **Jean Monnet** (1888–1979) was a French businessman who was asked to take charge of the French economy after the war.

> **Robert Schuman** (1886–1963) was the French foreign minister; he had fought in the resistance movement against the Germans during World War II.

> **Konrad Adenauer** (1876–1967) was an anti-Nazi German politician who, in 1949, became chancellor (prime minister) of the new West German republic.

**Resistance movement**
Secret group working to free an occupied country.

---

**KS**
### Activity 1

Examine these sources and then answer the questions below.

SOURCE 18.1: **Jean Monnet**

SOURCE 18.2: **Robert Schuman**

SOURCE 18.3: **Konrad Adenauer**

1 Research the career of one of these men.

2 Choose six facts you have found out and prepare a PowerPoint presentation to show them to the class.

---

These men agreed that it was important to spread **democracy** and respect for **human rights**. Dictators such as Hitler, Mussolini and Stalin had caused great suffering by ignoring human rights and pursuing aggressive foreign policies. Democratic governments, on the other hand, usually respect human rights and promote peace in international relations.

> **Human rights**
> Basic rights, such as freedom of speech or freedom from wrongful imprisonment, which belong to all people.

**Economic cooperation** was also needed. Many people had voted for fascist or communist parties because these parties gave them hope for a better future. The democratic governments needed to work together to improve their economies. In this way people would not be tempted to support fascists or communists in the future. This economic cooperation between countries would also help to heal the divisions of the war.

## Examples of cooperation

After 1945 there were a number of examples of greater European cooperation as countries learned to work together.

> The Americans gave loans and grants, called **Marshall Aid**, to European governments to help their economies recover from the war. The **Organisation for European Economic Cooperation (OEEC)** was set up in 1948 to distribute the money. As a result of this investment, the economies of Western Europe, especially Germany, recovered quickly from the war.

> The **Benelux Union**, comprising **Belgium**, the **Netherlands** and **Luxembourg**, came into existence in 1948. Goods, people and money could pass freely between them. This was called a **customs union**. The union was a success and by 1950 these countries had become prosperous.

> In 1949 the **Council of Europe** was formed by ten European countries, including Ireland, to encourage democracy and respect for human rights. In 1953 its members agreed to the **European Convention on Human Rights**, which set out the basic freedoms that its citizens were guaranteed, such as freedom of speech.

**SOURCE 18.4:** European Court of Human Rights, Strasbourg

# What were the main steps in the formation of the EEC?

In 1950, noting the success of the Benelux Union, Monnet and Schuman proposed that **France** and **Germany** should cooperate in coal and steel production. This became known as the **Schuman Declaration**.

Adenauer agreed, and **Italy** and the **Benelux** countries supported the proposal. These six countries formed the **European Coal and Steel Community (ECSC)** in 1951. It proved to be a great success. The first step on the road to European unity had been taken.

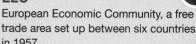

**EEC**
European Economic Community, a free trade area set up between six countries in 1957.

**EU**
European Union; the EEC became the EU after the Maastricht Treaty in 1992.

---

 **Activity 2**

Examine this source and then answer the questions below.

> In taking upon herself for more than 20 years the role of champion of a united Europe, France has always had as her essential aim the service of peace. A united Europe was not achieved and we had war. The coming together of the nations of Europe requires the elimination of the age-old opposition of France and Germany. Any action taken must in the first place concern these two countries.
>
> With this aim in view, the French Government proposes that action be taken immediately on one limited but decisive point. It proposes that Franco-German production of coal and steel as a whole be placed under a common High Authority, within the framework of an organisation open to the participation of the other countries of Europe. The pooling of coal and steel production should immediately provide for the setting up of common foundations for economic development as a first step in the federation of Europe.
>
> The solidarity in production thus established will make it plain that any war between France and Germany becomes not merely unthinkable, but materially impossible.

**SOURCE 18.5: Extract from the Schuman Declaration, 9 May 1950, taken from the EU's website**

1   According to Schuman, what has been the aim of France for 'more than 20 years'?
2   From the source, what key change does Schuman argue is important for the 'coming together of the nations of Europe'?
3   What proposal does Schuman make in the document? What is this proposal the first step towards?
4   What evidence is there in the source to support the view that the main aim of his proposal was to prevent another war between Germany and France?
5   Do you think this is a reliable source? Present evidence to support your view.

---

SOURCE 18.6: Signing the Treaty of Rome, 25 March 1957

## Treaty of Rome

With the success of the ECSC, the members decided to cooperate in other economic areas. After negotiations they agreed to the **Treaty of Rome** in 1957. This treaty established the **European Economic Community (EEC)**. The six countries agreed three central principles.

> To have no barriers on the movement of goods or people. This was called a **common market**.

> To protect rural communities through the **Common Agricultural Policy (CAP)**, which gave farmers **guaranteed prices** for their produce.

> To adopt a **social policy** whereby the richer countries would give money to help poorer ones.

In the longer term they would also work for political as well as economic unity.

**Common market**
An agreement between countries to have no barriers to trade between them. Some people also use this name to refer to the EEC/EU.

**Guaranteed price**
A good price that farmers would always be paid for their produce even if market prices fell.

# How were decisions reached in the EEC?

By the 1970s the main decision-making institutions of the EEC had been agreed by the member states.

| Council of Ministers | European Commission | European Parliament | Court of Justice |
|---|---|---|---|
| Government ministers, one from each member state, met to decide on the policies the EEC would follow | Commissioners, one from each member state, proposed changes in EEC law to the Council and carried out its decisions | Representatives of the people of each member state (the number depended on population size) advised the Council and Commission | Judges, one from each member state, ensured that the members followed the EEC's rules correctly |

### Activity 3

1  Find out about the current decision-making process in the EU. In your research, answer the following questions:

- Which institution has the power to propose legislation? Is it still the European Commission?
- How are the members of the European Parliament chosen? Have the parliament's powers increased?
- What is the European Council? What is the Council of the European Union?
- Name three other EU institutions and outline their roles.

2  Design a poster to illustrate where EU laws are proposed, developed and passed.

# How did the membership of the EEC/EU expand?

At first the **UK** did not want to join the EEC, but by 1960 it had changed its view. When the UK applied to join the EEC, **Ireland**, led by Taoiseach **Seán Lemass**, followed suit.

The French President, General **Charles de Gaulle** (1890–1970), blocked the UK's entry in 1963. He felt Britain was too close to the USA, which he did not trust. This meant that Ireland could not join either. He blocked a further application from Britain in 1967. After de Gaulle resigned in 1969, the UK and Ireland (along with **Denmark**) were admitted into the EEC on 1 January 1973. It was the first expansion of the community.

Since then, more countries have joined.

**SOURCE 18.7: Charles de Gaulle**

> **Greece**, **Spain** and **Portugal** joined in the 1980s. These countries were poorer than the other members and needed a lot of regional aid.
> In 1993 the EEC became the **European Union (EU)**.
> **Austria**, **Finland** and **Sweden** became members in 1995.

When communism fell in 1989, the countries of Eastern Europe applied to join the EU. The EU laid down the **Copenhagen criteria**, a set of conditions that countries applying to join the EU had to fulfil. These principles stated clearly the values that the EU promoted.

> They had to be democracies with the rule of law and good human rights.
> They had to have strong market economies where most economic decisions were made by private businesses.

It took a while for the economies of Eastern Europe to become strong enough. **Ten countries** became EU members in 2004, including **Poland**, **Lithuania** and the **Czech Republic**. **Romania** and **Bulgaria** became members in 2007. **Croatia** joined in 2013.

## Activity 4

Examine the map and then answer the questions below.

1   Find out in which year each EU member country on the map joined the EU.

2   Draw up a timeline showing this information.

SOURCE 18.8: **EU member states (in red), 2017**

## How has European cooperation developed?

The main aim of the EEC/EU since 1980 has been **closer integration** of members. At first the members of the EEC concentrated on **economic cooperation**. In 1979 the **European Monetary System** was introduced.

> Members agreed to try to reduce inflation and fix the value of their currencies in line with each other.

> This was to pave the way for the introduction of a shared currency in the future.

The **Single European Act** was signed in 1986. Its main aim was to remove any remaining barriers to trade and the free movement of people.

> As a result the **Single European Market** was established in 1993.

After lengthy negotiations, the **Maastricht Treaty** was signed in February 1992. Named after the Dutch town where it was signed, it was an important development in closer European cooperation.

> It changed the name of the EEC to the **European Union**.

> All people in the EU became **European citizens**.

> It brought much **closer political ties**, with greater cooperation in foreign policy, security and justice.

> A timetable for a **shared currency** was agreed.

> A **Social Charter** brought in policies to protect pay and conditions for workers in the EU.

On 1 January 2002 the shared or single currency, the **euro**, was introduced in twelve countries, including Ireland. It was the EU's most ambitious project to date.

> The **European Central Bank** was set up in 1998 to manage the new currency and to set interest rates for all members who adopted the euro.

> By 2017 nineteen members of the EU had adopted the single currency. They are known collectively as the **eurozone**.

**Integration**
Closer cooperation between members of an organisation.

**Inflation**
Rising prices for goods and services.

**DID YOU KNOW?**

1979 saw the first democratic elections to the European Parliament. These elections are held every five years. Each member state elects a number of **MEPs** (Members of the European Parliament) in proportion to the size of its population.

SOURCE 18.9: Jacques Delors, Head of the European Commission 1985–95

**DID YOU KNOW?**

Negotiations take a long time in the EU as all members have to agree on a new treaty. Member states have to consider their own interests as well as those of wider European cooperation.

KS 👥 **Activity 5**

1 Create a timeline of the main events that led to greater European cooperation between 1948 and 2002. Include ten major events.

2 In pairs, discuss whether the EU has had a positive or a negative overall effect on Europe. Give three reasons to justify your conclusion.

**Learning Outcome 3.12** 361

## Positive impacts

By 2017 the EU had become a political and economic union of twenty-eight European countries with a total population of over 500 million people. This union plays a major role in world affairs, promoting peace, international cooperation and human rights.

The EU has had a number of positive consequences for the countries of Europe.

> There has not been a major war in Europe in over seventy years. France and Germany are now close allies.

> All countries in the EU must be democracies, which has helped to stop any dictatorships.

> Protection of human rights remains a central theme, both within the EU and internationally.

> It has helped to integrate the economies of former communist countries and to improve the standard of living of the citizens of those countries.

> The EU is now a huge market in which people move and trade freely among member states. This has led to increased prosperity among members.

## Criticisms and Brexit

The aims and policies of the EU do not enjoy universal support within member states.

> Some people worry about its power over their lives. Some are concerned that their country has given up too much independence in the process of closer European cooperation. They criticise what they call a 'European superstate'.

> Some people are uncomfortable with the economic and social changes that have resulted from the free movement of people within the EU.

> These fears were shown in 2016 when the UK voted to leave the EU in what has been called **Brexit**.

SOURCE 18.10: Boris Johnson campaigning for Brexit, 2016

---

### DO YOU UNDERSTAND THESE KEY TERMS?

| | | |
|---|---|---|
| Benelux Union | EEC | human rights |
| CAP | EU | integration |
| common market | euro | Marshall Aid |
| Copenhagen criteria | European Commission | MEP |
| Council of Europe | European Convention on Human Rights | OEEC |
| Council of Ministers | European Court of Justice | Schuman Declaration |
| customs union | European Monetary System | Social Charter |
| ECSC | European Parliament | |

PowerPoint summary

---

## SELF-ASSESSMENT – CAN YOU?

**1** Explain why there were calls for European unity after World War II.

**2** Identify three men who helped to start the search for European unity.

**3** Comment on the importance of the European Coal and Steel Community.

**4** Examine the decisions agreed under the Treaty of Rome, 1957.

**5** Indicate why it was difficult for the UK to join the EU in the 1960s.

**6** Discuss the main stages in the expansion of the EU.

**7** Consider the need for the Copenhagen criteria.

**8** Explore the importance of the Single European Act in the development of the EU.

**9** Investigate the significance of the Maastricht Treaty for the EU.

**10** Discuss why the introduction of the single European currency was an important EU decision.

**11** Debate the positive and negative impacts of the EU.

# HOW DID IRELAND'S LINKS WITH EUROPE DEVELOP?

## LEARNING INTENTIONS

**At the end of this section, you should be able to:**

- Discuss why Ireland joined the EEC
- Outline the economic impact of EU membership on Ireland
- Describe how EU regulations affect the environment
- Outline the social impact of EU membership on Ireland.

SCHEME PARTLY FINANCED BY THE EUROPEAN REGIONAL DEVELOPMENT FUND

## Why did Ireland apply for membership of the EEC?

After the foundation of the Irish Free State in 1922 Ireland had very few links with Europe. Ireland joined the **League of Nations** in 1923, but remained neutral in World War II. In 1949 Ireland joined the newly formed **Council of Europe**.

A decision was taken to apply for membership of the EEC (see the previous section) in 1961. Taoiseach **Seán Lemass** applied to the EEC for membership at the same time as the UK. He believed that Ireland would become more prosperous through access to the common market, CAP and other EEC programmes. However, the French president, **Charles de Gaulle**, vetoed Britain's application for membership. Almost all Ireland's trade was with Britain so Ireland did not pursue EEC membership at that time.

In 1966 **Jack Lynch** succeeded Lemass as Taoiseach. Lynch negotiated Ireland's entry into the EEC in 1973. In the referendum on joining the EEC, 83 per cent voted yes. Ireland joined the EEC along with Denmark and the UK.

SOURCE 18.11: Jack Lynch and other EEC leaders at a summit in Dublin, 1979

# How did the Irish economy benefit from the EU?

The EU has played an important role in helping Ireland develop from a backward economy dependent on agriculture to a modern economy dominated by hi-tech industry and global exports. There have been negatives, however, and in the 1970s some Irish industries had to close down when they could not compete with foreign companies after tariffs (taxes) were lowered on imported goods.

EEC/EU membership has transformed the Irish economy in a number of ways.

> Irish businesses have easy access to a market of over 500 million people.

> The EU has invested tens of billions of euro in Ireland. Some of this money was used to create jobs, especially for young people.

> Being part of a free trade area makes it easier for Irish businesses to sell in European markets because there are no taxes on Irish exports. In 1973, 55 per cent of Ireland's exported goods went to Britain. By 2017 this figure had decreased to 16 per cent.

> The Single European Act in 1986 brought in the **single market**. This meant that all border controls on goods were abolished and that any remaining barriers to trade between member countries were removed. This led to hugely increased exports to the continent from Ireland. US companies were attracted to invest in Ireland to gain free access to the EU market. Billions of euro in **foreign direct investment** has created thousands of jobs in Ireland.

SOURCE 18.12: Intel opened its factory at Leixlip, Co. Kildare in 1989

> The single currency, the euro, came into effect in 2002. It meant that Irish companies did not have the added cost of currency fluctuations in the other eurozone countries.

> Ireland's recovery from the financial crisis that started in 2008 was helped by a joint EU and **IMF** assistance programme. As a result, when the programme ended in 2014, Ireland had the fastest growing economy in the EU.

**IMF**
International Monetary Fund, an international organisation that lends money to countries who are in financial difficulty.

---

**KS**             **Activity 1**

Examine this source and then answer the questions below.

| Year | Imports | Exports | Balance |
|------|---------|---------|---------|
| 1991 | 12,851 | 15,019 | 2,168 |
| 1993 | 14,885 | 19,830 | 4,945 |
| 1995 | 20,619 | 27,825 | 7,206 |
| 1997 | 25,882 | 35,336 | 9,454 |
| 1999 | 34,412 | 52,227 | 17,814 |

SOURCE 18.13: Central Statistics Office, 'Trade Statistics: Values in IR£m'

1 Draw a bar graph showing exports from 1991 to 1999.

2 What trend does the graph show?

3 Analyse the reasons for this trend.

4 Comment on why Britain is no longer Ireland's main export destination.

## Impact on agriculture

› Agriculture benefited most in the early years as farmers' incomes doubled between 1973 and 1979. This was due to the Common Agricultural Policy (CAP), which guaranteed high prices to farmers for their produce. CAP also gave grants to farmers to invest in modern farming methods and machinery. Today, EU payments help protect farmers' income. In 2016 farmers received a total of €1.2 billion through CAP.

› In 1973 Ireland's agriculture-based economy was totally dependent on the UK market. Nowadays, Ireland benefits from being able to trade easily with other EU countries (no tax on exports). EU prices are better than those in other parts of the world.

› The vast majority of Ireland's beef exports are to other EU countries. Most of these exports are high-value products.

› In 1973 Ireland was poor with high unemployment and emigration, and 24 per cent of workers were employed in agriculture. Today the agri-food industry employs 8.4 per cent of the working population.

**Agri-food industry**
Agriculture, forestry, fishing and food and beverage production.

› Between 2007 and 2013 €5.7 billion was provided to develop poorer agricultural areas such as the West of Ireland.

› The EU's food safety standards and rules on animal feed and welfare help keep Ireland's food supply safe to eat.

› In a 2016 survey 69 per cent of Irish people agreed that the EU fulfils its role in ensuring a fair standard of living for farmers and that agricultural products are of good quality, healthy and safe.

### Activity 2

Examine these sources and then answer the question below.

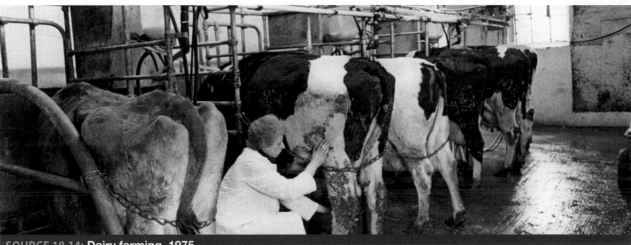

SOURCE 18.14: **Dairy farming, 1975**

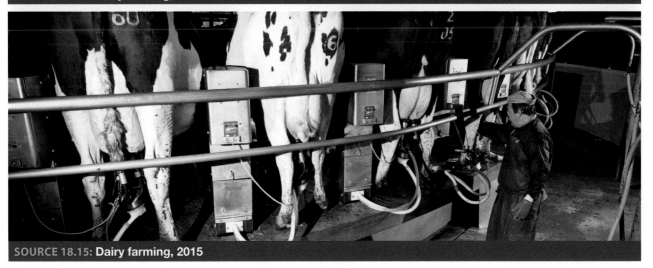

SOURCE 18.15: **Dairy farming, 2015**

1 Explain the differences between the two photographs.

## Impact on fishing

> In 1973 there were 6,000 fishermen in Ireland, some full time and some part time. Due to a lack of investment, most Irish fishermen used small boats and fished close to shore.

> Fishermen felt that unfair concessions had been made in fishing when Ireland joined the EEC (in order to gain better terms under the CAP). All EEC members were given equal access to each other's fishing waters. This meant that other countries with bigger and more modern boats could fish off Ireland's shores.

> The fishing industry faced a major challenge when Spain and Portugal joined the EEC in 1986. Both countries had large modern fishing fleets. The large Spanish trawlers could catch huge amounts of fish in Irish waters.

> **Quotas** were introduced to conserve some fish species. This reduced catch loads for all, including Irish fishermen.

**Quota**
In fishing, the number of fish of a certain species (e.g. cod) that fishermen are allowed to catch in a given year.

> The EEC gave grants and loans to fishermen to invest in bigger boats. By 1990 the fishing industry was thriving due to investment by the EU.

---

**Activity 3**

Examine these sources and then answer the question below.

SOURCE 18.16: Fishing boats, 1960s

SOURCE 18.17: Fishing boats, 2010

1  List two differences between fishing boats in the 1960s and in 2010.

## Impact on infrastructure

> The EEC provides grants to improve transport systems, communications technology and other infrastructure. This helps industry to prosper. Products can be delivered to their markets more quickly and cheaply.

> Ireland's main roads have benefited from EU funding. For example, the M1 between Dublin and Northern Ireland and the M4 between Dublin and the West have greatly reduced travel times between major centres of population.

> Projects such as the Port Tunnel and the Luas system were partly financed by the EU.

> In tourism, many amenities such as the Cliffs of Moher interpretive centre received EU funding.

**Infrastructure**
The facilities needed for a country to function (e.g. transport networks, communication systems, power supplies, buildings).

SOURCE 18.18: **Visitor centre at the Cliffs of Moher, Co. Clare**

### Activity 5

1   In groups of four, investigate and prepare a presentation about the impact of EU regulations on the environment. Include an account of how your local environment has been affected by these regulations.

# How have EU regulations affected the environment?

The EU has some of the world's highest environmental standards.

> It protects natural habitats by ensuring that air and water are clean.

> It is committed to ensuring that the **Paris Agreement** on climate change is implemented.

> Ireland and the other members of the EU have to cut **greenhouse gases** by 20 per cent by 2020.

> By 2020, **renewable energy** sources must be 20 per cent of all energy used.

> It is reducing the amount of rubbish being stored in dumps (landfills). This will decrease the pollution of surface water, soil and air by these dumps.

SOURCE 18.19: **The Poolbeg Waste to Energy plant converts waste into energy, which provides electricity for 80,000 homes and can also heat another 50,000 homes in the Dublin area. The plant will use 600,000 tonnes of non-recyclable waste from landfills each year.**

**Greenhouse gases**
Gases that trap heat in the atmosphere, which leads to global warming.

**Renewable energy**
Energy that comes from sources that can be used again and again, such as wind power and solar energy.

### Activity 4

1   Investigate the Paris Agreement. Write a paragraph on your findings.

### Activity 6

1   Visit the DWTE website.

2   Draw a diagram to show how waste is converted into energy at the Poolbeg plant. Write a paragraph describing what is happening in your diagram.

3   Using the internet and other sources, investigate whether there are any disadvantages to living near the Poolbeg plant.

# How has Irish society been affected by EU membership?

## Consumers

> No visas are needed to travel anywhere within the EU. There is no need to worry about exchange rates while travelling in the euro zone.

> Under EU regulations, all labels on processed food must supply nutritional information.

> Details of the origin of unprocessed meat from pigs, sheep and poultry must be shown on labels.

> The EU's **European Consumer Agenda** is making it safer for Irish citizens to buy goods and services.

---

**Activity 7**

1  In pairs, find out how many supermarkets in Ireland are run by non-Irish companies.

2  Make a list of them.

---

## Status of women in the workplace

> In 1973 women made up 34 per cent of the workforce; by 2014 the figure was 56 per cent.

> European legislation on equality states that men and women must get equal pay for doing the same job, and must receive equal and fair treatment at work.

> Women are now entitled to maternity leave.

> However, women are still behind when it comes to equal opportunities and income. Men remain the major decision makers in business and politics. The pay gap has narrowed but still exists: in 1973 women got 47 per cent of a man's wage on average; by 2013 it was 86 per cent.

# Summary: Impact of the EU on Ireland

Many people argue that joining the EEC was the single most important event in Ireland since independence. Reasons include:

> Ireland's links with Europe have become much closer.

> The single market has allowed Irish exports and Irish people free access to the other member states of the EU. This has transformed and modernised Ireland's economy.

> Ireland's infrastructure has been modernised with support from the EU.

> EU regulations have led to an improved environment.

> EU regulations are improving the status of women in the workplace.

> Today, Ireland is a modern country with a very successful economy. The EU plays a major role in Ireland's economic success.

It is clear that EU membership transformed many areas of Irish life. Ireland today is unrecognisable from the isolated, poor, agriculture-dominated country it was in 1973.

---

**Activity 8**

1  Take part in a class debate on the motion: 'That EU membership has always been good for Ireland.'

---

**DO YOU UNDERSTAND THESE KEY TERMS?**

| | |
|---|---|
| agri-food industry | infrastructure |
| foreign direct investment | pay gap |
| IMF | quota |

---

 Chapter summary     Weblinks    PowerPoint summary

**Pay gap**
Average difference between wages paid to men and wages paid to women.

---

# SELF-ASSESSMENT – CAN YOU?

1  Explain why Ireland applied for membership of the EEC.

2  Outline the impact of the CAP on Irish agriculture.

3  Outline how the Irish fishing industry has been affected by EU membership.

4  Explain how EU regulations affect the environment.

5  Explain how improved infrastructure helps industry.

6  Describe how the EU has improved the position of women in the workplace.

7  List the current members of the EU.

# 19 THE 1960s – A CRUCIAL DECADE

## Why was the 1960s an important decade?

## How did Ireland change in the 1960s?

# WHY WAS THE 1960s AN IMPORTANT DECADE?

## LEARNING INTENTIONS

**At the end of this section, you should be able to:**

◎ Outline the main political developments in the 1960s

◎ Discuss the main developments in society in the 1960s

◎ Describe the main technological developments in the 1960s.

## What were the main political developments in the 1960s?

The 1960s was one of the most dramatic decades in world history. It was an era of Cold War tensions, African independence and social protests. Events in one country, the USA, were to dominate the decade.

### Cold War

The Cold War between the USSR and the USA dominated international relations (see Section 17).

❯ The dispute between the superpowers over **Berlin** developed into a major crisis in 1961.

❯ 1962 saw the worst crisis of the Cold War, the **Cuban Missile Crisis**. After the crisis, relations between the two countries improved. In 1963 both agreed to end atmospheric nuclear testing.

❯ In the Arab-Israeli **Six-Day War** in 1967, the USA supported the Israelis, and the USSR backed the Arabs. When Israel won the war it acquired the Sinai Peninsula, the Golan Heights, the West Bank and East Jerusalem. The consequences of this war are still being felt today.

❯ In 1968 the USSR sent troops into **Czechoslovakia** to crush an attempt to reform the communist system there. The USA protested but did not take any action as to do so might have led to another world war.

### DID YOU KNOW?

**John F. Kennedy** (1917–1963) was the youngest US president, elected at the age of forty-three. A member of a rich Irish-American family, he served in the US Army during World War II. He was elected to the US Senate in 1953 for the Democratic Party. He defeated vice-president

SOURCE 19.1: **Kennedy's funeral procession, Washington**

Richard Nixon to win the 1960 presidential election. His presidency was mainly focused on relations with the USSR. He showed leadership in the crises over Berlin and Cuba. His final year in office saw an improvement in relations with Moscow. He supported civil rights reform and promised to land a man on the moon by the end of the 1960s. He visited Ireland in 1963. During his time in office he had the highest average approval ratings of any US president in recent history. He was **assassinated** in Dallas on 22 November 1963.

SOURCE 19.2: **Soviet tanks in Prague, 1968**

## Vietnam War

One of the events that strongly influenced the 1960s was the **Vietnam War**.

> Vietnam had been a French colony and was divided in 1954 when the French left. The north was communist and the south had a pro-American government.

> The USA bombed North Vietnam in 1964 and sent in troops in 1965.

> The USA wanted to defeat the **Viet Cong**, which was conducting a guerrilla campaign in South Vietnam. Over 500,000 US troops were fighting there by 1968.

The war strongly divided opinion in America and throughout the world.

> It was covered widely on TV and the daily pictures of death and destruction shocked viewers.

> A very strong **anti-war movement** developed in the USA and in Europe.

> Many leading figures such as **Muhammad Ali** and **Martin Luther King** opposed US intervention in South Vietnam. Protest marches against the war became very common.

**Activity 1**

Examine this source and then answer the questions below.

SOURCE 19.3: **US troops in Vietnam**

1 Identify evidence from the picture that indicates the nature of the fighting in Vietnam.

2 Is this picture a reliable source? Explain your answer.

In 1968 the North Vietnamese and their southern allies the Viet Cong launched the **Tet offensive**. Most Americans now wanted to leave Vietnam. US President **Lyndon B. Johnson** (1908–1973) decided not to contest the upcoming presidential election. His successor, **Richard Nixon** (1913–1994), would eventually pull US troops out of Vietnam in 1973. Vietnam was united under the control of the communist north in 1975.

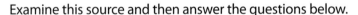

KS **Activity 2**

Examine this source and then answer the questions below.

We have been too often disappointed by the optimism of the American leaders, both in Vietnam and Washington, to have faith any longer in the silver linings they find in the darkest clouds … For it seems now more certain than ever that the bloody experience of Vietnam is to end in a stalemate …To say that we are closer to victory today is to believe, in the face of the evidence, the optimists who have been wrong in the past … To say that we are mired [stuck] in stalemate seems the only realistic, yet unsatisfactory, conclusion. On the off chance that military and political analysts are right, in the next few months we must test the enemy's intentions, in case this is indeed his last big gasp before negotiations. But it is increasingly clear to this reporter that the only rational way out then will be to negotiate, not as victors, but as an honourable people who lived up to their pledge to defend democracy, and did the best they could.

SOURCE 19.4: **Edited extract from Walter Cronkite's 'We Are Mired In Stalemate' Broadcast, 27 February 1968**

1 Does Cronkite believe that the Americans can win in Vietnam? Justify your answer using evidence from the source.

2 According to the source, what do the military and political analysts say about the Tet offensive?

3 What does Cronkite call on America to do now?

4 Do you consider this source to be factual? Explain your answer.

## Africa

The 1960s saw the rapid **decolonisation** of Africa as most African countries became independent. This process was not without problems. Military takeovers became an all too common feature of African politics throughout the decade.

In the **Congo**, the region of **Katanga** declared independence in 1960. This was the first crisis to hit an independent African country. The **United Nations (UN)** sent troops, including Irish soldiers, to the Congo to end the crisis. In the **Niemba ambush**, nine Irish soldiers were killed in an attack by local tribesmen. In 1963 Katanga rejoined the rest of the country. In 1965 **General Mobutu** (1930–1997) seized power and ended democracy.

Freedom for African countries was delayed where there was a large European settler population. In **Algeria**, for example, the French fought a vicious war against those seeking Algerian independence. In 1962 President Charles de Gaulle of France agreed to a ceasefire and France left Algeria.

In **South Africa**, the white (European) population was the largest in Africa. A policy of separating the races, known as **apartheid**, saw the majority black population treated as second-class citizens in their own country.

**Decolonisation**
Process by which European countries ceded independence to colonies that they had controlled.

### Activity 3

Research online and make a list of ten African countries that gained independence in 1960.

### DID YOU KNOW?

The **United Nations** is an international body established after World War II to preserve world peace. Its headquarters are in New York. The organisation is influential as no country likes to be condemned by the UN. Every member country attends the UN Assembly. However, the main decision-making body is the smaller Security Council. The **UN Security Council** originally had eleven members, but this was expanded to fifteen in 1965. There are five permanent members: France, China, UK, USA and Russia. Each of these countries has a veto and can stop any measure it does not like.
The head of the UN is called the secretary-general. In 1961 UN Secretary-General **Dag Hammarskjöld** was killed in a plane crash. He was trying to bring an end to the violence in the Congo.

### DID YOU KNOW?

The most prominent opponent of apartheid was **Nelson Mandela** (1918–2013). Imprisoned for his opposition in 1964, he became a symbol of resistance to the apartheid government. He was released in 1990. In 1994 he became the first president of a multi-racial South Africa.

SOURCE 19.5: Nelson Mandela, 1961

The white government of **Rhodesia** (modern-day Zimbabwe) declared independence rather than share power with the majority African population. A war broke out that saw the end of white rule in 1979.

**Apartheid**
Political system that discriminated against the black population in South Africa.

SOURCE 19.6: Celebrating independence, Algiers, 1962

## China

The communist government led by **Mao Zedong** (1893–1976) implemented economic reforms to modernise China. This policy was known as the **Great Leap Forward**. The reforms were a complete failure and led to famine and mass executions. Historians estimate that 30 million people lost their lives. Mao was forced to abandon the policy in the face of opposition from his own party.

In 1966 Mao brought in a new policy called the **Cultural Revolution**. It targeted those who were seen as opponents of communism in Chinese society. Millions of people were arrested. They faced public humiliation, torture, imprisonment, seizure of property and in some cases execution. Cultural and historical sites were destroyed. No one is sure how many people were victims of this policy as few official figures were kept, but it is likely that between 400,000 and 2 million people died.

SOURCE 19.7: Mao Zedong

# What were the main developments in society in the 1960s?

The 1960s saw major social changes throughout the Western world, starting with the USA. Young adults born after World War II began to question the values of their parents and to challenge traditional views of what was best for society. Some people turned to socialism or communism as answers to the problems that society faced. Partly influenced by events in Vietnam, there were strong anti-American views in many Western European countries.

## Women's rights

> **Feminism**
> Belief that women should have the same rights as men.

Many women felt restricted by the traditional view of a woman's role as homemaker. They wanted an alternative to staying at home to mind the children. This view led to the growth of **feminism**. The feminist movement campaigned for **equal rights for women**, especially in the workplace. Women wanted to pursue careers just as men did and to be paid the same as men. By the end of the 1960s this movement had improved the status of US and European women.

Families began to get smaller as couples were marrying later and having fewer children. This trend was very obvious in Western Europe, where birth rates fell in countries such as Germany. The increased availability of **contraception**, including the birth control pill, contributed to this development.

## Struggle for racial equality in the USA

Another demand for equal treatment that caught the popular imagination in the 1960s was that of African-Americans. US laws treated African-Americans very unfairly. In some states, African-Americans also found it very difficult to vote in elections.

The **civil rights movement** led by **Martin Luther King Jr** (1929–1968) made headlines at home and abroad. His policy of peaceful resistance to discrimination won admirers throughout the world.

> In 1963 King led a protest against racial discrimination in Birmingham, Alabama.
> The pictures on TV of peaceful protesters being brutally attacked by police won further sympathy for their cause.

> **Racial segregation**
> Separating people of different races (e.g. white people sitting at the front of the bus and black people at the back).

### DID YOU KNOW?

Martin Luther King rose to prominence as the leader of the **Montgomery Bus Boycott**. The boycott arose after **Rosa Parks** (1913–2005) refused to give up her seat to a white man on a bus.

SOURCE 19.8: Rosa Parks

This incident occurred in 1955 in the city of Montgomery, Alabama. Parks was arrested and fined. African-Americans decided they would not take the bus until **racial segregation** ended. The year-long boycott drew attention to the treatment of African-Americans in the southern states of America.

> In late 1963 King led a march to Washington, where he gave his famous 'I have a dream' speech.

> In 1964 he won the Nobel Peace Prize in recognition of his work in fighting racial discrimination through non-violent resistance.

> In 1965 he organised a march from Selma to Montgomery in Alabama campaigning for the right of African-Americans to vote.

---

**Activity 4**

1. In pairs, search on YouTube for footage of King's 'I have a dream' speech and answer these questions:

   - What was King's dream?
   - Was King an effective speaker? Give reasons for your answer.
   - Describe King's audience. How did they respond to his words?

2. 'Marches are an effective way to fight for equality.' Write a paragraph challenging or agreeing with this statement.

---

> The Civil Rights Act passed by President Lyndon B. Johnson in 1964 ended discrimination against African-Americans regarding jobs. The Voting Rights Act passed in 1965 made it easier for African-Americans to vote in US elections.

> African-Americans remained the poorest group in US society and not everyone was satisfied with King's peaceful message of racial harmony.

> Many African-Americans lived in areas called ghettos in the larger US cities. In the late 1960s riots broke out in many of these ghettos in protest at the poverty that existed there.

> King worked hard to deal with this poverty.

> However, he was assassinated in Memphis, Tennessee, in 1968. Today his birthday is celebrated as a US national holiday every January.

## Television

In general, people in Europe and America saw their standard of living rise during the 1960s. Most households could afford their own television. TV proved to be an important contributor to change.

First developed in the years before World War II, TVs became popular in the USA in the 1950s, where 86 per cent of households had a TV by 1959. This popularity spread to Europe during the 1960s, particularly Western Europe. Most TVs had black and white pictures, but colour TVs were becoming more common.

Families gathered in front of the TV to enjoy programmes and get the latest news. Long-accepted views were challenged on TV and that led to a greater questioning of traditional values. Events such as US civil rights protests and the Vietnam War were beamed into living rooms across the world.

SOURCE 19.9: **Family watching TV, 1965**

SOURCE 19.10: **King (centre) leading the Selma–Montgomery march, 1965**

SOURCE 19.11: Audience at a Rolling Stones concert, 1964

## Youth culture

Another major development was the growth of popular music and rock music in particular. At the time rock and roll was criticised by many as a bad influence on young people. This criticism did not diminish its popularity. By the mid-1960s English bands such as The Beatles and the Rolling Stones led to a growth in what became called **youth culture**. Their songs challenged traditional views of what was best for society. Young people copied the look and in some cases the lifestyle of their heroes.

**Youth culture**
Young people's interests, music, beliefs and clothes.

## Religion

During the 1960s the influence of religion began to decline in both the USA and Western Europe. As church attendances fell, the Catholic Church held the **Vatican II** conference of leading churchmen to modernise the Church. This led to a greater role for ordinary Catholics in the Church.

# What were the main technological developments in the 1960s?

## Computers

One major technological development of the 1960s was the use of **computers** in businesses. The first commercial computers had been developed in the late 1940s. They were very large and very expensive. They were also very slow. By the 1960s they had become quicker and smaller. Quicker meant that they could process information with greater speed. They were called **mainframes** and were used by businesses for tasks such as accounting and sending bills to customers.

SOURCE 19.12: IBM mainframe computer

By 1965 there were approximately 20,000 computers in the world. Computers with monitors came into use during the 1970s. The establishment of companies such as Apple and Microsoft saw the development of personal computers for home use. The laptop (1980s) and touchscreen technology (2000s) were still a long way from development.

### DID YOU KNOW?

US research during the 1960s led to what would eventually become the **Internet**. This technology was being developed for the US military to allow messages to be sent in the event of a nuclear war. The first test message between two computers was sent on 29 October 1969.

## Space exploration

Another major technological development was the **space race**. This was a contest between the USSR and USA in the area of space exploration. The USSR had the first successes with the launch of the first satellite in 1957, **Sputnik 1**. They also put the first person, **Yuri Gagarin**, into space in 1961.

The USA set up the **National Aeronautics and Space Administration (NASA)** in 1958 to manage US space exploration. President Kennedy promised that the USA would land a man on the moon by the end of the 1960s. His vision was fulfilled when the **Apollo XI** mission landed on the moon in 1969. This event had the largest television audience in the world up to that time, over half a billion people. The USA had won the space race.

An important outcome of the space race was the launching of commercial satellites. This development saw a revolution in communications, with TV pictures being beamed throughout the world.

### Activity 5

1   Research online either (a) Yuri Gagarin, the first man in space, or (b) the moon landing of 1969.
2   Identify five facts about your chosen topic that interest you.

## Banking

Technological developments during the 1960s allowed banks to automate some customer transactions. These **automated teller machines (ATMs)** were first used to take customer deposits, but later they were able to dispense cash as well.

**SOURCE 19.13:** Launch of the Barclaycash machine, London, 1967

## Medicine

There were also a number of very important medical developments in the 1960s. **Vaccines** were developed for measles, mumps and polio. These were to prove very important in reducing deaths, especially of children. Heart, lung and liver **transplants** were performed for the first time. These medical developments improved the **life expectancy** of people living in the USA and Western Europe.

**Life expectancy**
Age you can expect to live to when you are born.

### Activity 6

1 Draw a spider diagram showing key technological developments during the 1960s.

### DO YOU UNDERSTAND THESE KEY TERMS?

| | | |
|---|---|---|
| anti-war movement | decolonisation | space race |
| apartheid | feminism | Tet offensive |
| assassination | Great Leap Forward | United Nations |
| ATM | life expectancy | Viet Cong |
| civil rights movement | mainframe | youth culture |
| Cultural Revolution | NASA | |

PowerPoint summary

## SELF-ASSESSMENT – CAN YOU?

1 Discuss the importance of the Vietnam War.

2 Outline the main events in the Congo in the 1960s.

3 Explain what happened in African colonies with a large European settler population.

4 Describe the role of feminism in the 1960s.

5 Evaluate the success of the US civil rights movement.

6 Demonstrate the influence of TV in the 1960s.

7 Analyse the growth of youth culture in the 1960s.

8 Indicate how computer technology developed in the 1960s.

9 Comment on the main developments in the space race.

10 Explore the impact of medical improvements introduced in the 1960s.

# HOW DID IRELAND CHANGE IN THE 1960s?

## ⊚ LEARNING INTENTIONS

**At the end of this section, you should be able to:**

◎ Describe Ireland at the start of the 1960s

◎ Outline the main changes that occurred during the 1960s

◎ Discuss some of the key Irish events and personalities of the 1960s.

## What was Ireland like at the start of the 1960s?

Ireland was a very **conservative** country in 1960. In other words, it was a place where things had remained the same for decades. The Catholic Church dominated Irish society and Irish governments had to consult it on moral issues. People obeyed their bishops and priests without question.

There was an atmosphere of economic despair in Ireland. The **protectionist** policies that had been followed since the 1930s had failed. More than 400,000 people had emigrated during the 1950s to find a job and a better life elsewhere. If such high rates of emigration continued, some feared that the Irish as a race would disappear.

When **Seán Lemass** (1899–1971) became Taoiseach in 1959, he realised that a change of direction was needed. The new policies he introduced created an **economic boom**, which in turn led to dramatic changes in many areas of Irish life during the 1960s.

> **Moral issues**
> Issues dealing with what is right or wrong.

> **Protectionism**
> Putting taxes (tariffs) on imports, making foreign goods more expensive than home-produced goods.

> **Economic boom**
> Increased activity in the economy (e.g. more items are produced, sales increase, wages improve, prices rise).

**SOURCE 19.14: Seán Lemass**

### Activity 1 ✎

Using the Internet and other sources, write a paragraph on the career of Seán Lemass up to 1959.

### Activity 2 ✎

Examine this source and then answer the questions below.

> It is accepted on all sides that we have come to a critical and decisive point in our economic affairs. It is only too clear that the policies that we have hitherto followed have not resulted in a viable economy. It is equally clear that we face economic decay and the collapse of our political independence if we elect to shelter behind a protectionist blockade.
>
> **SOURCE 19.15:** Excerpt from a Department of Finance document, 'Economic Development', T. K. Whitaker, 1958

1 What is the writer's opinion of the economic policies being pursued at that time?

2 What does the writer think will happen if there is no change in policy?

3 Do you agree with this opinion? Use information from this textbook to support your answer.

# Why was there an economic boom in the 1960s?

Lemass decided on a new economic policy. It was based on a plan called the *First Programme for Economic Expansion*. This plan was drawn up by a civil servant, **T. K. Whitaker** (1916–2017).

**Activity 3**

In pairs, research the career of T. K. Whitaker and write a report on your findings.

**Aims of the programme:**

> To **attract foreign industry** into Ireland by offering grants to companies to set up factories in Ireland; not taxing their profits; and building industrial estates to provide factories for these companies. The **IDA (Industrial Development Authority)** was given the job of attracting these industries to Ireland.

> To **make Irish firms more efficient** by giving them grants to modernise. This would enable them to export their goods.

This programme was very successful. The government set a target of 2 per cent growth per year in the five years of the programme. However, it achieved 4 per cent growth per year.

Between 1960 and 1968, 656 overseas companies set up in Ireland. Many of these companies came from America, Britain and Japan. Unemployment fell by 40 per cent between 1961 and 1966. In the 1960s the Irish population grew for the first time since the Famine.

A second programme followed between 1963 and 1970. It was not as successful as the first programme, but the rate of growth remained high for the rest of the decade.

# What changes occurred in education?

In 1960 only 30 per cent of children went to secondary school. To continue its economic progress, Ireland needed an educated workforce. In 1967 **free post-primary education** was introduced by Minister for Education **Donogh O'Malley** (1921–1968). This meant that all school fees would be abolished.

There was a huge increase in the number of children attending secondary school. Free school transport for all second-level students also led to an increase in numbers. These policies created a well-educated workforce, which attracted more foreign companies to invest in Ireland. In 1966/7 there were 148,000 secondary school pupils; by 1968/9 the figure was 185,000.

**Activity 4**

Calculate the approximate percentage increase in the number of secondary school students between 1966/7 and 1968/9.

SOURCE 19.16: **T. K. Whitaker**

SOURCE 19.17: Donogh O'Malley

In 1968 grants were introduced for third-level education for students whose parents' income was below a certain level. This increased the numbers attending university.

New state-owned secondary schools, called **community schools**, were set up. This challenged the control of the Catholic Church over education. Up to this point the Church had had total control over schools.

All these reforms led to young people becoming more questioning and more critical. This was to have a major impact on the way young people viewed the Catholic Church.

# Why did the Catholic Church's influence decline in the 1960s?

At the beginning of the 1960s the Catholic Church dominated Irish society. In 1959 the new pope, **John XXIII**, called a **Vatican Council** of bishops to modernise the Catholic Church. Known as Vatican II, its reforms included: Mass being said in the language of the people of the country (rather than Latin); and recognition of the role of ordinary Catholics in the Church for the first time. Ordinary people could now join parish councils to help run the parish.

Up to this time the bishops and priests had run the Church. People looked up to them and obeyed them without question. These changes in the Church gave ordinary Catholics an opportunity to question the Church's teachings and to criticise the bishops and priests. However, it is important to realise that the vast majority of Catholics continued to obey the bishops and priests without question. Over 80 per cent of Catholics attended Mass every Sunday, and there was very little power given to the ordinary Catholics in Ireland during the 1960s.

SOURCE 19.18: Pope John XXIII

## Activity 5

Examine this source and then answer the question below.

> There are many parish councils, but no evidence that any significant number have been given decisive powers in matters of importance.
>
> SOURCE 19.19: **Kevin O'Kelly, RTÉ religious affairs correspondent 1985, quoted in 'A Church in Crisis'** (*History Ireland*, **Issue 3, Autumn 2000, Volume 8), James S. Donnelly Jr**

1   Suggest who would have been members of the parish councils and who would have prevented the parish councils having more power. Give reasons for your answers.

When **Pope Paul VI** condemned the use of contraceptives in 1968, many young Catholics in Ireland ignored his teaching on this matter.

**Contraceptive**
Artificial birth control.

## Activity 6

Examine this source and then answer the questions below.

> The gradual decline, later precipitous decline in Catholic power in the Republic was just about visible in the mid-1960s and was to become very obvious in the following decades. Priests were just beginning to become ordinary or even comic figures rather than being seen as revered teachers, men to be feared or even loved gurus.
>
> SOURCE 19.20: **Tom Garvin, *Preventing the Future* (Gill and Macmillan, 2004)**

1   What type of source is this? Explain your answer.
2   What is Garvin's main point in this extract?
3   According to Garvin, did everyone in the Catholic Church share this view in the 1960s?

## What was the impact of RTÉ on Irish society?

On New Year's Eve 1961 **Telefís Éireann** made its first broadcast. It had a major impact on the culture and values of Irish people. Television helped bring about changes in the way people lived and thought.

One programme in particular had a huge impact on the way people thought. It was called **The Late Late Show**. It was a live chat show hosted by **Gay Byrne**. Controversial matters such as divorce and contraceptives were discussed. The Church and its leaders were questioned by the audience. The programme was often criticised by priests at Sunday Mass. The vast majority of Catholics still supported the Church's teachings on these matters but slowly public opinion began to change. RTÉ played a major role in bringing about this change.

In 1966 380,000 households were watching RTÉ and this figure had increased to 536,000 by 1971. Many of the programmes were brought in from America and Britain. People were influenced by the cultures of these two countries. As a result, Ireland became a less religious but a more materialistic society. The majority of people, however, especially in rural areas, kept the traditional values.

### Activity 7

Find out who else has presented *The Late Late Show*. When did Ryan Tubridy take over?

**Materialism**
Focusing on becoming better-off, and ignoring religious values.

## How did Irish culture change in the 1960s?

Young people, in particular, were influenced by their access to cultures from abroad. They copied American and British **youth culture**. Pop music became very popular. The Beatles were mobbed when they played in Ireland in 1963. Men began to wear long hair and to copy how these pop bands dressed.

SOURCE 19.21: The Beatles at the Adelphi, Dublin, 1963

The 1960s also saw the emergence of the showbands. They played popular music in dance halls all over Ireland. This led to a decline in more traditional Irish music.

SOURCE 19.22: The Capitol Showband on RTÉ, 1967

Advertisements in newspapers and on TV changed the way young people dressed. The mini-skirt became popular, much to the disgust of the older generation. They saw it as a sign that moral standards were dropping.

SOURCE 19.23: Fashion models, 1967

### Activity 8

1 Find out how older people reacted to the new fashions.
2 Have you ever had a similar reaction to the clothes that you wear?

Increased income allowed people to socialise more and to buy more consumer goods. Many people went on foreign holidays and were exposed to other cultures.

The availability of washing machines and vacuum cleaners cut down on work in the home and women had more time for other activities. Their position in society was slowly beginning to improve in the 1960s.

TV also influenced young people in protesting about issues that affected them and others. They held protest marches to support the abolition of apartheid. They sought a reduction in the voting age (it was lowered to eighteen following a referendum in 1972).

Many people were afraid that because of all these changes, Irish culture would disappear over time.

**Apartheid**
Racial discrimination by the government of South Africa.

**Referendum**
A vote held to get the opinion of the people on an important issue.

SOURCE 19.24: **Anti-drug protest**

### Activity 9

Examine this source and then answer the questions below.

> The 1960s were indeed a time when everything changed in Ireland, for better or worse. Free mass second and third-level education, together with the influence of television, foreign travel and higher standards of living, transformed Irish society, a transformation that was foreseen with nervousness, anger and foreboding by some of the older generation of leaders and by many traditionalists.

SOURCE 19.25: **Tom Garvin,** *Preventing the Future* **(Gill and Macmillan, 2004)**

1 List the reasons that caused the changes Garvin refers to in Ireland in the 1960s.
2 Who, according to the excerpt, did not agree with these changes? Using this textbook, give reasons why they did not agree with these changes.
3 Draw a spider diagram showing the changes in Ireland in the 1960s.

## How did Ireland emerge from isolation in the 1960s?

### Ireland and the EEC

Lemass realised that the prosperity of the Irish economy depended on building links with European countries, especially the **European Economic Community (EEC)**. Closer ties would mean increased trade. Ireland, along with Britain, applied to join the EEC. The French president, **Charles de Gaulle**, vetoed the applications. Ireland would have to wait until 1973 to join. (See Section 18)

### Ireland and Britain

Ireland's most important market was Britain. In 1965 the **Anglo-Irish Free Trade Area Agreement** was signed by Lemass and Harold Wilson, the British prime minister.

Tariffs between the two countries would be abolished over a ten-year period. By 1975 there would be free trade between Ireland and the UK.

**Isolationism**
Not taking part in international affairs.

**Tariff**
Tax on imports.

## Ireland and Northern Ireland

Lemass also tried to work towards better north–south relations. He tried to establish closer economic links in areas such as tourism and fishing. Northern Ireland Prime Minister Terence O'Neill invited Lemass to Belfast on 14 January 1965. The next month O'Neill visited Dublin. This was followed by other ministers meeting to discuss economic matters such as agriculture and tourism. With such a huge change in north–south relations, there was an inevitable backlash from more extreme unionists in Northern Ireland who felt that O'Neill was betraying them. This closer economic cooperation was ended by the Troubles (see Section 12).

## Ireland and the United Nations

Ireland had joined the United Nations (UN) in 1955. The most important UN function Ireland had was peacekeeping. Ireland's first peacekeeping role was in the **Congo** in Africa, 1960–64. On 8 November 1960 nine Irish soldiers were killed in an ambush in Niemba. An estimated 300,000 people lined the route of their funerals in Dublin. Twenty-six Irish soldiers died in four years in the Congo.

Ireland took part in seven peacekeeping missions in the 1960s. Irish people were proud that their soldiers were involved in such international operations. They raised Ireland's profile on the world stage.

| DO YOU UNDERSTAND THESE KEY TERMS? | | |
| --- | --- | --- |
| Anglo-Irish Free Trade Agreement | economic boom | protectionism |
| | IDA | referendum |
| apartheid | isolationism | tariff |
| community school | materialism | Vatican Council |

### Activity 10

Examine this source and then answer the question below.

SOURCE 19.26: Funeral of soldiers killed in the Niemba ambush

1 In pairs, research the Niemba ambush and write a report on it.

### Activity 11

1 Draw a timeline showing how Ireland emerged from isolation in the 1960s. Write a short note on each of the key events.

### Activity 12

1 In groups of three or four, choose one of the following topics as they relate to the 1960s: (a) education, (b) the Catholic Church, (c) culture, (d) international affairs, (e) the economy of Ireland.

2 Assign a role to each member of the group.

3 Research your chosen topic.

4 Make a presentation to the class, lasting no more than one minute, on your topic.

 Chapter summary  Weblinks  PowerPoint summary

## SELF-ASSESSMENT – CAN YOU?

**1** Explain why there was an economic boom in the 1960s.

**2** Determine whether the First Programme for Economic Expansion was a success, giving three pieces of evidence to support your view.

**3** Outline the changes that occurred in education during the 1960s.

**4** Outline the impact of these changes.

**5** Describe the impact of RTÉ on Irish society.

**6** Describe how Irish culture changed in the 1960s.

**7** Explain why the influence of the Catholic Church declined in the 1960s.

**8** Outline the ways in which Ireland began to participate in international affairs during the 1960s.

**9** Describe north–south relations during the 1960s.

# 20 PATTERNS OF CHANGE

**The GAA and Irish life** — 385

**Crime and punishment over time** — 393

# THE GAA AND IRISH LIFE

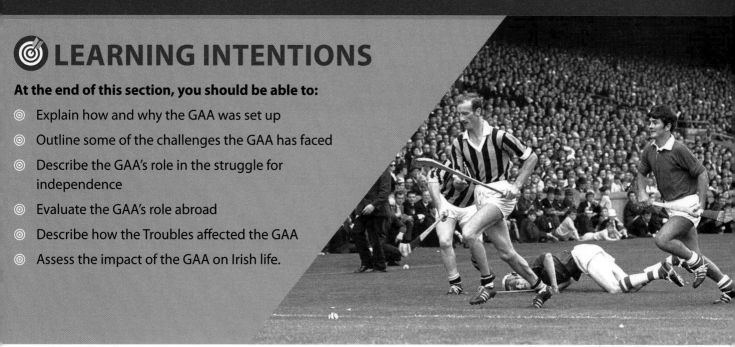

## LEARNING INTENTIONS

**At the end of this section, you should be able to:**

◎ Explain how and why the GAA was set up

◎ Outline some of the challenges the GAA has faced

◎ Describe the GAA's role in the struggle for independence

◎ Evaluate the GAA's role abroad

◎ Describe how the Troubles affected the GAA

◎ Assess the impact of the GAA on Irish life.

## What led to the establishment of the GAA?

**Cultural nationalism** stressed the cultural differences between Ireland and Britain (see Section 12). One area of difference was the sports people played. **Anglicisation** saw more and more Irish people playing British sports such as cricket, soccer and rugby. Traditional Irish sports were being neglected. To address this, a small group of cultural nationalists decided to set up the **Gaelic Athletic Association (GAA)**.

| Activity 1 |
| --- |

Examine this source and then answer the questions below.

> Dear Sir – I am much pleased to see that you take an interest in Irish Athletics. It is time that a handbook was published with rules &c., for all Irish games. The English Handbooks of Athletics are very good in their way, but they do not touch on many of the Irish games which, although much practiced, are not included in the events and programmes of athletic sports ... Irish football is a great game, and worth going a very long way to see, when played on a fairly laid-out ground and under proper rules. Many old people say that hurling exceeded it as a trial of men. I would not care to see either game now, as the rules stand at present. I may say there are no rules, and therefore, those games are dangerous. I am anxious to see both games revived under regular rules ...
>
> If a movement such as you advise is made for the purpose of reviving and encouraging Irish games and drafting rules &c., I will gladly lend a hand if I can be of any use.

**SOURCE 20.1: Extract from Maurice Davin's letter in the *United Ireland* newspaper, October 1884, replying to Michael Cusack's proposal to set up the GAA**

1 Is this a primary or a secondary source? Explain your answer.
2 What is the main point Davin is making?
3 Which two Irish games does he mention?
4 What offer does he make to Michael Cusack?
5 How useful is this document to historians? Explain your answer.

## First meeting

On 1 November 1884 **Michael Cusack** invited six men to meet him in Hayes Hotel, Thurles, Co. Tipperary. It was to be the first meeting of the GAA.

## First members

**Maurice Davin** became the first president of the organisation; Michael Cusack became one of the secretaries; **Archbishop Croke of Cashel**, and prominent politicians **Charles Stewart Parnell** and **Michael Davitt** became patrons. Four of the seven men present were members of the IRB.

## Aims

> To increase the number of people playing hurling and Gaelic football.
> To draw up rules for these games.
> To organise competitions.

SOURCE 20.2: Hayes Hotel, Thurles

### Activity 2

Examine this source and then answer the questions below.

1   There shall not be less than 15 or more than 21 players a side.
2   There shall be two umpires and a referee. Where the umpires disagree the referee's decision is final.
3   The ground shall be at least 120 yards long by 80 in breadth and properly marked by boundary lines. Boundary lines must be at least five yards from the fences.
4   The goal posts shall stand at each end in the centre of the goal line. They shall be 15 feet apart with a crossbar eight feet from the ground.
5   The captains of each team shall toss for choice of sides before commencing play and the players shall stand in two ranks opposite each other until the ball is thrown up, each man holding the hand of one of the other side.
6   Pushing or tripping from behind, holding from behind or butting with the head shall be deemed foul and the player so offending shall be ordered to stand aside and may not afterwards take part in the match, nor can his side substitute another man.
7   The time of actual play shall be one hour. Sides can be changed only at half time.
8   The match shall be decided by the greater number of goals. If no goals be kicked, the match is a draw. A goal is when the ball is kicked through the goal posts under the crossbar.
9   When the ball is kicked over the sideline it shall be thrown back by a player of the opposite side to him who kicked it over. If kicked over the goal line by a player whose goal-line it is, it shall be directly thrown back in any direction by a player of the other side. If kicked over the goal-line by a player of the other side, the goalkeeper whose line it crosses shall have a free kick. No player of the other side to approach nearer than 25 yards of him till the ball is kicked.
10  The umpires and referee shall have during the match, full power to disqualify any player or order him to stand aside and discontinue play, for any act which they consider unfair as set out in Rule 6.

SOURCE 20.5: **First set of rules for Gaelic football, 1885**

1   In groups of four, compare the rules for Gaelic football drawn up in 1885 with today's rules. Discuss what you think has been the biggest change in the rules.
2   Which rules would you prefer to play under? Give reasons for your answer.

SOURCE 20.3: **Michael Cusack**

SOURCE 20.4: **Maurice Davin**

## Immediate impact

> Ordinary people felt encouraged to play sports. Up to this time only the middle and upper classes took part in organised sport.

> Soon there were GAA clubs in almost every parish. Cusack said that 'it spread like a prairie fire'. It made people proud of their parish.

> It was the first experience that many Irish people had of running a democratic organisation.

### Activity 3

Using the Internet and other sources, write a short paragraph on the history of your local GAA club.

# What challenges has the GAA overcome?

The GAA has been a split organisation on more than one occasion. However, it has always managed to survive such divisions.

## Political divisions

The first major crisis occurred in 1887. The GAA split into two groups: one supported the Home Rule Party and the other backed the IRB's plans to achieve full independence by violent means. The IRB had infiltrated the GAA from the start. These fit young athletes were just the kind of men it needed for a rebellion against British rule.

At the GAA's annual congress in 1887 the IRB candidate defeated Maurice Davin for the GAA presidency. The Home Rule supporters threatened to set up a rival organisation. However, Archbishop Croke reunited the two sides and Davin was reinstated as president in 1888.

### DID YOU KNOW?

- The first All-Ireland championships were played in 1887: Tipperary, represented by Thurles Blues, won the hurling; and Limerick's Commercials won the football. The county club champions represented their county in the All-Ireland series until 1891.

- To honour the memory of Archbishop Thomas Croke, who had died in 1902, funds were raised (by running tournaments) to buy a sports ground on Jones' Road, Dublin. It cost £3,500 in 1913 and was renamed **Croke Park**.

SOURCE 20.6: **Archbishop Croke**

### Activity 4

Examine this source and then answer the questions below.

The GAA has been represented by nationalists as a purely non-political body organised solely for the revival and development of national pastimes.

The public is in no way deceived by its preference to be non-political … It is principally officered by well-known Fenians (IRB).

The Macroom branch of the Association passed the following resolution 'That we, the members of the Macroom GAA condemn the prosecution of Messrs F B Dineen* and T J Mahoney, two well-known athletes, is intended to strike a blow at the GAA, in our struggle for national independence ….'

* F B Dineen of the IRB bought the field in Jones' Road, Dublin that later became Croke Park.

SOURCE 20.7: **Extract from an article in *The Times*, September 1888**

1 What type of source is this?
2 Outline the main points made in the extract.
3 What evidence is offered in support of the accusation made against the GAA?
4 How useful is this article to historians? Give reasons for your answer.

## Charles Stewart Parnell

The GAA was further weakened by the Parnellite split in 1890 (see Section 12). This split occurred in the Home Rule Party. The IRB-led GAA sided with Parnell. When Parnell died, GAA members formed a guard of honour at his funeral. Many anti-Parnellites left the association as a result. It took ten years for the GAA to recover.

## 'The Ban'

**Rule 21** was introduced in 1897 to prevent members of the RIC (Royal Irish Constabulary) or the British Army joining the GAA. It remained in place until 2001.

**Rule 27**, commonly known as **'the Ban'**, was introduced in 1901. Members of the GAA were not allowed to play foreign games such as soccer or rugby. If they were caught playing such games they were expelled from the association. This rule aimed to ensure that Irish people played Irish sports only, which would in turn strengthen their Irish identity.

In 1938 **Douglas Hyde**, President of Ireland, was removed as patron of the GAA because he had attended a soccer match. 'The Ban' ended in 1971.

# Had the GAA a role in the 1916 Rising?

Although the GAA was not officially involved, many GAA members took part in the Rising as they were either in the IRB or the Irish Volunteers. Among these were **Michael Collins** and **Harry Boland**. The **Rebellion Commission** set up by the British government after the Rising alleged that the GAA was involved. The GAA issued a statement strongly denying this and claiming to be a non-political organisation.

However, with the change in public opinion after the Rising, the GAA became involved in politics through the **Political Prisoners Amnesty Association**. It helped fundraise for the families of those who had been imprisoned after the Rising. In November 1916 it ran an All-Ireland competition to raise money for the families.

## Commemorating 1916

> In 1938 the GAA commemorated the Easter Rising by inviting the 350 survivors of the GPO in 1916 to Croke Park on All-Ireland final day. There were four Fianna Fáil ministers in the group.

> In 1966 a pageant was performed to mark the fiftieth anniversary. Written by Bryan McMahon, it was about the lives of the seven signatories of the Proclamation.

> In 2016 the GAA celebrated the centenary of the Rising with a pageant called 'Laochra', held in Croke Park. It highlighted the GAA's role in the story of Ireland.

These events show that the GAA is not merely a sporting organisation but is involved in many other areas of Irish life.

---

**Activity 6**

**SOURCE 20.9:** 1916 centenary celebrations in Croke Park, 2016

1 Watch the RTÉ coverage of this event and describe it in your own words.

---

**Activity 5**

Examine the source and then answer the question below.

**SOURCE 20.8:** Michael Collins starting a match at Croke Park, 1921

1 What was unusual about the way the games were started?

---

# Why is Bloody Sunday a key event?

During the War of Independence many members of the GAA were involved in the fight for freedom. On the morning of 21 November 1920, Michael Collins' 'Squad' killed thirteen British spies. In retaliation, the Auxiliaries entered Croke Park that afternoon looking for the killers in the crowd watching a challenge football match between Dublin and Tipperary. The proceeds from the game were to be given to the Irish Republican Prisoners' Fund. The Auxiliaries opened fire, killing fourteen people. One of those killed was the Tipperary player **Michael Hogan**. The Hogan Stand in Croke Park is named after him. This atrocity increased public support for the IRA.

---

## Activity 7

Examine these sources and then answer the questions below.

**A** The spectators were startled by a volley of shots fired from inside the turnstile entrances. Armed and uniformed men were seen entering the field, and immediately firing broke out scenes of the wildest confusion took place. The spectators made a rush for the far side of Croke Park and shots were fired over their heads and into the crowd.

SOURCE 20.10: *Freeman's Journal*, 22 November 1920

**B** Learning on Saturday that a number of these gunmen were present in Croke Park, the Crown forces went to raid the field. It was the original intention that an officer would go to the centre of the field and speaking from a megaphone, invite the assassins to come forward. But on their approach, armed pickets [sentries keeping look-out] gave warning. Shots were fired to warn the wanted men, who caused a stampede and escaped in the confusion.

SOURCE 20.11: **Press release from the British forces in Dublin Castle, 21 November 1920**

1. Who does the *Freeman's Journal* blame for what happened?
2. What is the British version of what happened in Croke Park?
3. How useful is each of these documents? Explain your answers.
4. Which one, do you think, is more credible? Give reasons for your answer.
5. Imagine you were a spectator at the match. Write a paragraph describing what happened and how you felt.

---

# What were the Tailteann Games?

The Tailteann Games was the Irish Free State's answer to the Olympic Games. It was a sign of Ireland's independence. Among the sports included in 1924 were athletics, hurling, Gaelic football, sailing and swimming. Competitors came from countries where the Irish had emigrated to. The event also attracted tourists from abroad. The government had given the GAA £10,000 to improve Croke Park for the event. A new stand, called the Hogan Stand, was built. The Tailteann Games were also held in 1928 and 1932.

SOURCE 20.12: **Athletics at the 1928 Tailteann Games**

# What role does the GAA play abroad?

As early as 1888 the GAA went to America with two hurling teams and athletes. Its aim was to establish the GAA in America and also to raise money for staging the Tailteann Games in Ireland. However, the tour was a financial disaster.

In 1947 the All-Ireland Gaelic football final was played in New York. This created great interest among the Irish-American community. New clubs were formed and the GAA made a profit of £10,000. Cavan beat Kerry.

In 1958 the British GAA rented Wembley Stadium for exhibition matches. It was an annual event until 1975. Forty thousand people attended in 1962.

At present there are over 400 clubs all over the world. When the recession hit Ireland in 2008 thousands of young people emigrated to look for work. Many went to America, Australia and Britain. The GAA clubs provide connections for Irish emigrants looking for work. They also provide friendship for newly arrived Irish people.

## Activity 8

Examine this source and then answer the questions below.

[T]he game is flourishing overseas, with GAA clubs across Europe, North America, Asia, Australia and New Zealand enriched by the influx of young and talented Irish players … who are eager to maintain their connection with Ireland by playing their national sport … It can provide invaluable connections for Irish emigrants seeking work and friends when they arrive in an unfamiliar place … [Clubs] become hubs for the Irish community …

We help them find jobs and homes … We provide a place for them to train and to play the games they love, and we provide a shoulder to cry on when they are jilted or lonely or upset. We become their family and friends, because essentially, we are all any of us have.

SOURCE 20.13: Ciara Kenny, Philip O'Connor, *Irish Times*, 27 April 2012

1 Name three areas where the clubs are flourishing.
2 State two ways in which the GAA clubs help Irish immigrants to settle into their new environment.
3 Give three reasons why the new arrivals join the local GAA club.

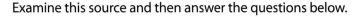

SOURCE 20.14: Football match at Gaelic Park, New York, 2017

SOURCE 20.15: Army watchtower overlooking Crossmaglen Rangers

## How did the Troubles affect the GAA?

In Northern Ireland both the unionists and the security forces suspected that there were close links between the IRA and the GAA. Weapons finds in some GAA grounds seemed to confirm this opinion.

The GAA encountered a number of difficulties during the Troubles. For example:

> The British Army took over part of the GAA ground at Crossmaglen, Co. Armagh, to use as a base. This angered the nationalist community.
> Unionist-led councils refused to give money to improve GAA facilities.
> GAA clubs were targeted in sectarian attacks.
> Players were stopped and searched many times on their way to training or matches.

Since the end of the Troubles in 1998 life has returned to normal for members of the GAA.

## What has been the impact of the GAA?

> Hurling and Gaelic football have been successfully revived and organised.
> It helped develop the organisational skills of its members. This, in turn, provided a training ground for democracy. People gained administrative experience that helped them in local and national politics.
> It played an important part in creating a national identity. It made people aware of being Irish and proud of their culture. These people were more likely to take part in the fight for independence from the British.
> It has also nurtured community identity. People feel proud of their parish due to the inter-club matches.
> Significant commemorations of the 1916 Rising have taken place in Croke Park.
> The GAA has also encouraged Irish music and culture.
> In the past fifty years €2.6 billion has been invested in sports grounds. Between 1993 and 2005 Croke Park was transformed into one of the most modern stadiums in the world, with a capacity of 82,300.

› The GAA has become more inclusive. In 2005 soccer and rugby matches were played in Croke Park during the redevelopment of the stadium at Lansdowne Road. This had a positive impact on north–south relations.

› The GAA has provided a focal point for Irish emigrants over the years. Many of them depend on it for building links in a new country and for help finding employment.

Today, the GAA is one of the greatest amateur sporting organisations in the world. It is part of Irish life and its influence goes beyond promoting Irish games. It remains an amateur association that depends on volunteers to run it and fundraise for it. As the GAA goes from strength to strength, the future looks bright for Ireland's native games.

**SOURCE 20.16: Croke Park**

---

### Activity 9

1 Draw a timeline showing key events in the history of the GAA and write a short note on each event.

---

**DO YOU UNDERSTAND THESE KEY TERMS?**

| | | |
|---|---|---|
| anglicisation | cultural nationalism | Rule 27 |
| 'the Ban' | GAA | |
| Bloody Sunday | Rule 21 | |

 PowerPoint summary

---

## SELF-ASSESSMENT – CAN YOU?

1 Outline the aims of the GAA when it was set up.

2 Describe the immediate impact of the GAA.

3 Discuss how the Parnellite split affected the GAA.

4 Examine why the GAA decided to build Croke Park.

5 Explain what happened on Bloody Sunday.

6 Comment on the role played by the GAA abroad.

7 Explore the GAA's role in commemorating 1916.

8 Indicate how the Troubles impacted on the GAA.

9 Analyse the impact of the GAA on Irish society.

# CRIME AND PUNISHMENT OVER TIME

## 🎯 LEARNING INTENTIONS

**At the end of this section, you should be able to:**

◎ Describe and compare systems of crime and punishment in different historical periods.

## Crime and punishment

Over the last few years you have learned about many changes in the way people lived in the past. In this section you will investigate how our ideas of crime and punishment have changed over time. We will focus on three eras that you have already studied:

> Europe in the Middle Ages
> Seventeenth-century Ireland during the plantations
> Twentieth-century totalitarian states under Hitler and Stalin.

## Crime and punishment in the Middle Ages

> The lord/baron was in charge of keeping law and order.
> Bailiffs, guilds and corporations enforced the law.
> Common crimes: poaching, fighting, drunkenness, running away from the master, stealing, gossiping, getting pregnant before marriage, not working hard enough, not paying taxes, witchcraft.
> Common punishments: hanging, hands cut off, a fine, stocks, pillory, ducking stool, burned at stake.
> Availability of sanctuary in churches.

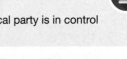
**Totalitarian**
Where one political party is in control of everything.

**SOURCE 20.17: Witches being burned at the stake**

---

### Activity 1 (KS 👥) ✏️

Read the summary above for the Middle Ages and look back at Section 4.

1  Write down five types of crime and five types of punishment in the Middle Ages.

2  Try to match the crimes with the type of punishment you think they would receive.

3  Which of these crimes do we not have today in Europe?

4  Which of these punishments do we not have today in Europe?

5  Who was in charge of law and order in a town or village? How is that system different from today's justice system?

6  Was this a better or worse legal system than the one we have today, in your view? Justify your answer.

7  What was sanctuary?

---

### Activity 2 ✏️

Examine this source and then answer the question below.

**SOURCE 20.18: Ducking stool**

1  What crimes was the ducking stool used to punish?

## Activity 3

Examine this source and then answer the question below.

SOURCE 20.19: **Public burnings and hangings**

1   Why were these punishments new in Gaelic Ireland?

# Crime and punishment in plantation Ireland

> Brehon law (and the éiric) changed to common law. Common law is common to 'all the king's subjects'.
> Courts and judges enforced the law in courthouses.
> Constables kept order on the streets.
> Common crimes: stealing, attacking settlers, murder, divorce, pregnancy outside marriage, being a Catholic.
> Common punishments: beheading, hanging, stocks, pillory, ducking stool, burned at stake, jail.

## Activity 4

Read the summary above for plantation Ireland and look back at Section 8.

1   What was an éiric?
2   Write down four differences between the old Brehon Law and the new English common law in seventeenth-century Ireland.
3   What new type of punishment did the English introduce to Ireland that had not been there under Brehon law?
4   Who enforced the common law in Ireland?
5   Which of these seventeenth-century offences are not crimes in Europe today?
6   Which of these punishments do we not have in Europe today?

# Crime and punishment under Hitler and Stalin

> State/dictator makes all the laws.

> Laws enforced using propaganda and terror (e.g. secret police, show trials).

> Common crimes: stealing, murder, criticising the government, giving a personal opinion, belief in God.

> Common punishments: execution, jail, concentration camps, Gulag, torture, Great Purge, beating.

SOURCE 20.20: Gulag (prison camp), Russia, 1930

 **Activity 5**

Read the summary for crime and punishment under Hitler and Stalin and look back at Section 14.

1 Name three types of crime and three types of punishment in Nazi Germany.

2 Name three types of crime and three types of punishment in the USSR under Stalin.

3 Explain the terms 'concentration camp', 'Gulag', 'show trial' and 'Holocaust'.

4 Name two crimes listed on the left that you would not find in a democracy.

5 Name two punishments listed on the left that you would not find in a democracy.

 **Activity 6**

1 'Punishments were more brutal before the twentieth century.' Would you agree? In pairs, prepare two arguments for and two arguments against this statement.

  **Activity 7**

In groups, select any three or four eras from those you have studied in this book and describe the changes that have taken place over time in one of the following: (a) clothing/fashion; (b) health and medicine; (c) work and leisure; (d) food and drink.

Chapter summary    Weblinks    PowerPoint summary

# SELF-ASSESSMENT – CAN YOU?

1 Name the most common way people are punished today for a crime and explain how that has changed over time, referring to three punishments from the past that we do not have today.

2 Debate which punishment listed in the summaries above was the most cruel, and justify your opinion.

# INDEX